Honey
So Sweet

6

Story and Art by
Amu Meguro

Contents

#26 Birthday Crisis! 3

#27 Who's He? 41

#28 Back in Junior High 77

#29 Miyabi Nishigaki 113

#30 What Is Love? 151

Story Thus Far

Soon after starting high school, the fearsome-looking Onise asks Nao to be his girlfriend. At first Nao is afraid, but once she discovers that Onise is actually a gentle soul, Nao asks him out and their blissful relationship begins.

Nao and Onise plan to have their first date on Christmas, but all their friends invite themselves over to Onise's place for a party. Worried about Onise after he eats some whiskey bonbons, Nao ends up staying the night and forgets to let Sou know where she is! She apologizes to Sou the next day, and he insists he isn't upset even though he is. Onise comes to the rescue and helps them through their argument.

Nao and Onise exchange chocolates on Valentine's Day, and their relationship is stronger than ever.♥

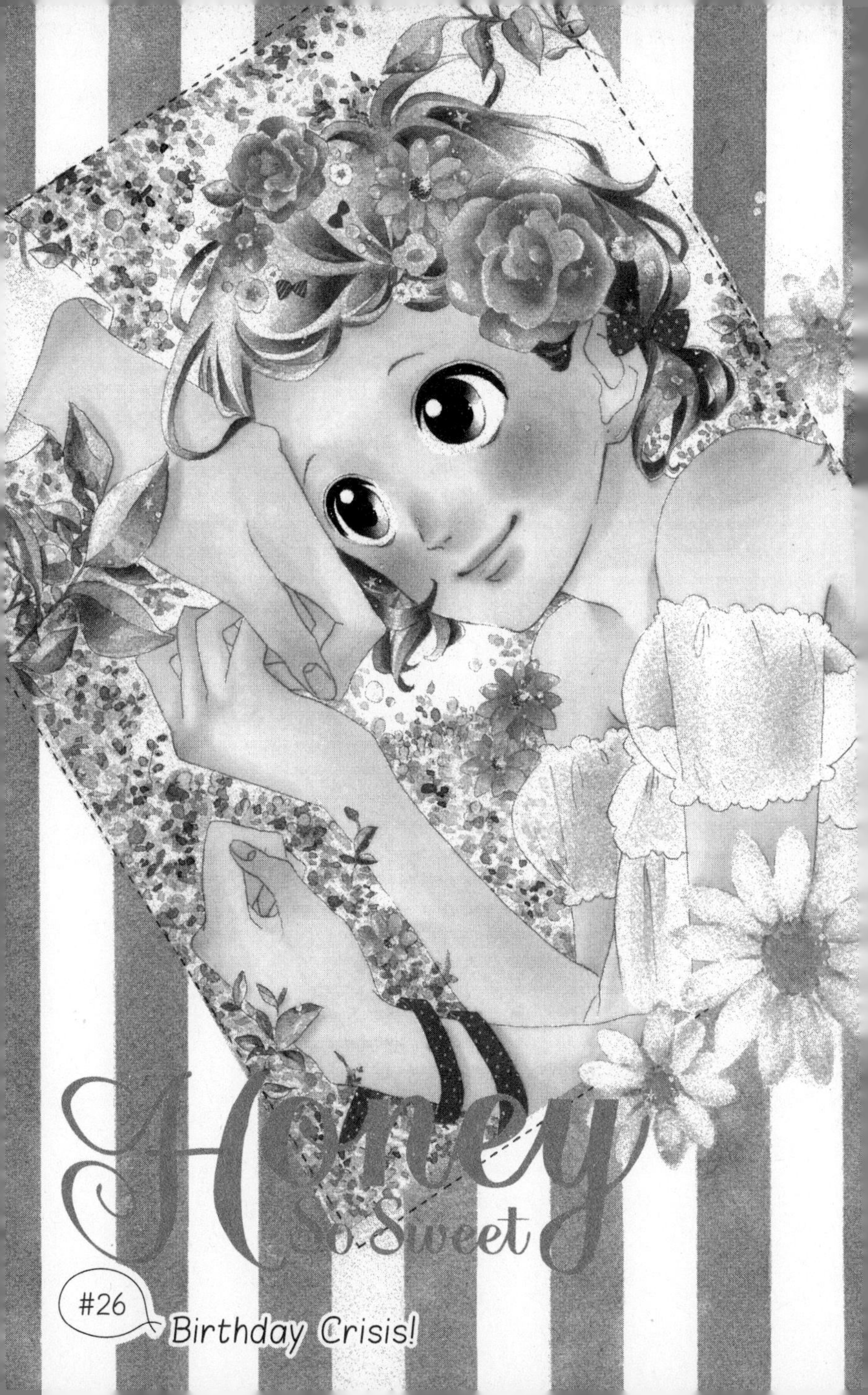
Honey So Sweet
#26
Birthday Crisis!

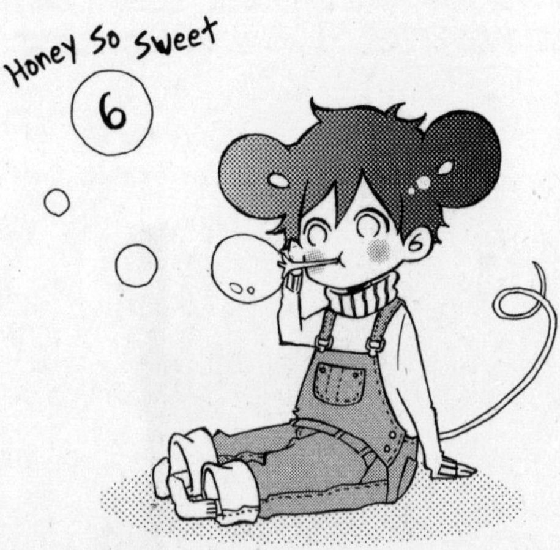
Honey So Sweet
6

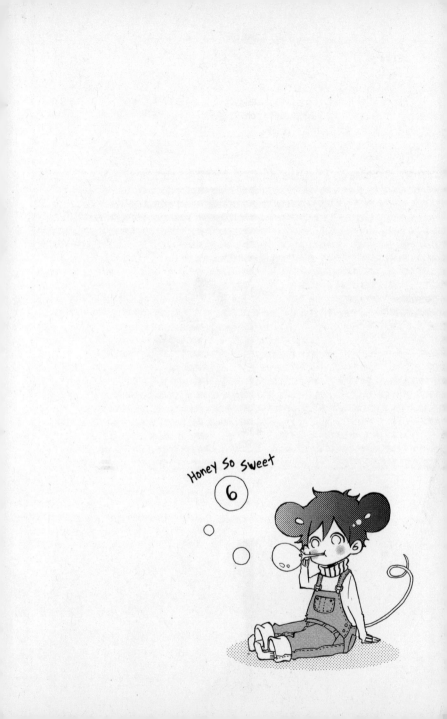

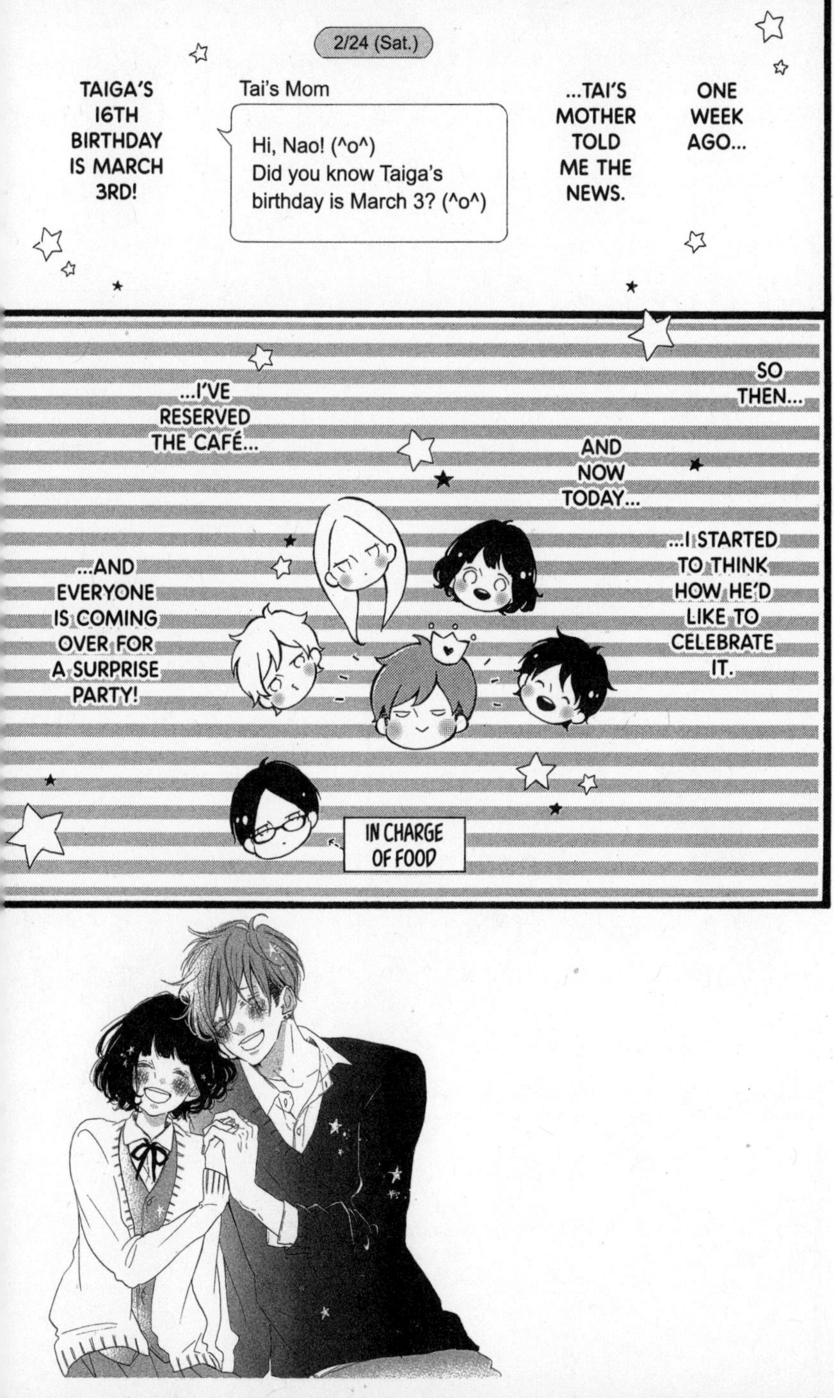
ONE WEEK AGO...
...TAI'S MOTHER TOLD ME THE NEWS.
2/24 (Sat.)
Tai's Mom
Hi, Nao! (^o^)
Did you know Taiga's birthday is March 3? (^o^)
TAIGA'S 16TH BIRTHDAY IS MARCH 3RD!
SO THEN...
...I STARTED TO THINK HOW HE'D LIKE TO CELEBRATE IT.
AND NOW TODAY...
...I'VE RESERVED THE CAFÉ...
...AND EVERYONE IS COMING OVER FOR A SURPRISE PARTY!
IN CHARGE OF FOOD

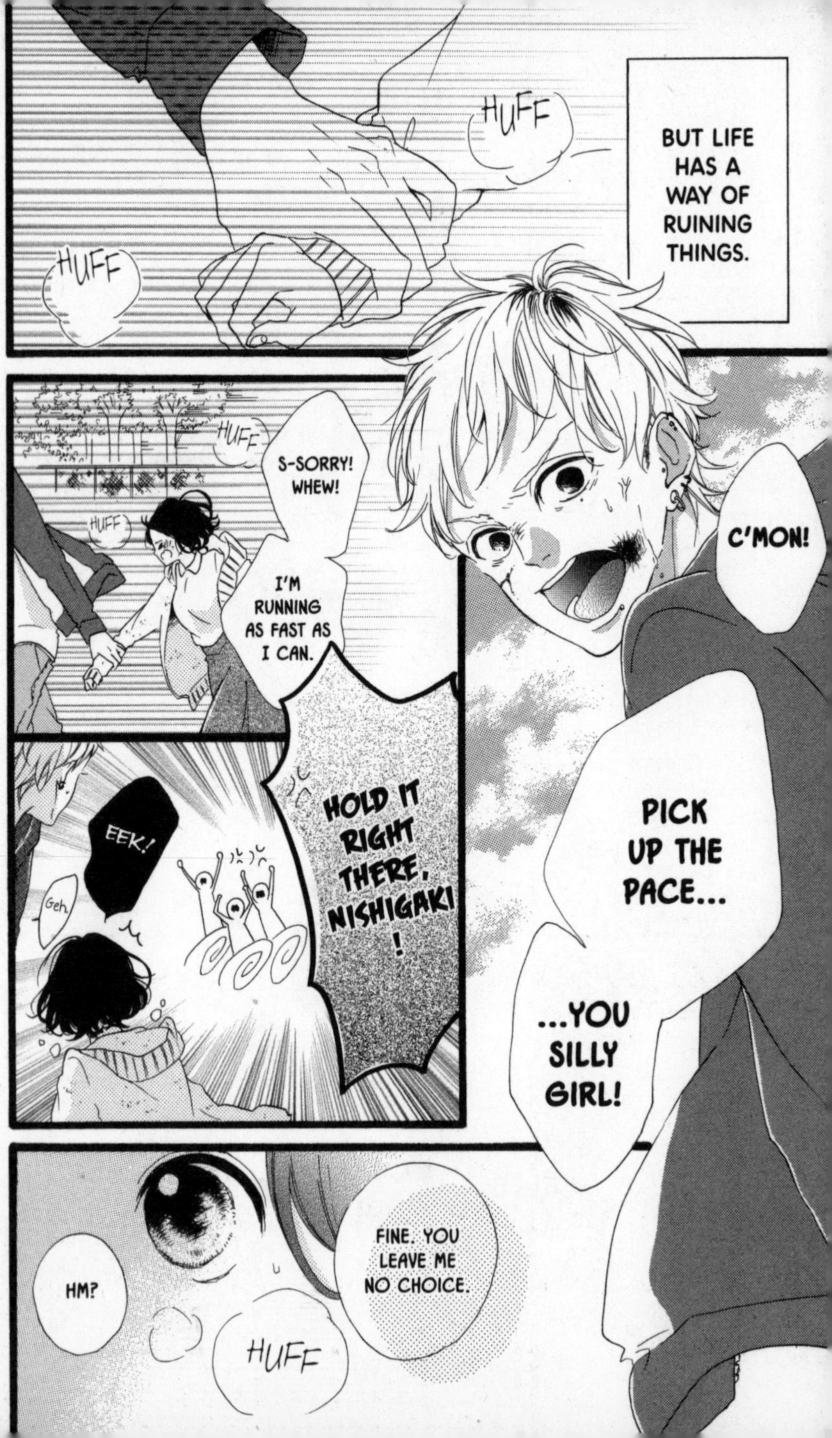
BUT LIFE HAS A WAY OF RUINING THINGS.
HUFF
HUFF
C'MON!
PICK UP THE PACE...
...YOU SILLY GIRL!
S-SORRY! WHEW!
I'M RUNNING AS FAST AS I CAN.
HUFF
HUFF
HOLD IT RIGHT THERE, NISHIGAKI!
EEK!
Geh.
FINE. YOU LEAVE ME NO CHOICE.
HM?
HUFF

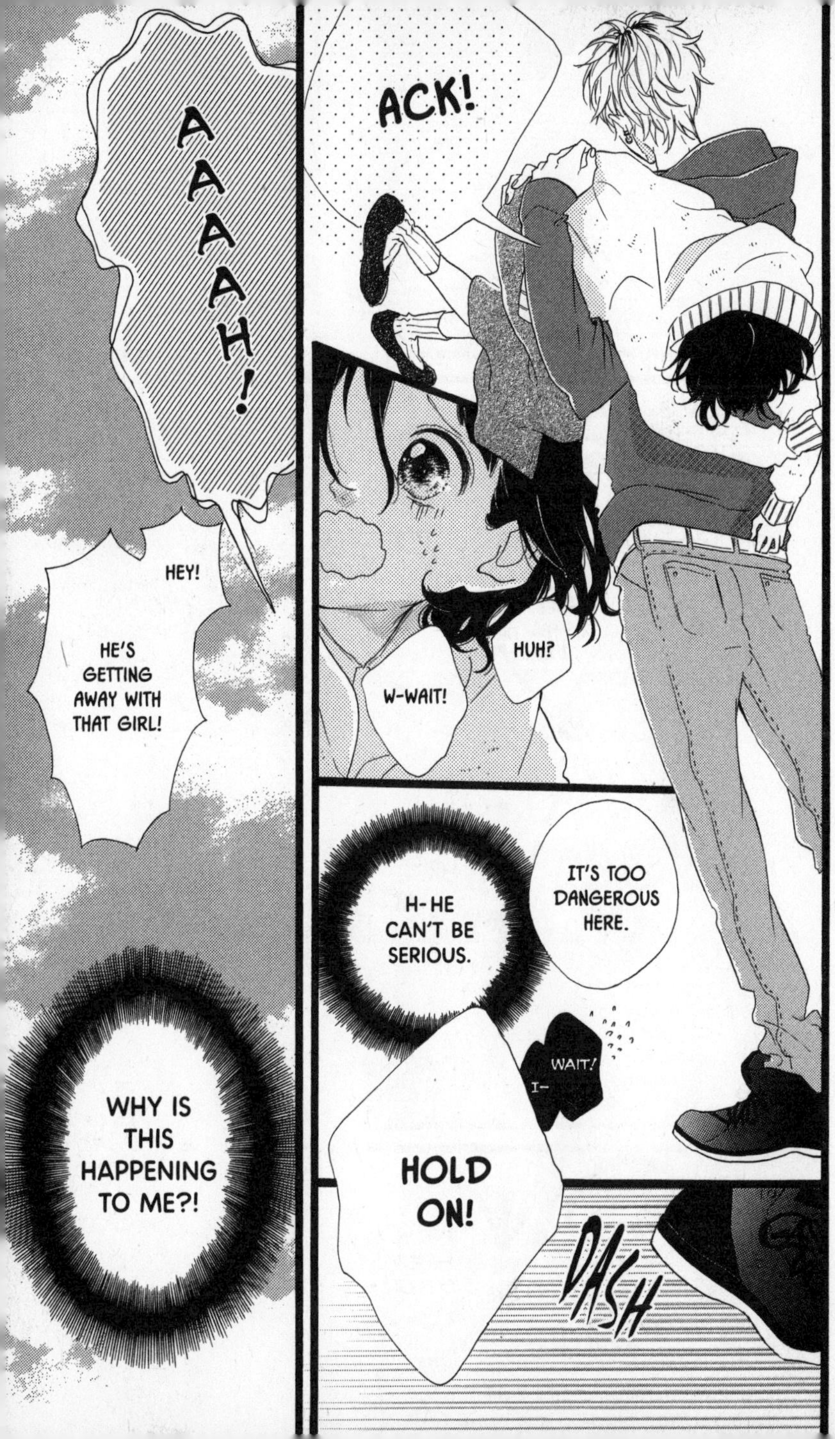
ACK!
HUH?
W-WAIT!
IT'S TOO DANGEROUS HERE.
H-HE CAN'T BE SERIOUS.
WAIT! I-
HOLD ON!
DASH
AAAAH!
HEY!
HE'S GETTING AWAY WITH THAT GIRL!
WHY IS THIS HAPPENING TO ME?!

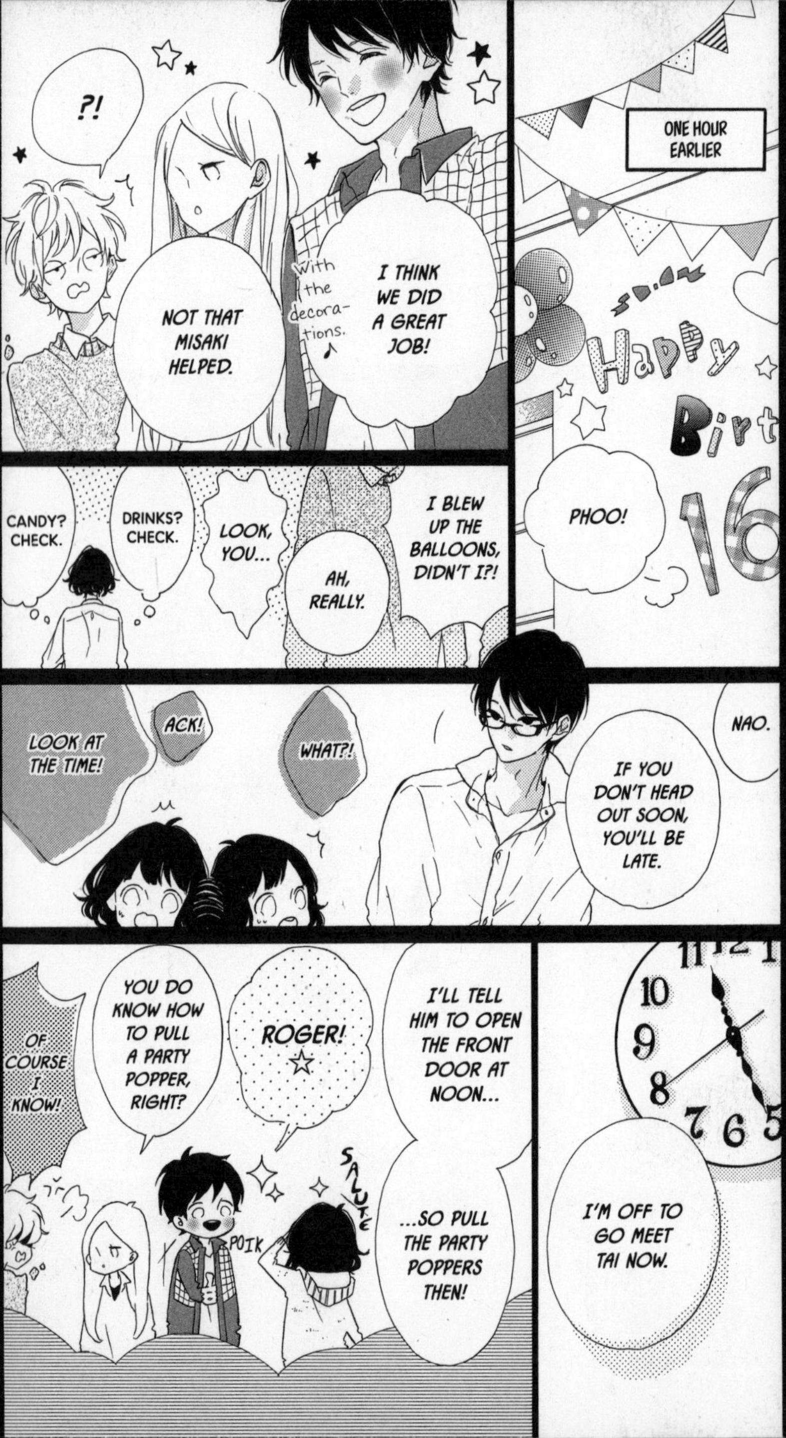
ONE HOUR EARLIER
Happy Birt
16
PHOO!
I THINK WE DID A GREAT JOB!
With the decorations. ♪
NOT THAT MISAKI HELPED.
?!
I BLEW UP THE BALLOONS, DIDN'T I?!
AH, REALLY.
LOOK, YOU...
DRINKS? CHECK.
CANDY? CHECK.
NAO.
IF YOU DON'T HEAD OUT SOON, YOU'LL BE LATE.
WHAT?!
ACK!
LOOK AT THE TIME!
I'M OFF TO GO MEET TAI NOW.
I'LL TELL HIM TO OPEN THE FRONT DOOR AT NOON...
...SO PULL THE PARTY POPPERS THEN!
ROGER! ☆
SALUTE
YOU DO KNOW HOW TO PULL A PARTY POPPER, RIGHT?
POIK
OF COURSE I KNOW!

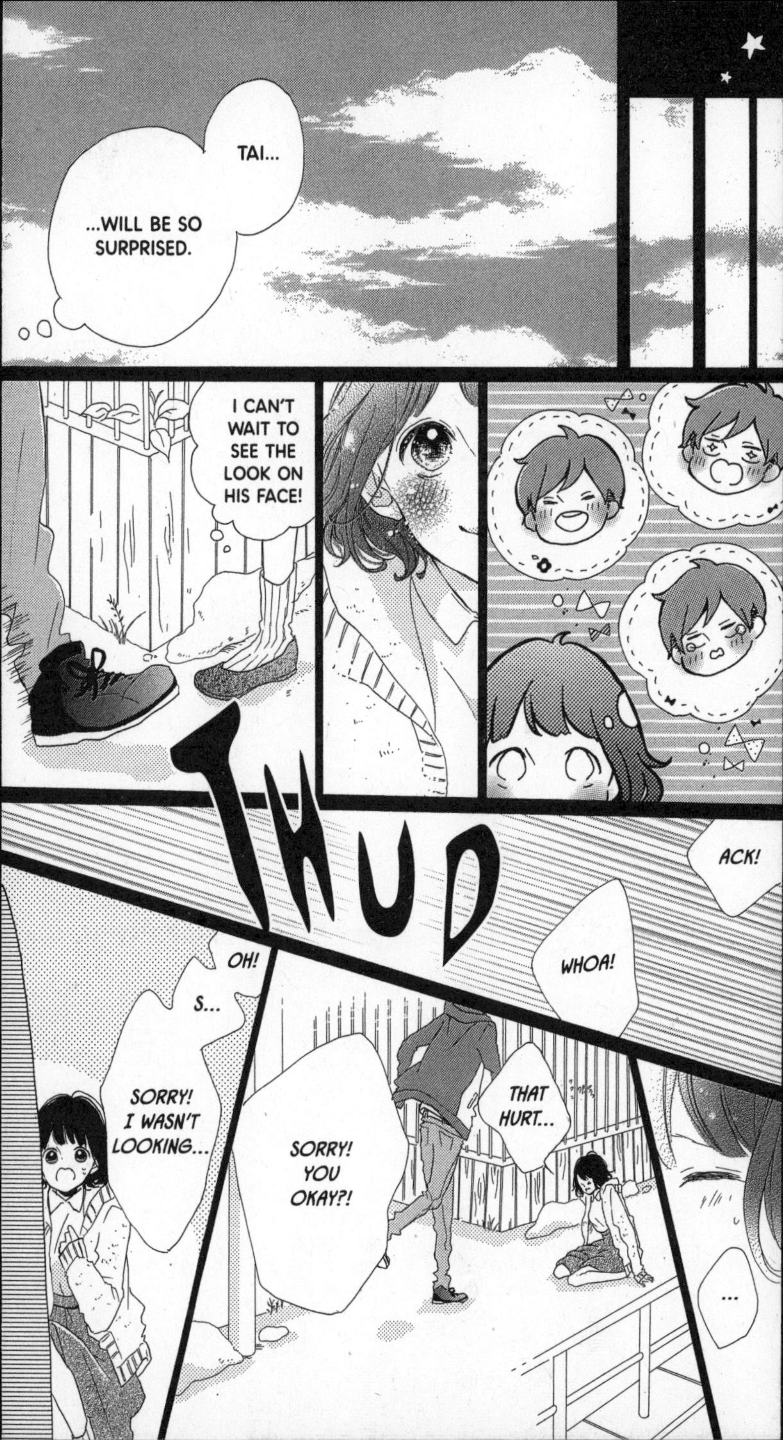
TAI...
...WILL BE SO SURPRISED.
I CAN'T WAIT TO SEE THE LOOK ON HIS FACE!
THUD
ACK!
WHOA!
...
THAT HURT...
SORRY! YOU OKAY?!
OH!
S...
SORRY! I WASN'T LOOKING...

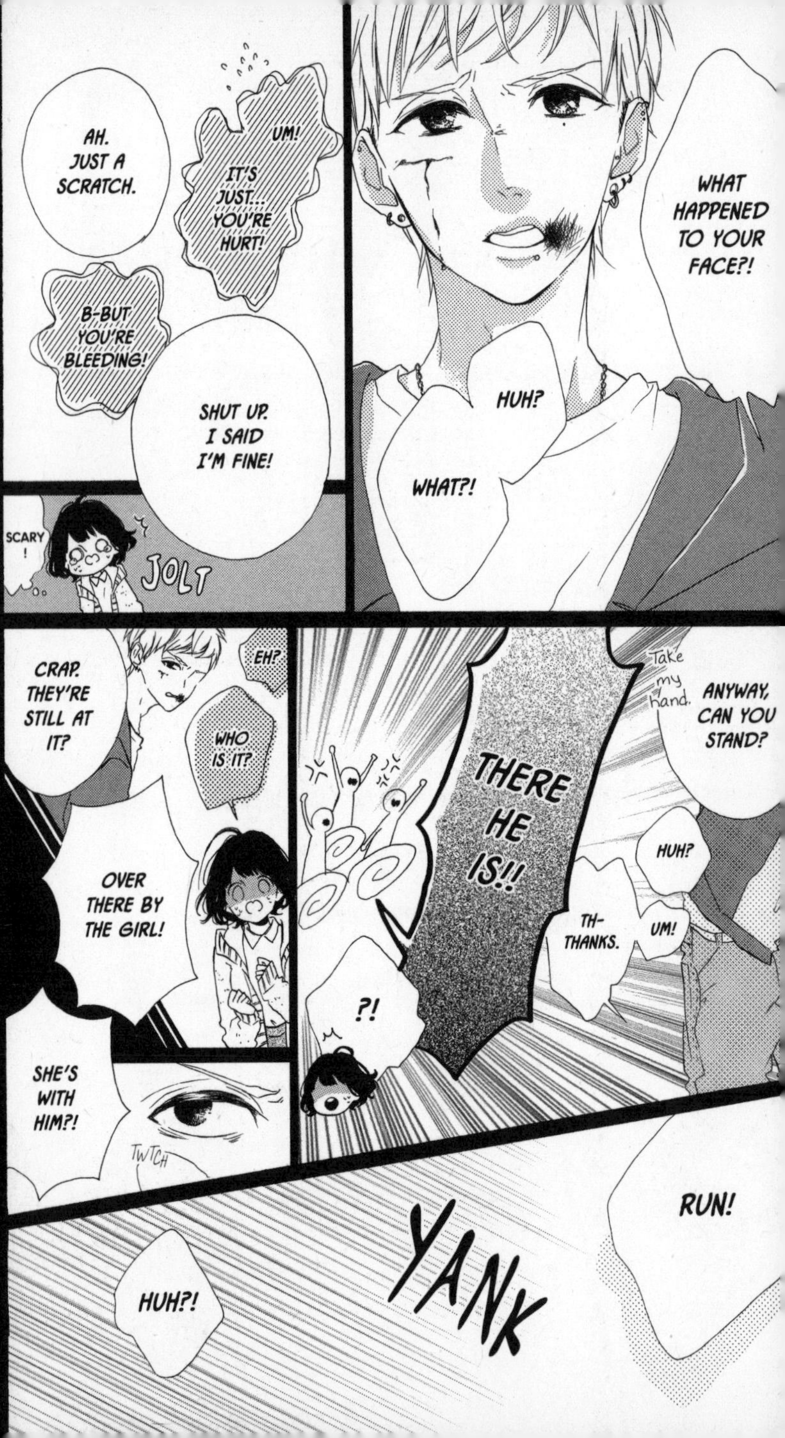
WHAT HAPPENED TO YOUR FACE?!
HUH?
WHAT?!
UM!
IT'S JUST... YOU'RE HURT!
AH. JUST A SCRATCH.
B-BUT YOU'RE BLEEDING!
SHUT UP. I SAID I'M FINE!
SCARY!
JOLT
Take my hand.
ANYWAY, CAN YOU STAND?
HUH?
UM!
TH-THANKS.
THERE HE IS!!
?!
EH?
CRAP. THEY'RE STILL AT IT?
WHO IS IT?
OVER THERE BY THE GIRL!
SHE'S WITH HIM?!
TWITCH
RUN!
YANK
HUH?!

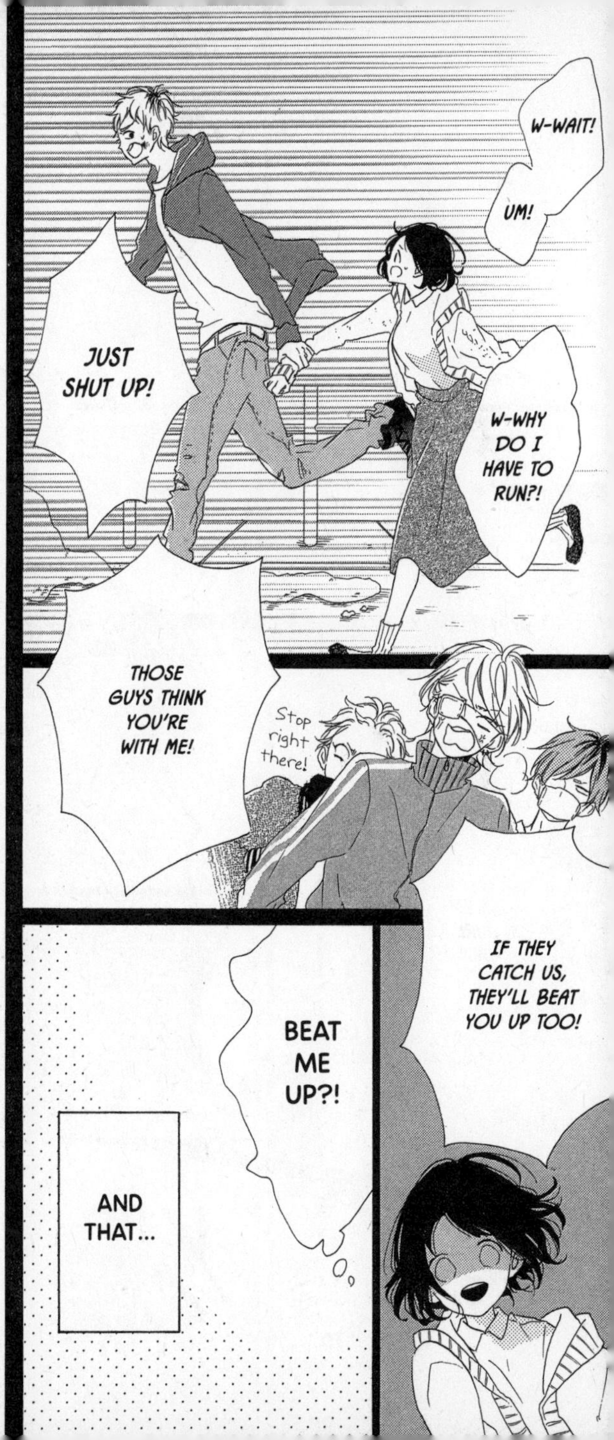
W-WAIT!
UM!
W-WHY DO I HAVE TO RUN?!
JUST SHUT UP!
THOSE GUYS THINK YOU'RE WITH ME!
Stop right there!
IF THEY CATCH US, THEY'LL BEAT YOU UP TOO!
BEAT ME UP?!
AND THAT...
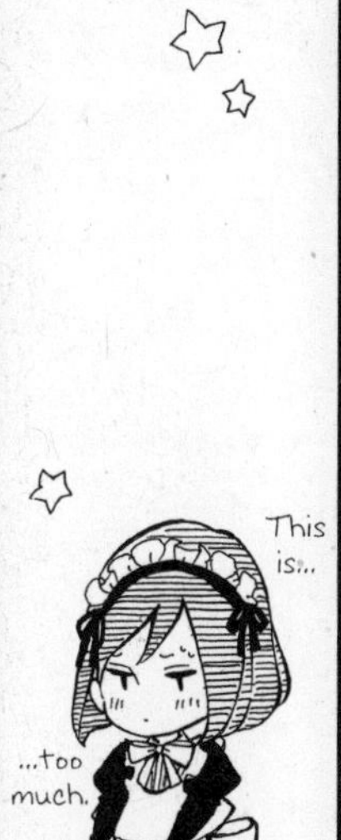
This is...
...too much.

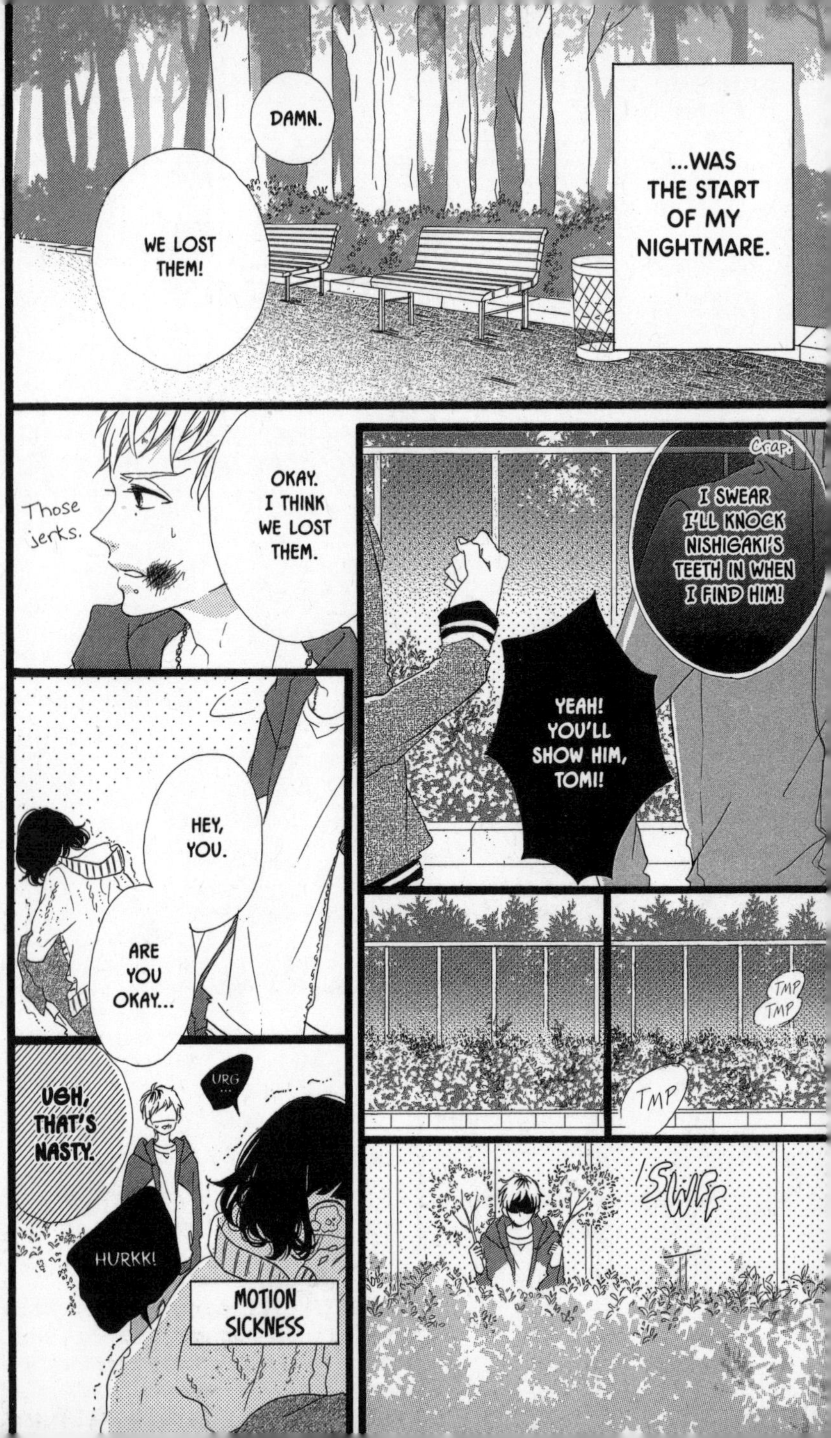
...WAS THE START OF MY NIGHTMARE.
DAMN.
WE LOST THEM!
Crap.
I SWEAR I'LL KNOCK NISHIGAKI'S TEETH IN WHEN I FIND HIM!
YEAH! YOU'LL SHOW HIM, TOMI!
OKAY. I THINK WE LOST THEM.
Those jerks.
TMP TMP
TMP
SWFF
HEY, YOU.
ARE YOU OKAY...
URG...
UGH, THAT'S NASTY.
HURKK!
MOTION SICKNESS

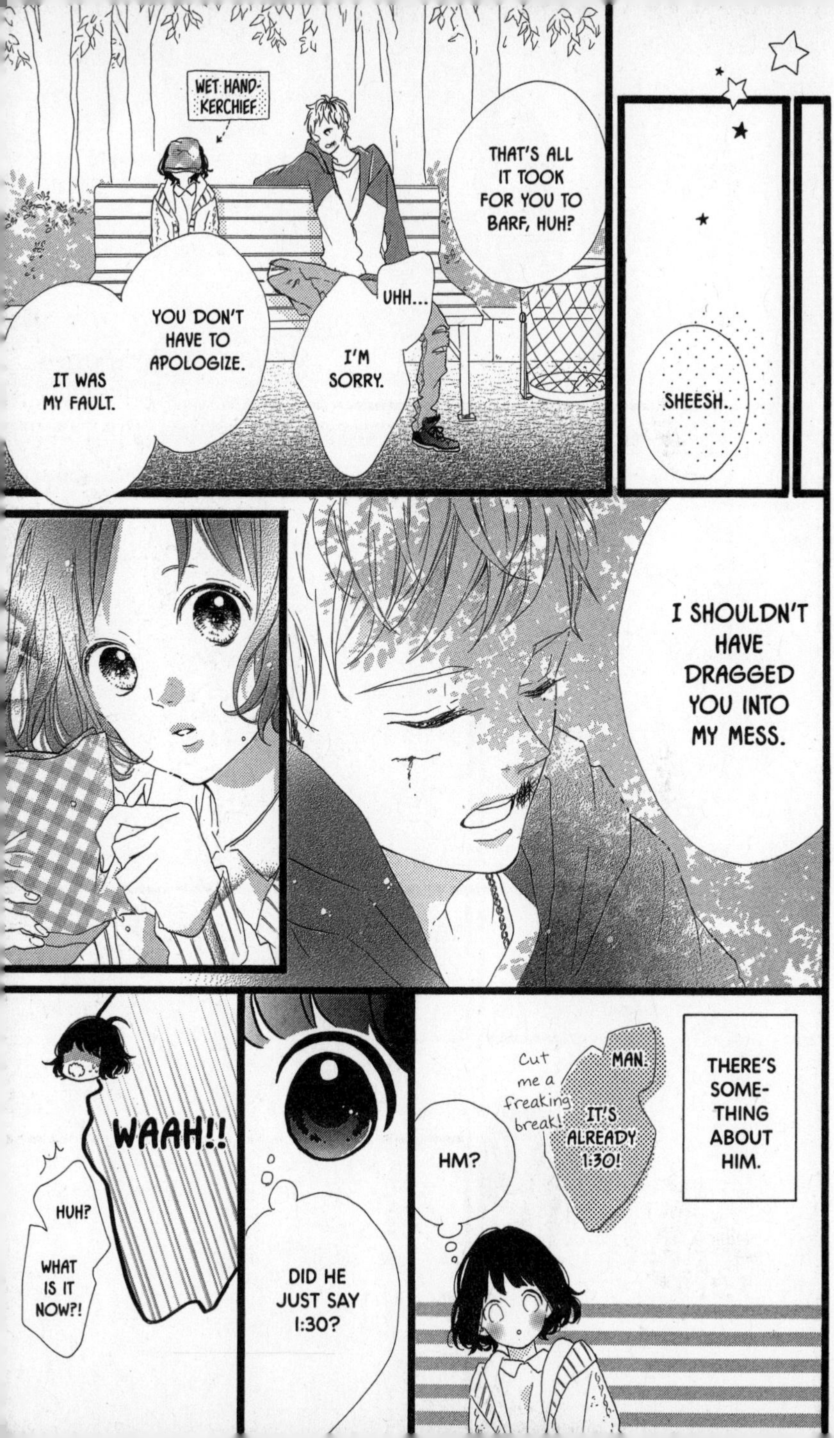
SHEESH.
THAT'S ALL IT TOOK FOR YOU TO BARF, HUH?
WET HAND-KERCHIEF
UHH...
I'M SORRY.
YOU DON'T HAVE TO APOLOGIZE.
IT WAS MY FAULT.
I SHOULDN'T HAVE DRAGGED YOU INTO MY MESS.
THERE'S SOME-THING ABOUT HIM.
MAN.
IT'S ALREADY 1:30!
Cut me a freaking break!
HM?
DID HE JUST SAY 1:30?
WAAH!!
HUH?
WHAT IS IT NOW?!

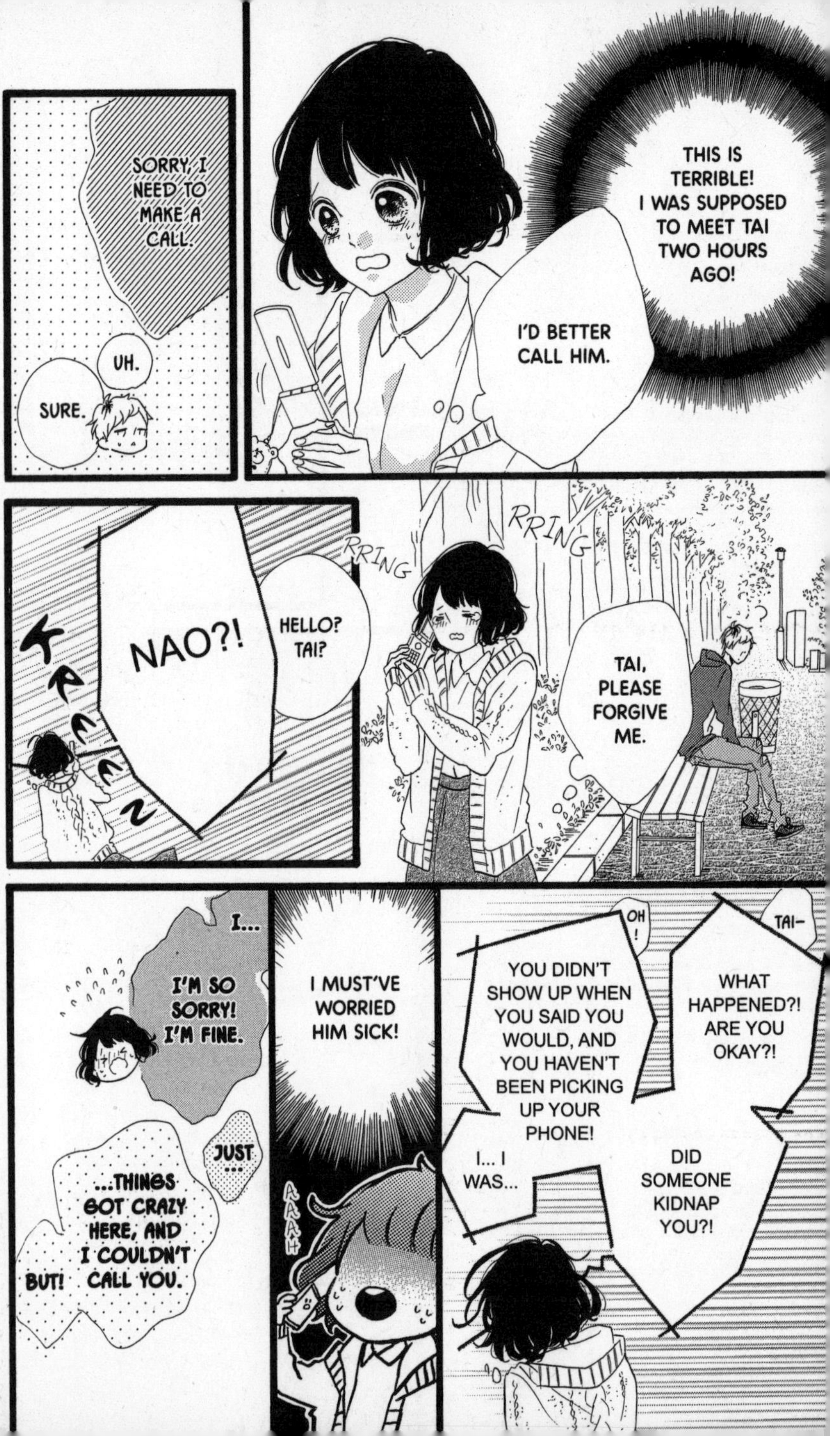

THIS IS TERRIBLE! I WAS SUPPOSED TO MEET TAI TWO HOURS AGO!
I'D BETTER CALL HIM.
SORRY, I NEED TO MAKE A CALL.
UH.
SURE.
RRING
RRING
TAI, PLEASE FORGIVE ME.
HELLO? TAI?
NAO?!
KREEN
TAI—
OH!
WHAT HAPPENED?! ARE YOU OKAY?!
YOU DIDN'T SHOW UP WHEN YOU SAID YOU WOULD, AND YOU HAVEN'T BEEN PICKING UP YOUR PHONE!
DID SOMEONE KIDNAP YOU?!
I... I WAS...
I MUST'VE WORRIED HIM SICK!
AAAAH
I...
I'M SO SORRY! I'M FINE.
JUST...
...THINGS GOT CRAZY HERE, AND I COULDN'T CALL YOU.
BUT!

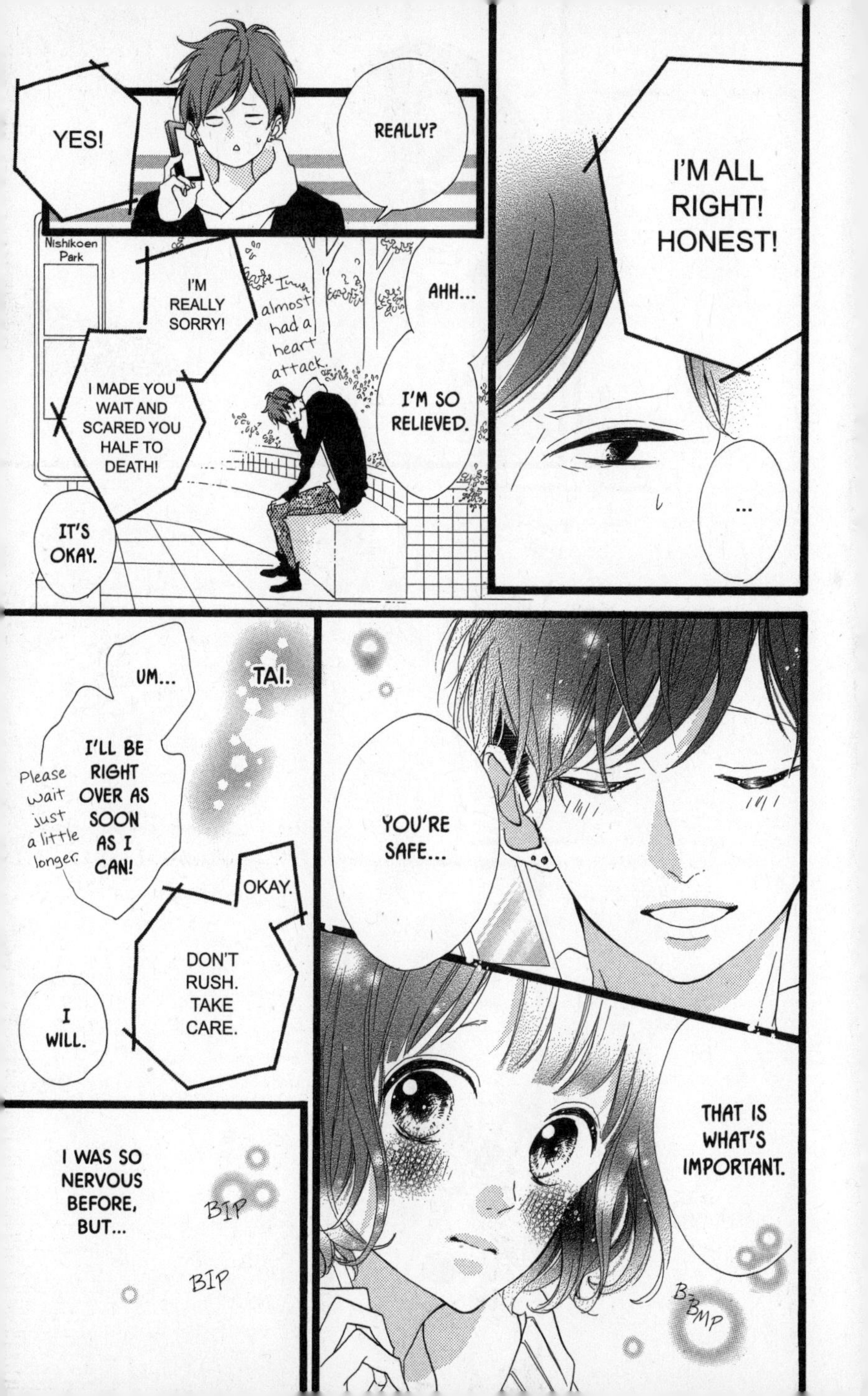
I'M ALL RIGHT! HONEST!
...
REALLY?
YES!
AHH...
I'M SO RELIEVED.
I almost had a heart attack.
Nishikoen Park
I'M REALLY SORRY!
I MADE YOU WAIT AND SCARED YOU HALF TO DEATH!
IT'S OKAY.
YOU'RE SAFE...
TAI.
UM...
I'LL BE RIGHT OVER AS SOON AS I CAN!
Please wait just a little longer.
OKAY.
DON'T RUSH. TAKE CARE.
I WILL.
THAT IS WHAT'S IMPORTANT.
B-BMP
I WAS SO NERVOUS BEFORE, BUT...
BIP
BIP

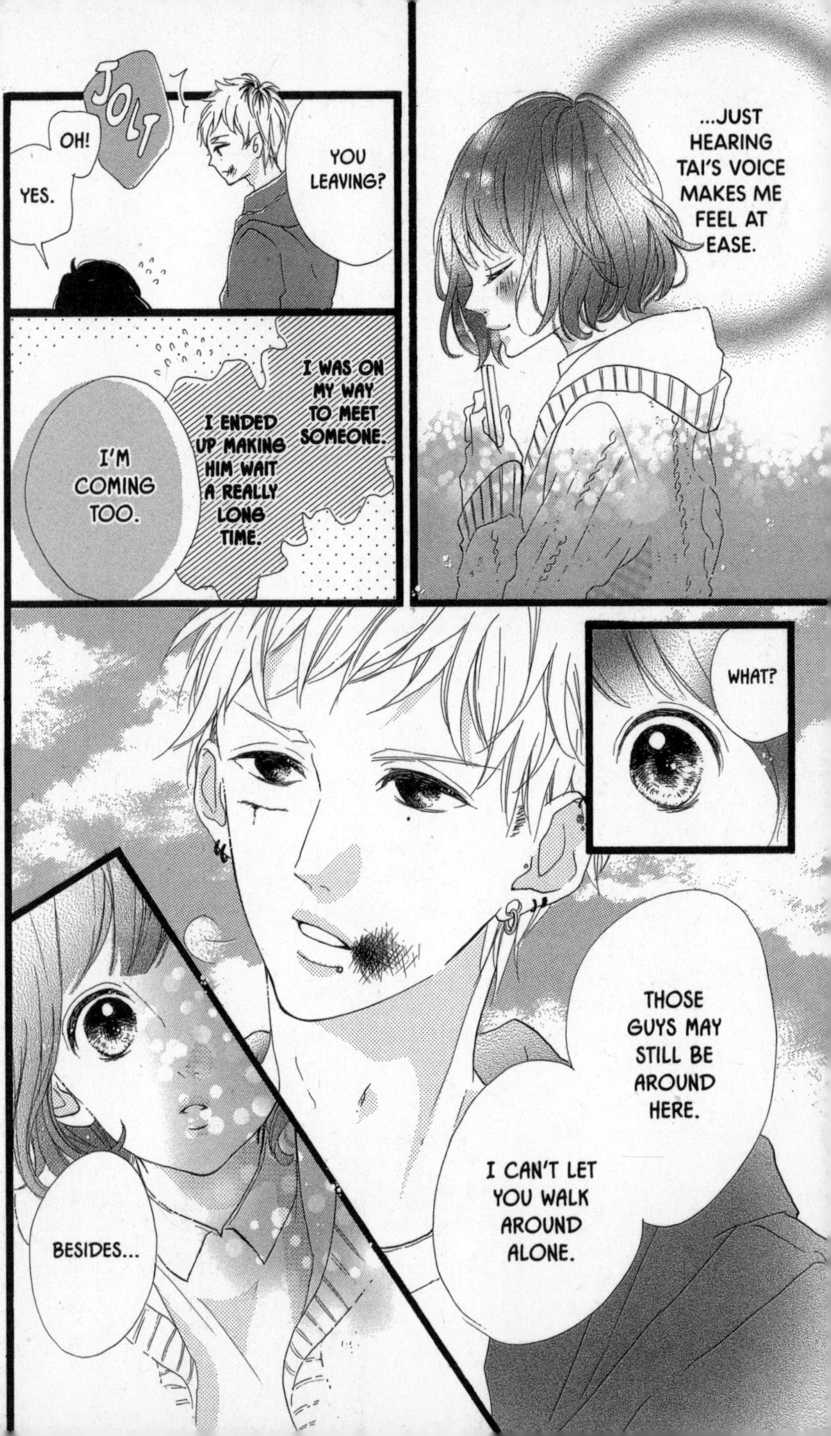
...JUST HEARING TAI'S VOICE MAKES ME FEEL AT EASE.
YOU LEAVING?
JOLT
OH!
YES.
I WAS ON MY WAY TO MEET SOMEONE.
I ENDED UP MAKING HIM WAIT A REALLY LONG TIME.
I'M COMING TOO.
WHAT?
THOSE GUYS MAY STILL BE AROUND HERE.
I CAN'T LET YOU WALK AROUND ALONE.
BESIDES...

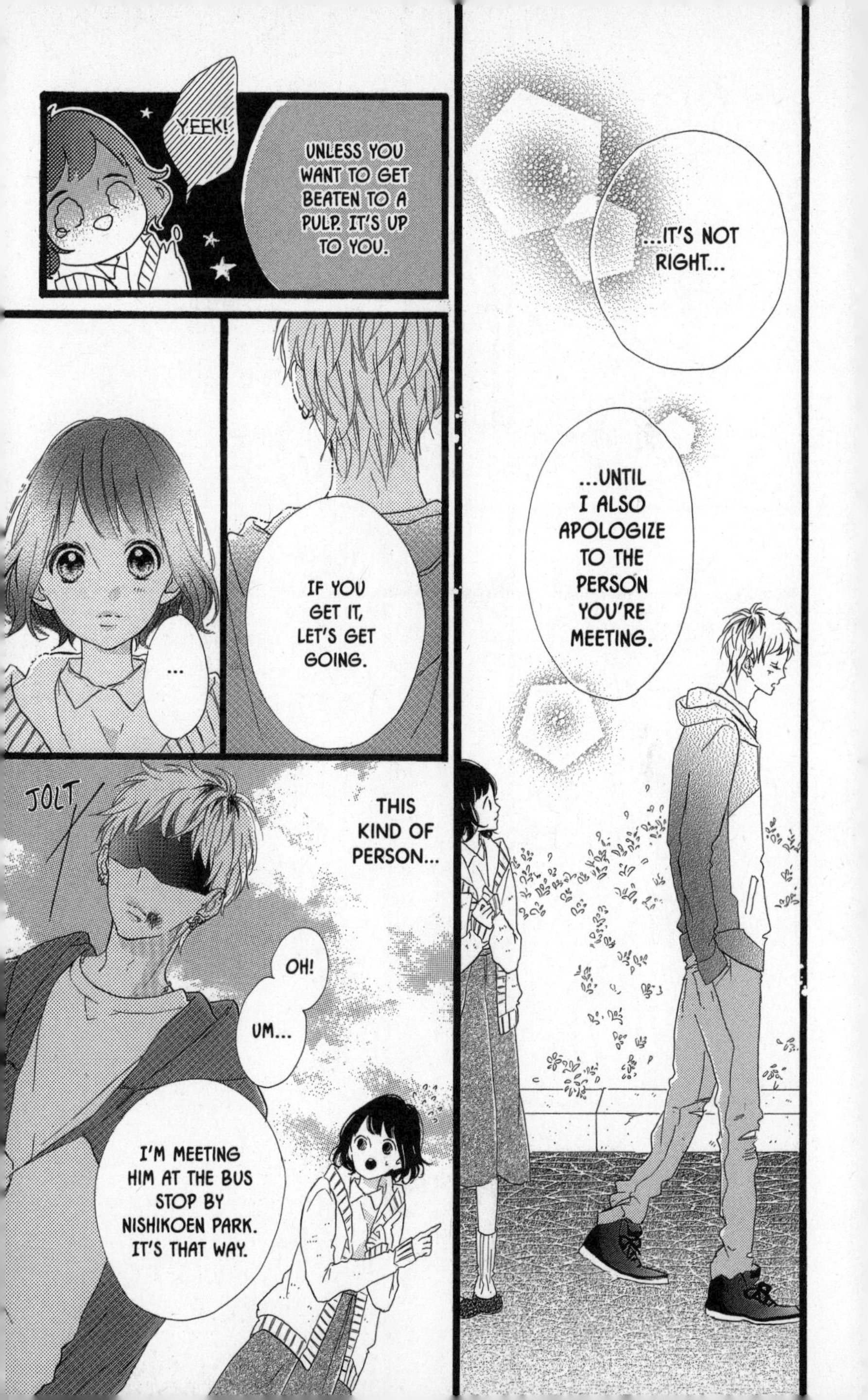
...IT'S NOT RIGHT...
...UNTIL I ALSO APOLOGIZE TO THE PERSON YOU'RE MEETING.
UNLESS YOU WANT TO GET BEATEN TO A PULP. IT'S UP TO YOU.
YEEK!
IF YOU GET IT, LET'S GET GOING.
...
JOLT
THIS KIND OF PERSON...
OH!
UM...
I'M MEETING HIM AT THE BUS STOP BY NISHIKOEN PARK. IT'S THAT WAY.

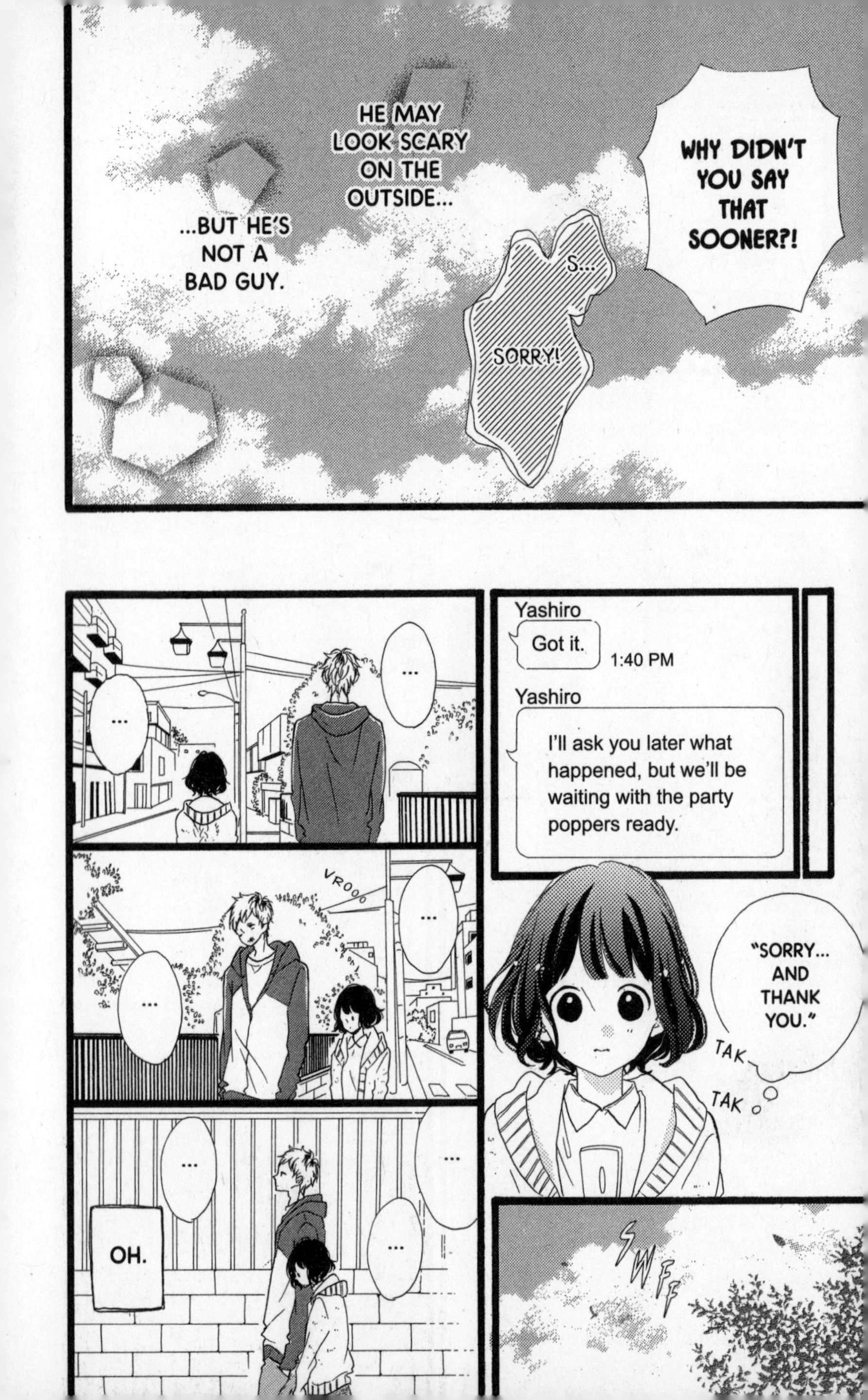
WHY DIDN'T YOU SAY THAT SOONER?!
S...
SORRY!
HE MAY LOOK SCARY ON THE OUTSIDE...
...BUT HE'S NOT A BAD GUY.
Yashiro
Got it.
1:40 PM
Yashiro
I'll ask you later what happened, but we'll be waiting with the party poppers ready.
"SORRY... AND THANK YOU."
TAK
TAK
SWFF
...
...
VROOO
...
...
...
...
OH.

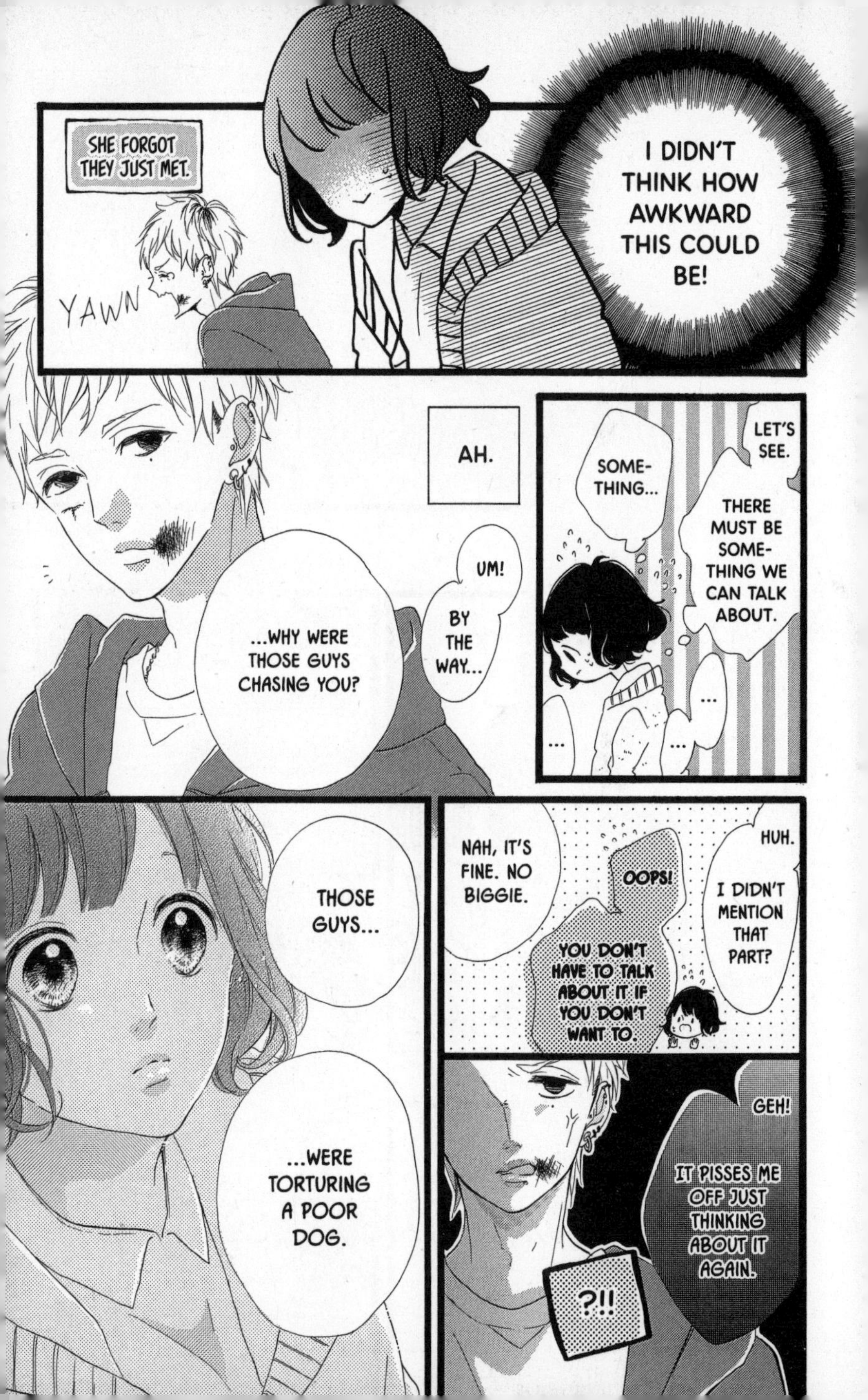
I DIDN'T THINK HOW AWKWARD THIS COULD BE!
SHE FORGOT THEY JUST MET.
YAWN
LET'S SEE.
SOME-THING...
THERE MUST BE SOME-THING WE CAN TALK ABOUT.
...
...
...
AH.
UM! BY THE WAY...
...WHY WERE THOSE GUYS CHASING YOU?
HUH. I DIDN'T MENTION THAT PART?
OOPS!
NAH, IT'S FINE. NO BIGGIE.
YOU DON'T HAVE TO TALK ABOUT IT IF YOU DON'T WANT TO.
GEH!
IT PISSES ME OFF JUST THINKING ABOUT IT AGAIN.
?!!
THOSE GUYS...
...WERE TORTURING A POOR DOG.

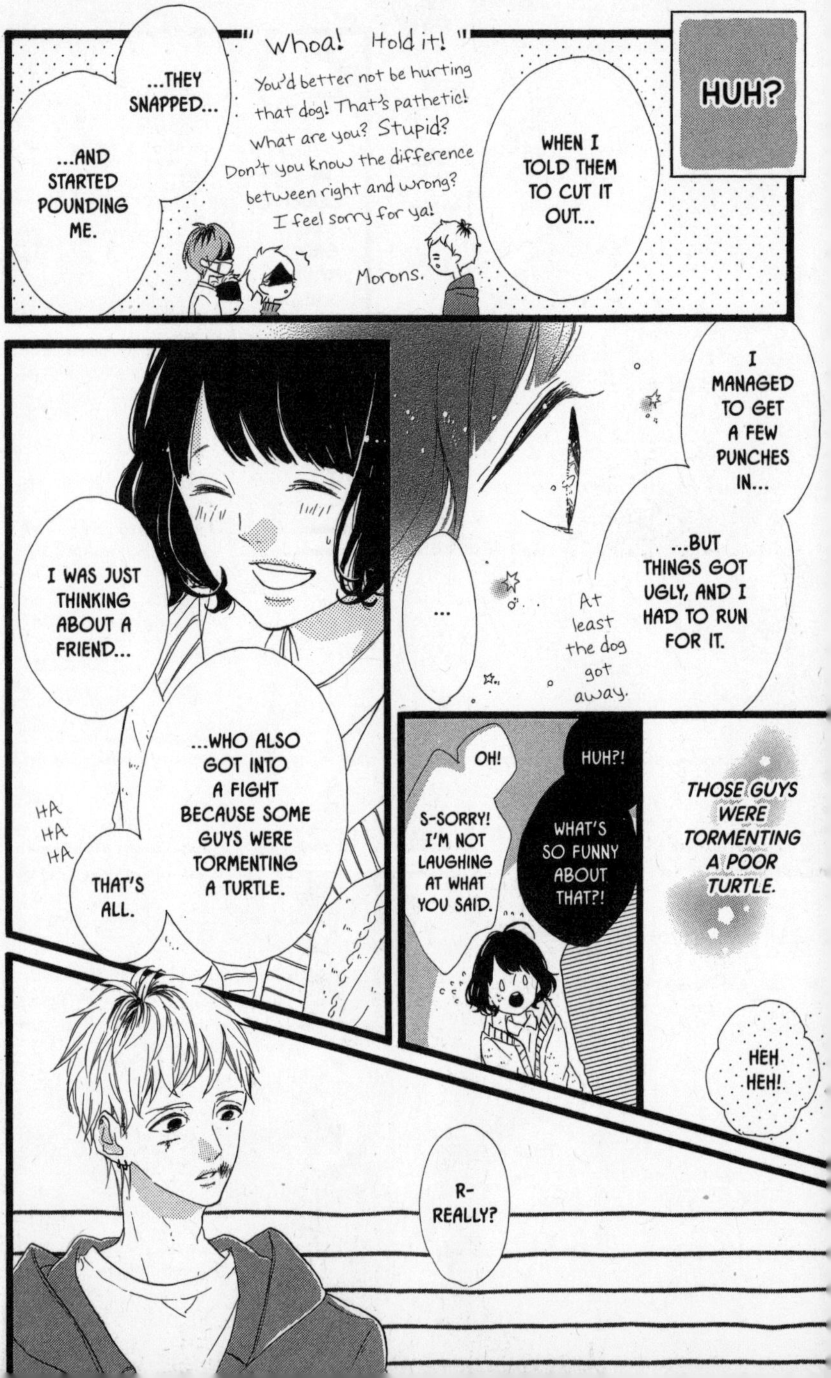
HUH?
WHEN I TOLD THEM TO CUT IT OUT...
"Whoa! Hold it!"
You'd better not be hurting that dog! That's pathetic! What are you? Stupid? Don't you know the difference between right and wrong? I feel sorry for ya!
Morons.
...THEY SNAPPED...
...AND STARTED POUNDING ME.
I MANAGED TO GET A FEW PUNCHES IN...
...BUT THINGS GOT UGLY, AND I HAD TO RUN FOR IT.
At least the dog got away.
...
I WAS JUST THINKING ABOUT A FRIEND...
...WHO ALSO GOT INTO A FIGHT BECAUSE SOME GUYS WERE TORMENTING A TURTLE.
HA HA HA
THAT'S ALL.
THOSE GUYS WERE TORMENTING A POOR TURTLE.
HEH HEH!
HUH?!
WHAT'S SO FUNNY ABOUT THAT?!
OH!
S-SORRY! I'M NOT LAUGHING AT WHAT YOU SAID.
R-REALLY?

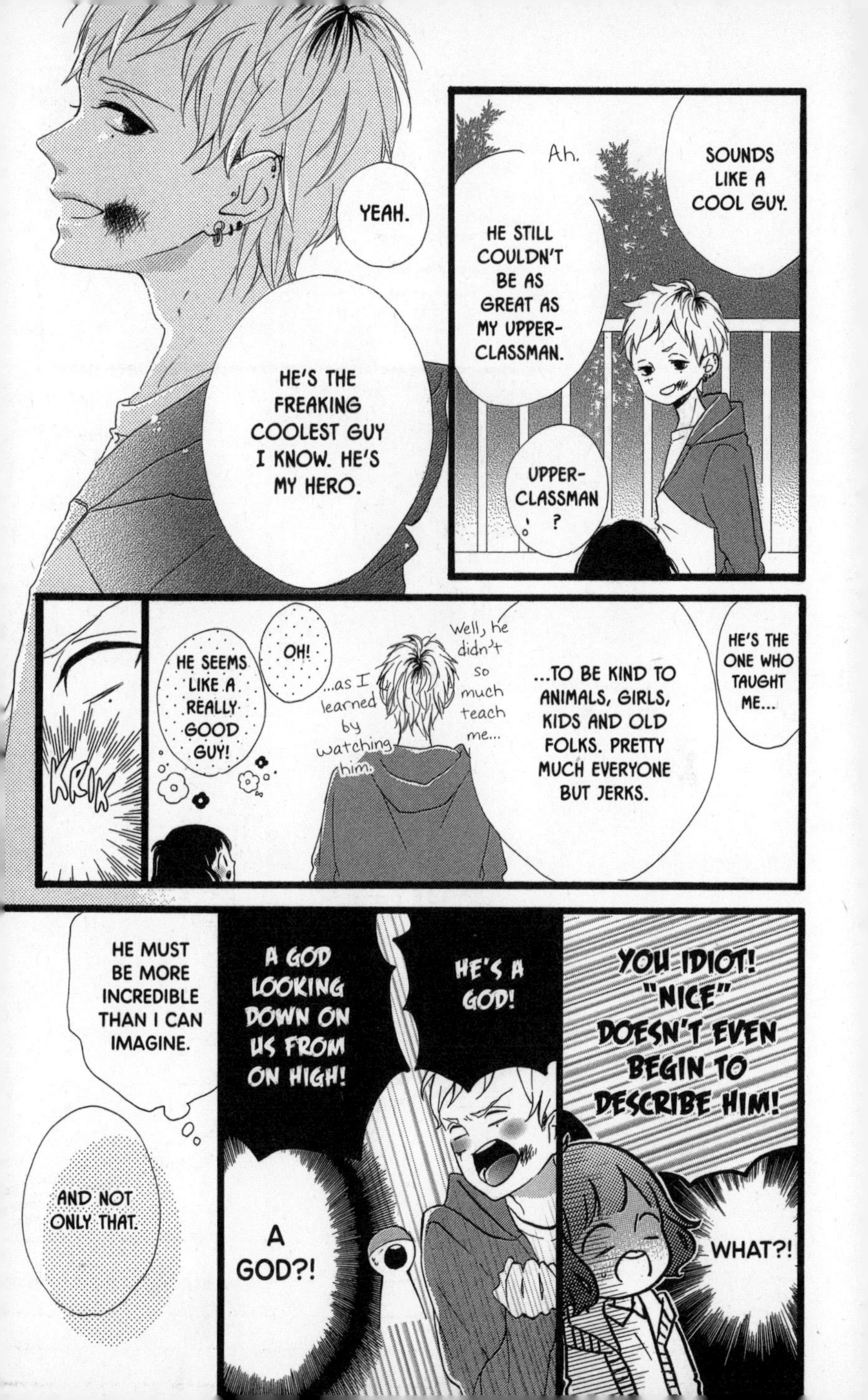
SOUNDS LIKE A COOL GUY.
Ah.
HE STILL COULDN'T BE AS GREAT AS MY UPPER-CLASSMAN.
UPPER-CLASSMAN?
YEAH.
HE'S THE FREAKING COOLEST GUY I KNOW. HE'S MY HERO.
HE'S THE ONE WHO TAUGHT ME...
...TO BE KIND TO ANIMALS, GIRLS, KIDS AND OLD FOLKS. PRETTY MUCH EVERYONE BUT JERKS.
Well, he didn't so much teach me...
...as I learned by watching him.
OH!
HE SEEMS LIKE A REALLY GOOD GUY!
KRIK
YOU IDIOT! "NICE" DOESN'T EVEN BEGIN TO DESCRIBE HIM!
WHAT?!
HE'S A GOD!
A GOD LOOKING DOWN ON US FROM ON HIGH!
A GOD?!
HE MUST BE MORE INCREDIBLE THAN I CAN IMAGINE.
AND NOT ONLY THAT.

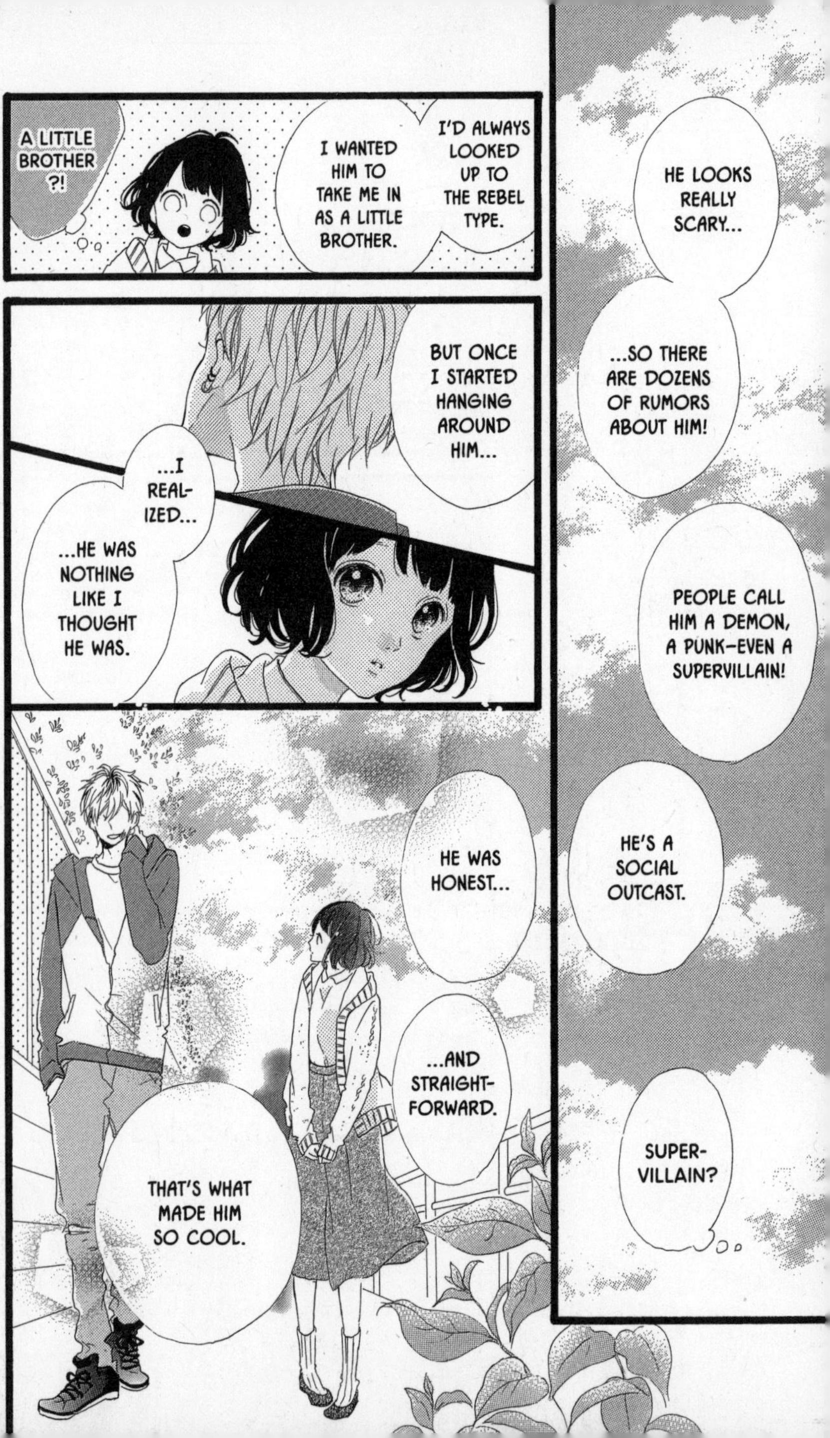
HE LOOKS REALLY SCARY...
...SO THERE ARE DOZENS OF RUMORS ABOUT HIM!
PEOPLE CALL HIM A DEMON, A PUNK—EVEN A SUPERVILLAIN!
HE'S A SOCIAL OUTCAST.
SUPERVILLAIN?
I'D ALWAYS LOOKED UP TO THE REBEL TYPE.
I WANTED HIM TO TAKE ME IN AS A LITTLE BROTHER.
A LITTLE BROTHER?!
BUT ONCE I STARTED HANGING AROUND HIM...
...I REALIZED...
...HE WAS NOTHING LIKE I THOUGHT HE WAS.
HE WAS HONEST...
...AND STRAIGHTFORWARD.
THAT'S WHAT MADE HIM SO COOL.

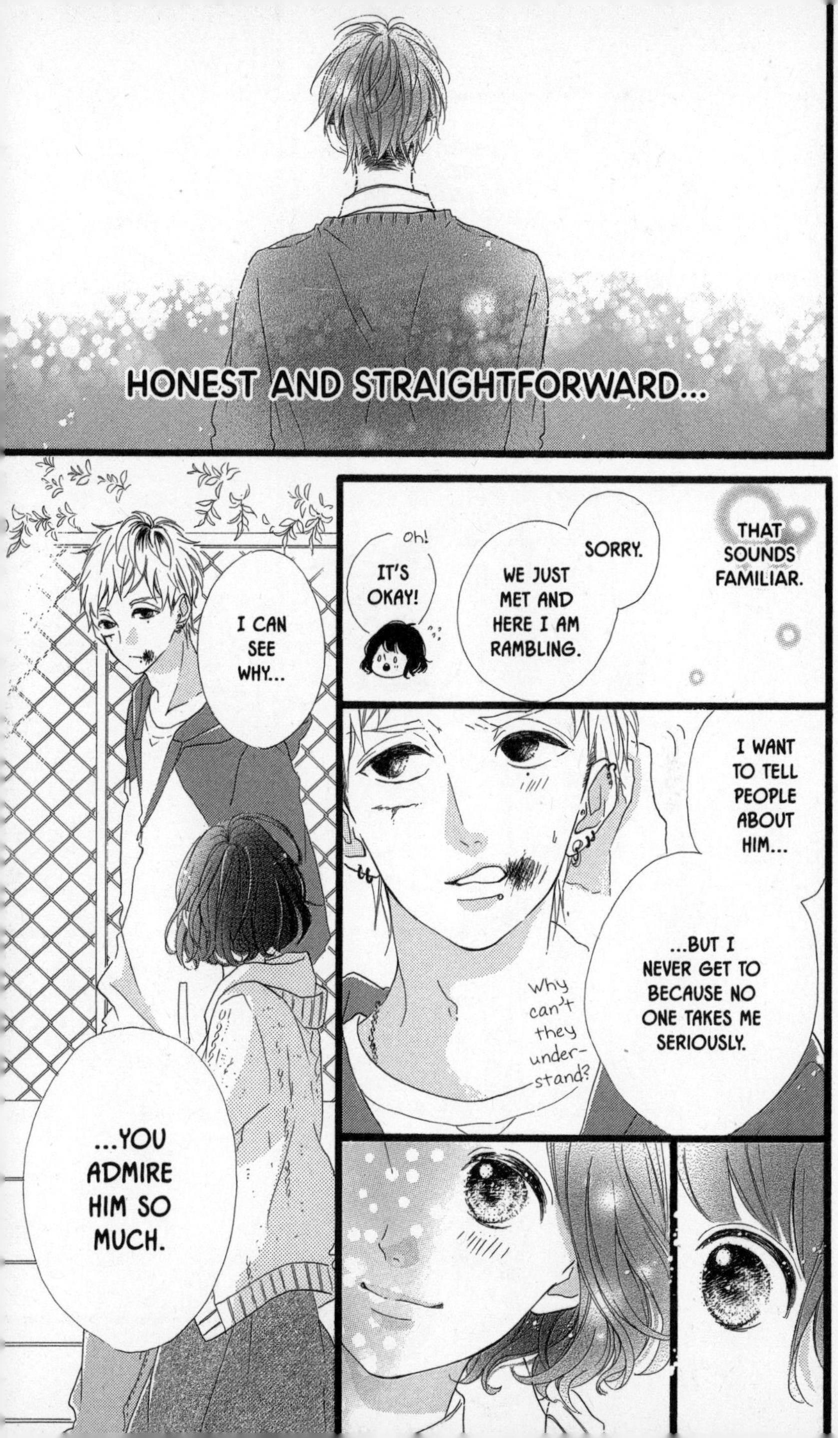
HONEST AND STRAIGHTFORWARD...
THAT SOUNDS FAMILIAR.
SORRY. WE JUST MET AND HERE I AM RAMBLING.
Oh! IT'S OKAY!
I WANT TO TELL PEOPLE ABOUT HIM...
...BUT I NEVER GET TO BECAUSE NO ONE TAKES ME SERIOUSLY.
Why can't they under-stand?
I CAN SEE WHY...
...YOU ADMIRE HIM SO MUCH.

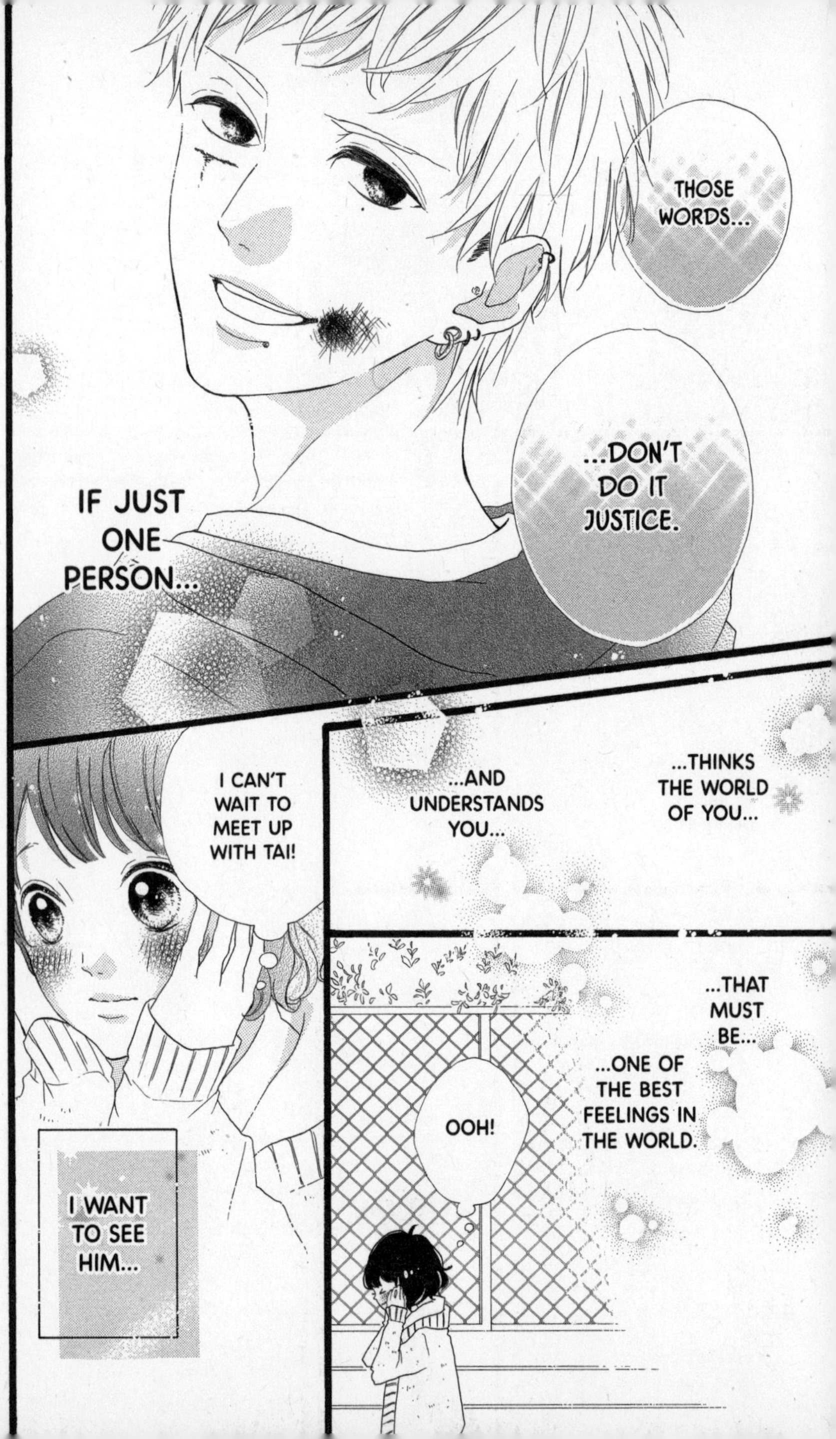
THOSE WORDS...
...DON'T DO IT JUSTICE.
IF JUST ONE PERSON...
...THINKS THE WORLD OF YOU...
...AND UNDERSTANDS YOU...
...THAT MUST BE...
...ONE OF THE BEST FEELINGS IN THE WORLD.
OOH!
I CAN'T WAIT TO MEET UP WITH TAI!
I WANT TO SEE HIM...

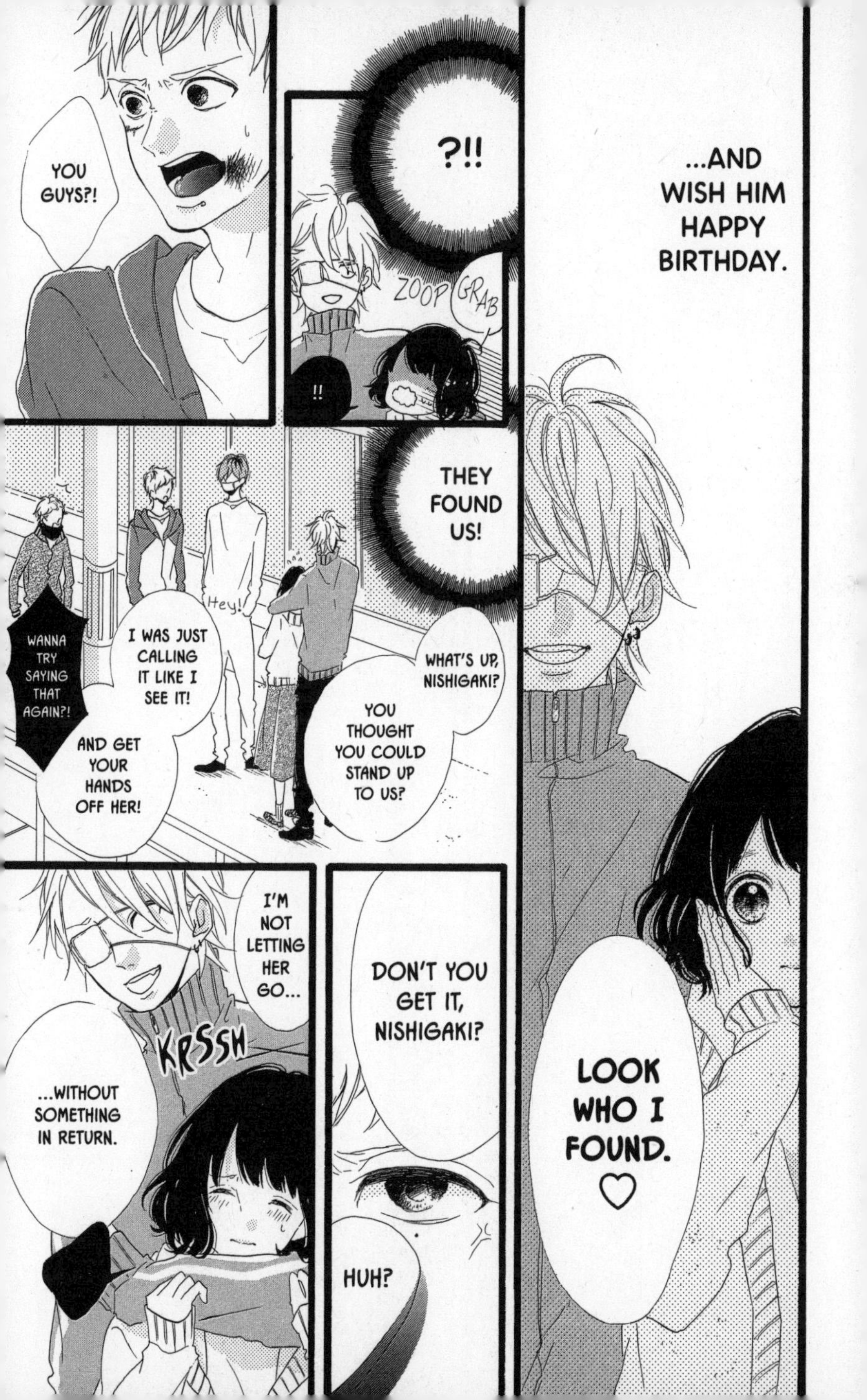
...AND WISH HIM HAPPY BIRTHDAY.
LOOK WHO I FOUND. ♡
?!!
ZOOP
GRAB
!!
YOU GUYS?!
THEY FOUND US!
WHAT'S UP, NISHIGAKI?
YOU THOUGHT YOU COULD STAND UP TO US?
Hey!
I WAS JUST CALLING IT LIKE I SEE IT!
AND GET YOUR HANDS OFF HER!
WANNA TRY SAYING THAT AGAIN?!
DON'T YOU GET IT, NISHIGAKI?
HUH?
I'M NOT LETTING HER GO...
KRSSH
...WITHOUT SOMETHING IN RETURN.

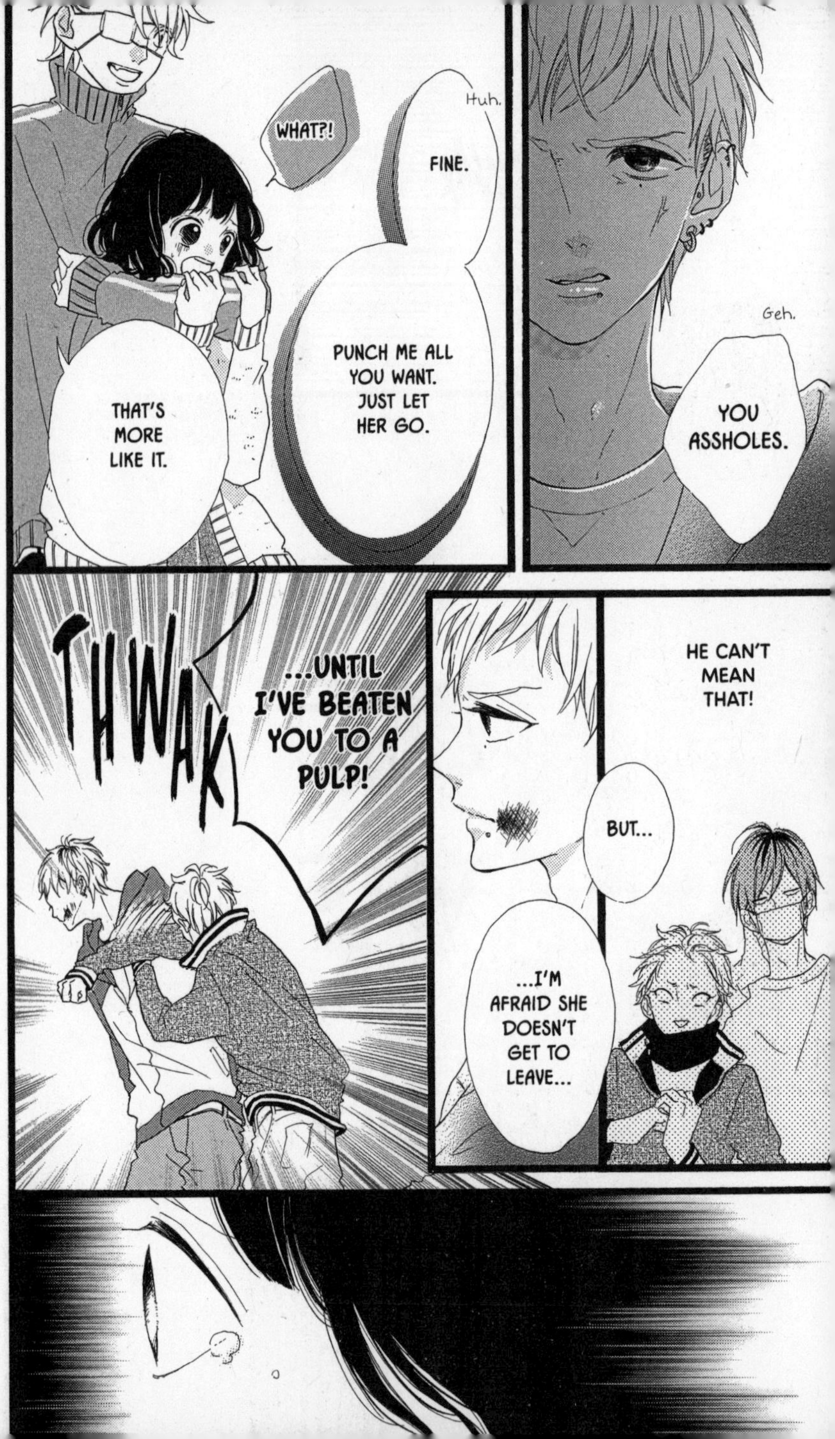
Geh.
YOU ASSHOLES.
Huh.
FINE.
WHAT?!
PUNCH ME ALL YOU WANT. JUST LET HER GO.
THAT'S MORE LIKE IT.
HE CAN'T MEAN THAT!
BUT...
...I'M AFRAID SHE DOESN'T GET TO LEAVE...
...UNTIL I'VE BEATEN YOU TO A PULP!
THWAK

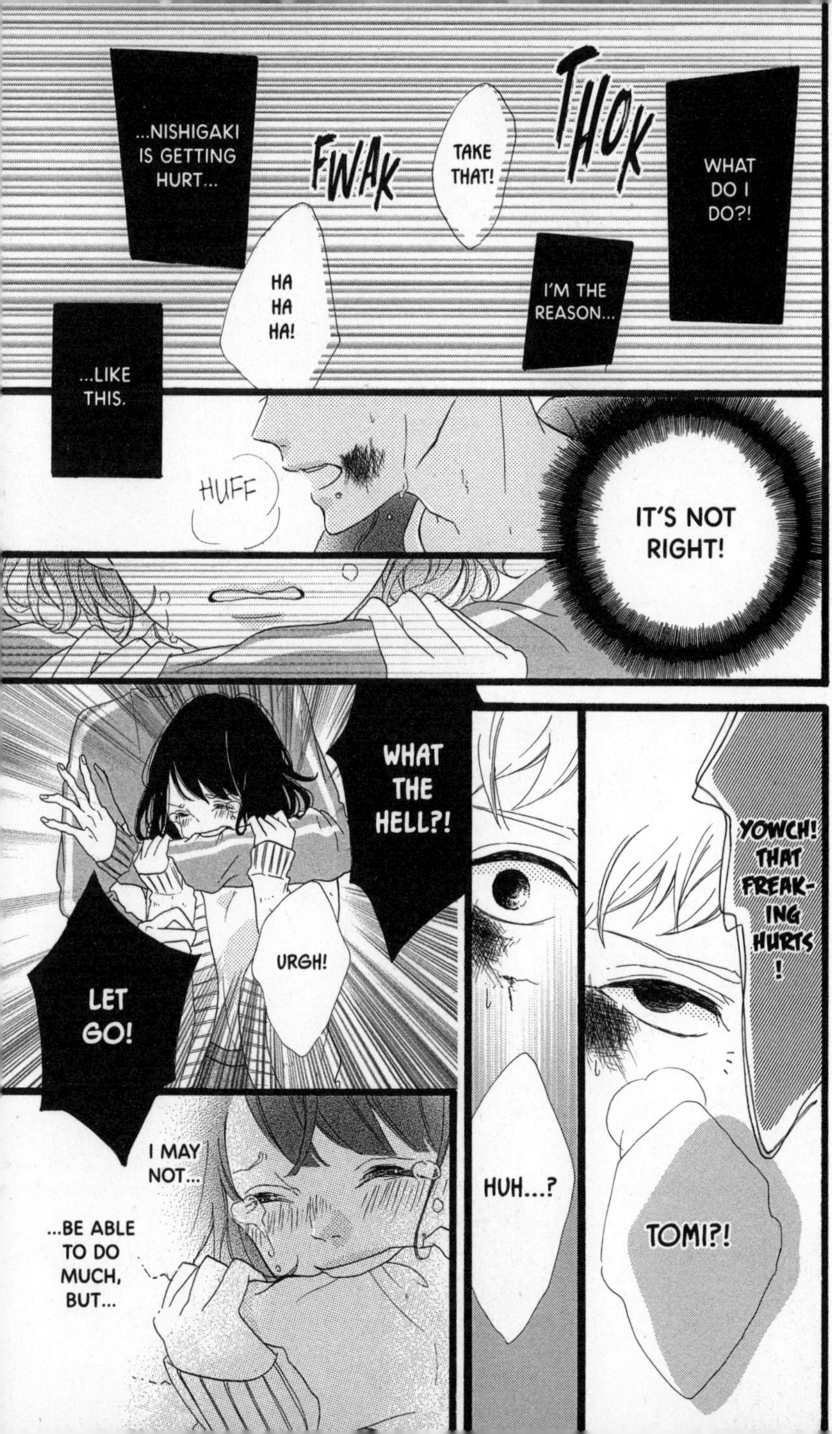
WHAT DO I DO?!
THOK
I'M THE REASON...
TAKE THAT!
FWAK
...NISHIGAKI IS GETTING HURT...
HA HA HA!
...LIKE THIS.
IT'S NOT RIGHT!
HUFF
YOWCH! THAT FREAK-ING HURTS!
TOMI?!
HUH...?
WHAT THE HELL?!
URGH!
LET GO!
I MAY NOT...
...BE ABLE TO DO MUCH, BUT...

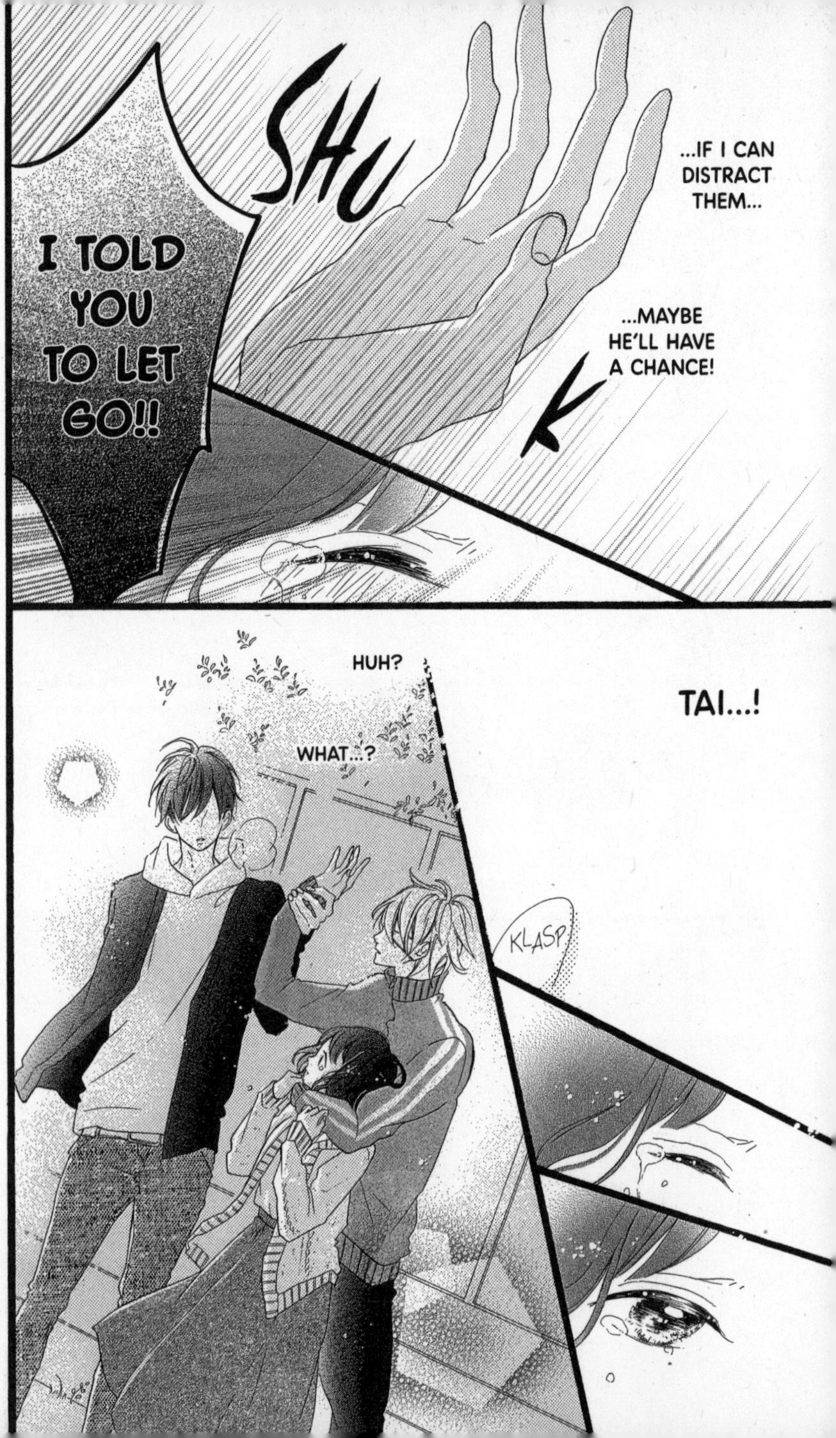
...IF I CAN DISTRACT THEM...
SHUK
...MAYBE HE'LL HAVE A CHANCE!
I TOLD YOU TO LET GO!!
TAI...!
KLASP
HUH?
WHAT...?

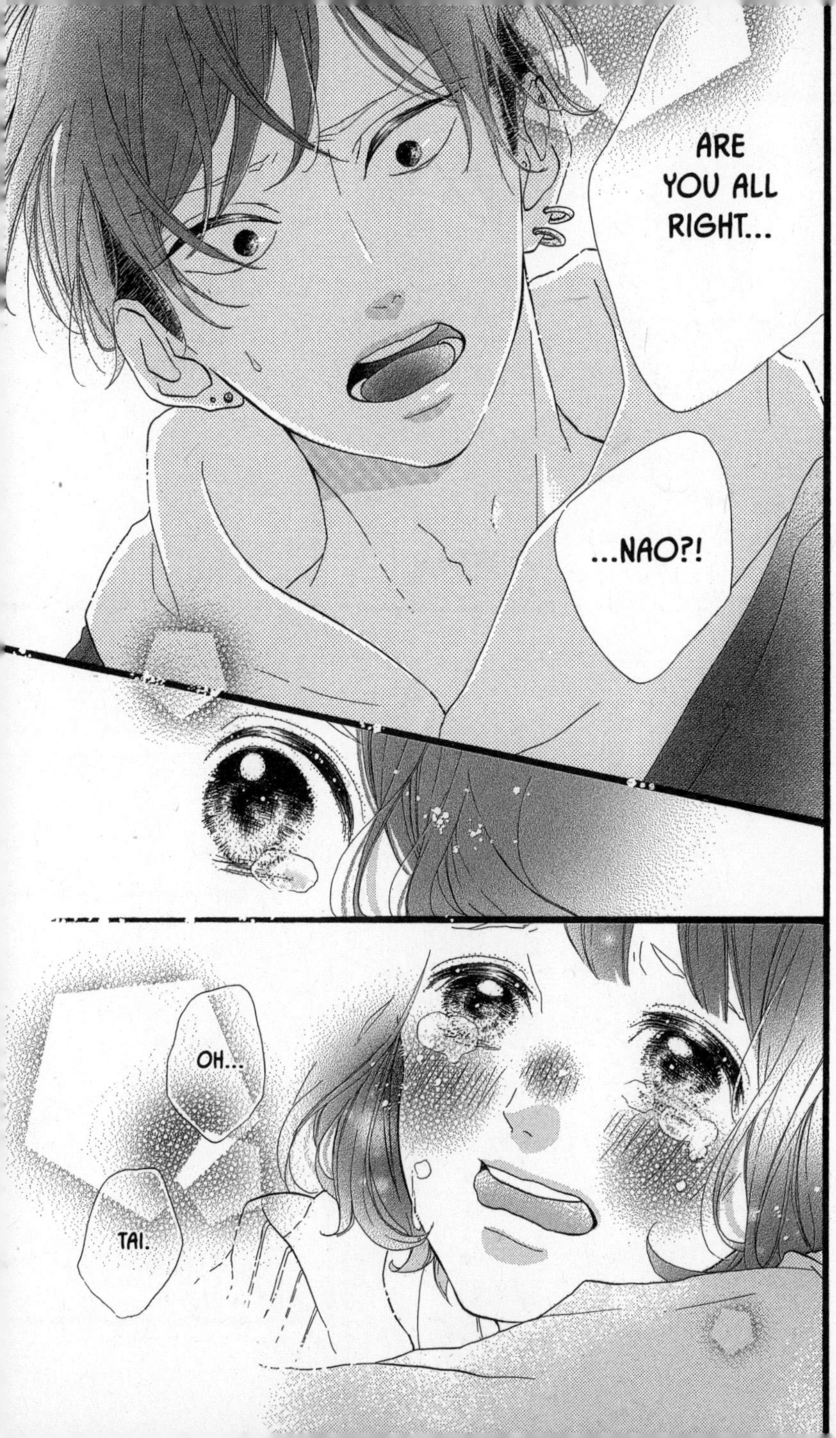
ARE YOU ALL RIGHT...
...NAO?!
OH...
TAI.

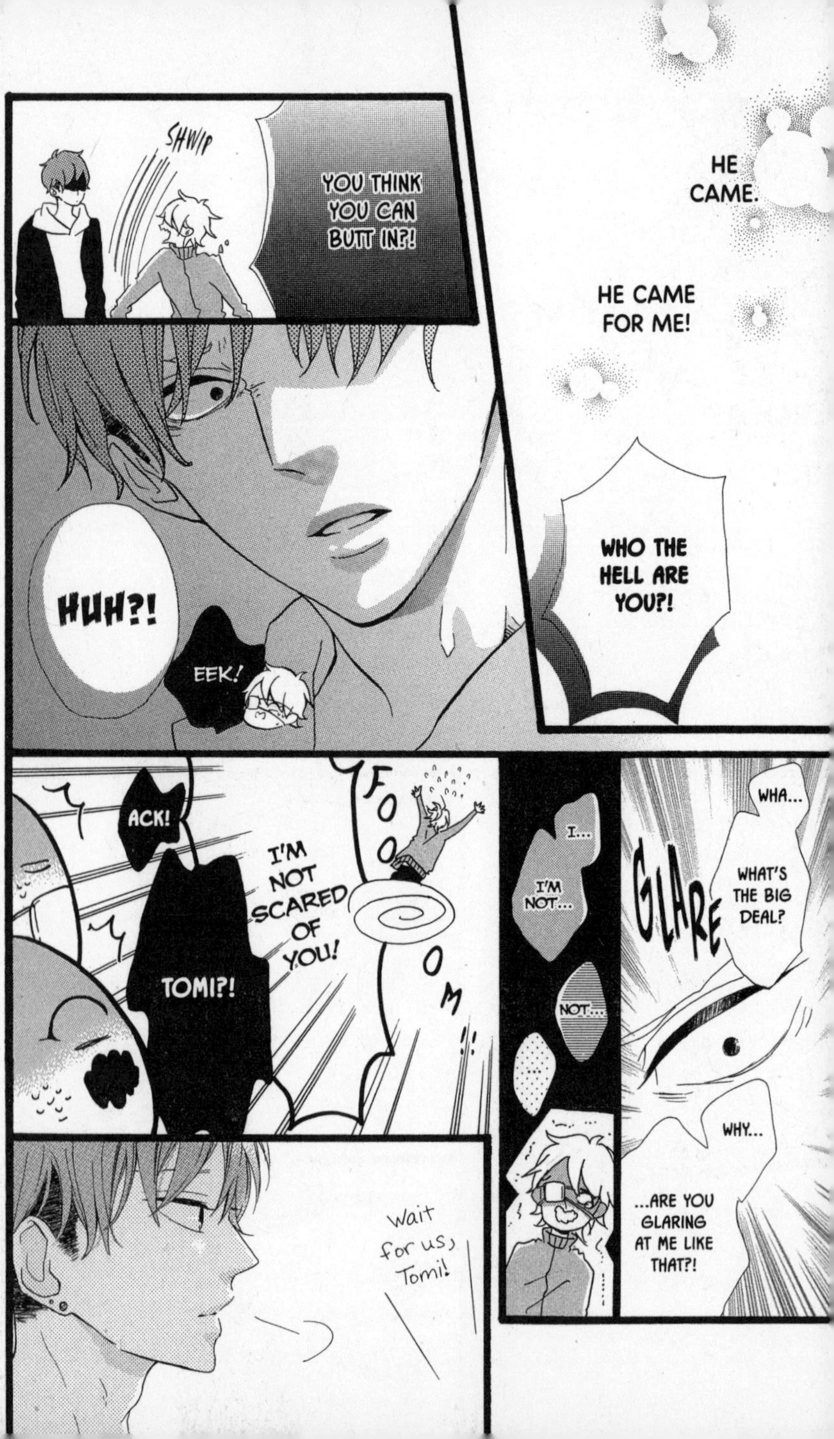
HE CAME.
HE CAME FOR ME!
WHO THE HELL ARE YOU?!
SHWIP
YOU THINK YOU CAN BUTT IN?!
HUH?!
EEK!
WHA...
GLARE
WHAT'S THE BIG DEAL?
WHY...
...ARE YOU GLARING AT ME LIKE THAT?!
I...
I'M NOT...
NOT...
FOOOOM!!
I'M NOT SCARED OF YOU!
ACK!
TOMI?!
Wait for us, Tomi!

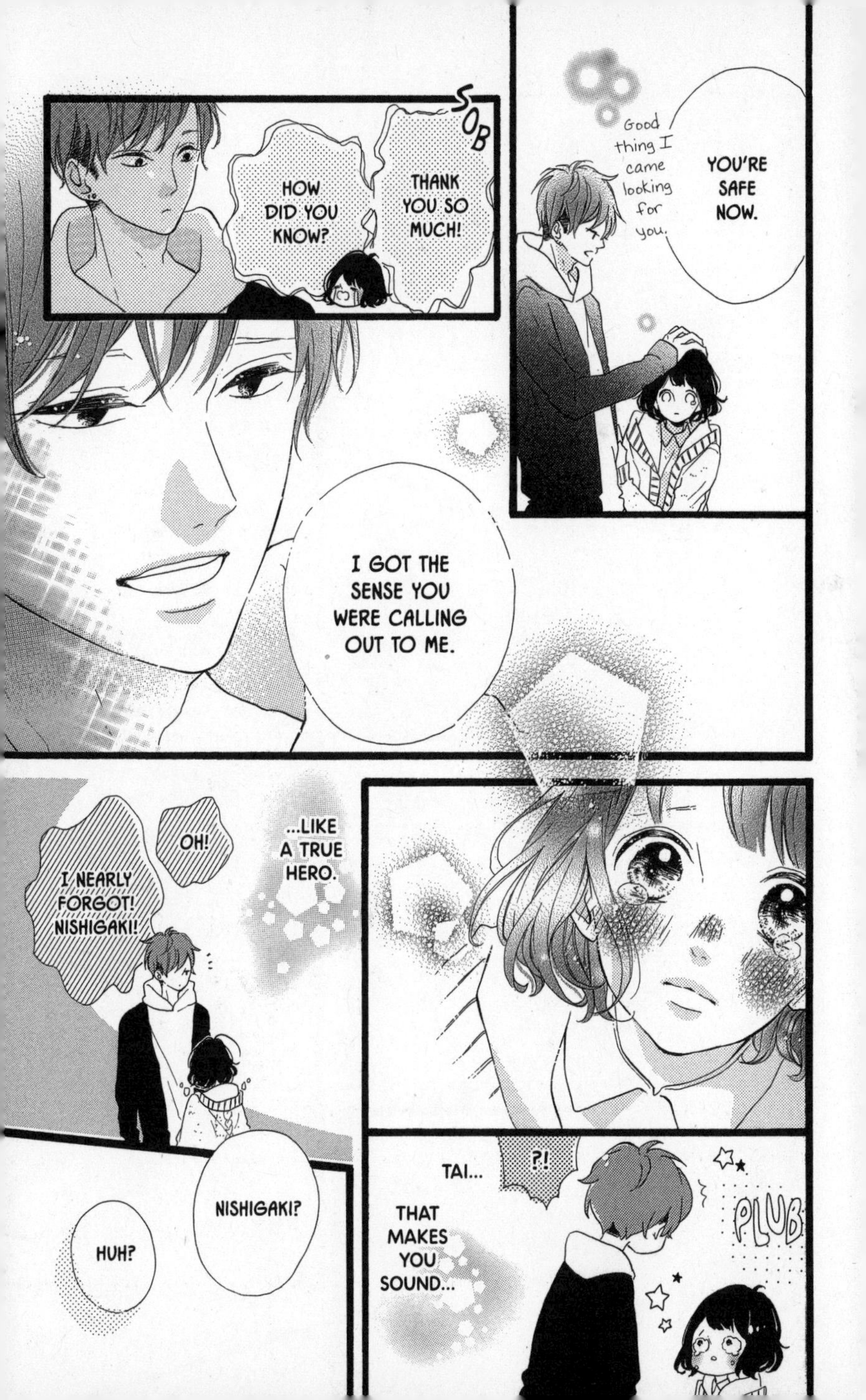
Good thing I came looking for you.
YOU'RE SAFE NOW.
SOB
THANK YOU SO MUCH!
HOW DID YOU KNOW?
I GOT THE SENSE YOU WERE CALLING OUT TO ME.
TAI...
THAT MAKES YOU SOUND...
?!
PLUB
...LIKE A TRUE HERO.
OH!
I NEARLY FORGOT! NISHIGAKI!
NISHIGAKI?
HUH?

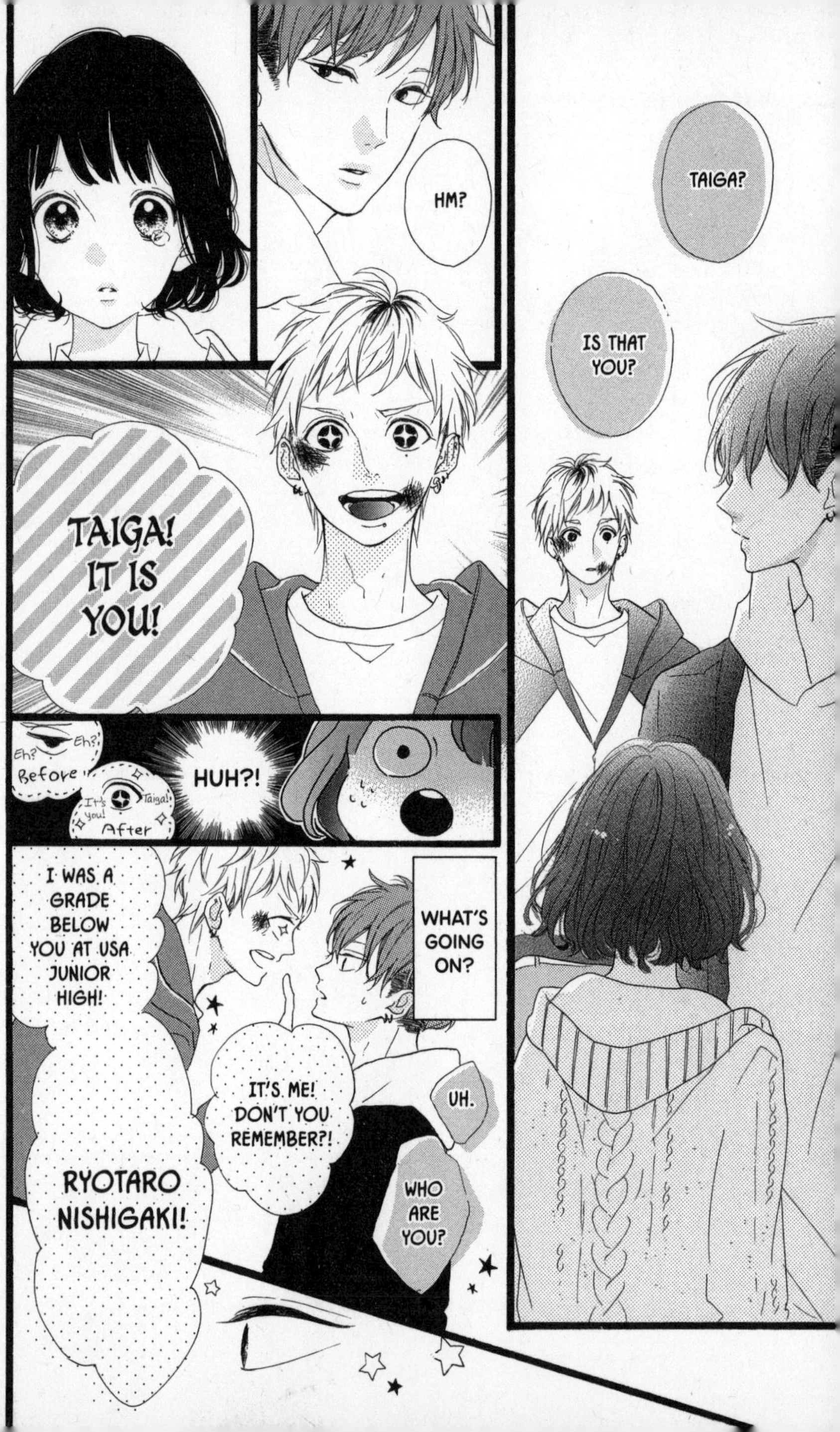
TAIGA?
IS THAT YOU?
HM?
TAIGA! IT IS YOU!
HUH?!
Eh? Eh? Before
It's you! Taiga! After
WHAT'S GOING ON?
I WAS A GRADE BELOW YOU AT USA JUNIOR HIGH!
IT'S ME! DON'T YOU REMEMBER?!
RYOTARO NISHIGAKI!
UH.
WHO ARE YOU?

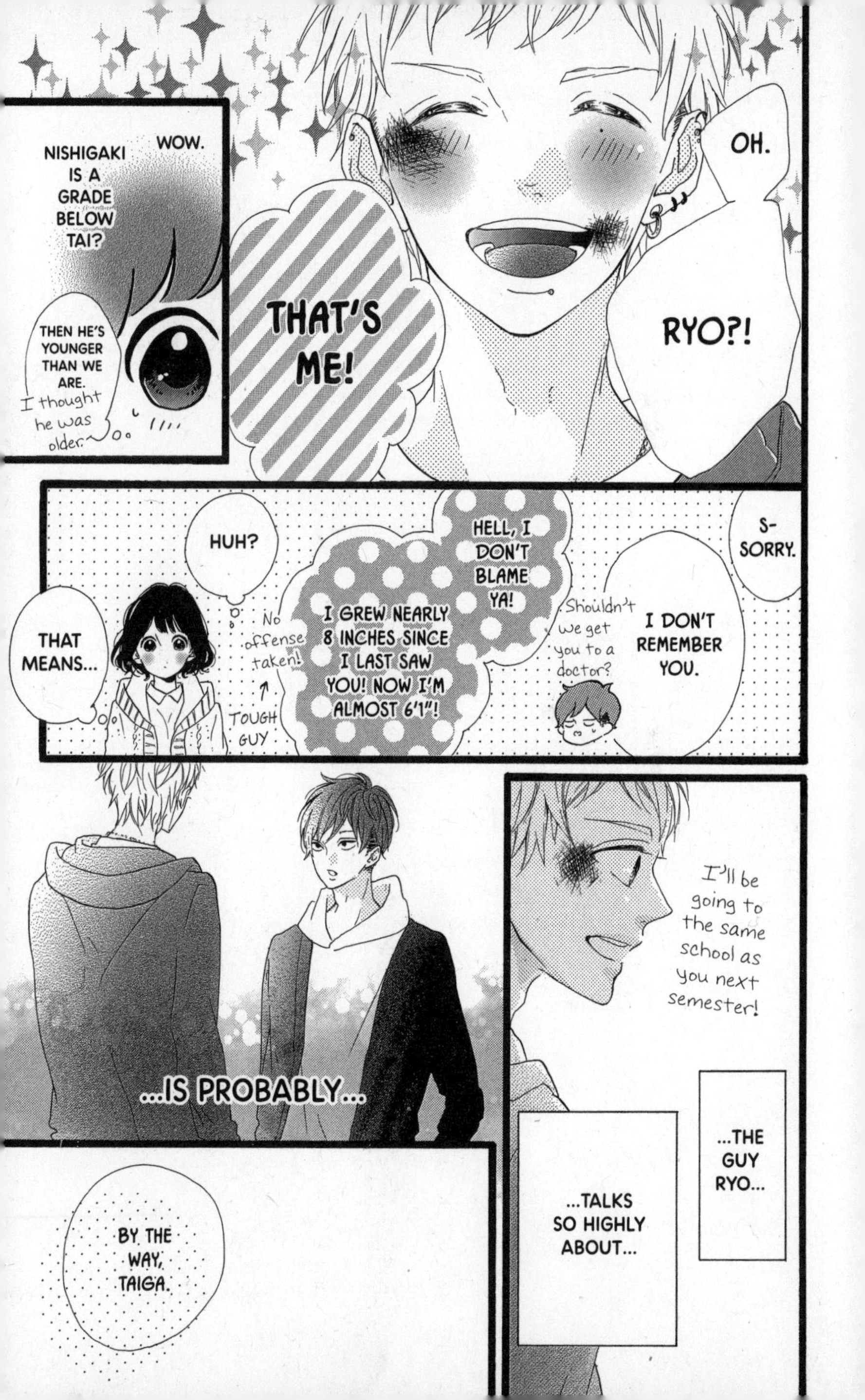
OH.
RYO?!
THAT'S ME!
WOW.
NISHIGAKI IS A GRADE BELOW TAI?
THEN HE'S YOUNGER THAN WE ARE.
I thought he was older.
S-SORRY.
I DON'T REMEMBER YOU.
Shouldn't we get you to a doctor?
HELL, I DON'T BLAME YA!
I GREW NEARLY 8 INCHES SINCE I LAST SAW YOU! NOW I'M ALMOST 6'1"!
No offense taken!
TOUGH GUY
HUH?
THAT MEANS...
I'll be going to the same school as you next semester!
...THE GUY RYO...
...TALKS SO HIGHLY ABOUT...
...IS PROBABLY...
BY THE WAY, TAIGA.

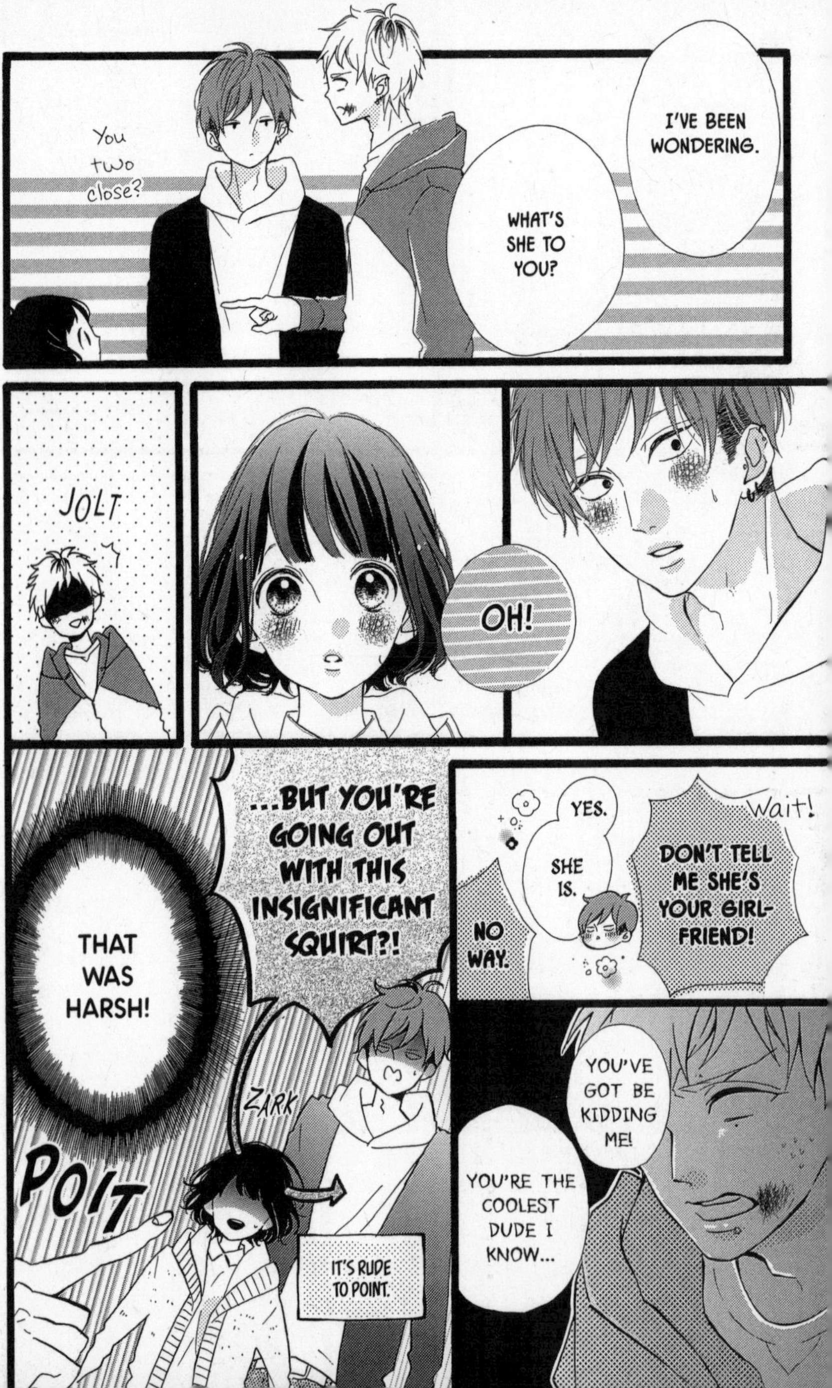
I'VE BEEN WONDERING.
WHAT'S SHE TO YOU?
You two close?
OH!
JOLT
Wait!
DON'T TELL ME SHE'S YOUR GIRL-FRIEND!
YES. SHE IS.
NO WAY.
YOU'VE GOT BE KIDDING ME!
YOU'RE THE COOLEST DUDE I KNOW...
...BUT YOU'RE GOING OUT WITH THIS INSIGNIFICANT SQUIRT?!
THAT WAS HARSH!
ZARK
POIT
IT'S RUDE TO POINT.

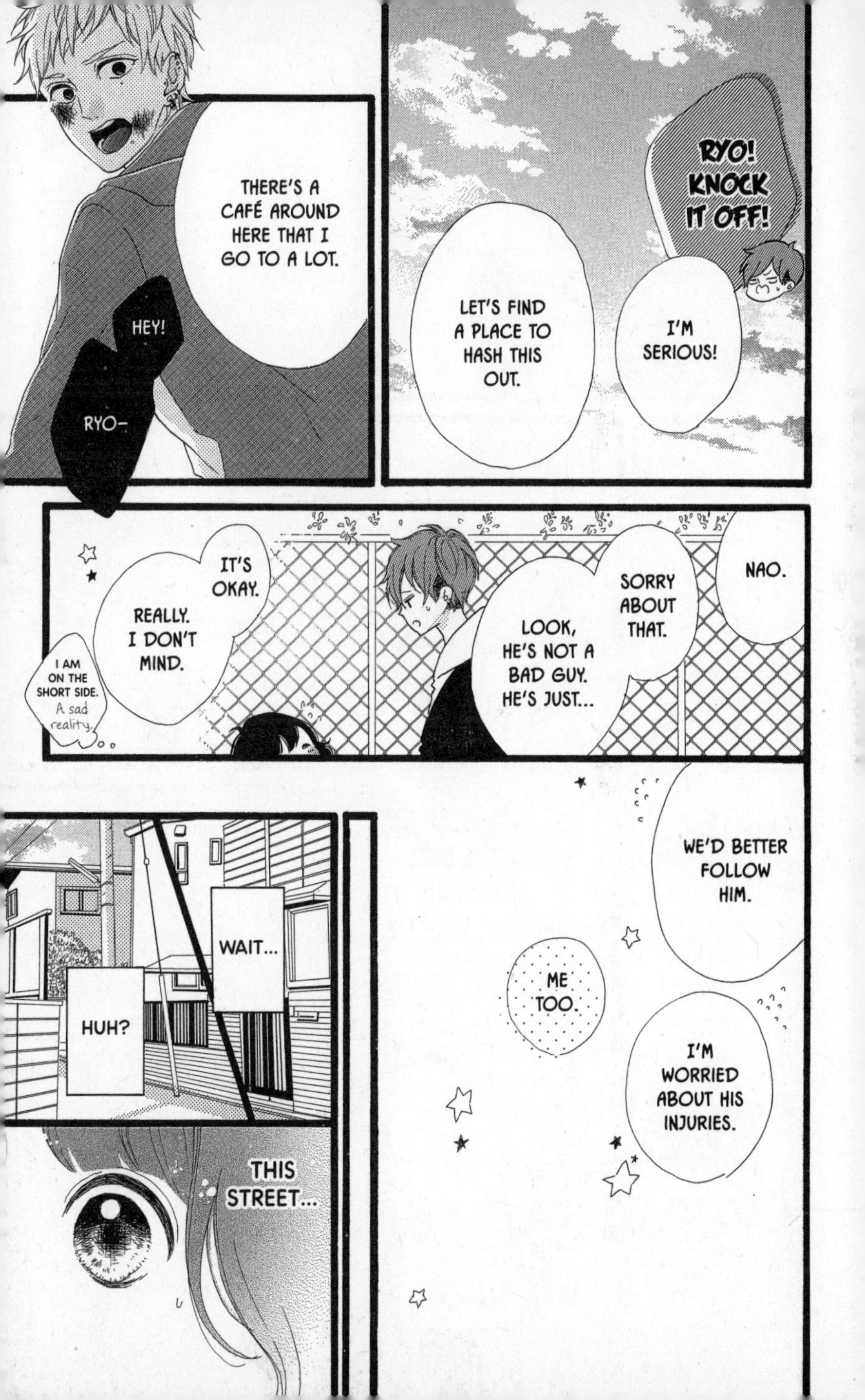
RYO! KNOCK IT OFF!
I'M SERIOUS!
LET'S FIND A PLACE TO HASH THIS OUT.
THERE'S A CAFÉ AROUND HERE THAT I GO TO A LOT.
HEY!
RYO-
NAO.
SORRY ABOUT THAT.
LOOK, HE'S NOT A BAD GUY. HE'S JUST...
IT'S OKAY.
REALLY. I DON'T MIND.
I AM ON THE SHORT SIDE. A sad reality.
WE'D BETTER FOLLOW HIM.
I'M WORRIED ABOUT HIS INJURIES.
ME TOO.
WAIT...
HUH?
THIS STREET...

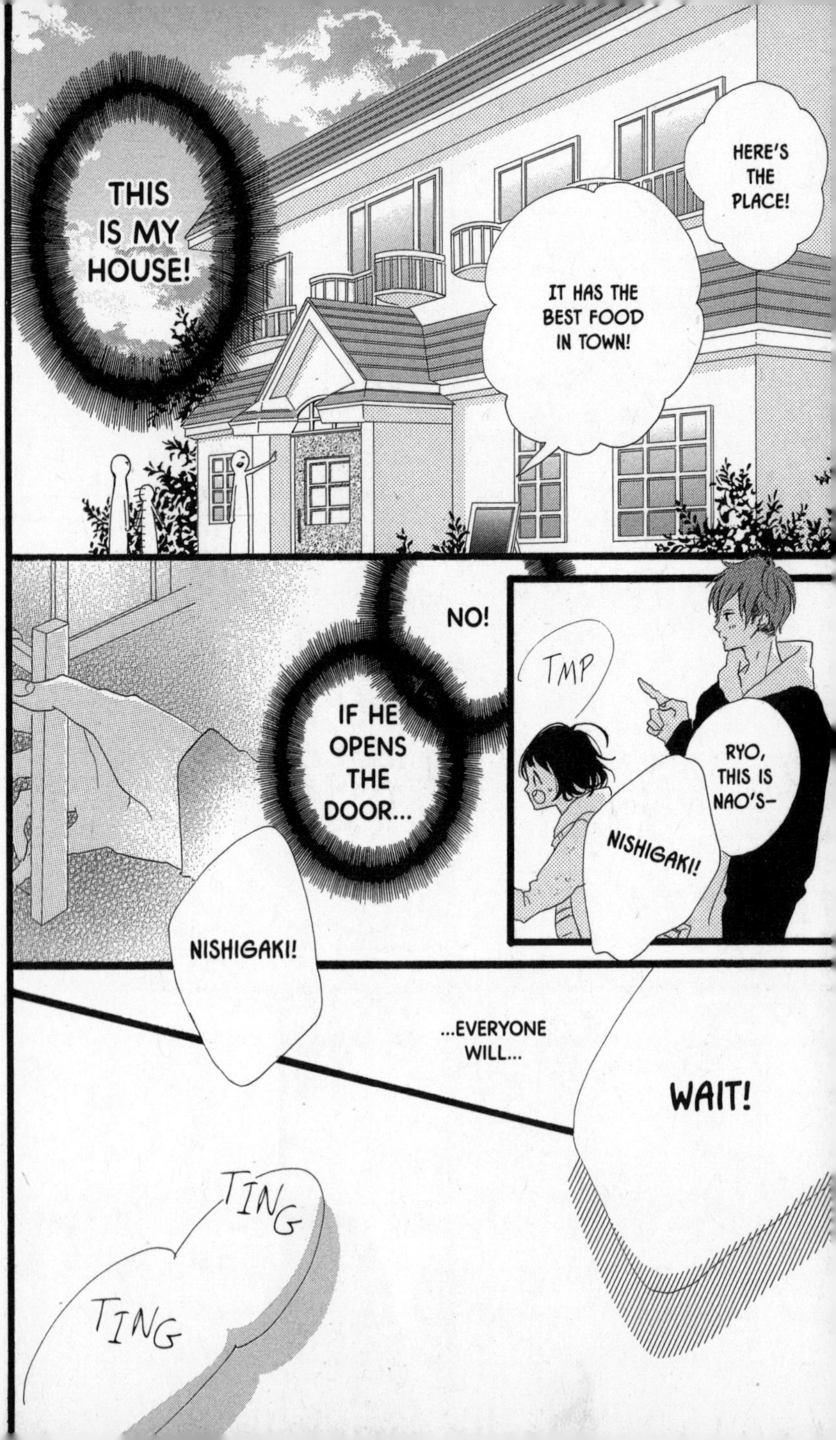
HERE'S THE PLACE!
IT HAS THE BEST FOOD IN TOWN!
THIS IS MY HOUSE!
TMP
RYO, THIS IS NAO'S–
NISHIGAKI!
NO!
IF HE OPENS THE DOOR...
NISHIGAKI!
WAIT!
...EVERYONE WILL...
TING
TING

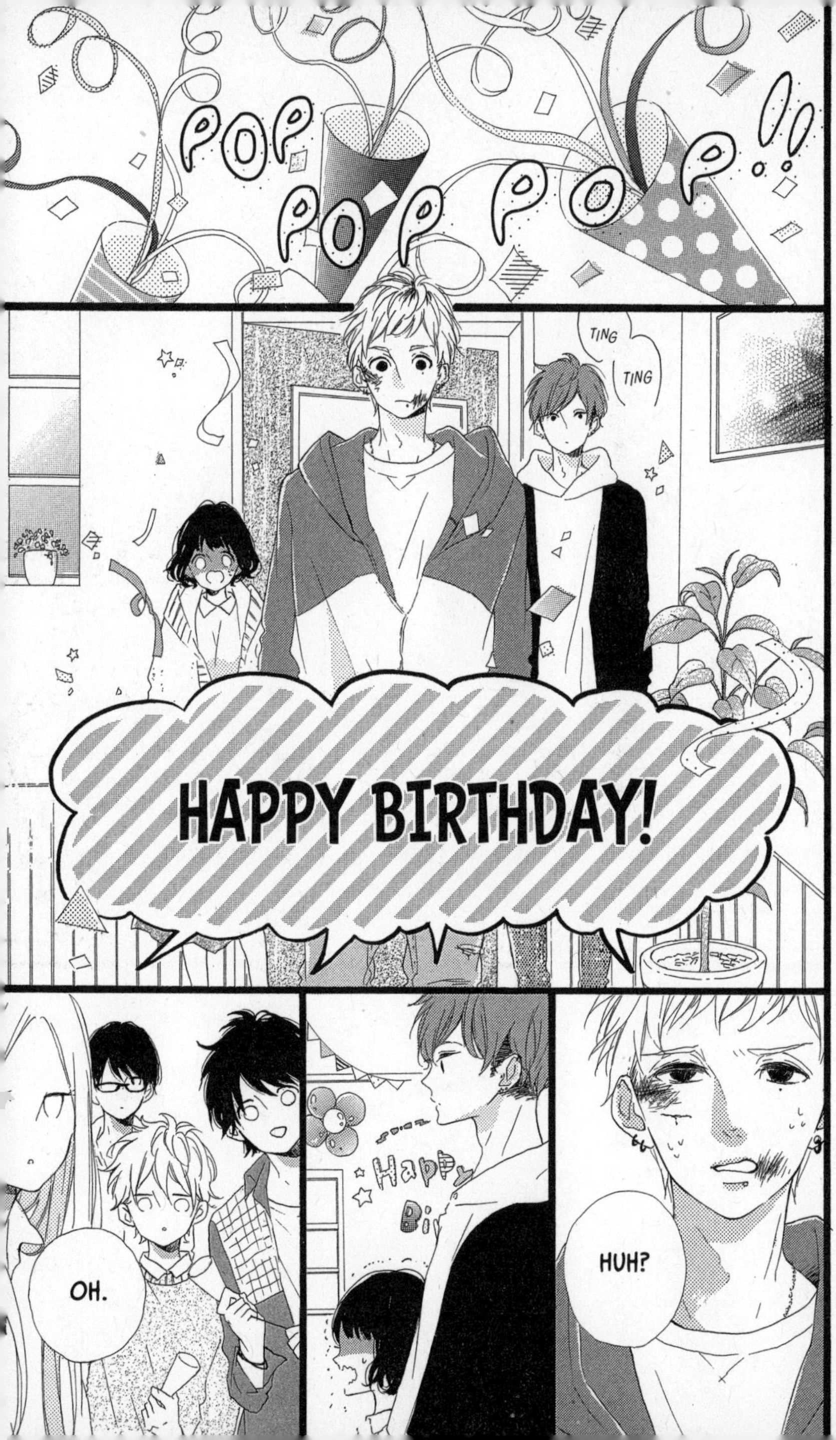
POP
POP POP!!
TING
TING
HAPPY BIRTHDAY!
HUH?
Happy
OH.

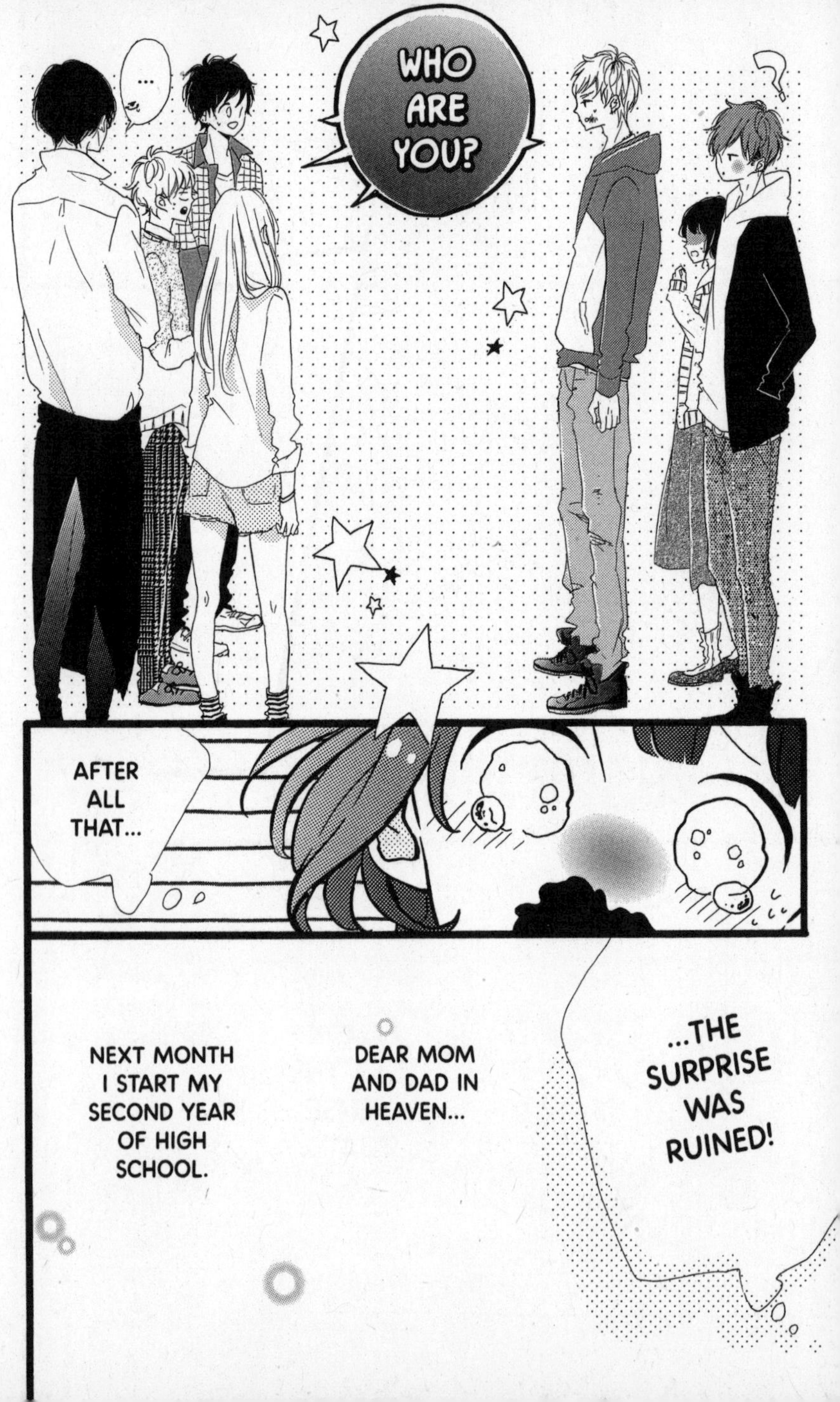
WHO ARE YOU?
...
AFTER ALL THAT...
...THE SURPRISE WAS RUINED!
DEAR MOM AND DAD IN HEAVEN...
NEXT MONTH I START MY SECOND YEAR OF HIGH SCHOOL.

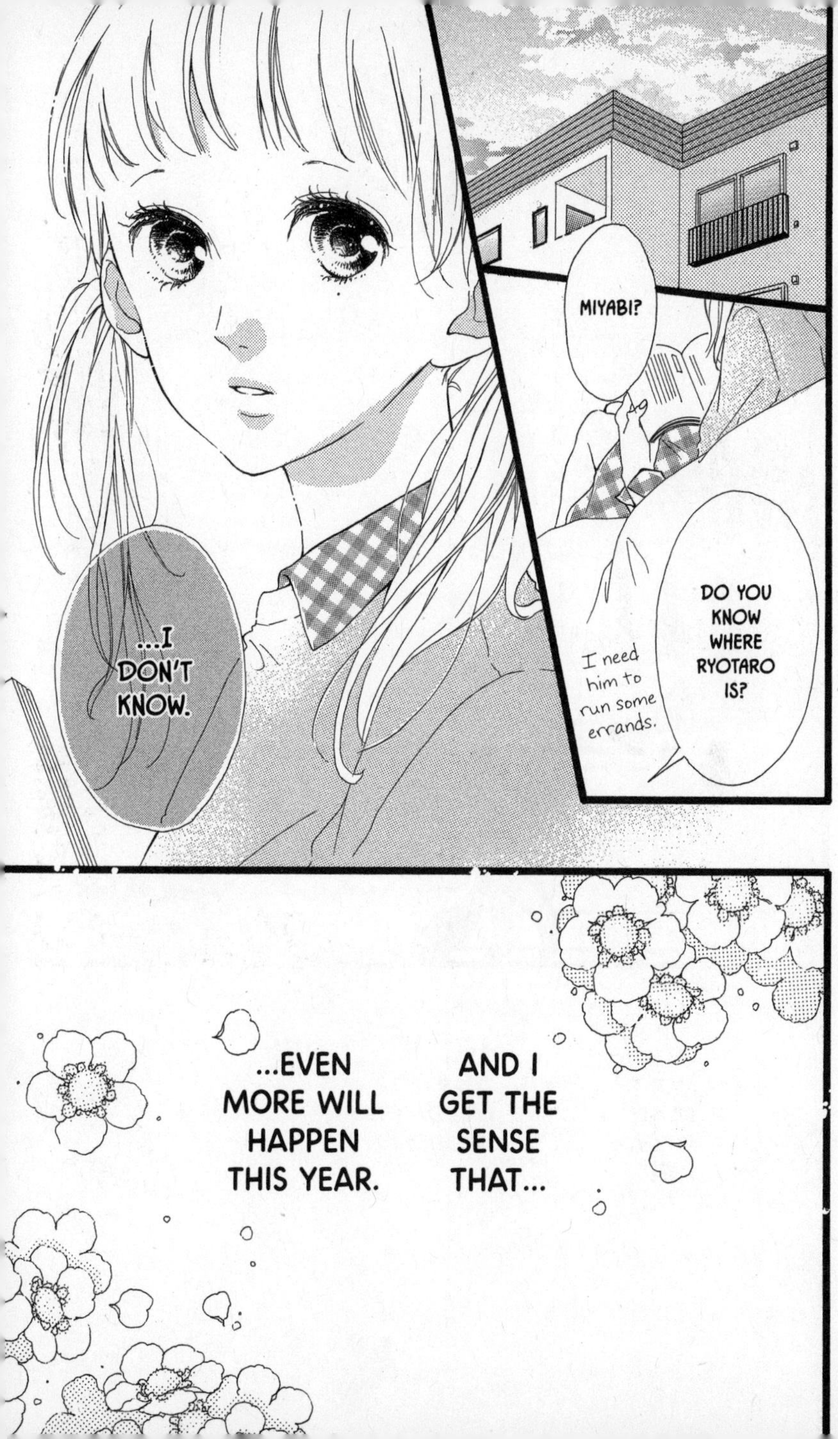
MIYABI?
DO YOU KNOW WHERE RYOTARO IS?
I need him to run some errands.
...I DON'T KNOW.
AND I GET THE SENSE THAT...
...EVEN MORE WILL HAPPEN THIS YEAR.

Expressionless Sou

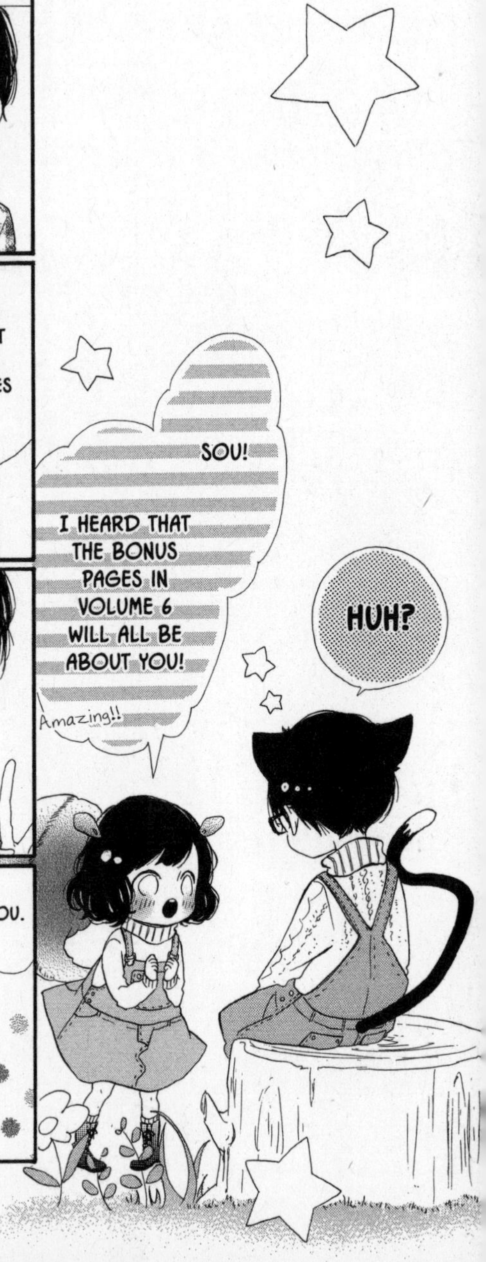
SOU!
I HEARD THAT THE BONUS PAGES IN VOLUME 6 WILL ALL BE ABOUT YOU!
Amazing!!
HUH?

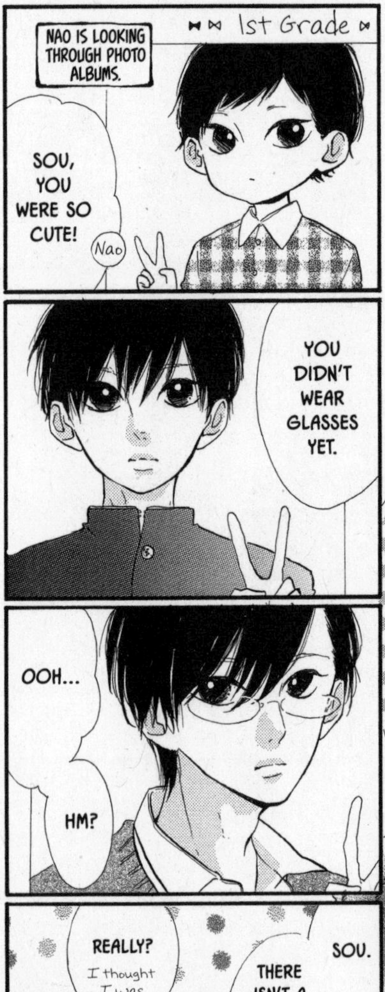
1st Grade
NAO IS LOOKING THROUGH PHOTO ALBUMS.
SOU, YOU WERE SO CUTE!
Nao
YOU DIDN'T WEAR GLASSES YET.
OOH...
HM?
SOU.
THERE ISN'T A SINGLE PICTURE OF YOU SMILING.
REALLY?
I thought I was smiling.

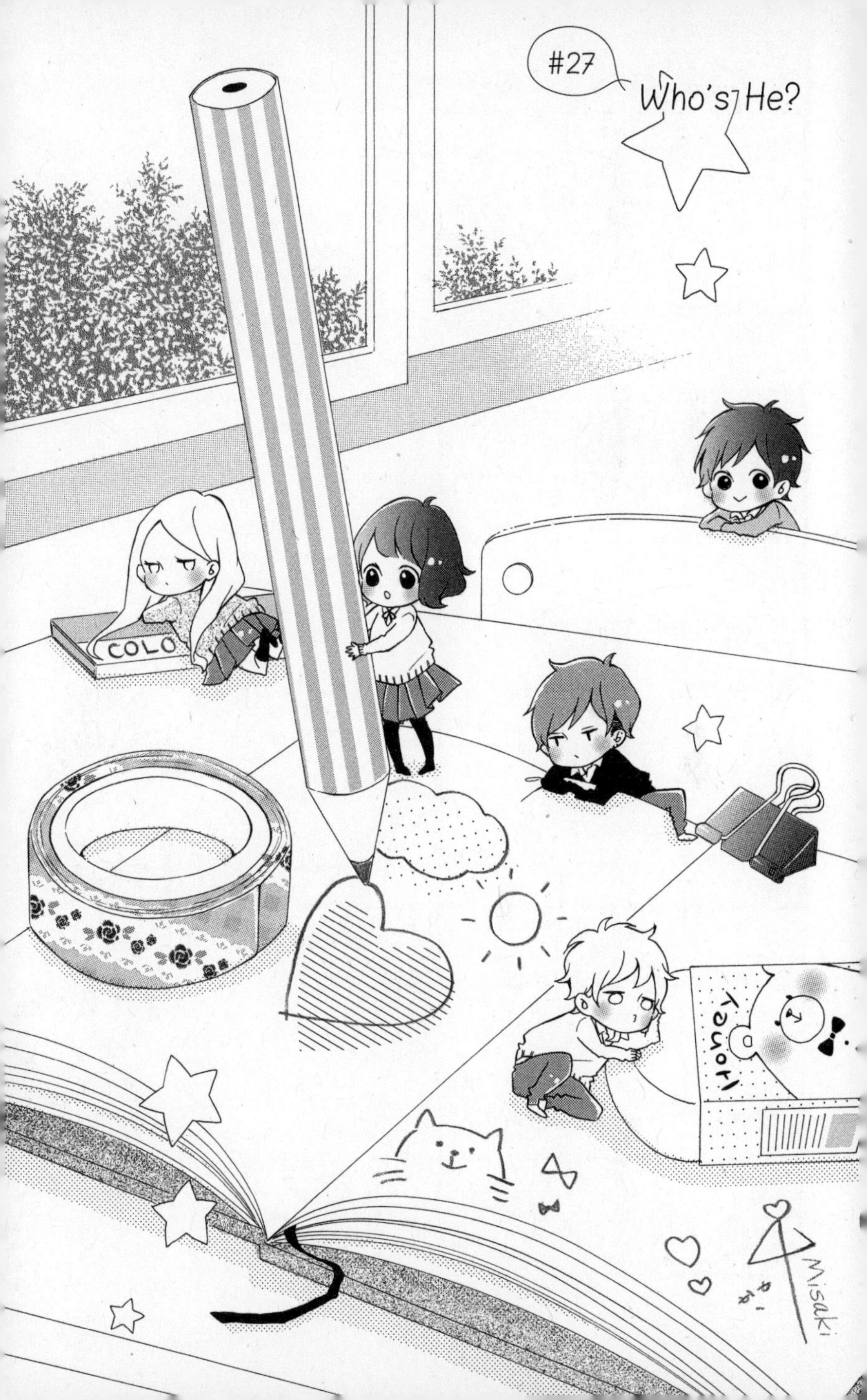

#27
Who's He?
COLO
Misaki

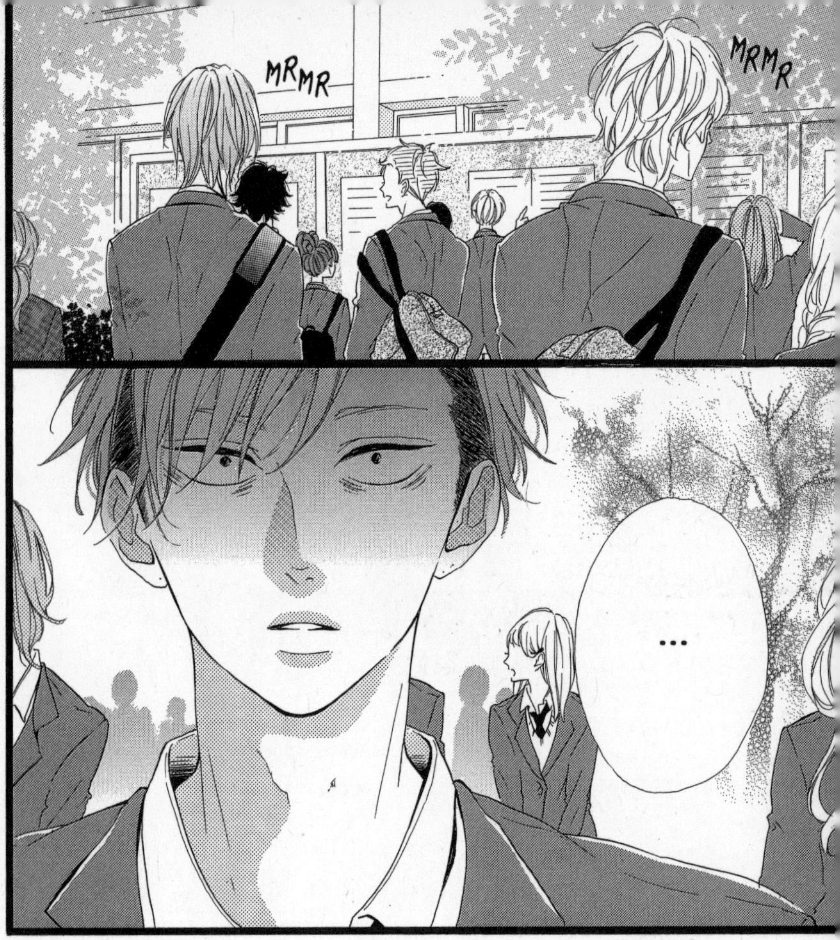
MRMR
MRMR
...

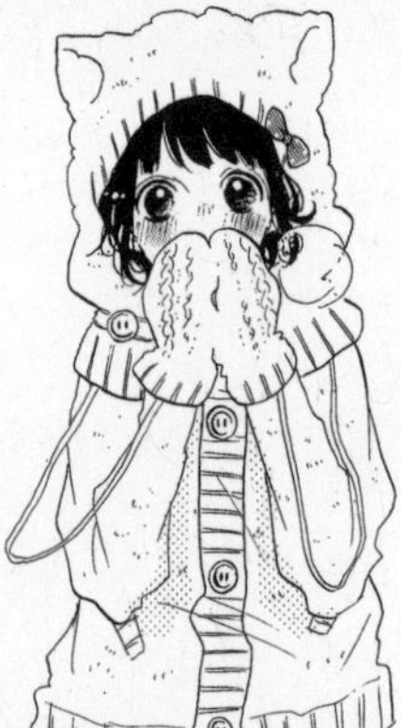

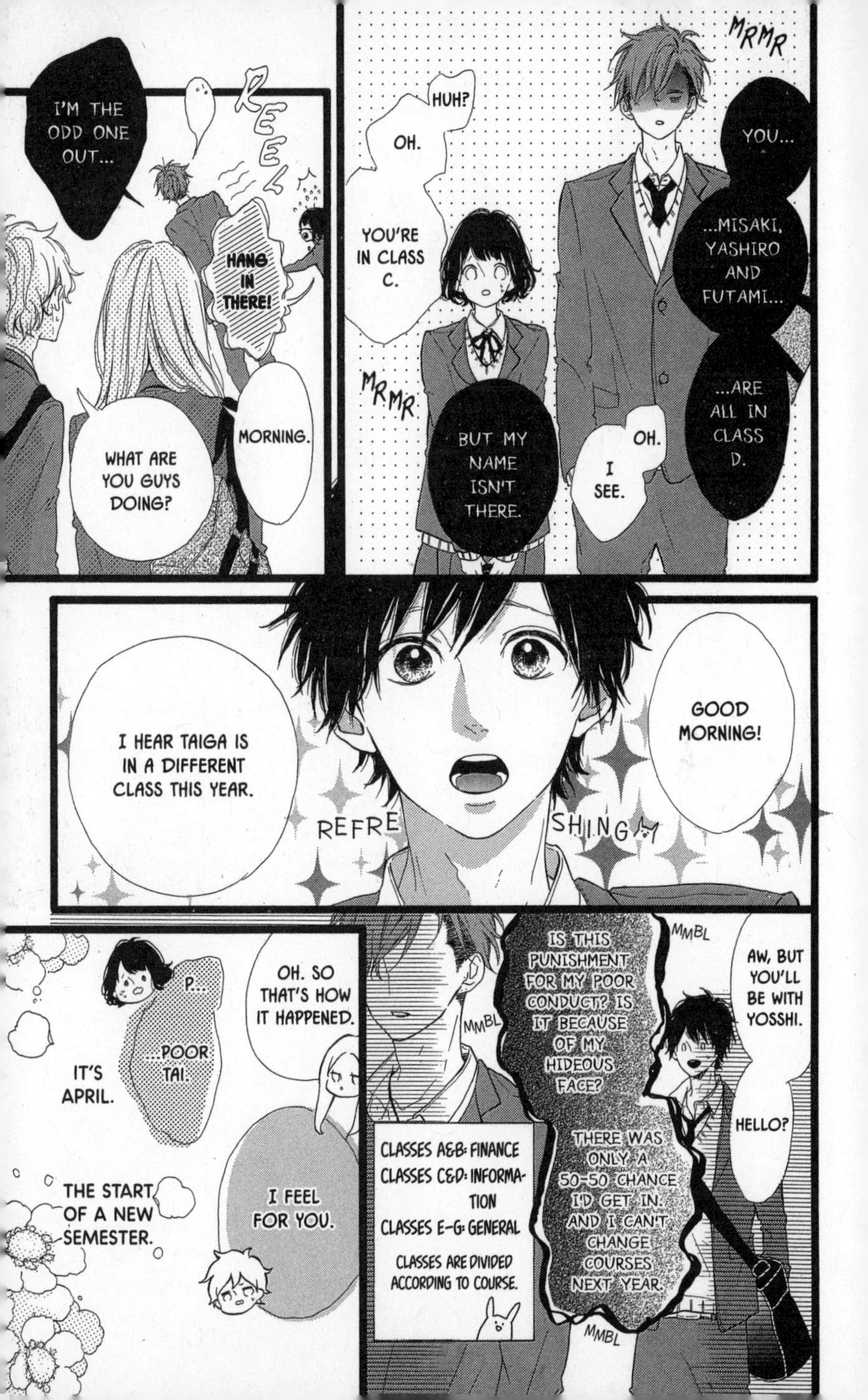

MRMR
YOU...
...MISAKI, YASHIRO AND FUTAMI...
HUH?
OH.
YOU'RE IN CLASS C.
...ARE ALL IN CLASS D.
OH. I SEE.
BUT MY NAME ISN'T THERE.
MRMR
REEL
I'M THE ODD ONE OUT...
HANG IN THERE!
MORNING.
WHAT ARE YOU GUYS DOING?
GOOD MORNING!
REFRESHING
I HEAR TAIGA IS IN A DIFFERENT CLASS THIS YEAR.
MMBL
AW, BUT YOU'LL BE WITH YOSSHI.
IS THIS PUNISHMENT FOR MY POOR CONDUCT? IS IT BECAUSE OF MY HIDEOUS FACE?
MMBL
HELLO?
THERE WAS ONLY A 50-50 CHANCE I'D GET IN. AND I CAN'T CHANGE COURSES NEXT YEAR.
MMBL
CLASSES A&B: FINANCE
CLASSES C&D: INFORMATION
CLASSES E-G: GENERAL
CLASSES ARE DIVIDED ACCORDING TO COURSE.
OH. SO THAT'S HOW IT HAPPENED.
P...
...POOR TAI.
IT'S APRIL.
I FEEL FOR YOU.
THE START OF A NEW SEMESTER.

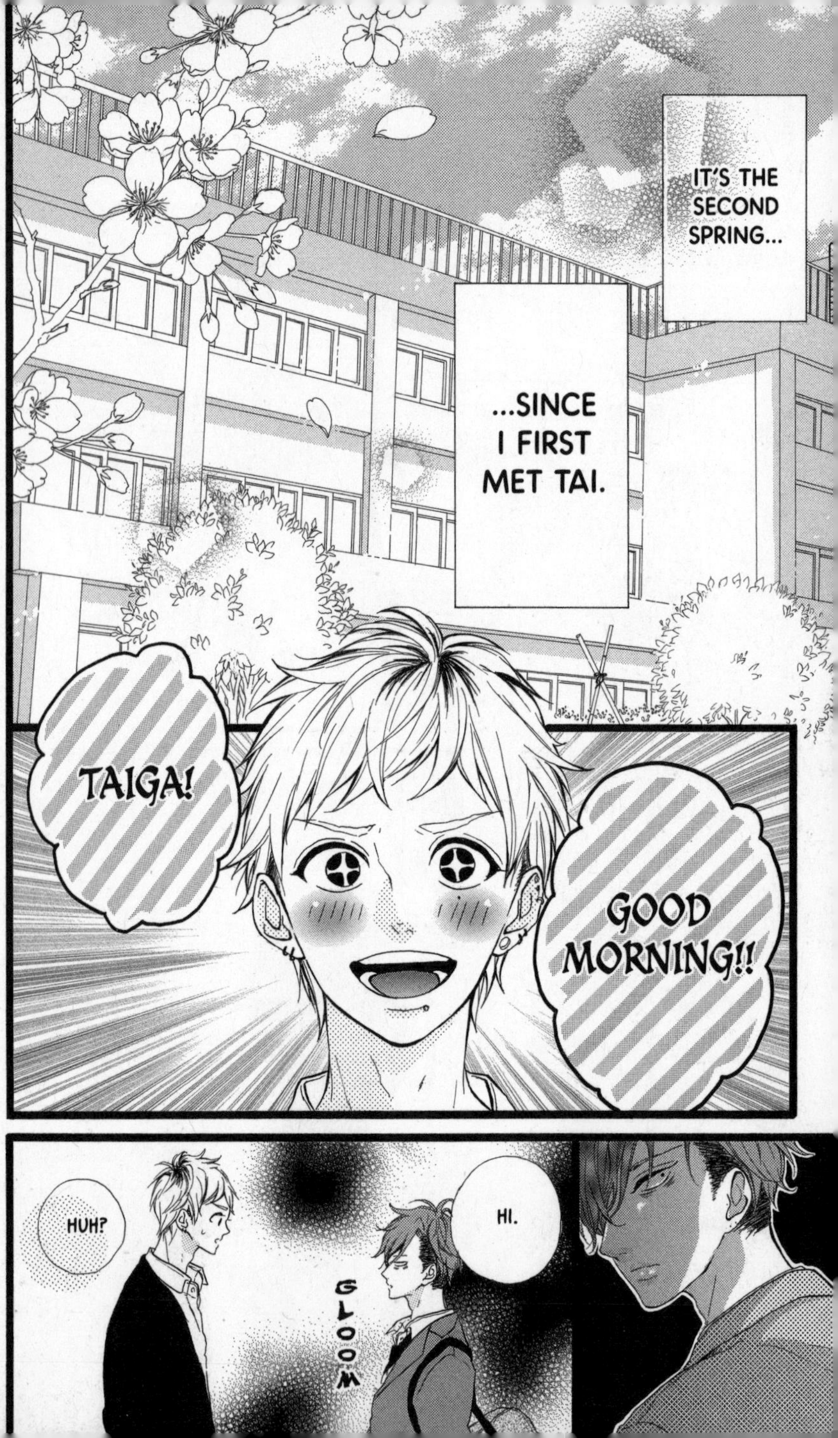
IT'S THE SECOND SPRING...
...SINCE I FIRST MET TAI.
GOOD MORNING!!
TAIGA!
HI.
GLOOM
HUH?

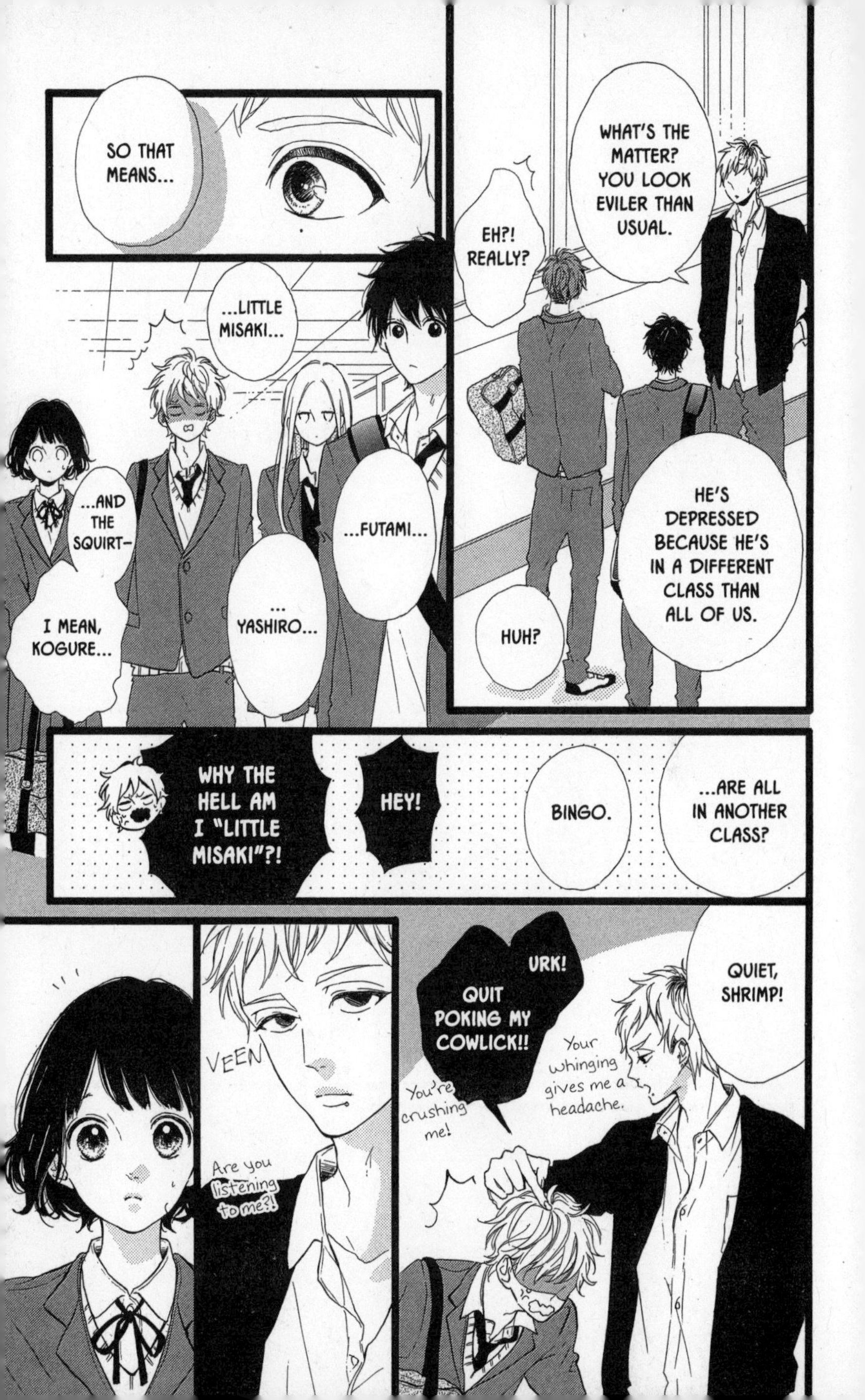
WHAT'S THE MATTER? YOU LOOK EVILER THAN USUAL.
EH?! REALLY?
HE'S DEPRESSED BECAUSE HE'S IN A DIFFERENT CLASS THAN ALL OF US.
HUH?
SO THAT MEANS...
...LITTLE MISAKI...
...FUTAMI...
...YASHIRO...
...AND THE SQUIRT—
I MEAN, KOGURE...
...ARE ALL IN ANOTHER CLASS?
BINGO.
HEY!
WHY THE HELL AM I "LITTLE MISAKI"?!
QUIET, SHRIMP!
Your whinging gives me a headache.
URK!
QUIT POKING MY COWLICK!!
You're crushing me!
VEEN
Are you listening to me?!

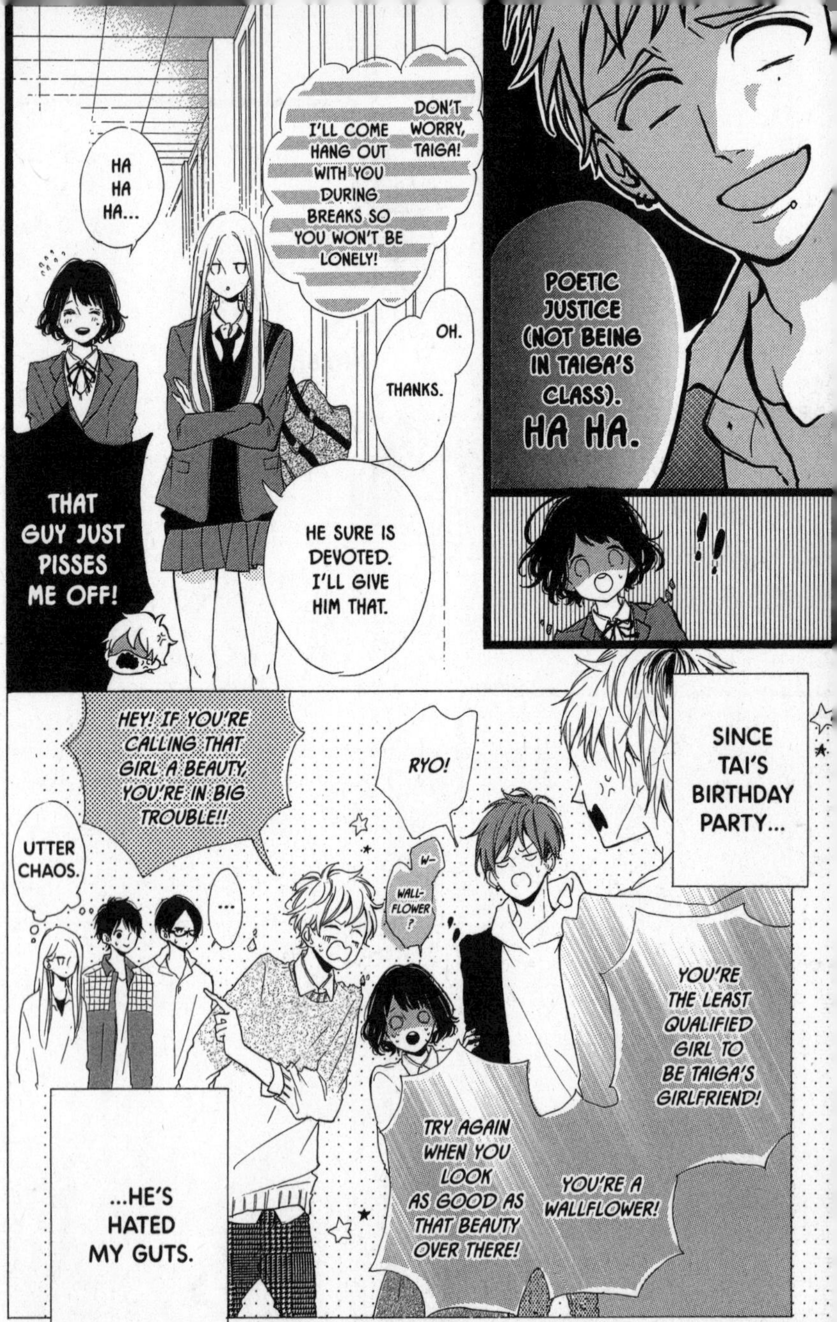
POETIC JUSTICE (NOT BEING IN TAIGA'S CLASS). HA HA.
!!
DON'T WORRY, TAIGA!
I'LL COME HANG OUT WITH YOU DURING BREAKS SO YOU WON'T BE LONELY!
HA HA HA...
OH. THANKS.
HE SURE IS DEVOTED. I'LL GIVE HIM THAT.
THAT GUY JUST PISSES ME OFF!
SINCE TAI'S BIRTHDAY PARTY...
RYO!
HEY! IF YOU'RE CALLING THAT GIRL A BEAUTY, YOU'RE IN BIG TROUBLE!!
UTTER CHAOS.
W- WALL-FLOWER?
...
YOU'RE THE LEAST QUALIFIED GIRL TO BE TAIGA'S GIRLFRIEND!
YOU'RE A WALLFLOWER!
TRY AGAIN WHEN YOU LOOK AS GOOD AS THAT BEAUTY OVER THERE!
...HE'S HATED MY GUTS.

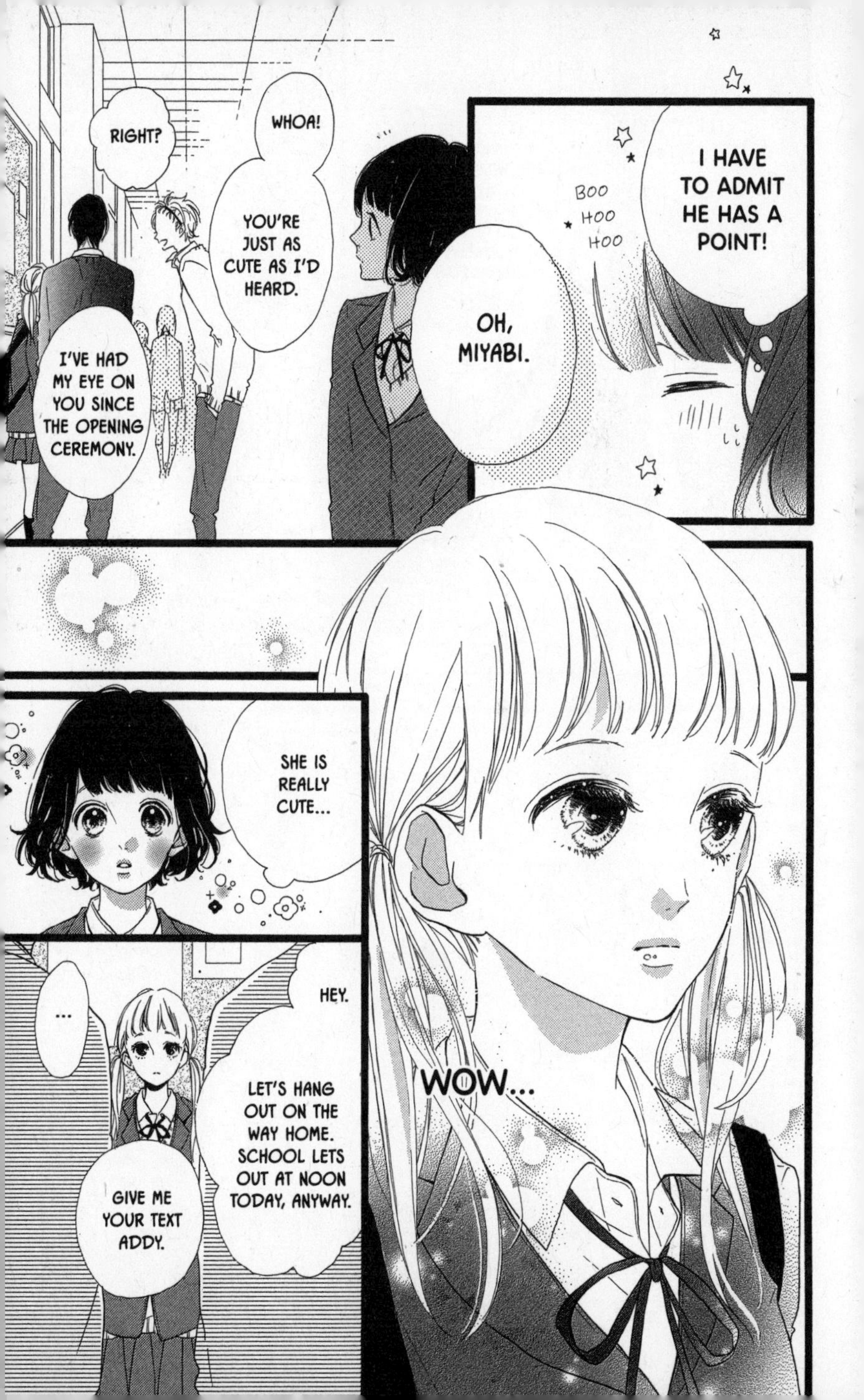
I HAVE TO ADMIT HE HAS A POINT!
BOO HOO HOO
WHOA!
YOU'RE JUST AS CUTE AS I'D HEARD.
RIGHT?
I'VE HAD MY EYE ON YOU SINCE THE OPENING CEREMONY.
OH, MIYABI.
WOW...
SHE IS REALLY CUTE...
HEY.
LET'S HANG OUT ON THE WAY HOME. SCHOOL LETS OUT AT NOON TODAY, ANYWAY.
GIVE ME YOUR TEXT ADDY.
...

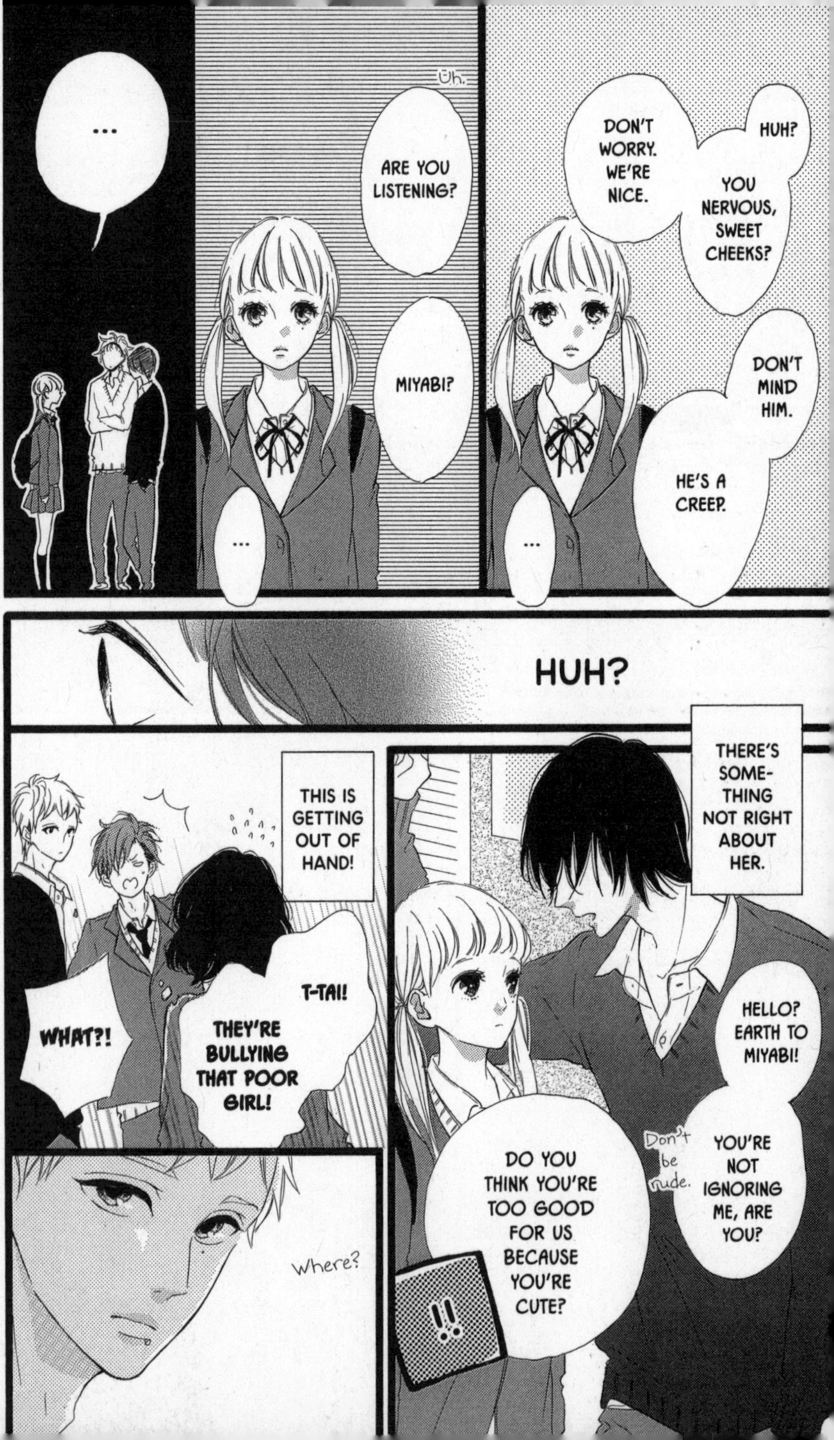
HUH? YOU NERVOUS, SWEET CHEEKS?
DON'T WORRY. WE'RE NICE.
DON'T MIND HIM. HE'S A CREEP.
...
Uh.
ARE YOU LISTENING?
MIYABI?
...
...
HUH?
THERE'S SOME-THING NOT RIGHT ABOUT HER.
HELLO? EARTH TO MIYABI!
YOU'RE NOT IGNORING ME, ARE YOU?
Don't be rude.
DO YOU THINK YOU'RE TOO GOOD FOR US BECAUSE YOU'RE CUTE?
!!
THIS IS GETTING OUT OF HAND!
T-TAI! THEY'RE BULLYING THAT POOR GIRL!
WHAT?!
Where?

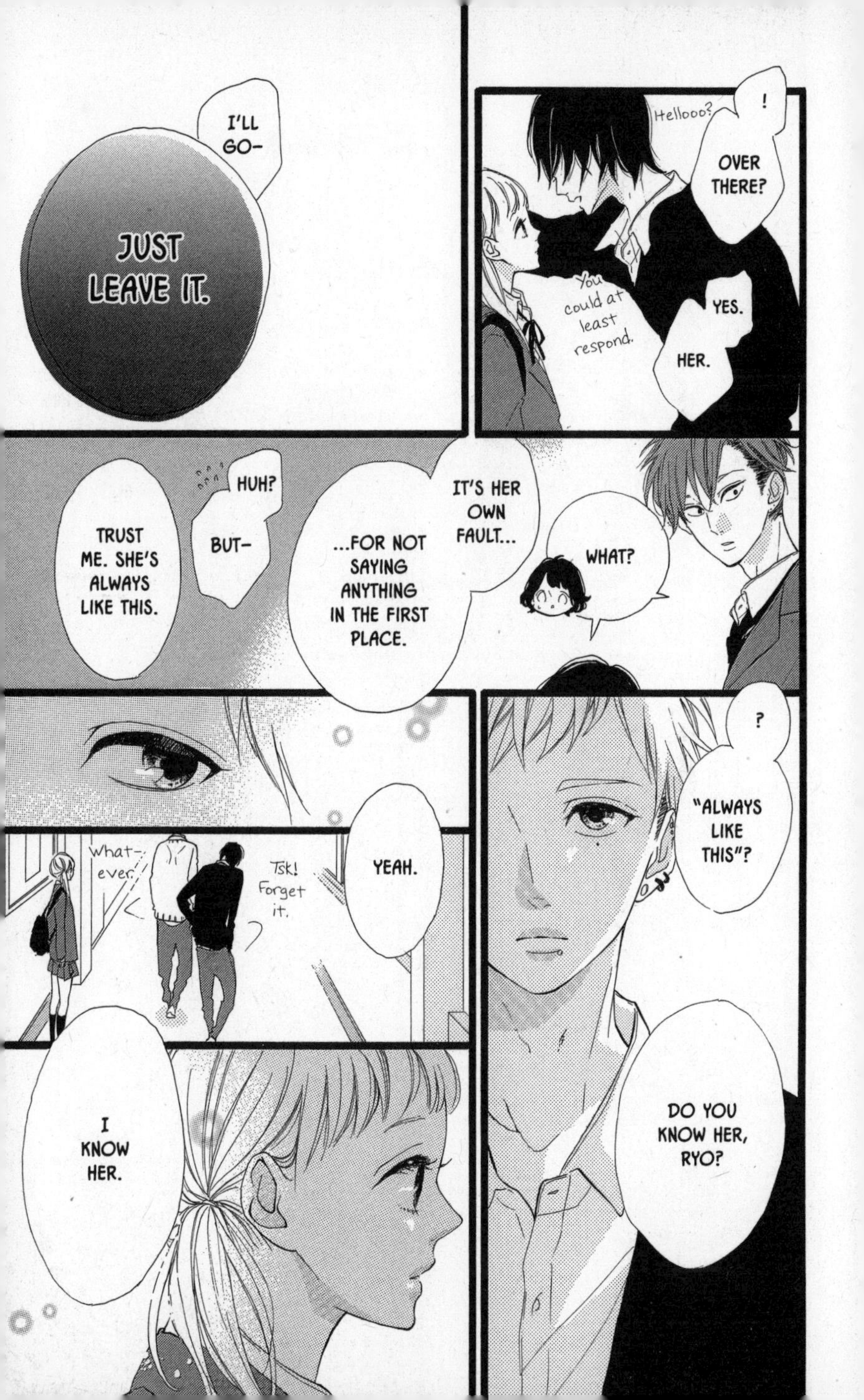
!
Hellooo?
OVER THERE?
YES.
You could at least respond.
HER.
I'LL GO-
JUST LEAVE IT.
WHAT?
IT'S HER OWN FAULT...
...FOR NOT SAYING ANYTHING IN THE FIRST PLACE.
HUH?
BUT-
TRUST ME. SHE'S ALWAYS LIKE THIS.
?
"ALWAYS LIKE THIS"?
DO YOU KNOW HER, RYO?
YEAH.
Tsk! Forget it.
What-ever.
I KNOW HER.

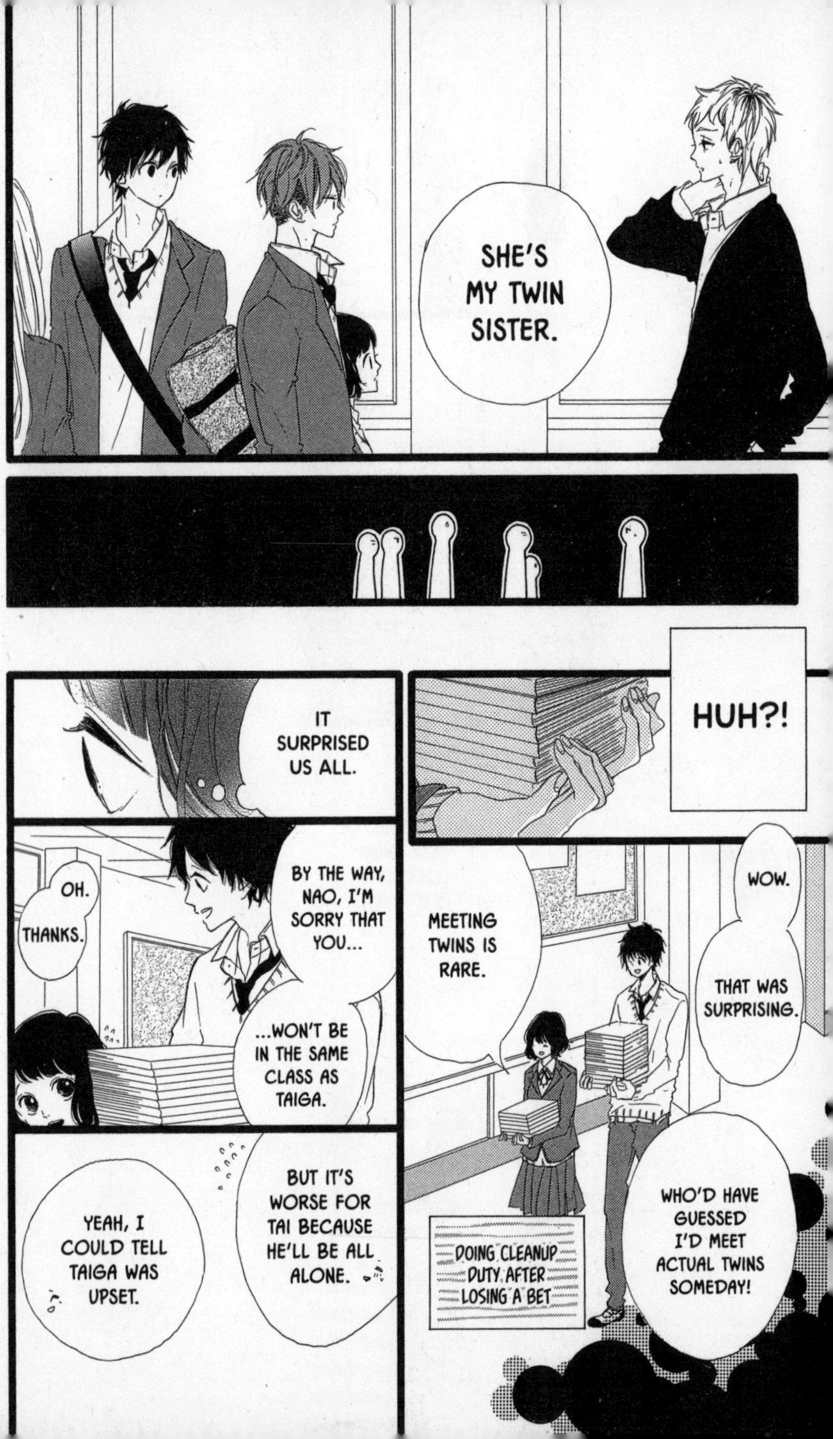
SHE'S MY TWIN SISTER.
HUH?!
IT SURPRISED US ALL.
WOW.
THAT WAS SURPRISING.
MEETING TWINS IS RARE.
WHO'D HAVE GUESSED I'D MEET ACTUAL TWINS SOMEDAY!
DOING CLEANUP DUTY AFTER LOSING A BET
BY THE WAY, NAO, I'M SORRY THAT YOU...
...WON'T BE IN THE SAME CLASS AS TAIGA.
OH.
THANKS.
BUT IT'S WORSE FOR TAI BECAUSE HE'LL BE ALL ALONE.
YEAH, I COULD TELL TAIGA WAS UPSET.

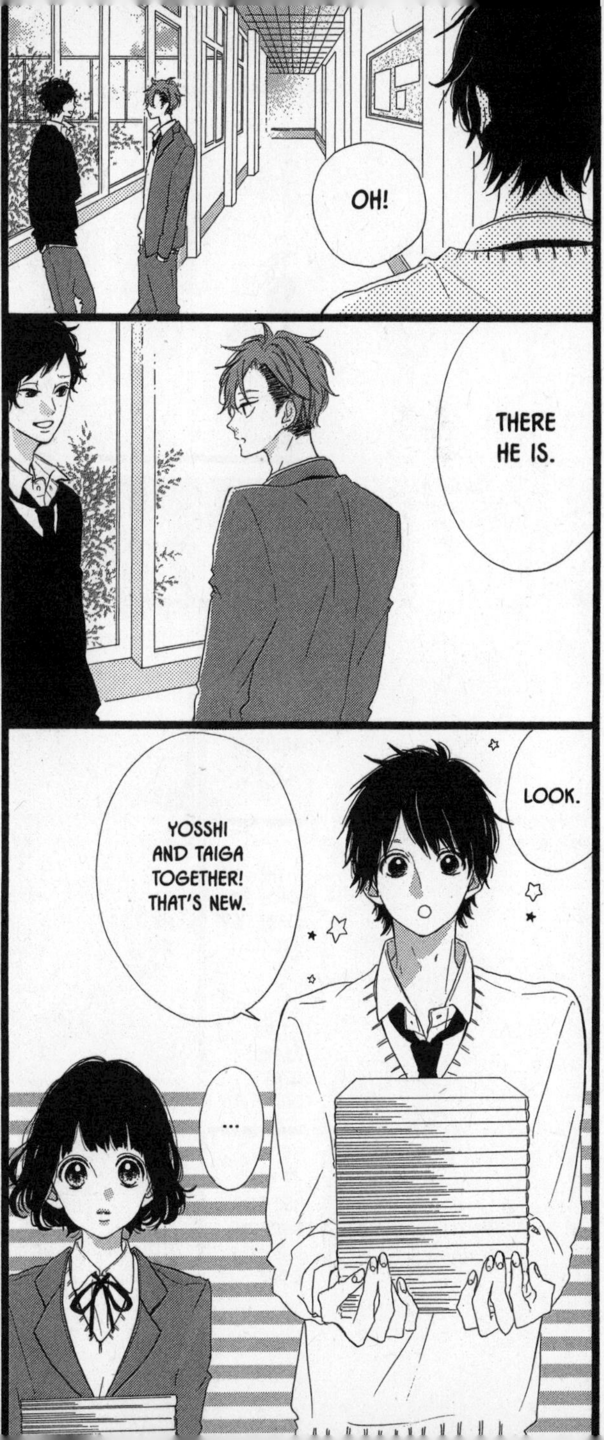
OH!
THERE HE IS.
LOOK.
YOSSHI AND TAIGA TOGETHER! THAT'S NEW.
...

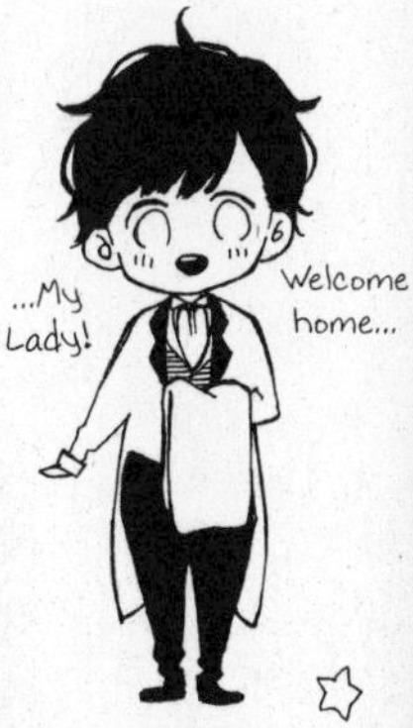
Welcome home...
...My Lady!

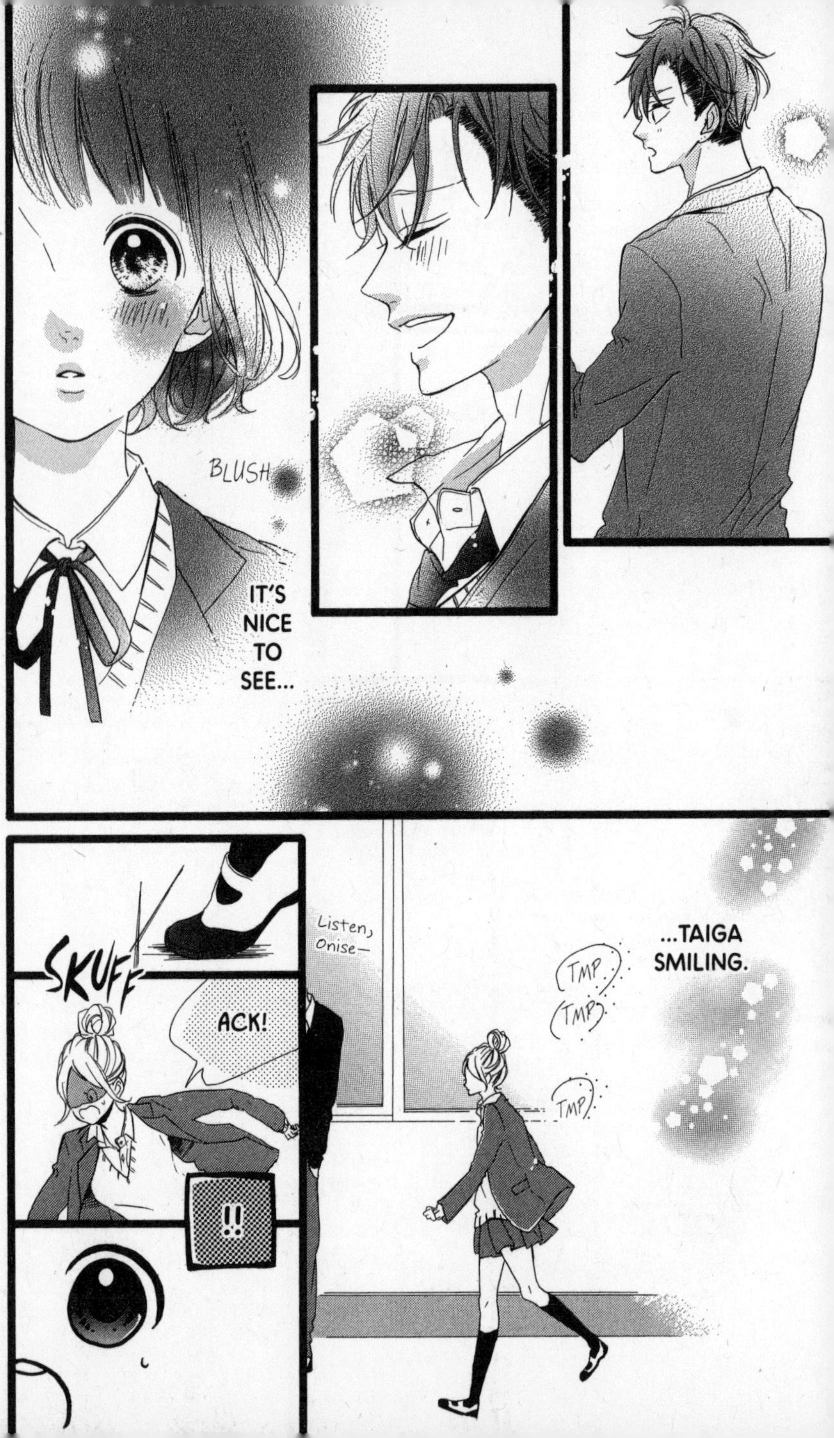
BLUSH
IT'S NICE TO SEE...
...TAIGA SMILING.
TMP
TMP
TMP
Listen, Onise—
SKUFF
ACK!
!!

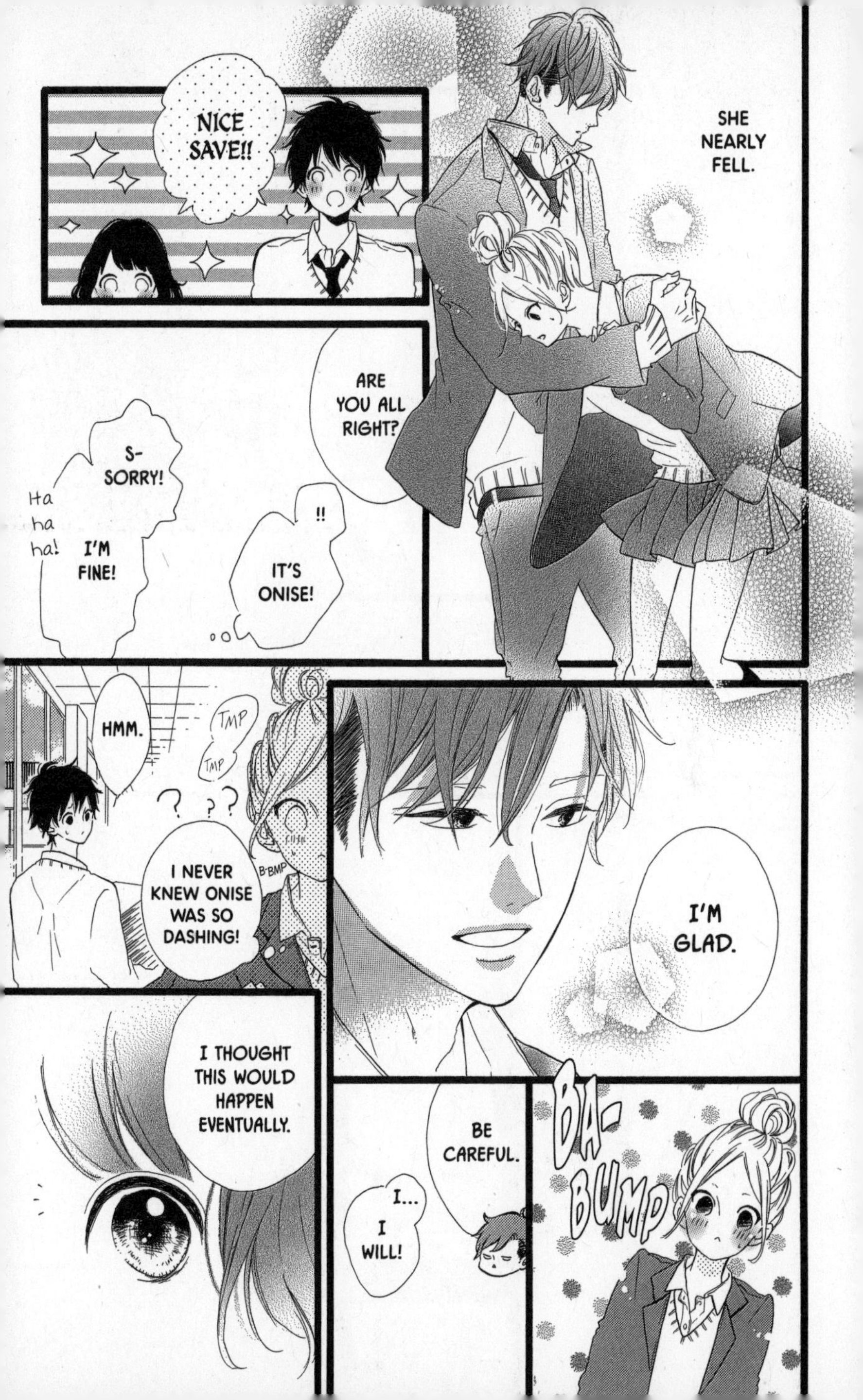

SHE NEARLY FELL.
NICE SAVE!!
ARE YOU ALL RIGHT?
S-SORRY! I'M FINE!
Ha ha ha!
!!
IT'S ONISE!
I'M GLAD.
BA-BUMP
BE CAREFUL.
I... I WILL!
HMM.
TMP
TMP
? ??
I NEVER KNEW ONISE WAS SO DASHING!
B-BMP
I THOUGHT THIS WOULD HAPPEN EVENTUALLY.

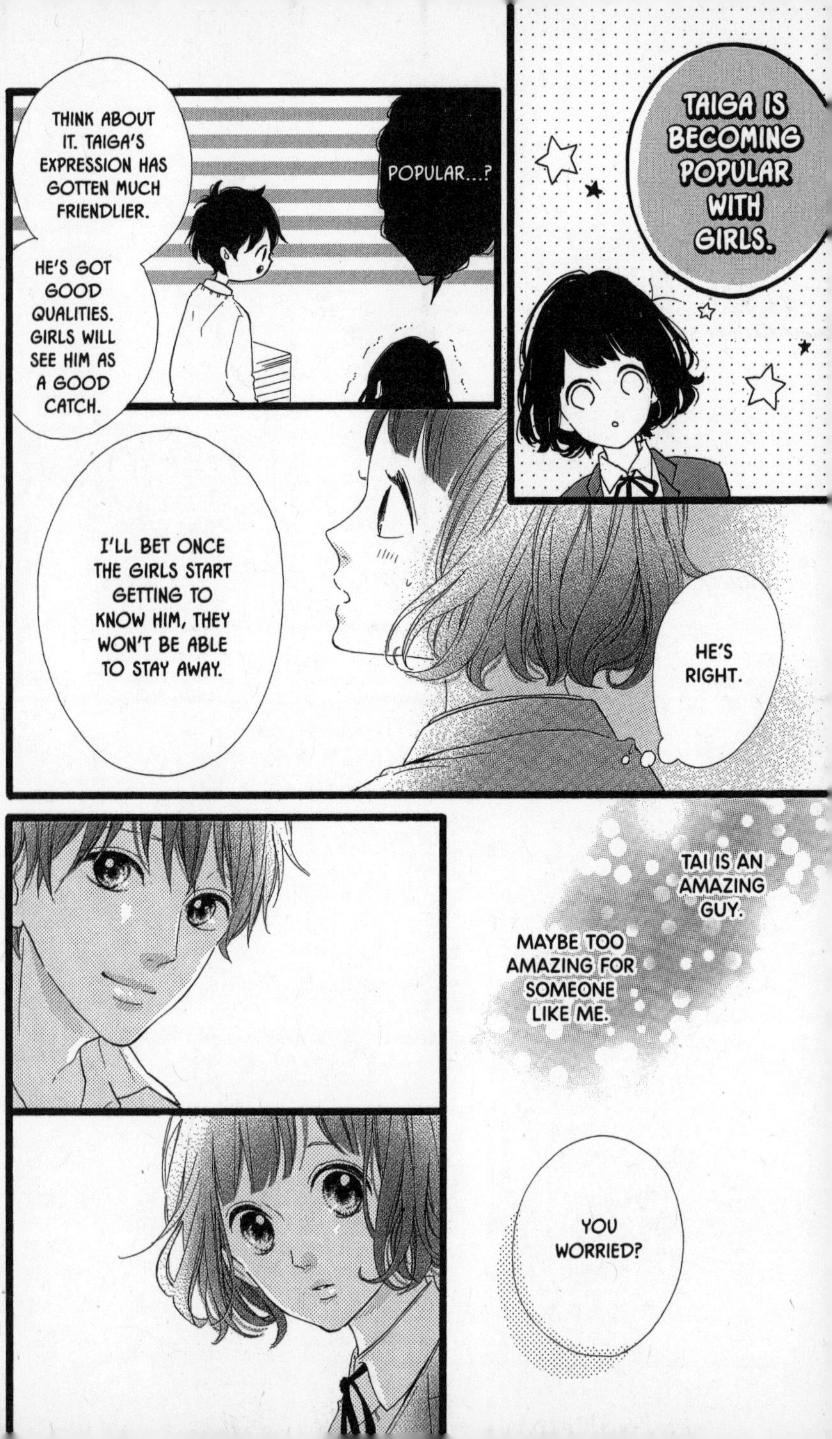
TAIGA IS BECOMING POPULAR WITH GIRLS.
POPULAR...?
THINK ABOUT IT. TAIGA'S EXPRESSION HAS GOTTEN MUCH FRIENDLIER.
HE'S GOT GOOD QUALITIES. GIRLS WILL SEE HIM AS A GOOD CATCH.
I'LL BET ONCE THE GIRLS START GETTING TO KNOW HIM, THEY WON'T BE ABLE TO STAY AWAY.
HE'S RIGHT.
TAI IS AN AMAZING GUY.
MAYBE TOO AMAZING FOR SOMEONE LIKE ME.
YOU WORRIED?

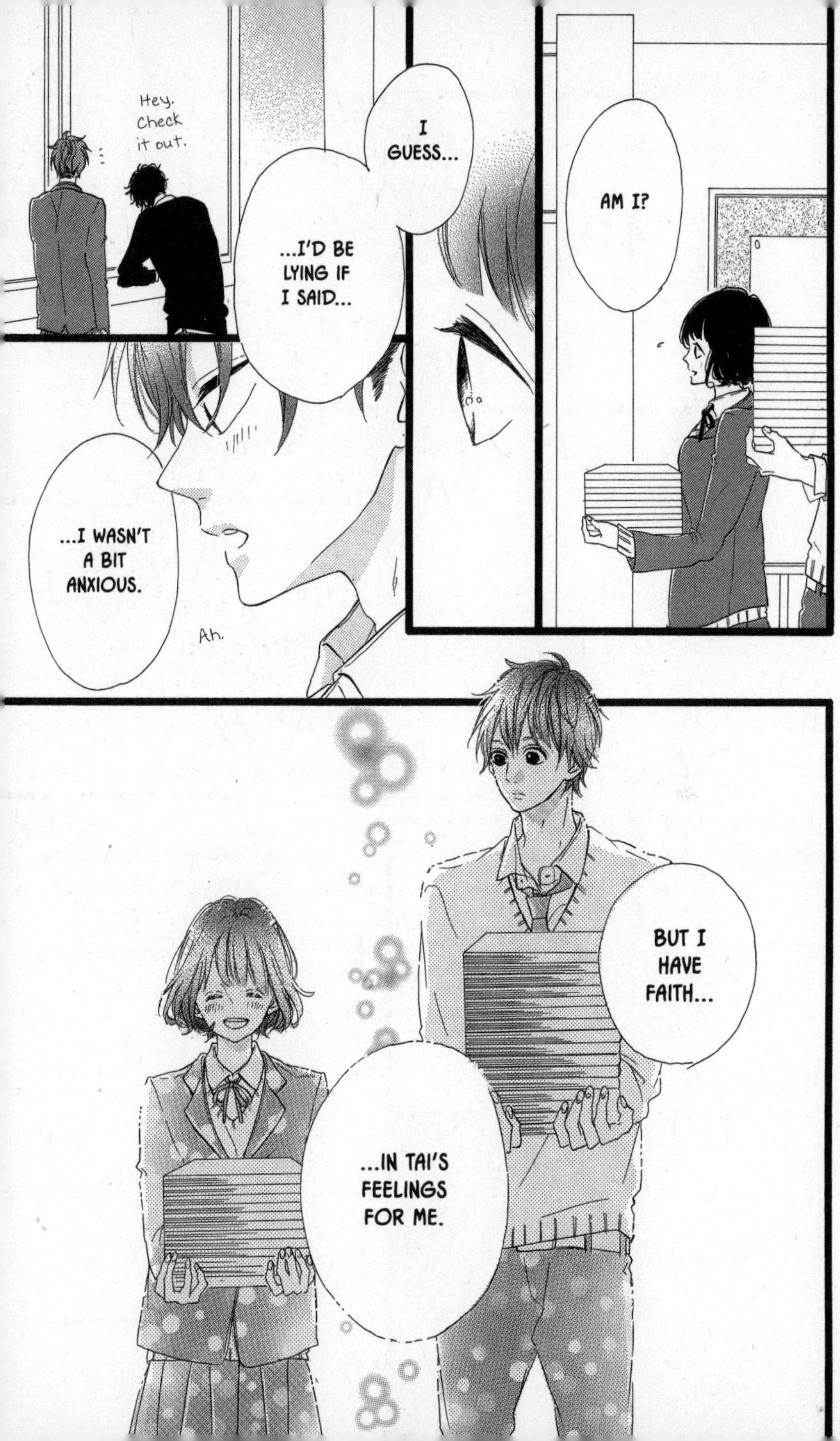
AM I?
I GUESS...
...I'D BE LYING IF I SAID...
...I WASN'T A BIT ANXIOUS.
Hey. Check it out.
Ah.
BUT I HAVE FAITH...
...IN TAI'S FEELINGS FOR ME.

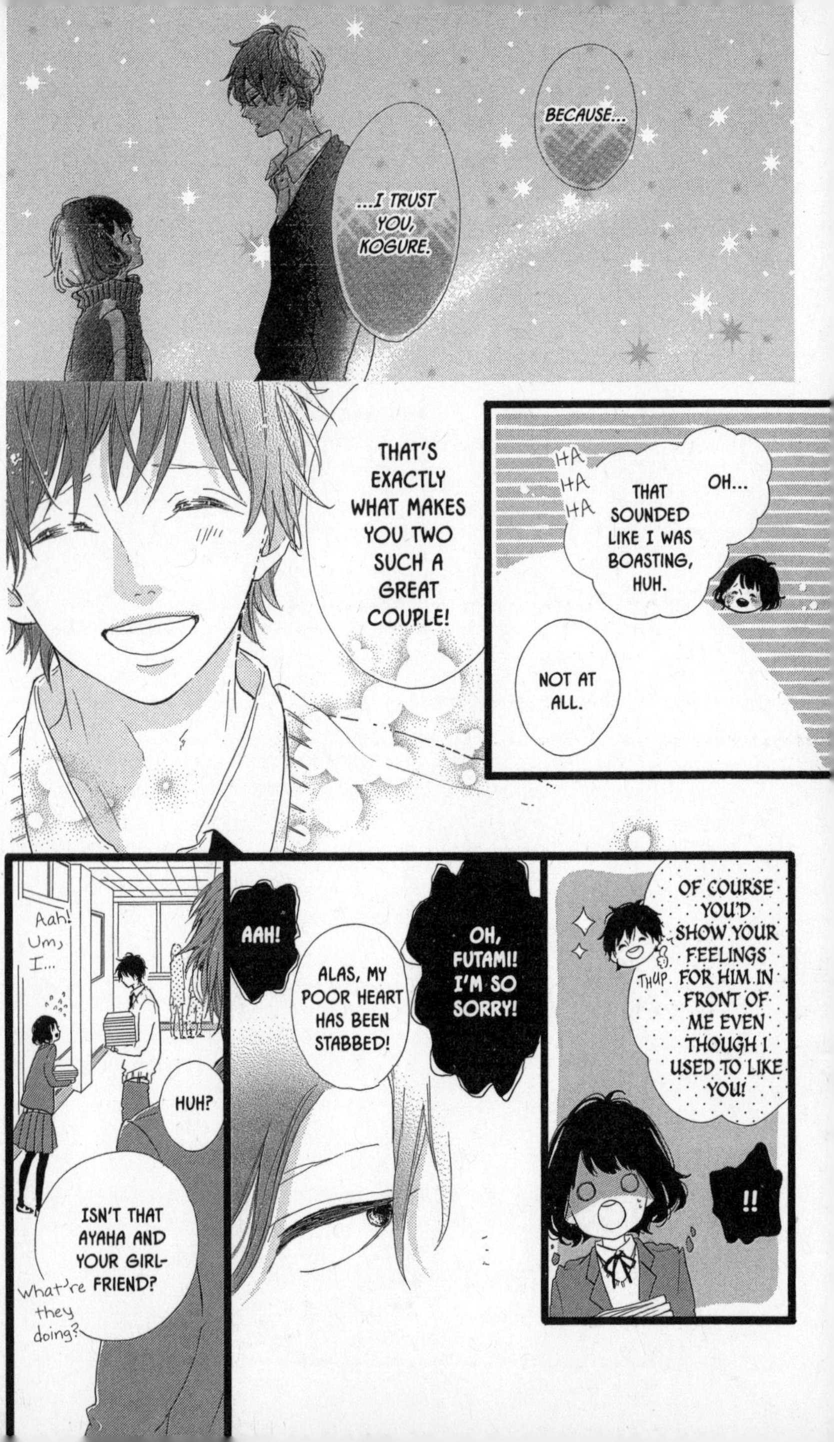
BECAUSE...
...I TRUST YOU, KOGURE.
OH...
HA HA HA
THAT SOUNDED LIKE I WAS BOASTING, HUH.
NOT AT ALL.
THAT'S EXACTLY WHAT MAKES YOU TWO SUCH A GREAT COUPLE!
OF COURSE YOU'D SHOW YOUR FEELINGS FOR HIM IN FRONT OF ME EVEN THOUGH I USED TO LIKE YOU!
THUP
!!
OH, FUTAMI! I'M SO SORRY!
ALAS, MY POOR HEART HAS BEEN STABBED!
AAH!
HUH?
Aah! Um, I...
ISN'T THAT AYAHA AND YOUR GIRL-FRIEND?
What're they doing?

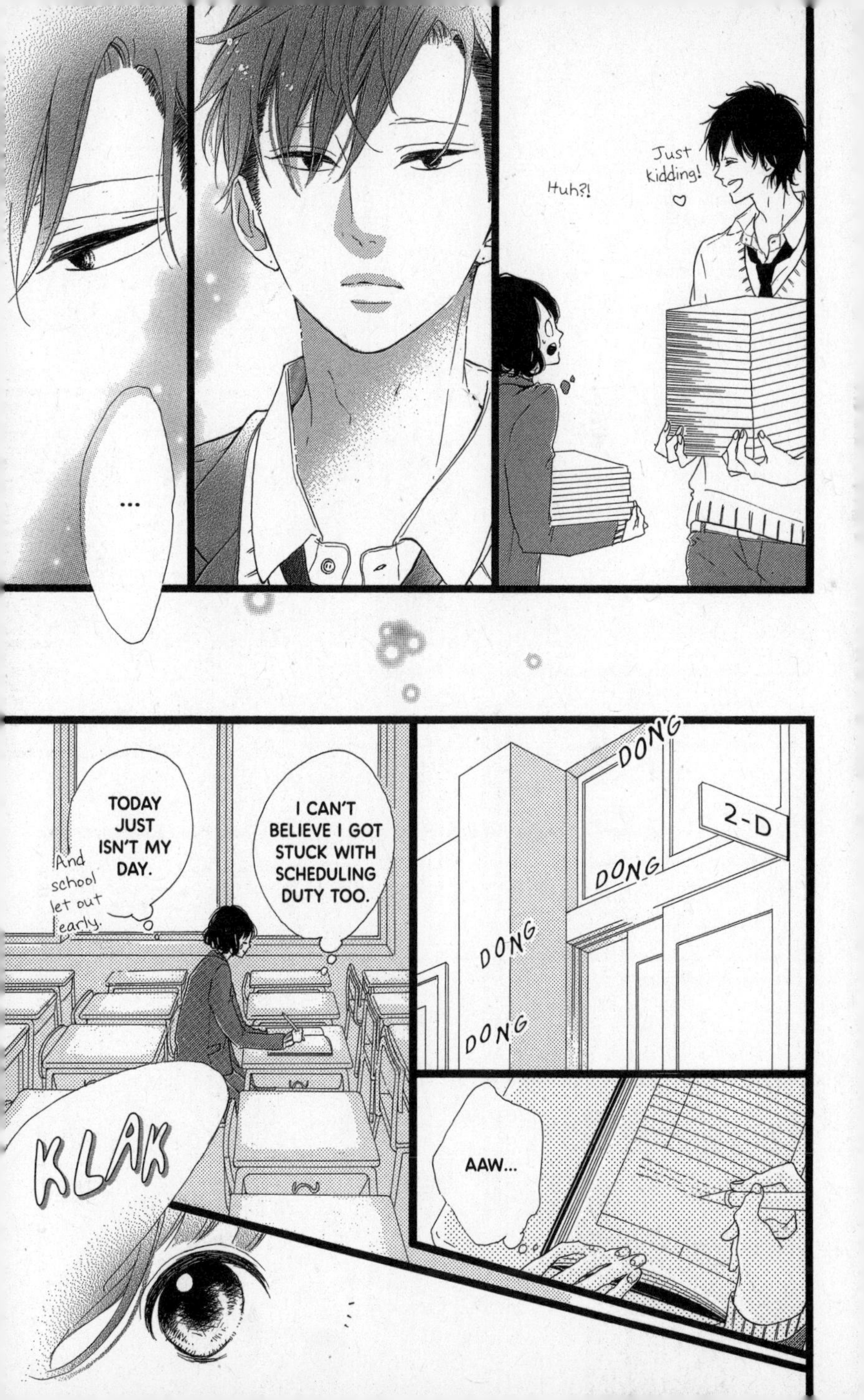
Just kidding!
Huh?!
...
DONG
2-D
DONG
DONG
DONG
AAW...
I CAN'T BELIEVE I GOT STUCK WITH SCHEDULING DUTY TOO.
TODAY JUST ISN'T MY DAY.
And school let out early.
KLAK

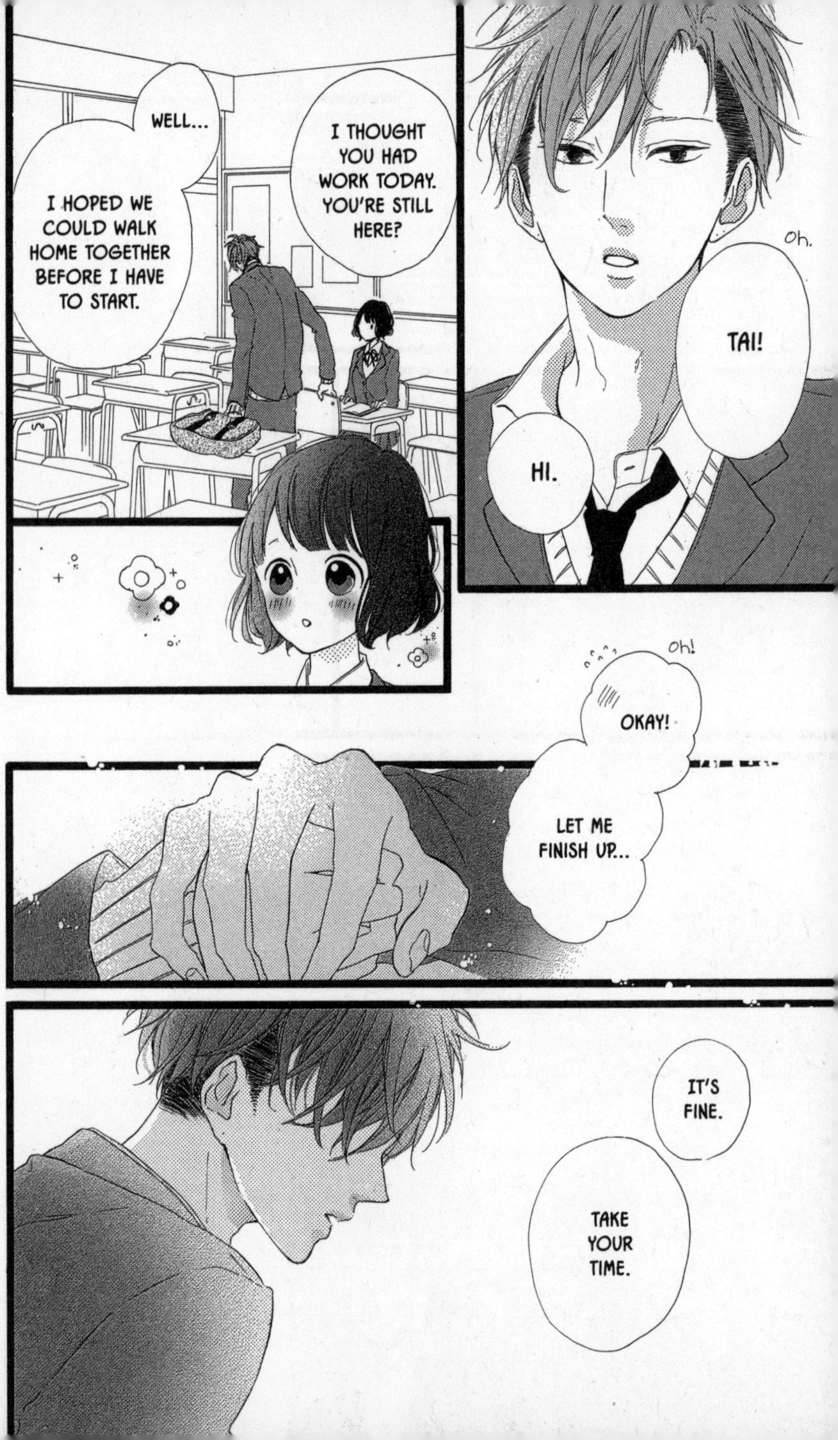
Oh.
TAI!
HI.
I THOUGHT YOU HAD WORK TODAY. YOU'RE STILL HERE?
WELL...
I HOPED WE COULD WALK HOME TOGETHER BEFORE I HAVE TO START.
Oh!
OKAY!
LET ME FINISH UP...
IT'S FINE.
TAKE YOUR TIME.

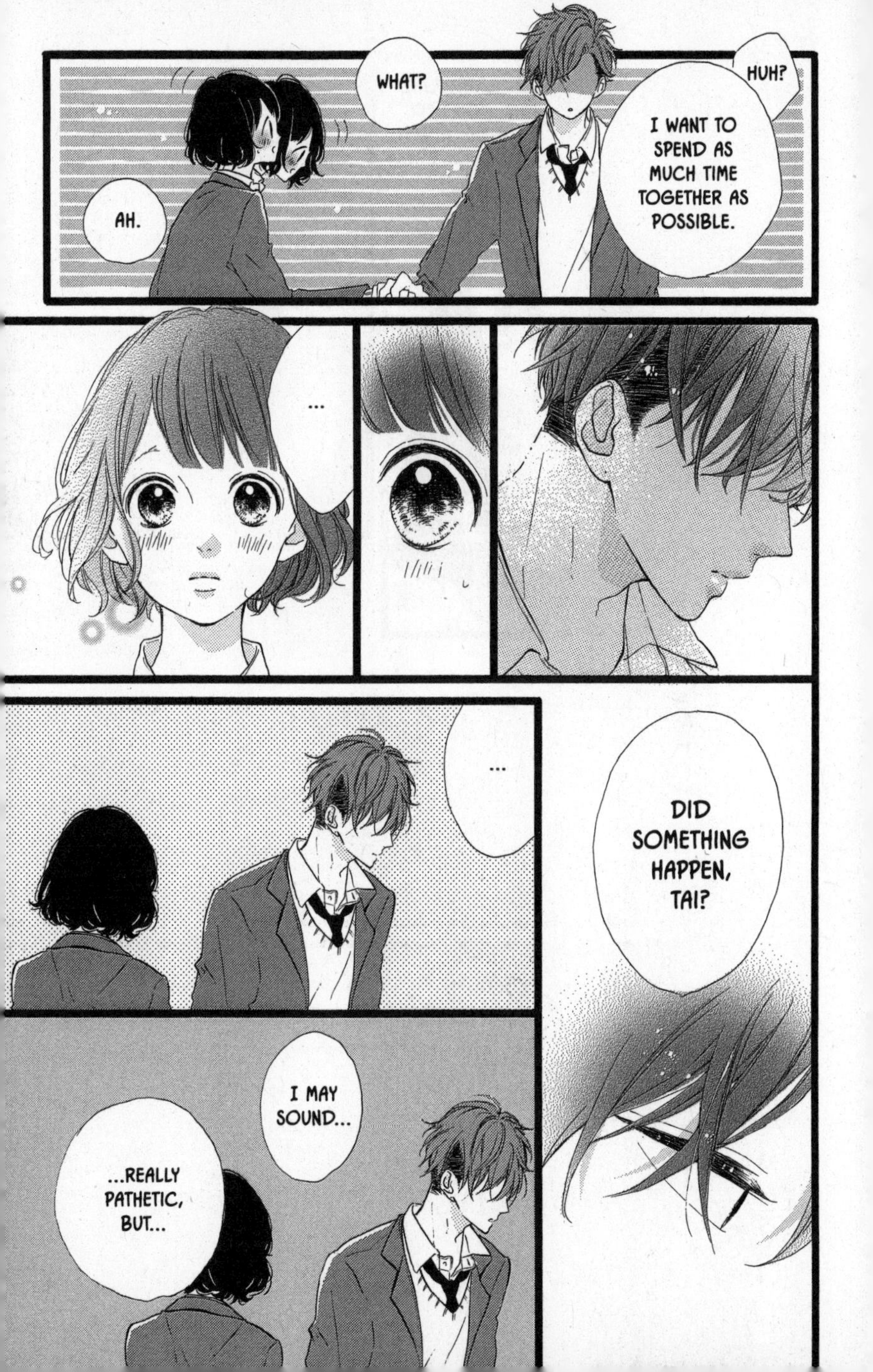
HUH?
I WANT TO SPEND AS MUCH TIME TOGETHER AS POSSIBLE.
WHAT?
AH.
...
DID SOMETHING HAPPEN, TAI?
...
I MAY SOUND...
...REALLY PATHETIC, BUT...

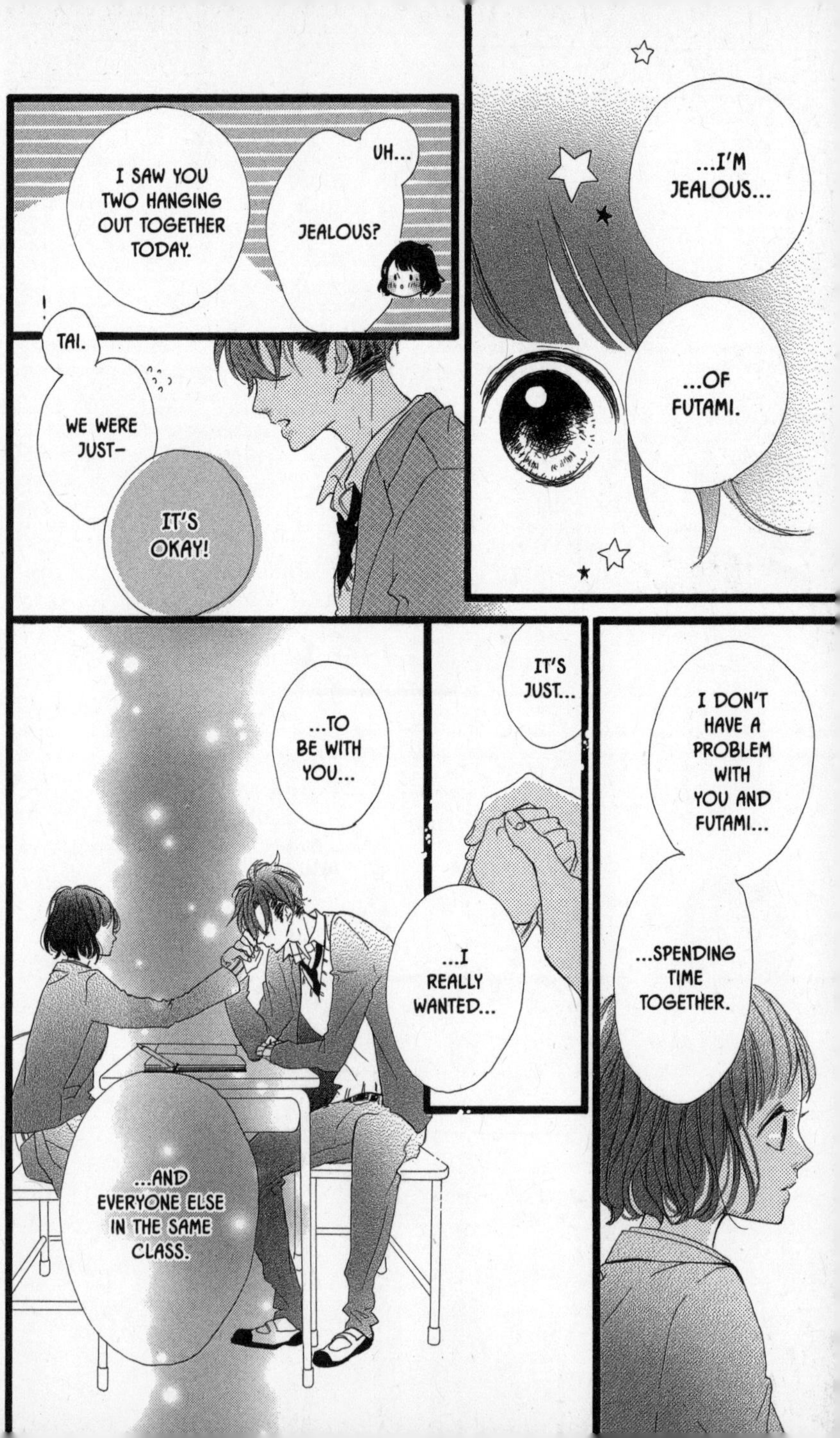
...I'M JEALOUS...
...OF FUTAMI.
UH...
JEALOUS?
I SAW YOU TWO HANGING OUT TOGETHER TODAY.
!
TAI.
WE WERE JUST–
IT'S OKAY!
I DON'T HAVE A PROBLEM WITH YOU AND FUTAMI...
...SPENDING TIME TOGETHER.
IT'S JUST...
...I REALLY WANTED...
...TO BE WITH YOU...
...AND EVERYONE ELSE IN THE SAME CLASS.

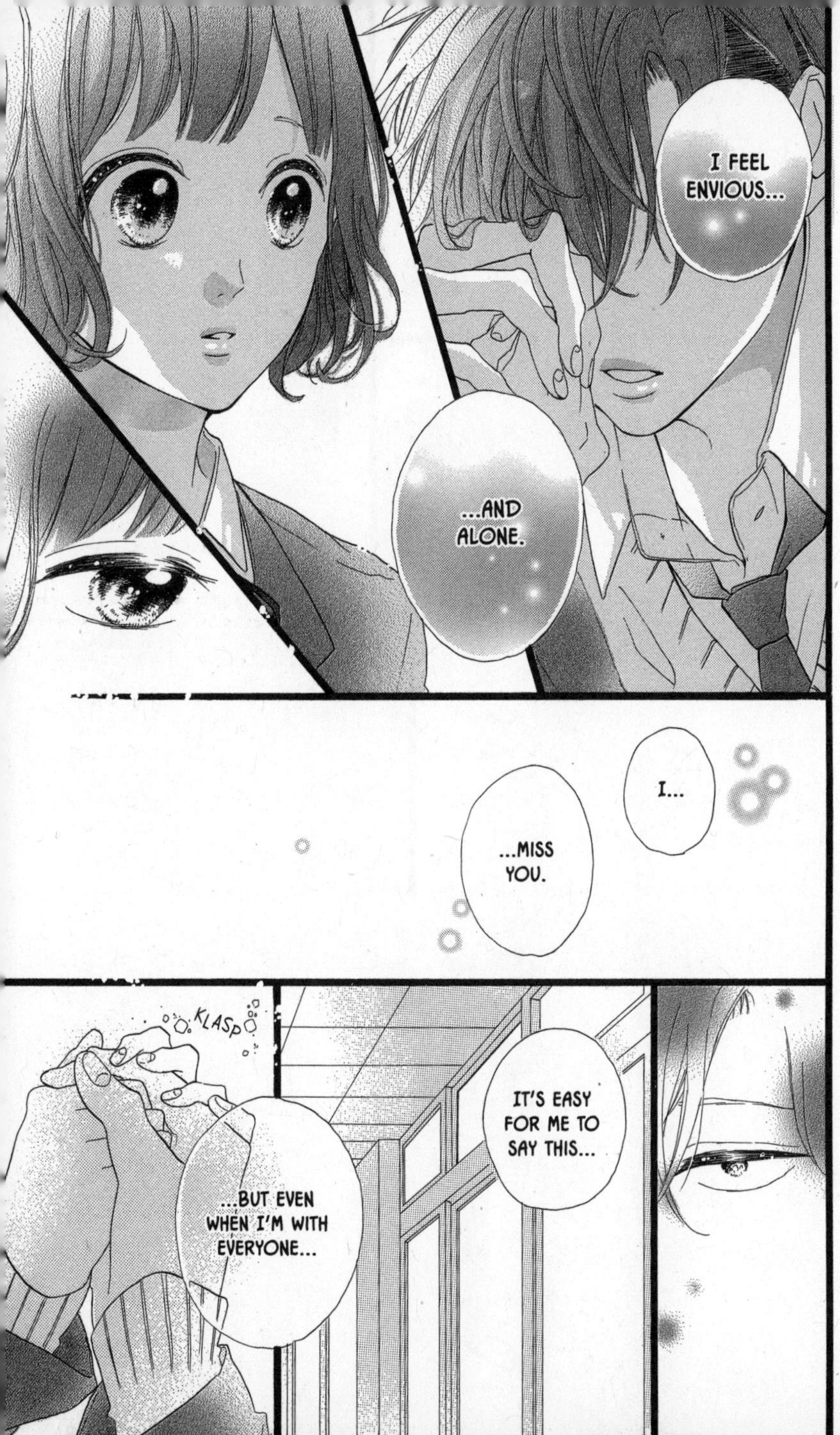
I FEEL ENVIOUS...
...AND ALONE.
I...
...MISS YOU.
IT'S EASY FOR ME TO SAY THIS...
KLASP
...BUT EVEN WHEN I'M WITH EVERYONE...

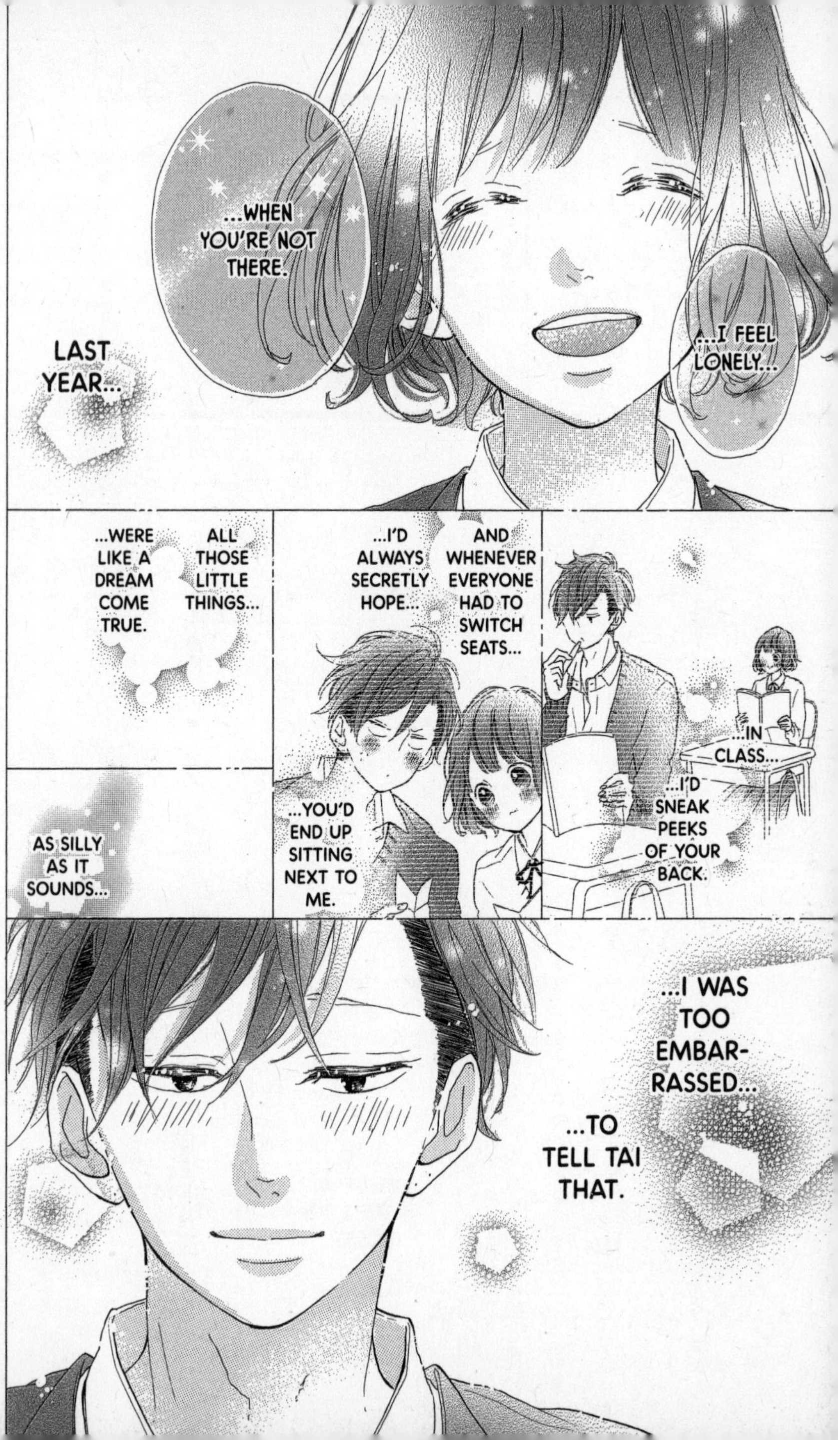
...I FEEL LONELY...
...WHEN YOU'RE NOT THERE.
LAST YEAR...
...IN CLASS...
...I'D SNEAK PEEKS OF YOUR BACK.
AND WHENEVER EVERYONE HAD TO SWITCH SEATS...
...I'D ALWAYS SECRETLY HOPE...
...YOU'D END UP SITTING NEXT TO ME.
ALL THOSE LITTLE THINGS...
...WERE LIKE A DREAM COME TRUE.
AS SILLY AS IT SOUNDS...
...I WAS TOO EMBAR-RASSED...
...TO TELL TAI THAT.

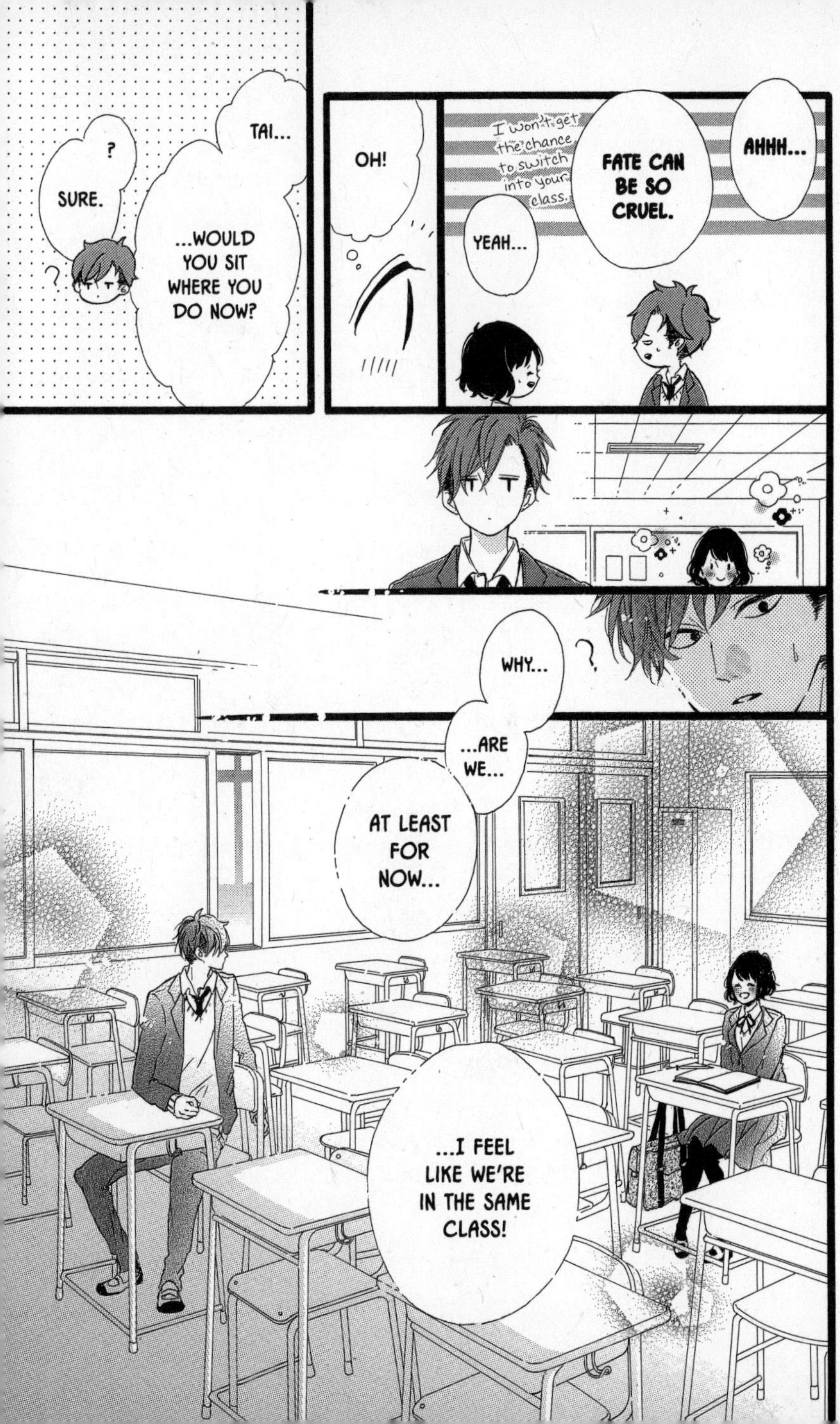
AHHH...
FATE CAN BE SO CRUEL.
I won't get the chance to switch into your class.
YEAH...
OH!
TAI...
...WOULD YOU SIT WHERE YOU DO NOW?
?
SURE.
WHY...
...ARE WE...
AT LEAST FOR NOW...
...I FEEL LIKE WE'RE IN THE SAME CLASS!

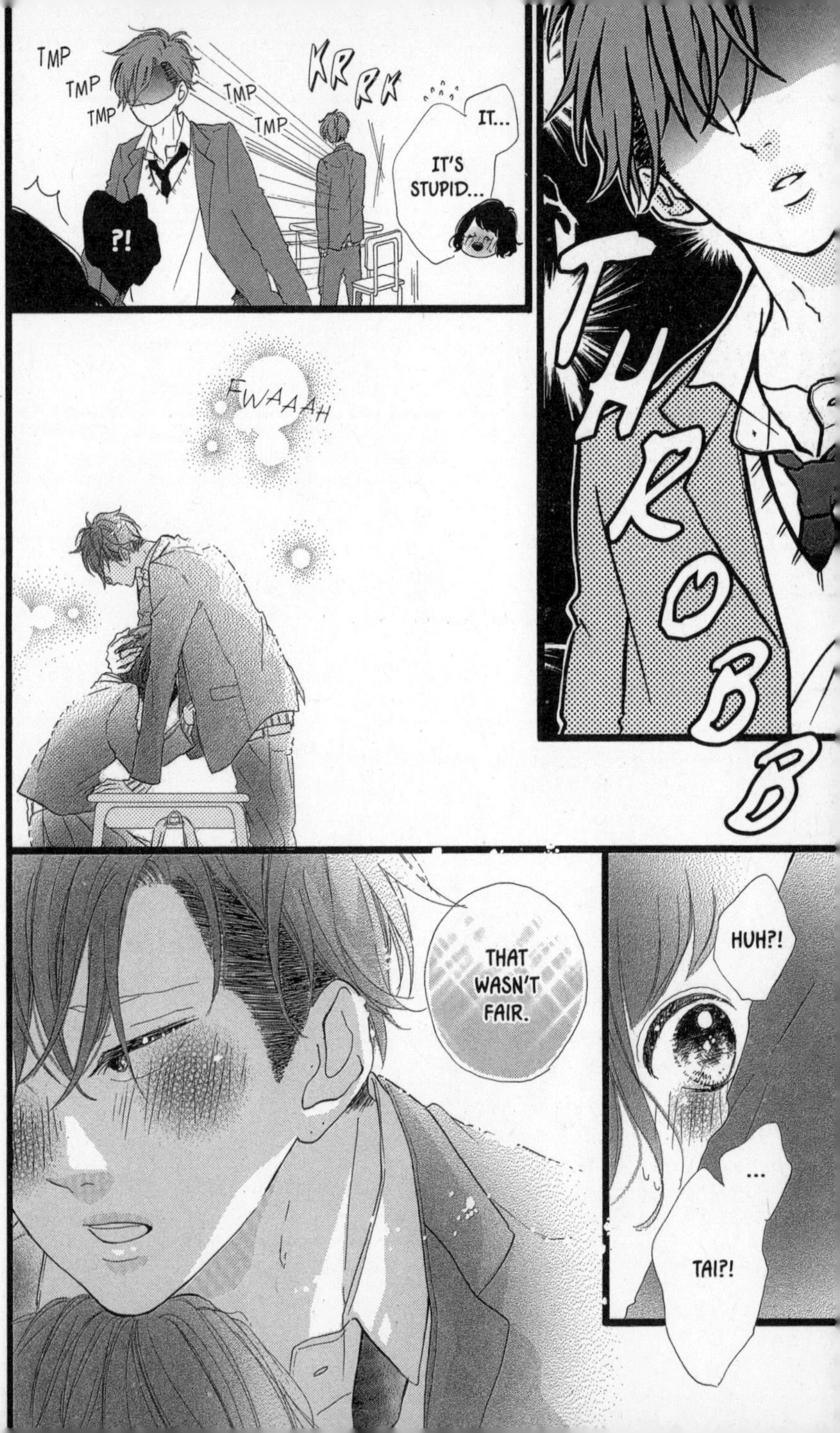
THROBB
IT...
IT'S STUPID...
KRRK
TMP
TMP
TMP
TMP
?!
FWAAAH
HUH?!
...
TAI?!
THAT WASN'T FAIR.

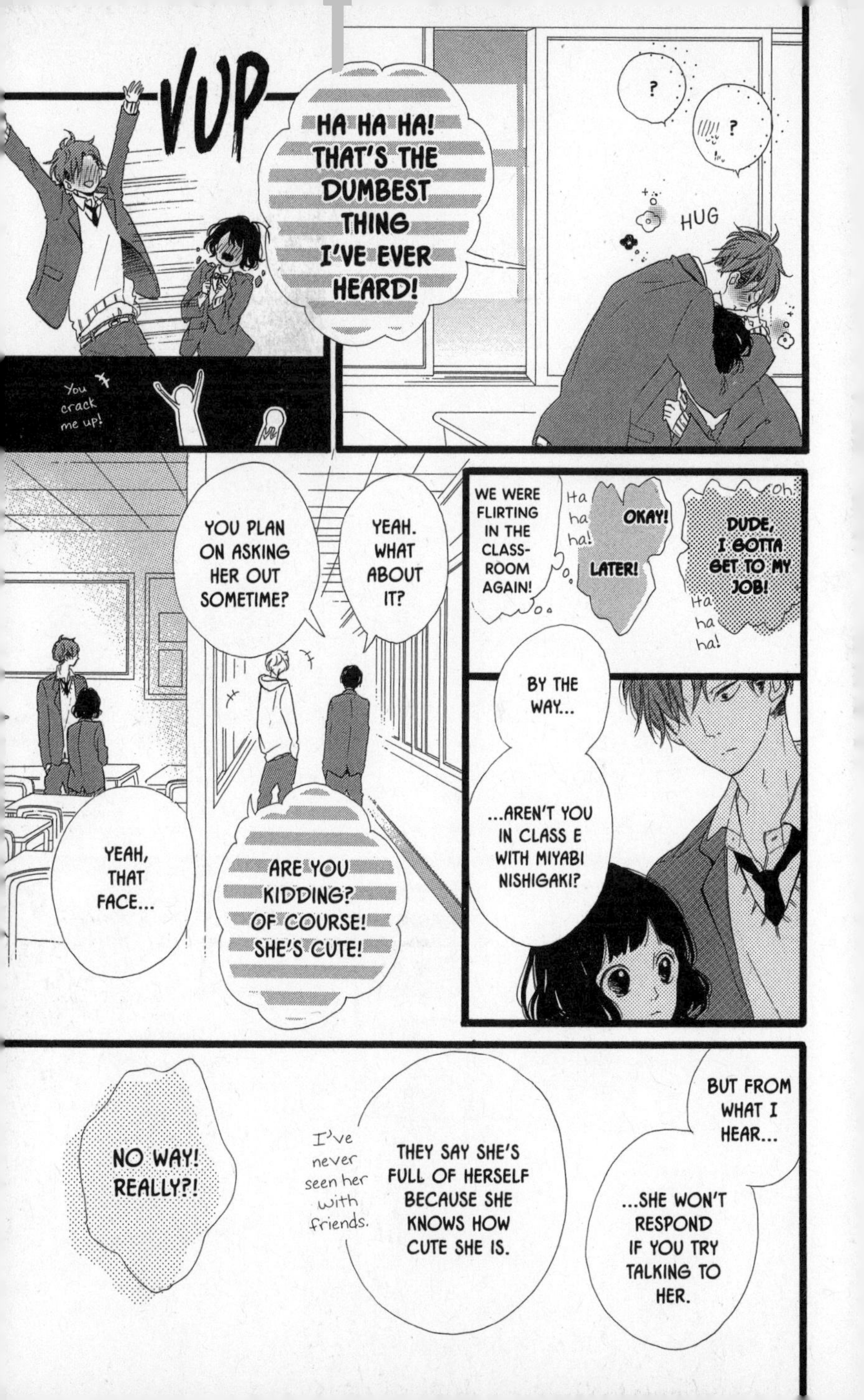

?
?
HUG
VUP
HA HA HA! THAT'S THE DUMBEST THING I'VE EVER HEARD!
You crack me up!
Oh.
DUDE, I GOTTA GET TO MY JOB!
Ha ha ha!
OKAY! LATER!
Ha ha ha!
WE WERE FLIRTING IN THE CLASSROOM AGAIN!
BY THE WAY...
...AREN'T YOU IN CLASS E WITH MIYABI NISHIGAKI?
YEAH. WHAT ABOUT IT?
YOU PLAN ON ASKING HER OUT SOMETIME?
ARE YOU KIDDING? OF COURSE! SHE'S CUTE!
YEAH, THAT FACE...
BUT FROM WHAT I HEAR...
...SHE WON'T RESPOND IF YOU TRY TALKING TO HER.
THEY SAY SHE'S FULL OF HERSELF BECAUSE SHE KNOWS HOW CUTE SHE IS.
I've never seen her with friends.
NO WAY! REALLY?!

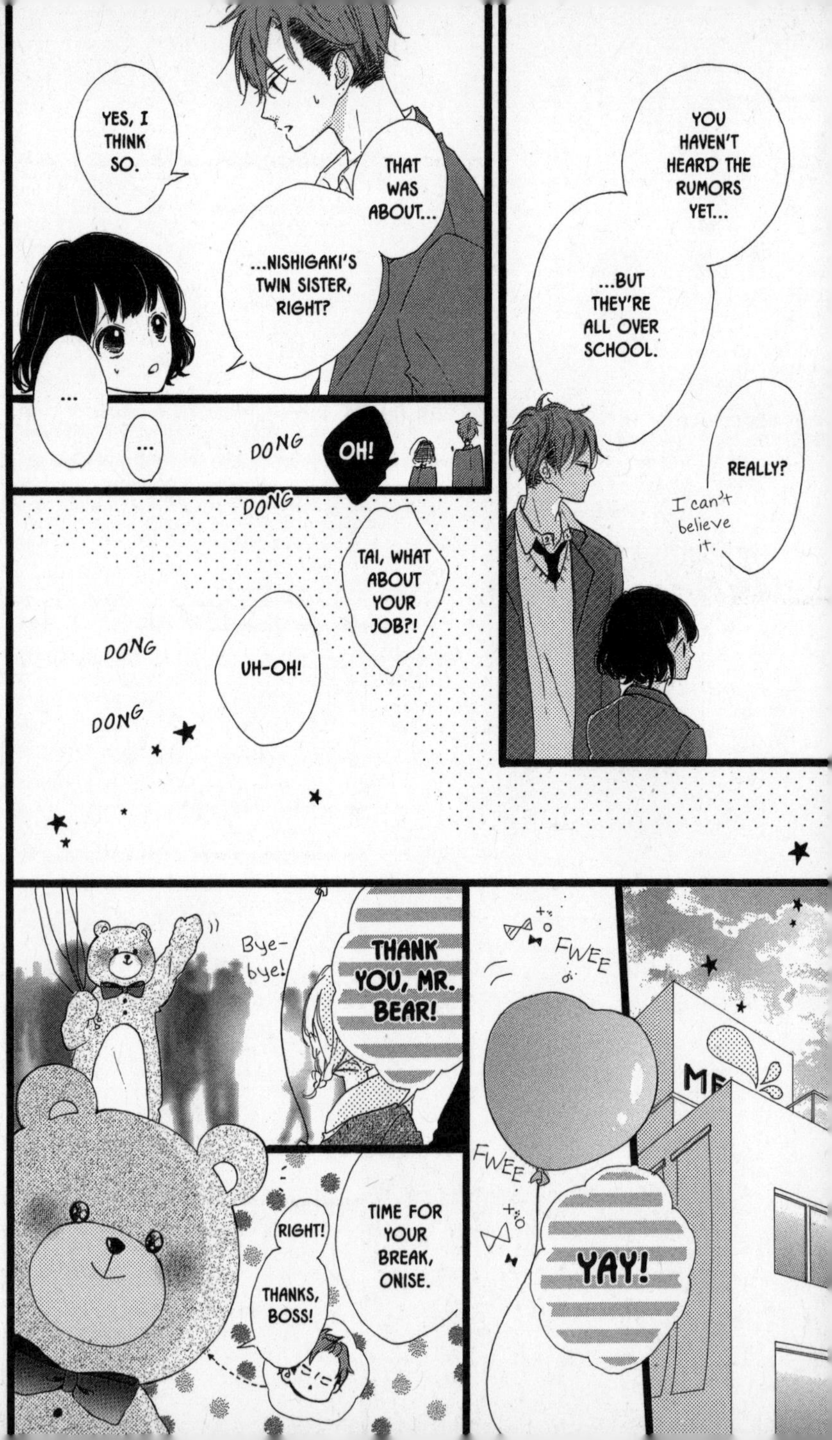
YOU HAVEN'T HEARD THE RUMORS YET...
...BUT THEY'RE ALL OVER SCHOOL.
REALLY?
I can't believe it.
THAT WAS ABOUT...
...NISHIGAKI'S TWIN SISTER, RIGHT?
YES, I THINK SO.
...
...
OH!
DONG
DONG
TAI, WHAT ABOUT YOUR JOB?!
UH-OH!
DONG
DONG
FWEE
FWEE
YAY!
THANK YOU, MR. BEAR!
Bye-bye!
TIME FOR YOUR BREAK, ONISE.
RIGHT!
THANKS, BOSS!

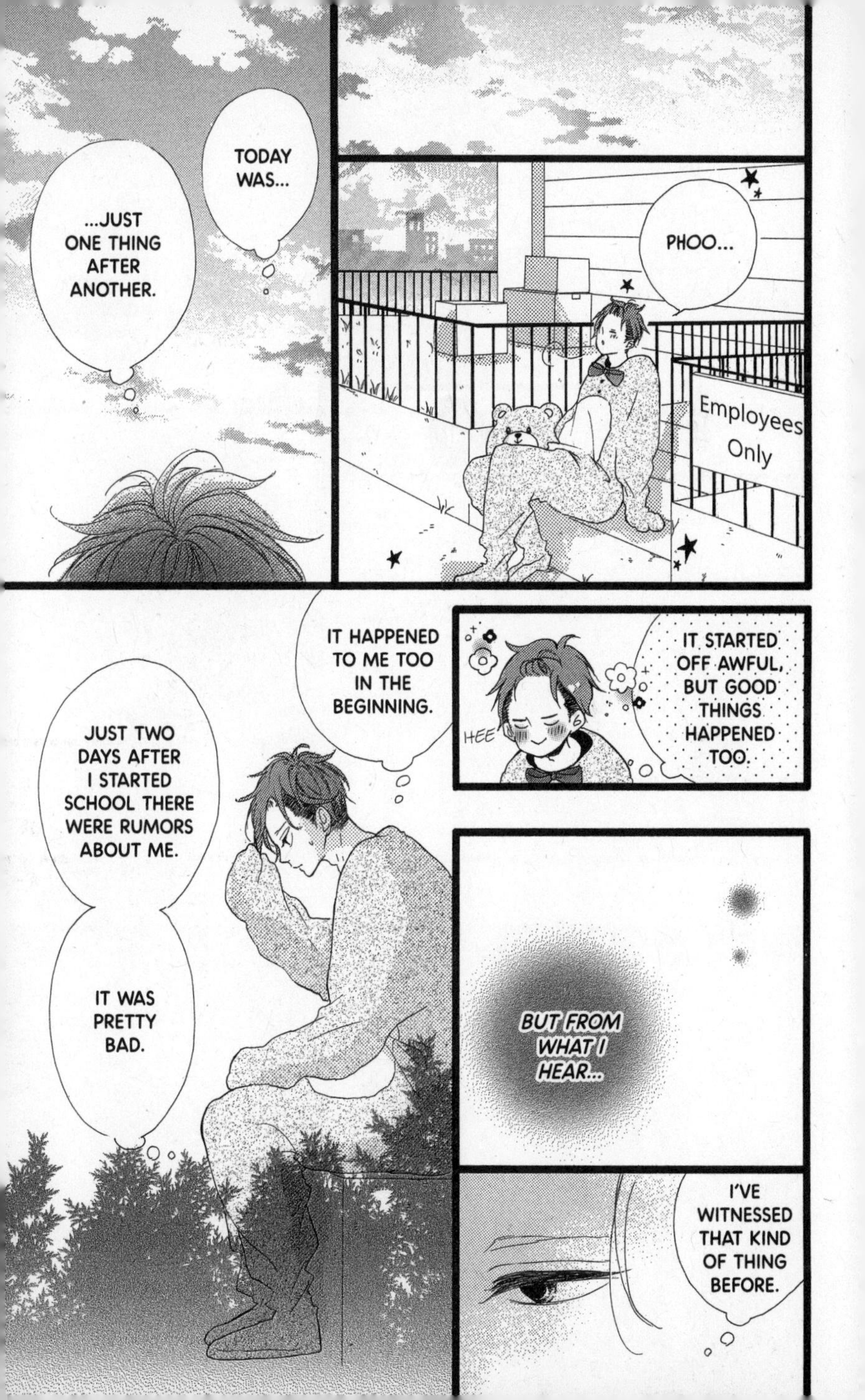
PHOO...
Employees Only
TODAY WAS...
...JUST ONE THING AFTER ANOTHER.
IT STARTED OFF AWFUL, BUT GOOD THINGS HAPPENED TOO.
HEE
BUT FROM WHAT I HEAR...
I'VE WITNESSED THAT KIND OF THING BEFORE.
IT HAPPENED TO ME TOO IN THE BEGINNING.
JUST TWO DAYS AFTER I STARTED SCHOOL THERE WERE RUMORS ABOUT ME.
IT WAS PRETTY BAD.

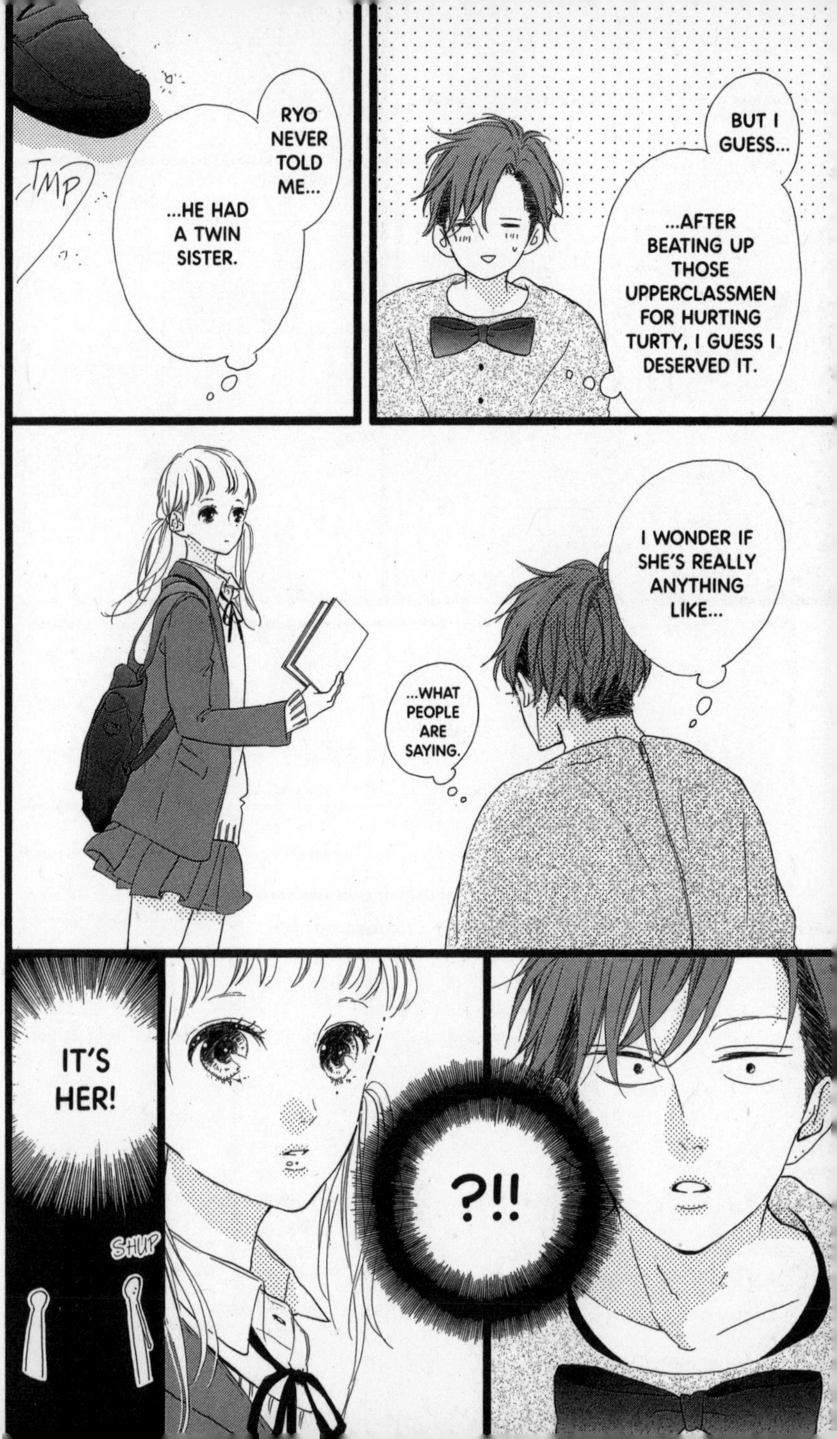
BUT I GUESS...
...AFTER BEATING UP THOSE UPPERCLASSMEN FOR HURTING TURTY, I GUESS I DESERVED IT.
RYO NEVER TOLD ME...
...HE HAD A TWIN SISTER.
TMP
I WONDER IF SHE'S REALLY ANYTHING LIKE...
...WHAT PEOPLE ARE SAYING.
?!!
IT'S HER!
SHUP

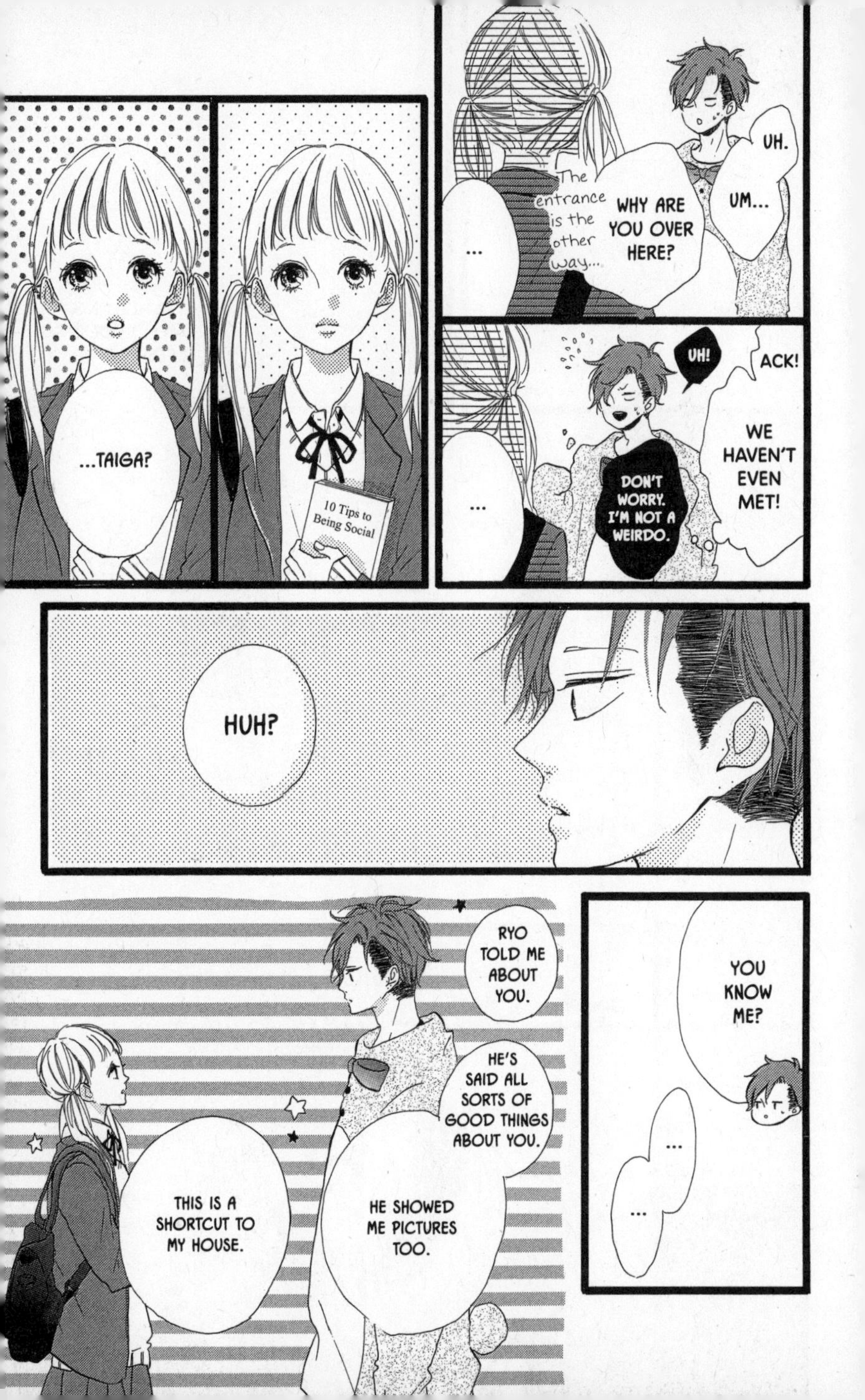
UH.
UM...
WHY ARE YOU OVER HERE?
The entrance is the other way...
...
ACK!
UH!
WE HAVEN'T EVEN MET!
DON'T WORRY. I'M NOT A WEIRDO.
...
10 Tips to Being Social
...TAIGA?
HUH?
YOU KNOW ME?
...
...
RYO TOLD ME ABOUT YOU.
HE'S SAID ALL SORTS OF GOOD THINGS ABOUT YOU.
HE SHOWED ME PICTURES TOO.
THIS IS A SHORTCUT TO MY HOUSE.

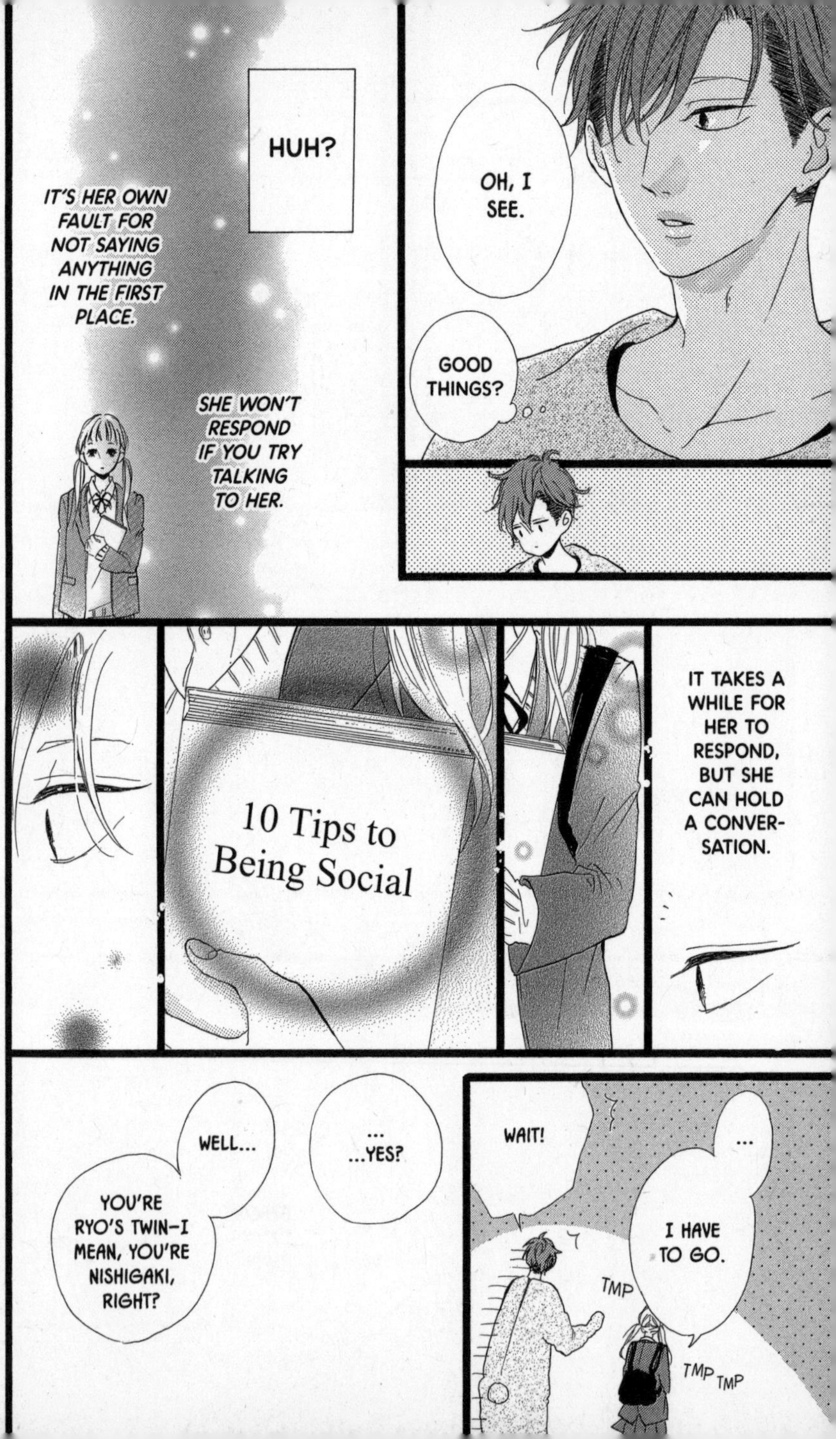
OH, I SEE.
GOOD THINGS?
HUH?
IT'S HER OWN FAULT FOR NOT SAYING ANYTHING IN THE FIRST PLACE.
SHE WON'T RESPOND IF YOU TRY TALKING TO HER.
IT TAKES A WHILE FOR HER TO RESPOND, BUT SHE CAN HOLD A CONVERSATION.
10 Tips to Being Social
...
I HAVE TO GO.
WAIT!
TMP
TMP TMP
...
...YES?
WELL...
YOU'RE RYO'S TWIN—I MEAN, YOU'RE NISHIGAKI, RIGHT?

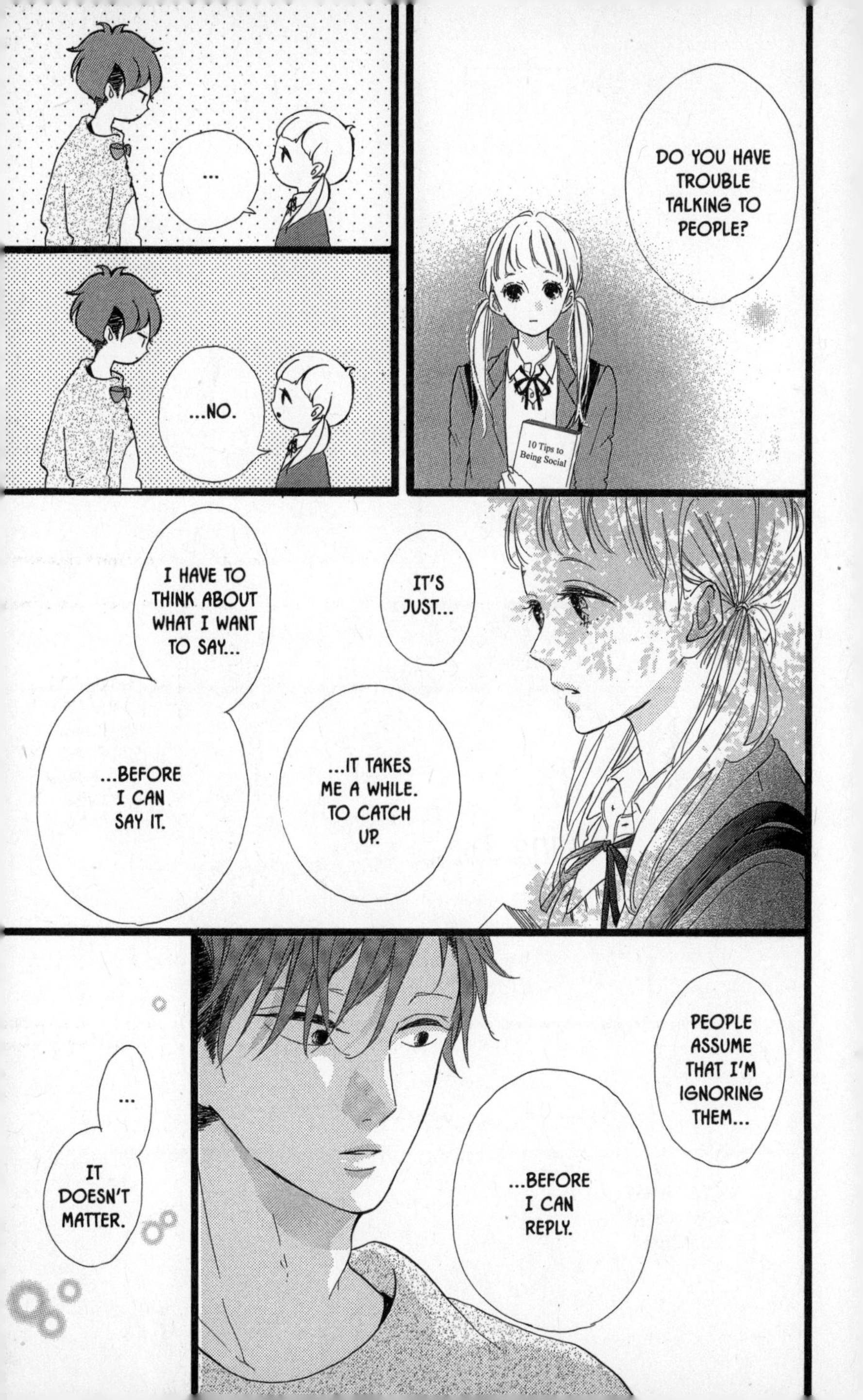
DO YOU HAVE TROUBLE TALKING TO PEOPLE?
10 Tips to Being Social
...
...NO.
IT'S JUST...
I HAVE TO THINK ABOUT WHAT I WANT TO SAY...
...BEFORE I CAN SAY IT.
...IT TAKES ME A WHILE. TO CATCH UP.
PEOPLE ASSUME THAT I'M IGNORING THEM...
...BEFORE I CAN REPLY.
...
IT DOESN'T MATTER.

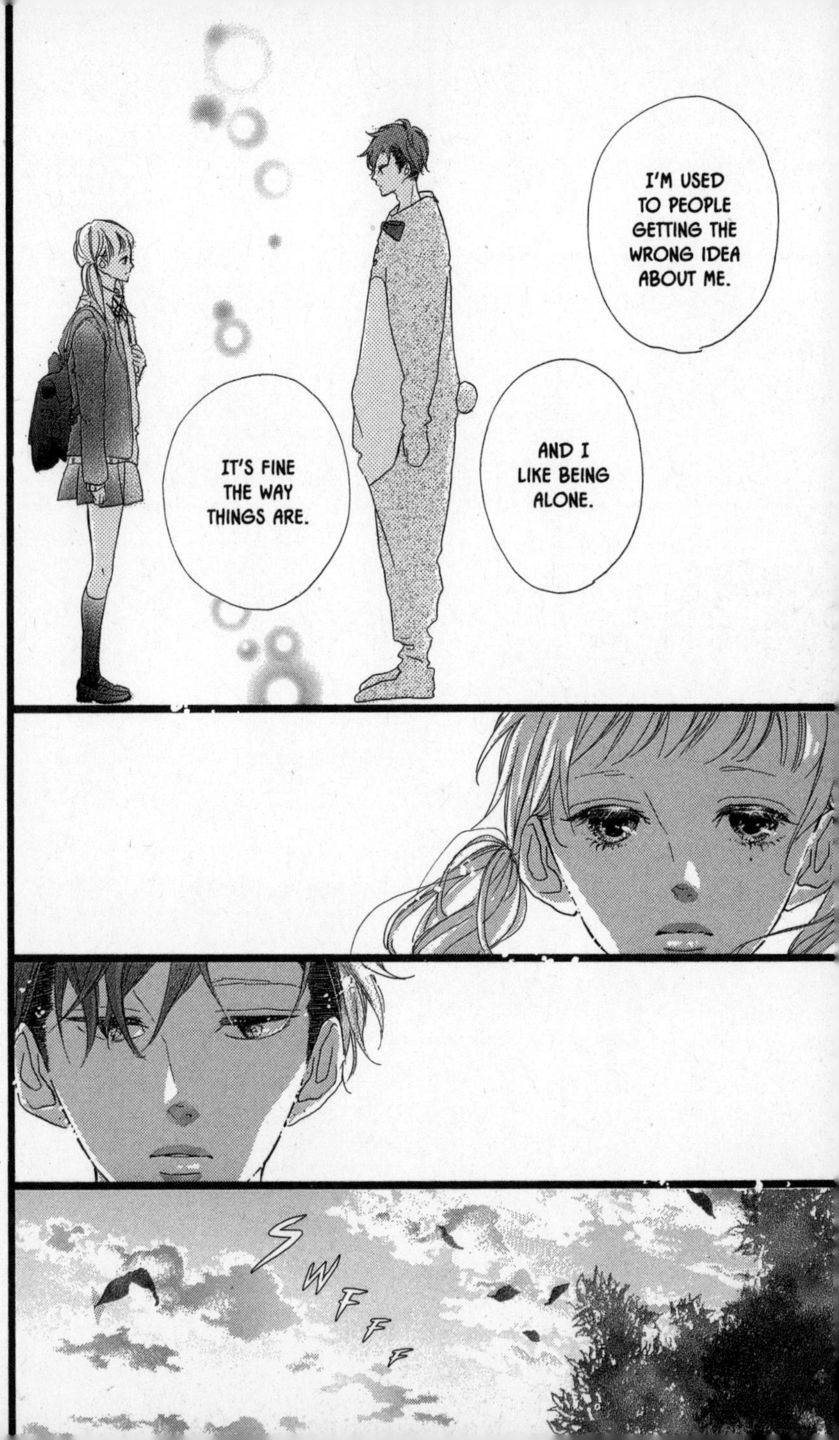
I'M USED TO PEOPLE GETTING THE WRONG IDEA ABOUT ME.
AND I LIKE BEING ALONE.
IT'S FINE THE WAY THINGS ARE.
SWFFF

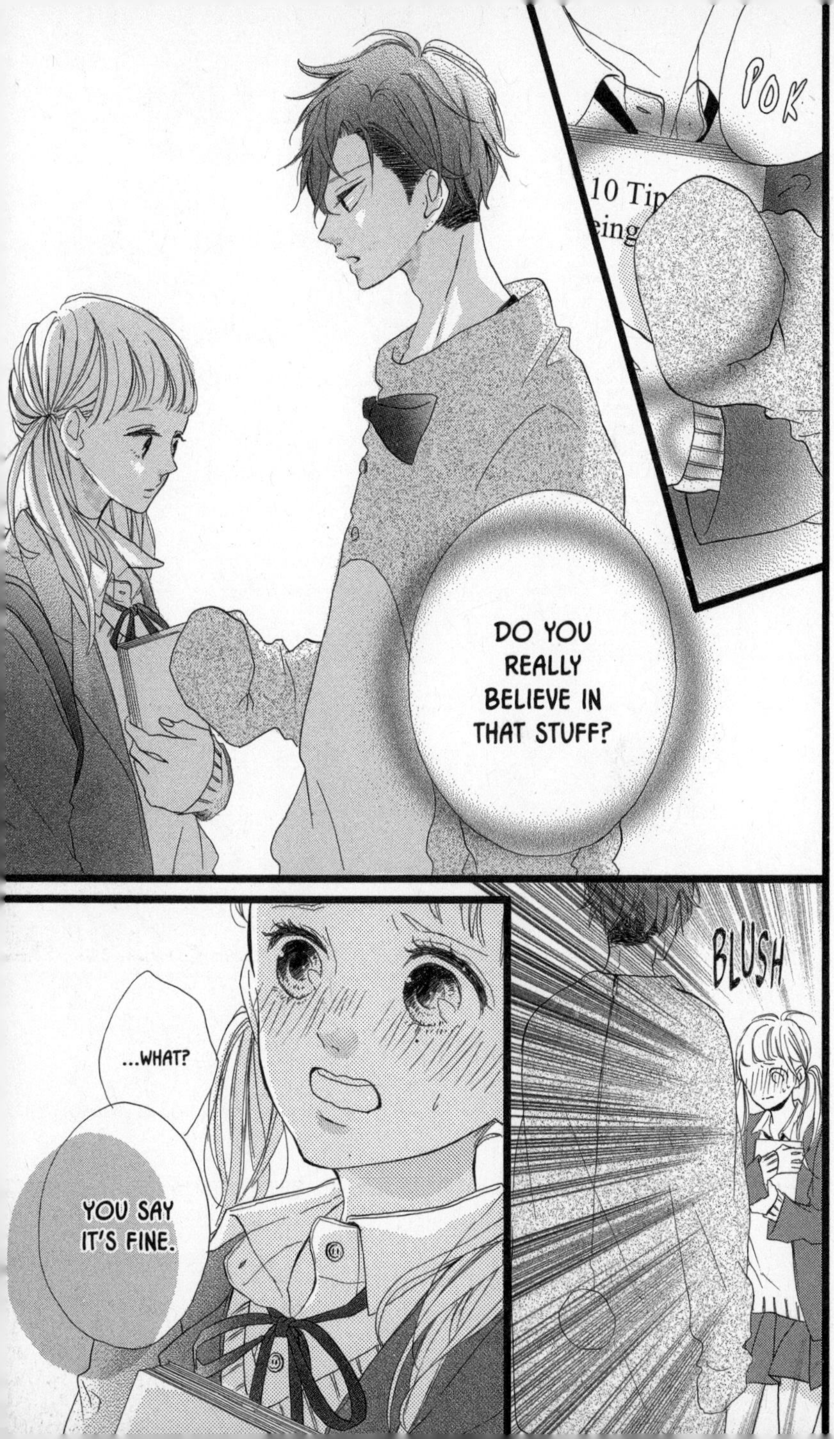
POK
10 Tip
eing
DO YOU REALLY BELIEVE IN THAT STUFF?
BLUSH
...WHAT?
YOU SAY IT'S FINE.

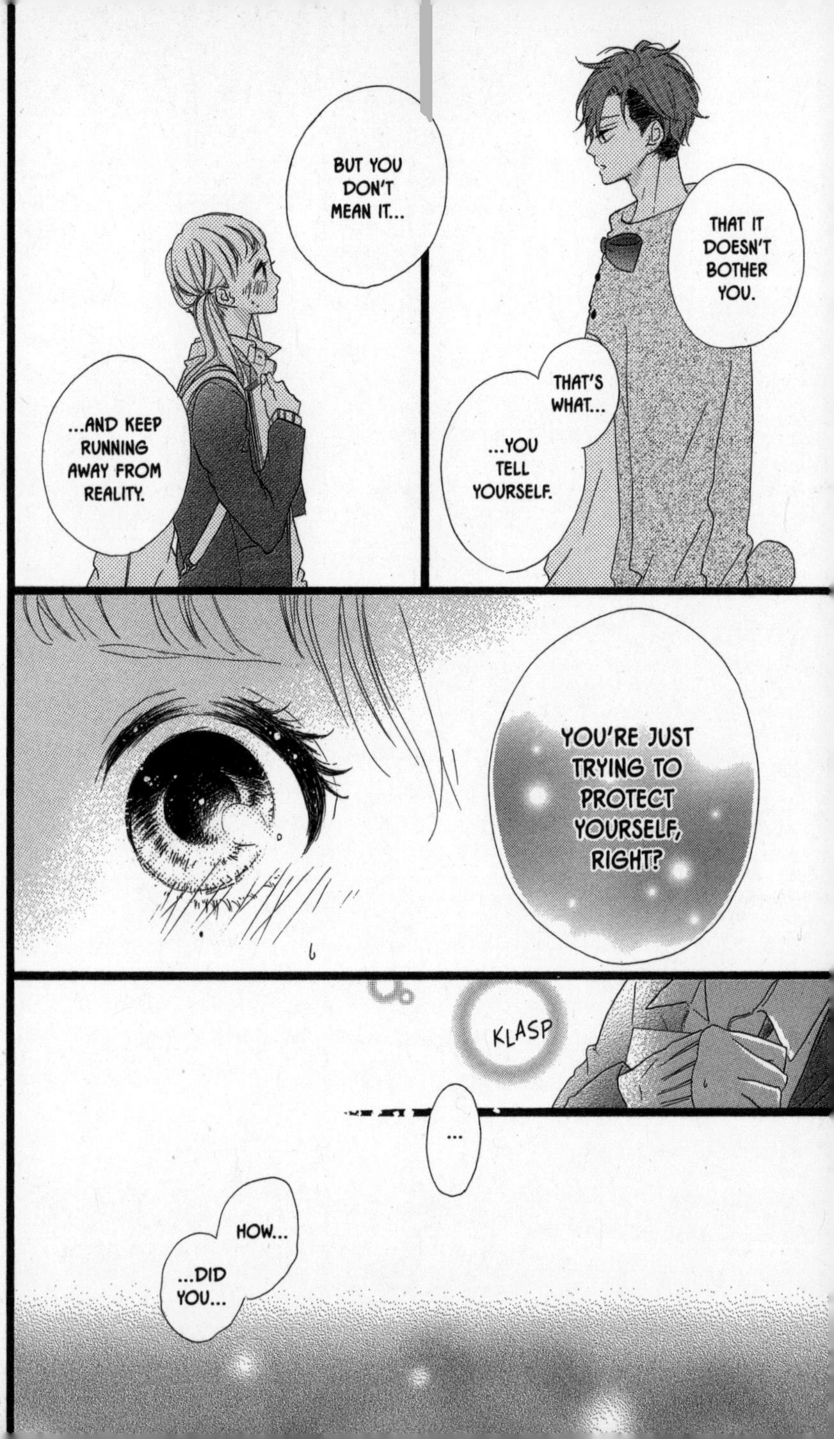
THAT IT DOESN'T BOTHER YOU.
THAT'S WHAT...
...YOU TELL YOURSELF.
BUT YOU DON'T MEAN IT...
...AND KEEP RUNNING AWAY FROM REALITY.
YOU'RE JUST TRYING TO PROTECT YOURSELF, RIGHT?
KLASP
...
HOW...
...DID YOU...

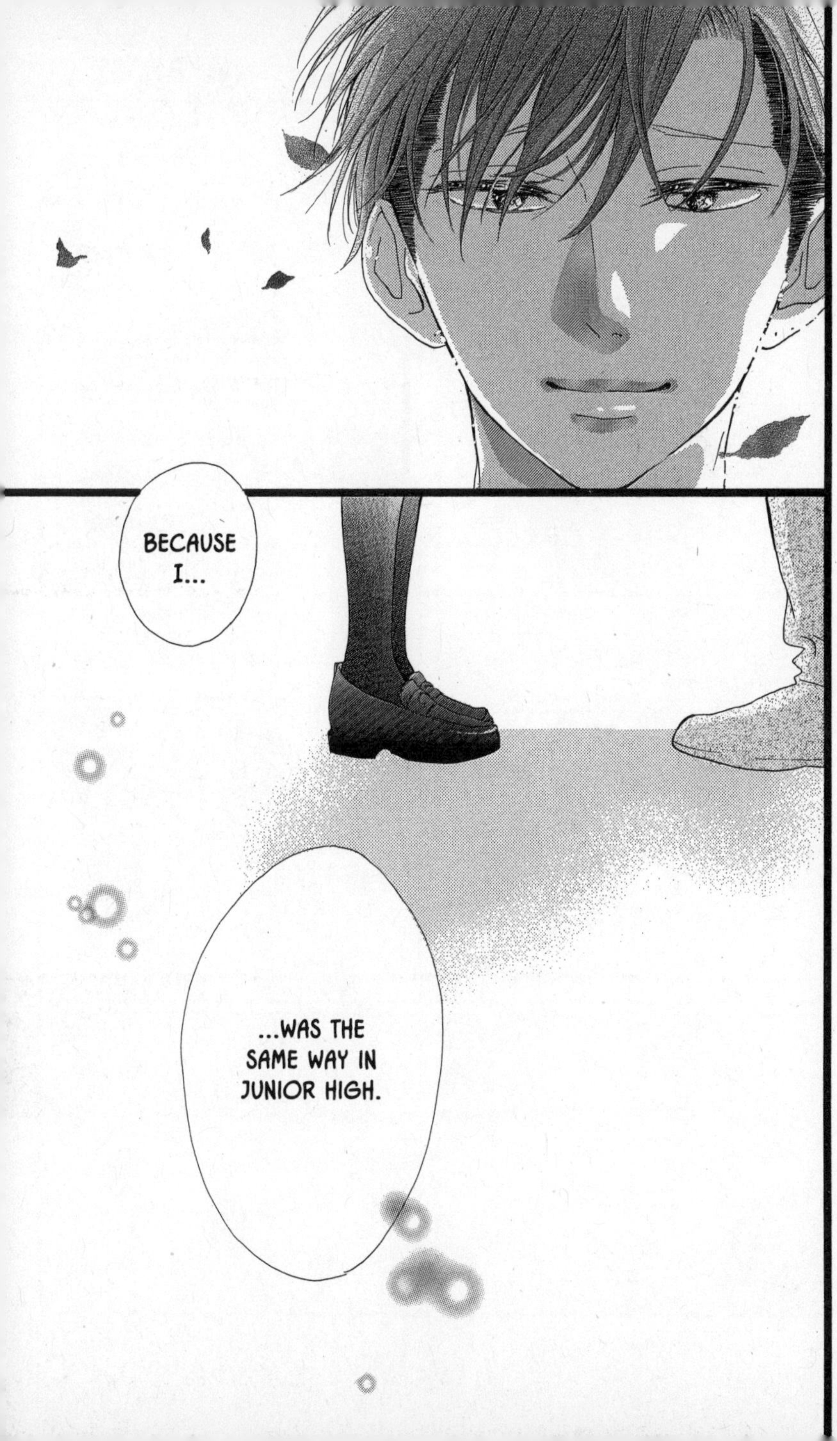
BECAUSE I...
...WAS THE SAME WAY IN JUNIOR HIGH.

Super Things (Age 29)

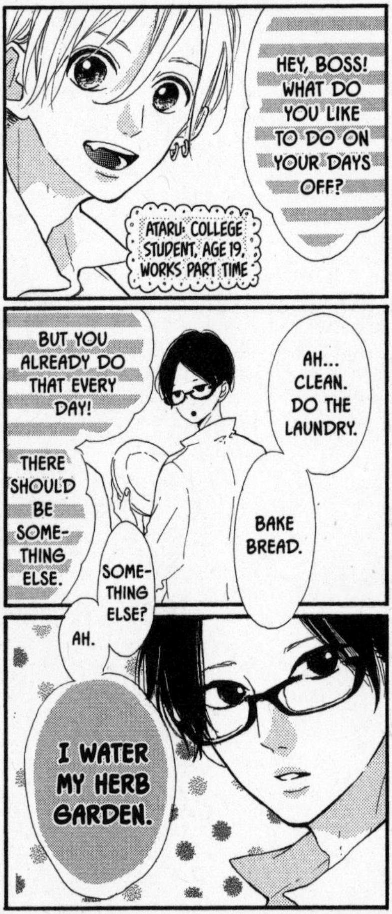
HEY, BOSS! WHAT DO YOU LIKE TO DO ON YOUR DAYS OFF?
ATARU: COLLEGE STUDENT, AGE 19, WORKS PART TIME
AH... CLEAN. DO THE LAUNDRY.
BAKE BREAD.
BUT YOU ALREADY DO THAT EVERY DAY!
THERE SHOULD BE SOME-THING ELSE.
SOME-THING ELSE?
AH.
I WATER MY HERB GARDEN.
I TAKE CARE OF THEM ON A DAILY BASIS, BUT...
...I TAKE EXTRA SPECIAL CARE OF THEM ON MY DAYS OFF.
MY RADISHES HAVE JUST SPROUTED.
I BET HE'D MAKE ONE HEAVENLY HUSBAND.
I could learn a thing or two from him.

Avant-Garde Sou

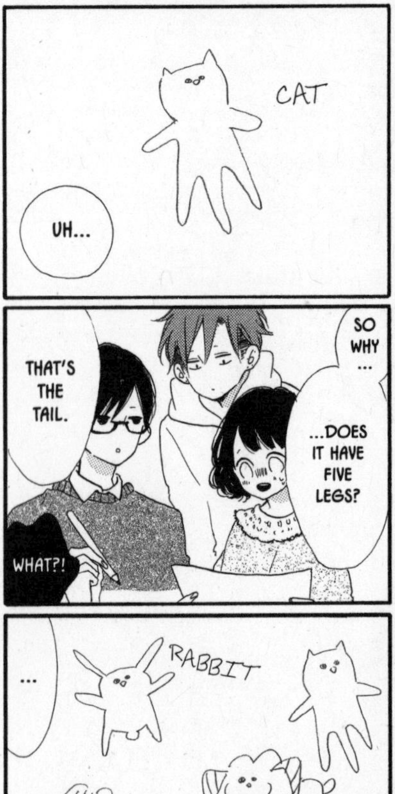
CAT
UH...
SO WHY ...
...DOES IT HAVE FIVE LEGS?
THAT'S THE TAIL.
WHAT?!
RABBIT
...
NAO
SHEEP
SOU, THIS IS SORT OF–
YOUR ARTWORK IS SO AVANT-GARDE!
AMAZING!!
TAI?!

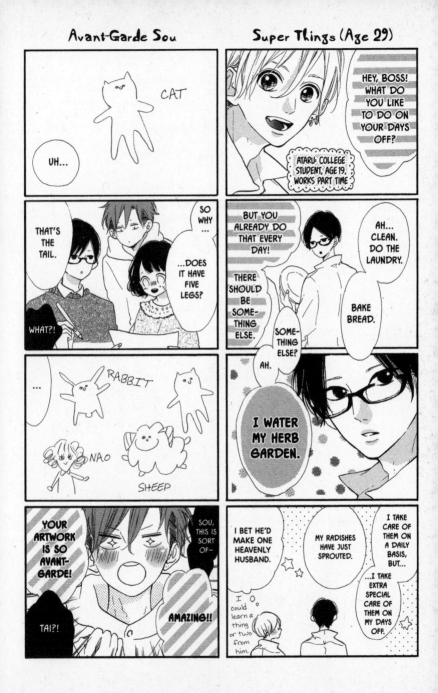

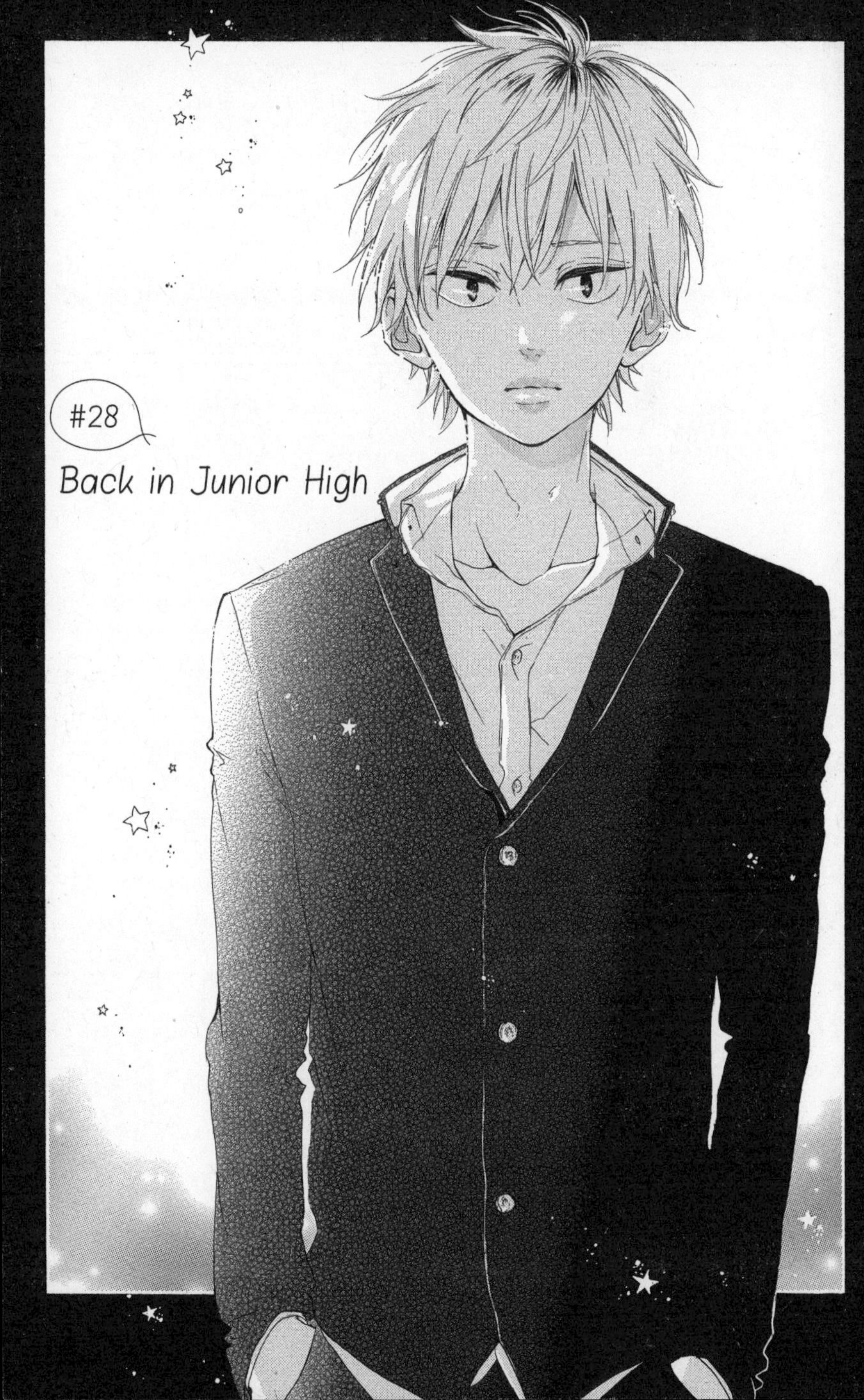
#28
Back in Junior High

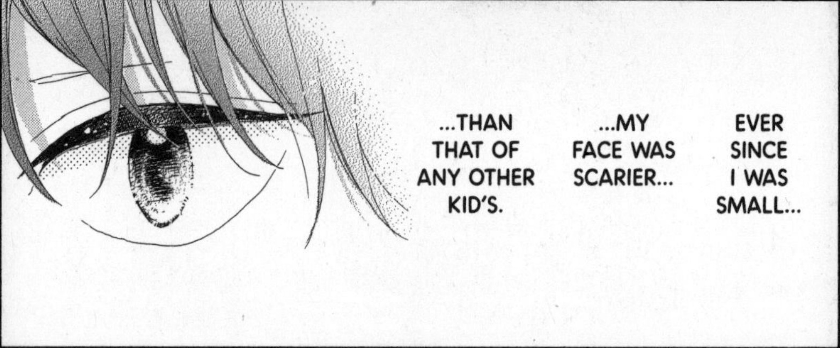
EVER SINCE I WAS SMALL...
...MY FACE WAS SCARIER...
...THAN THAT OF ANY OTHER KID'S.

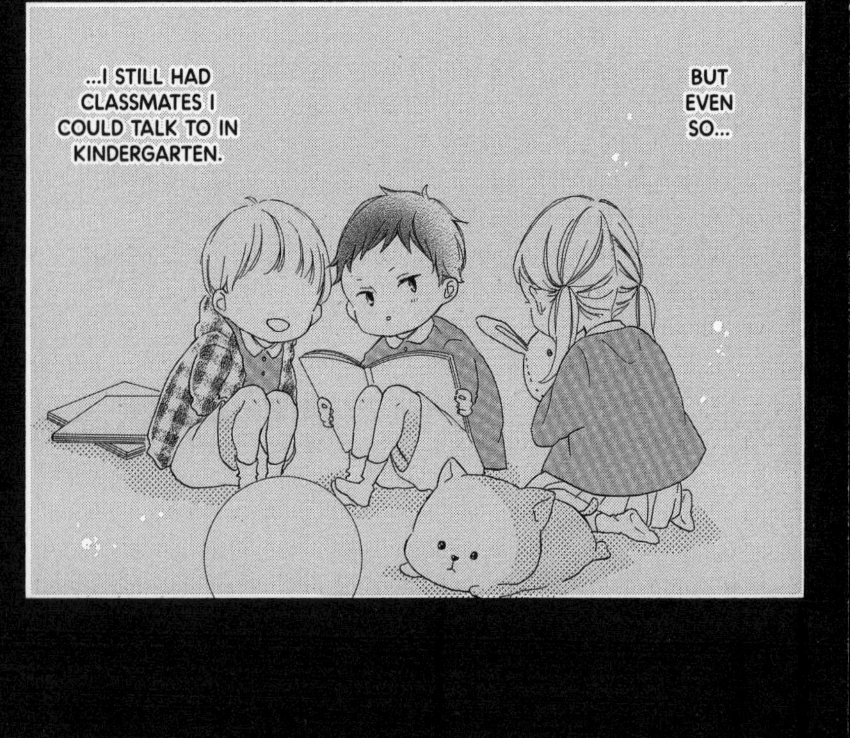
BUT EVEN SO...
...I STILL HAD CLASSMATES I COULD TALK TO IN KINDERGARTEN.

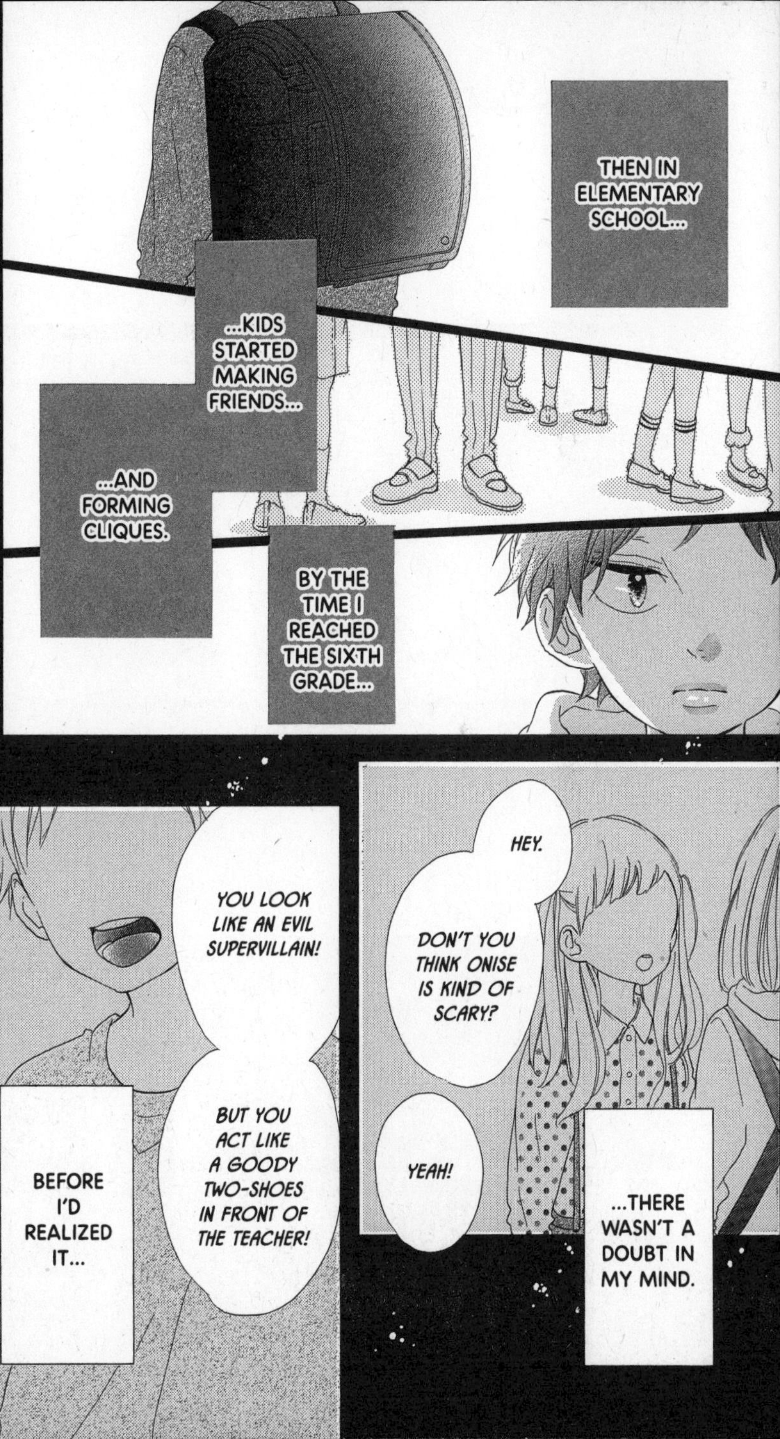
THEN IN ELEMENTARY SCHOOL...
...KIDS STARTED MAKING FRIENDS...
...AND FORMING CLIQUES.
BY THE TIME I REACHED THE SIXTH GRADE...
HEY.
DON'T YOU THINK ONISE IS KIND OF SCARY?
YEAH!
...THERE WASN'T A DOUBT IN MY MIND.
YOU LOOK LIKE AN EVIL SUPERVILLAIN!
BUT YOU ACT LIKE A GOODY TWO-SHOES IN FRONT OF THE TEACHER!
BEFORE I'D REALIZED IT...

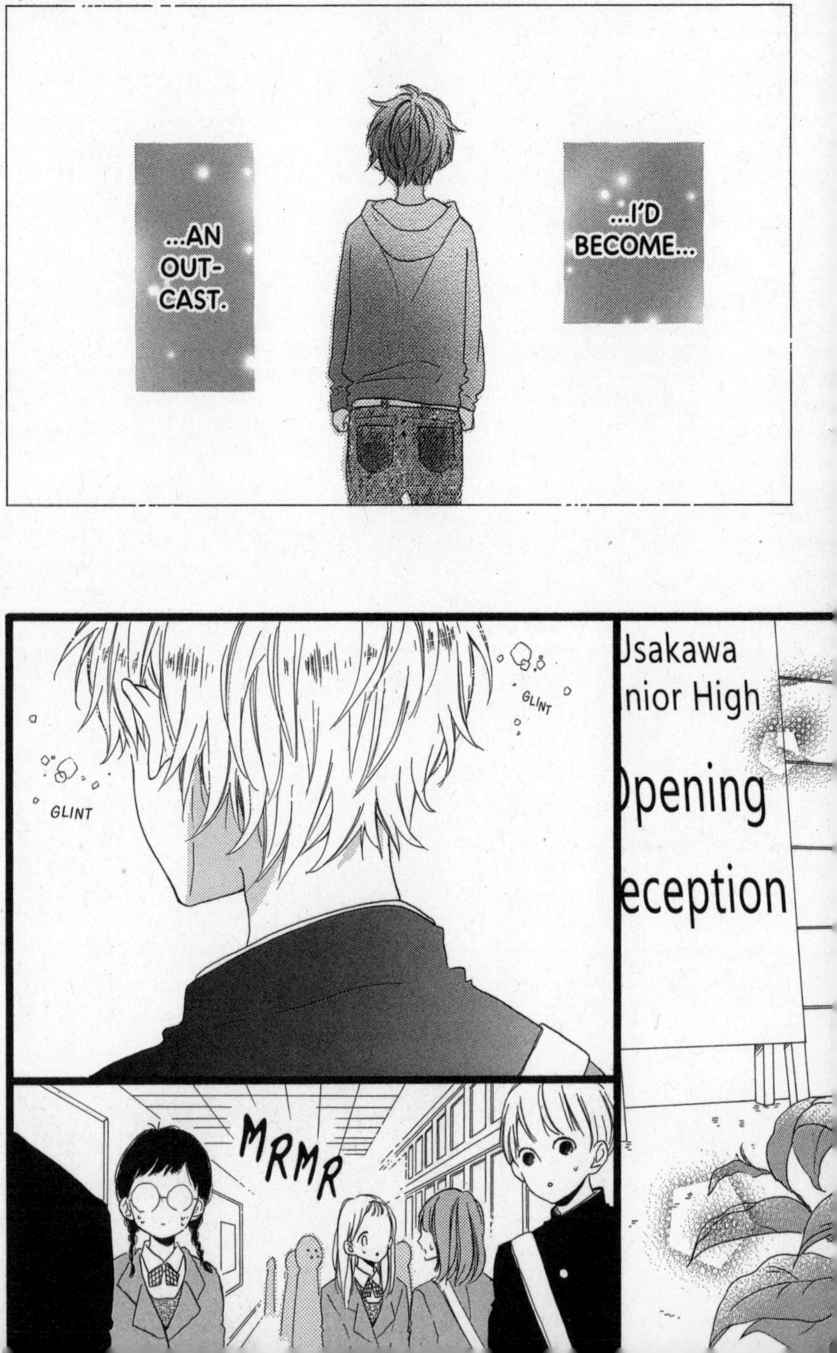
...I'D BECOME...
...AN OUT-CAST.
Usakawa
nior High
pening
eception
GLINT
GLINT
MRMR

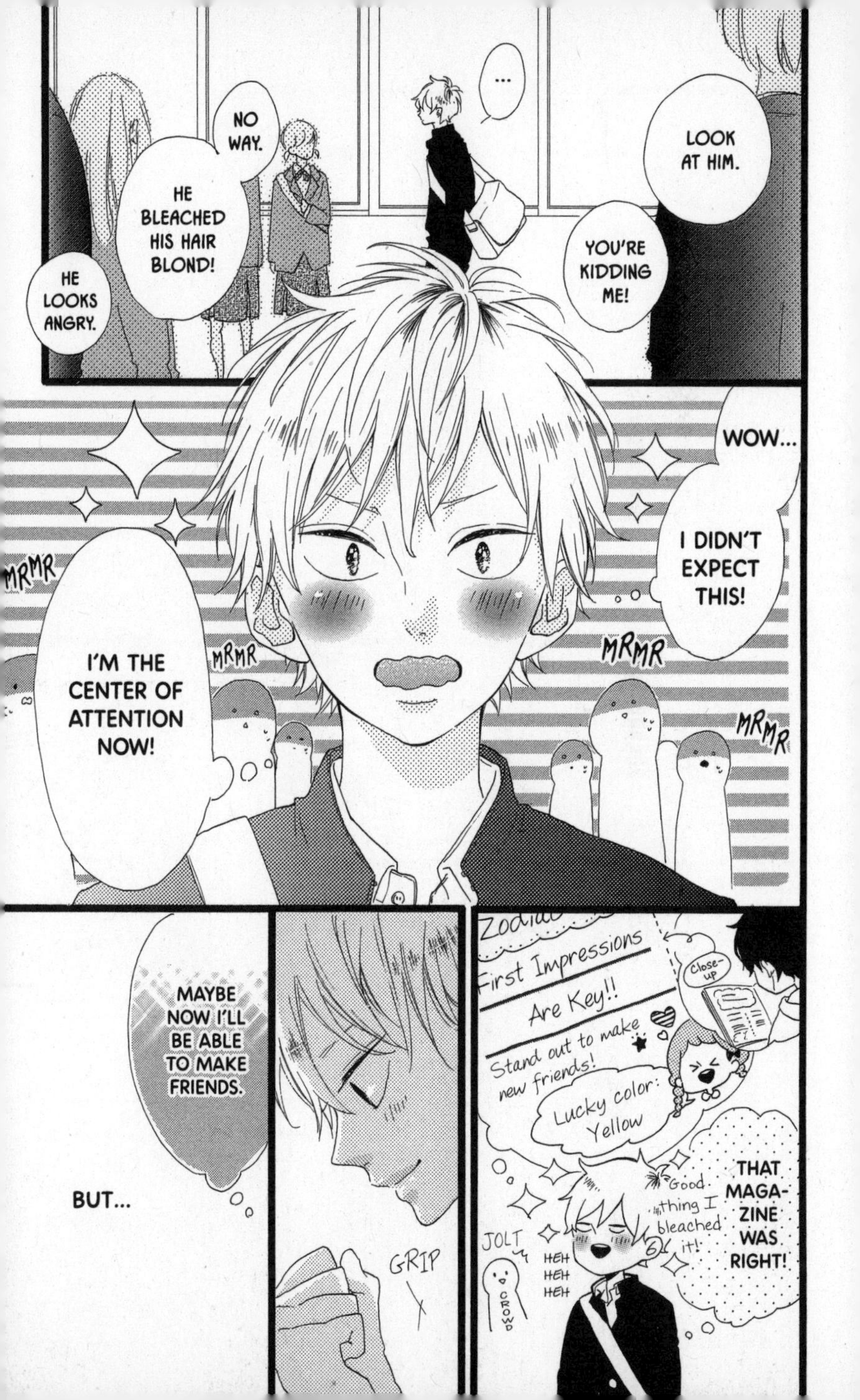
LOOK AT HIM.
...
NO WAY.
YOU'RE KIDDING ME!
HE BLEACHED HIS HAIR BLOND!
HE LOOKS ANGRY.
WOW...
I DIDN'T EXPECT THIS!
MRMR
MRMR
MRMR
MRMR
I'M THE CENTER OF ATTENTION NOW!
Close-up
First Impressions Are Key!!
Stand out to make new friends!
Lucky color: Yellow
THAT MAGAZINE WAS RIGHT!
Good thing I bleached it!
JOLT
HEH HEH HEH
CROWD
GRIP
MAYBE NOW I'LL BE ABLE TO MAKE FRIENDS.
BUT...

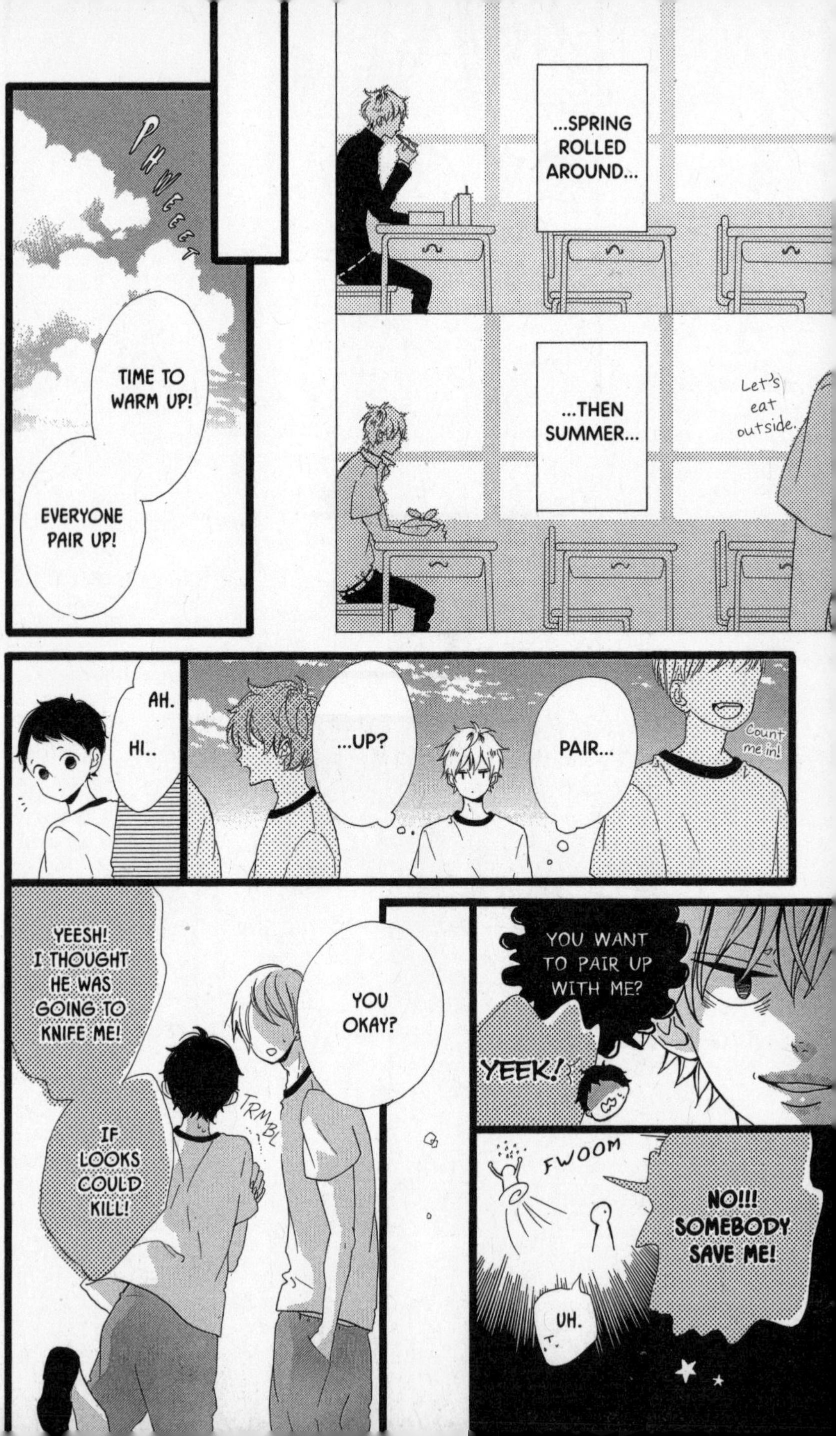
...SPRING ROLLED AROUND...
...THEN SUMMER...
Let's eat outside.
PHWEEET
TIME TO WARM UP!
EVERYONE PAIR UP!
Count me in!
PAIR...
...UP?
AH.
HI..
YOU WANT TO PAIR UP WITH ME?
YEEK!
FWOOM
NO!!! SOMEBODY SAVE ME!
UH.
YOU OKAY?
YEESH! I THOUGHT HE WAS GOING TO KNIFE ME!
TRMBL
IF LOOKS COULD KILL!

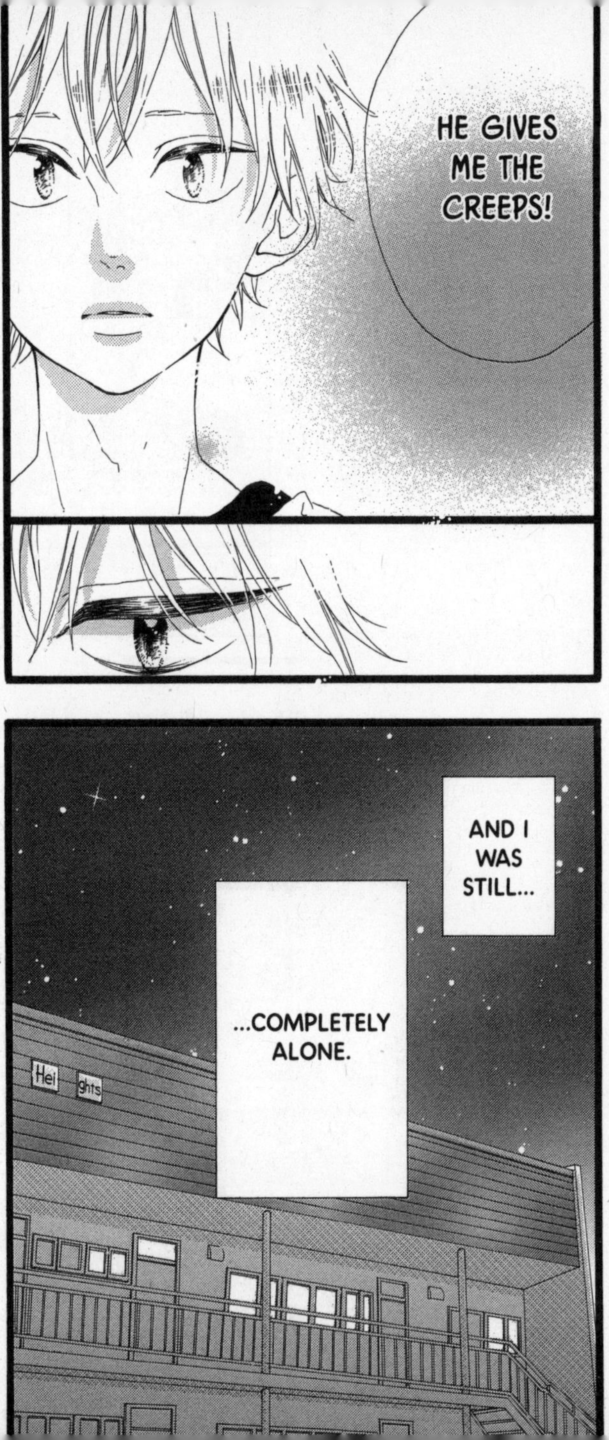
HE GIVES ME THE CREEPS!
AND I WAS STILL...
...COMPLETELY ALONE.
Hei
ghts

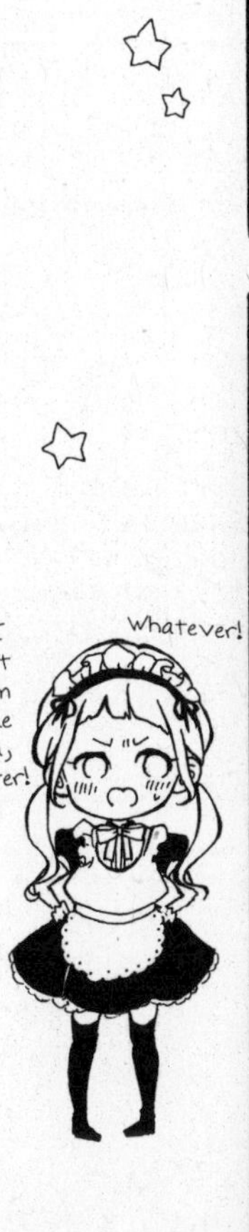
Whatever!
I-I don't even l-like you, Master!

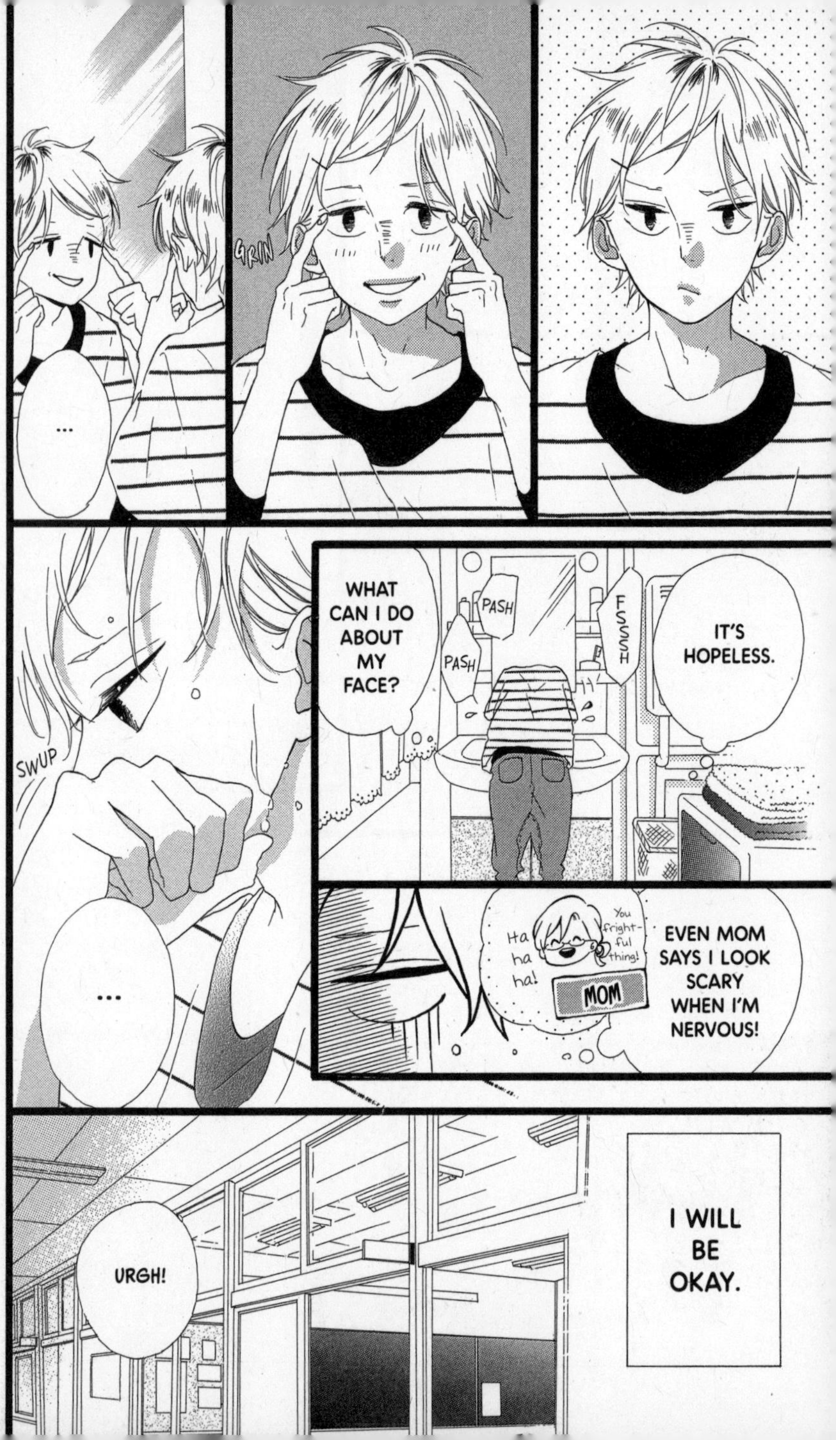
GRIN
...
IT'S HOPELESS.
FSSSH
PASH
PASH
WHAT CAN I DO ABOUT MY FACE?
EVEN MOM SAYS I LOOK SCARY WHEN I'M NERVOUS!
You frightful thing!
Ha ha ha!
MOM
SWUP
...
I WILL BE OKAY.
URGH!

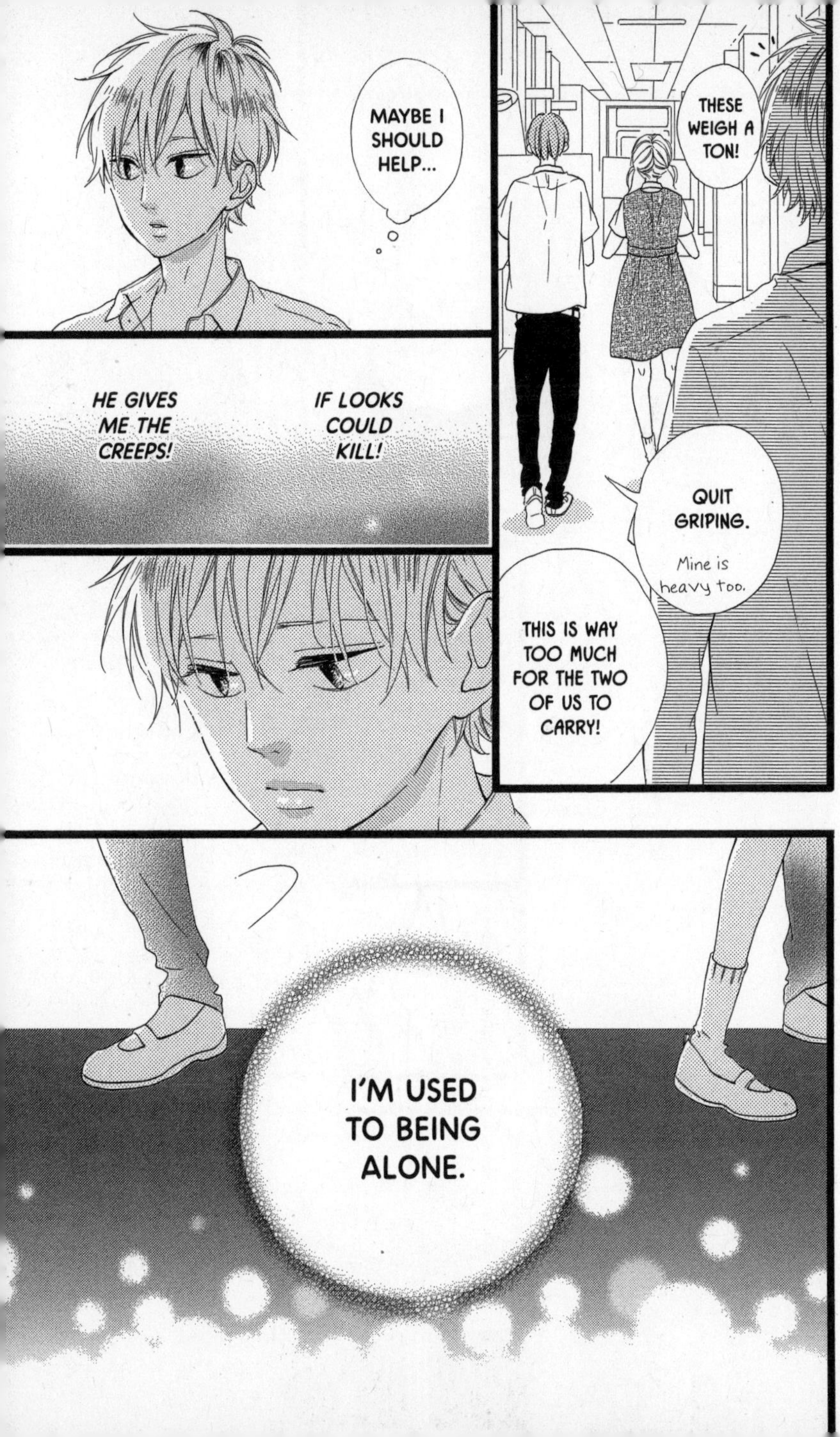
THESE WEIGH A TON!
QUIT GRIPING.
Mine is heavy too.
THIS IS WAY TOO MUCH FOR THE TWO OF US TO CARRY!
MAYBE I SHOULD HELP...
IF LOOKS COULD KILL!
HE GIVES ME THE CREEPS!
I'M USED TO BEING ALONE.

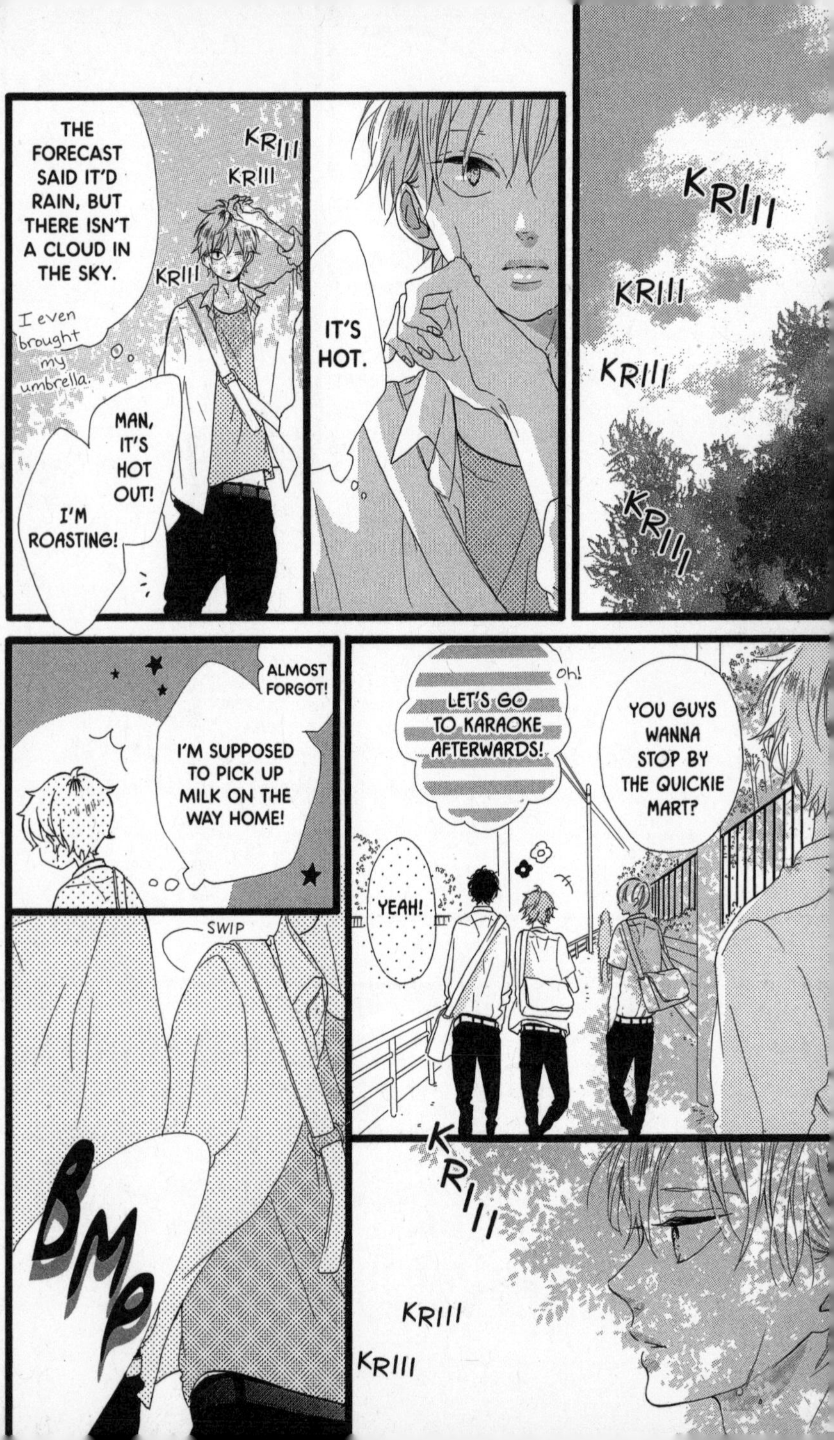
KRIII
KRIII
KRIII
KRIII
KRIII
IT'S HOT.
KRIII
KRIII
THE FORECAST SAID IT'D RAIN, BUT THERE ISN'T A CLOUD IN THE SKY.
KRIII
I even brought my umbrella.
MAN, IT'S HOT OUT!
I'M ROASTING!
YOU GUYS WANNA STOP BY THE QUICKIE MART?
Oh!
LET'S GO TO KARAOKE AFTERWARDS!
YEAH!
ALMOST FORGOT!
I'M SUPPOSED TO PICK UP MILK ON THE WAY HOME!
KRIII
KRIII
KRIII
SWIP
BMP

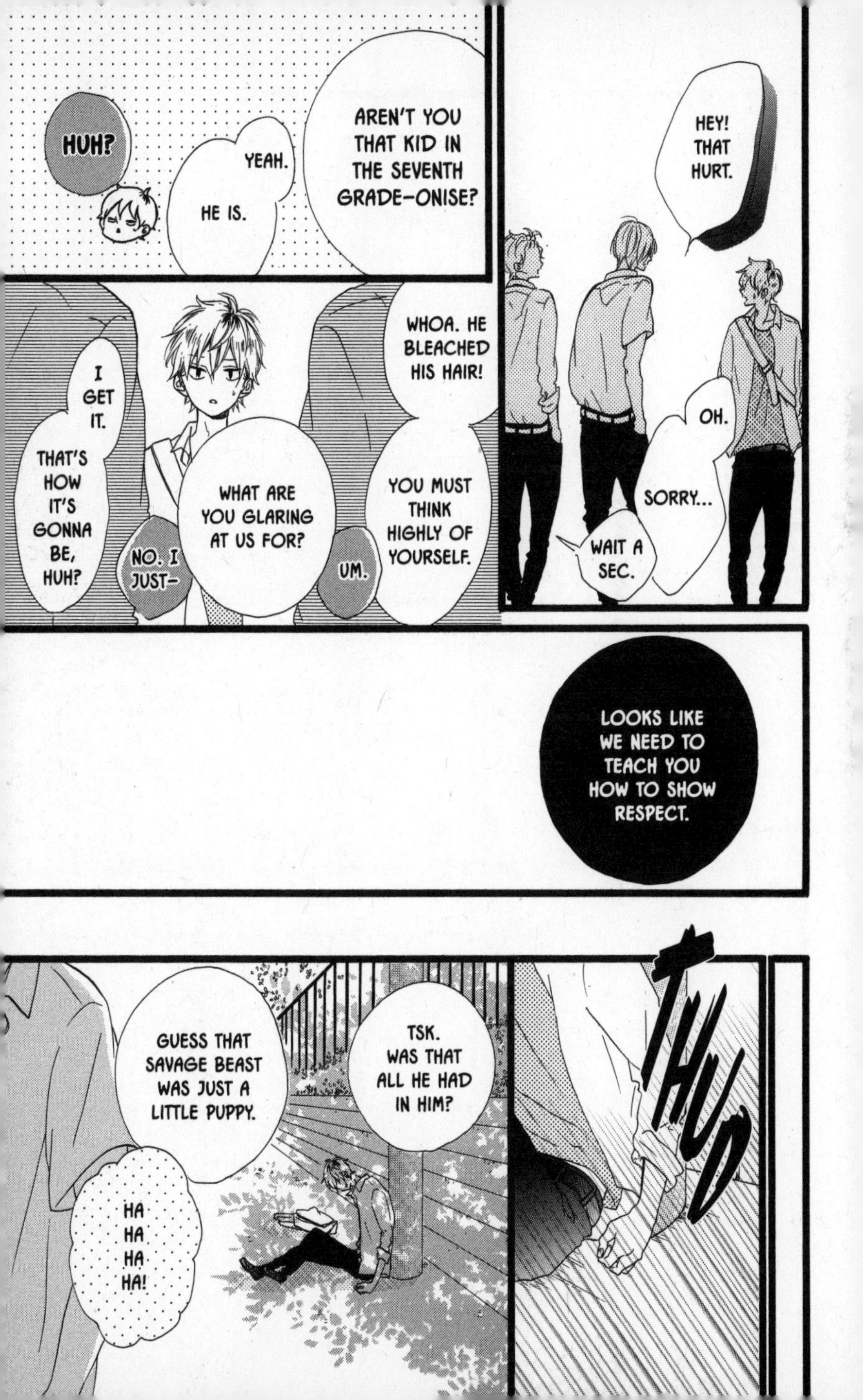

HEY! THAT HURT.
OH. SORRY...
WAIT A SEC.
AREN'T YOU THAT KID IN THE SEVENTH GRADE—ONISE?
YEAH. HE IS.
HUH?
WHOA. HE BLEACHED HIS HAIR!
YOU MUST THINK HIGHLY OF YOURSELF.
UM.
WHAT ARE YOU GLARING AT US FOR?
NO. I JUST—
I GET IT. THAT'S HOW IT'S GONNA BE, HUH?
LOOKS LIKE WE NEED TO TEACH YOU HOW TO SHOW RESPECT.
THUD
TSK. WAS THAT ALL HE HAD IN HIM?
GUESS THAT SAVAGE BEAST WAS JUST A LITTLE PUPPY.
HA HA HA HA!

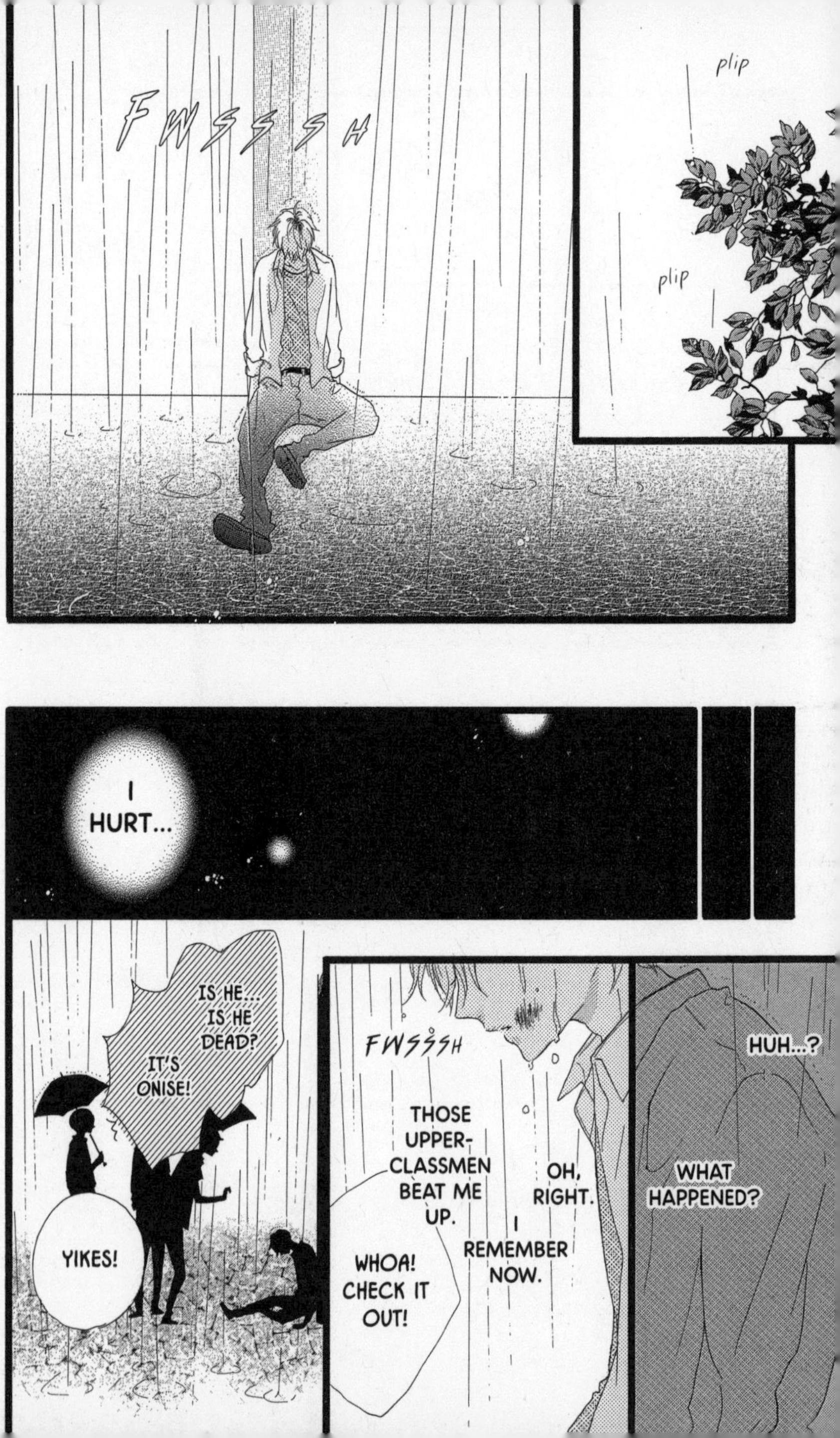
plip
plip
FWSSSH
I HURT...
HUH...?
WHAT HAPPENED?
FWSSSH
OH, RIGHT.
I REMEMBER NOW.
THOSE UPPER-CLASSMEN BEAT ME UP.
WHOA! CHECK IT OUT!
IS HE... IS HE DEAD?
IT'S ONISE!
YIKES!

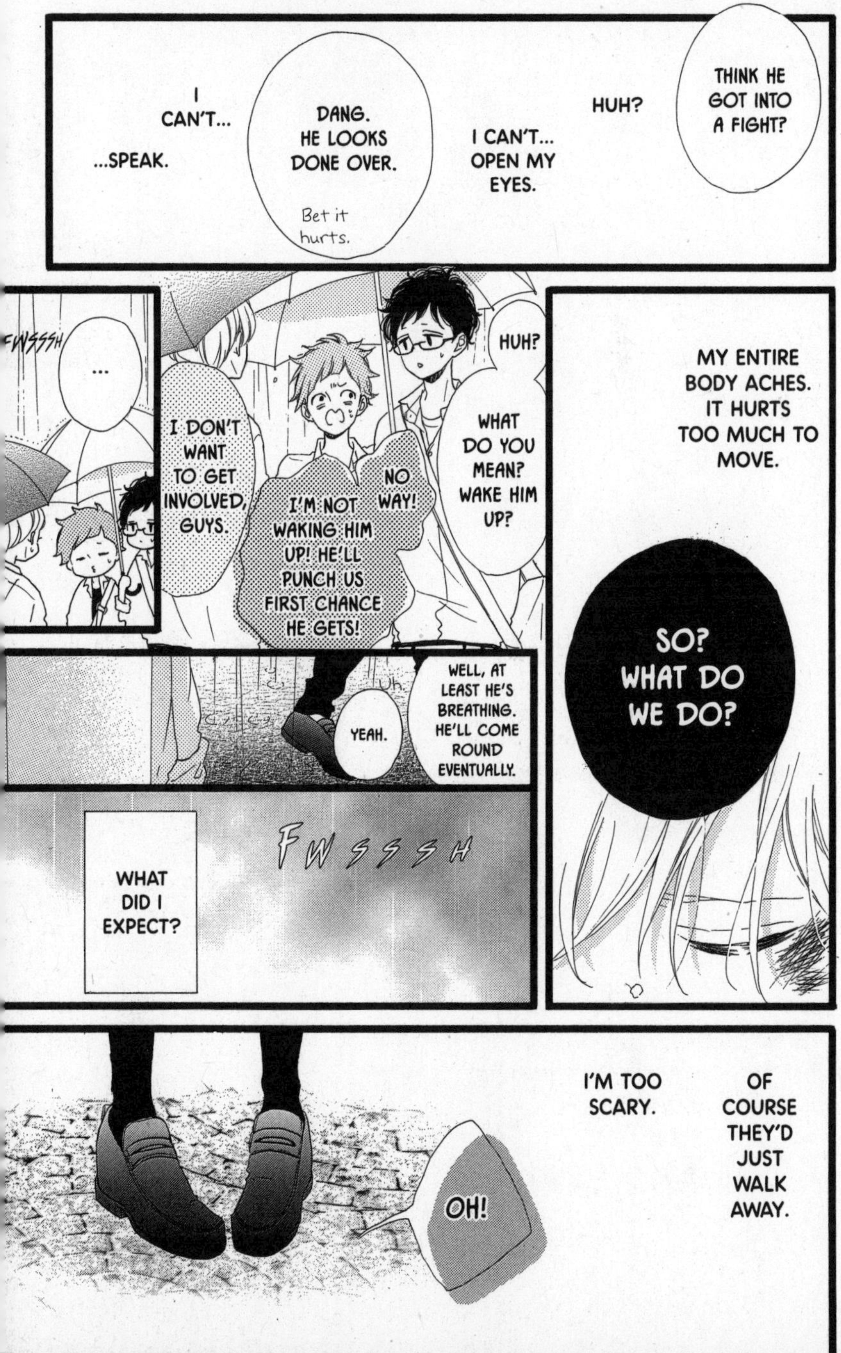
THINK HE GOT INTO A FIGHT?
HUH?
I CAN'T... OPEN MY EYES.
DANG. HE LOOKS DONE OVER.
Bet it hurts.
I CAN'T...
...SPEAK.
MY ENTIRE BODY ACHES. IT HURTS TOO MUCH TO MOVE.
SO? WHAT DO WE DO?
HUH?
WHAT DO YOU MEAN? WAKE HIM UP?
NO WAY!
I'M NOT WAKING HIM UP! HE'LL PUNCH US FIRST CHANCE HE GETS!
I DON'T WANT TO GET INVOLVED, GUYS.
FWSSSH
...
WELL, AT LEAST HE'S BREATHING. HE'LL COME ROUND EVENTUALLY.
Uh.
YEAH.
FWSSSH
WHAT DID I EXPECT?
OF COURSE THEY'D JUST WALK AWAY.
I'M TOO SCARY.
OH!

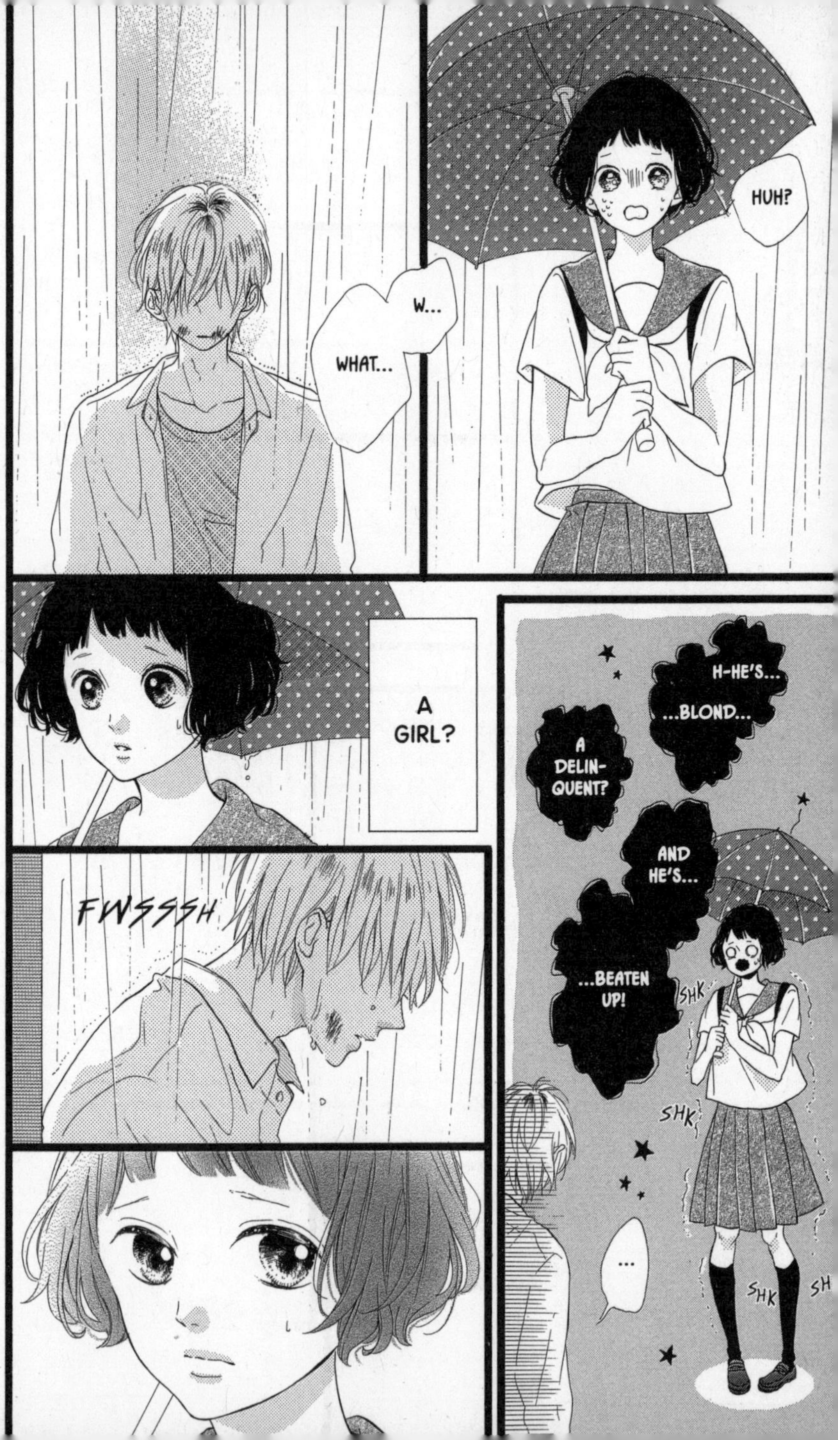
HUH?
W... WHAT...
H-HE'S... ...BLOND...
A DELINQUENT?
AND HE'S... ...BEATEN UP!
SHK
SHK
SHK
SH
...
A GIRL?
FWSSSH

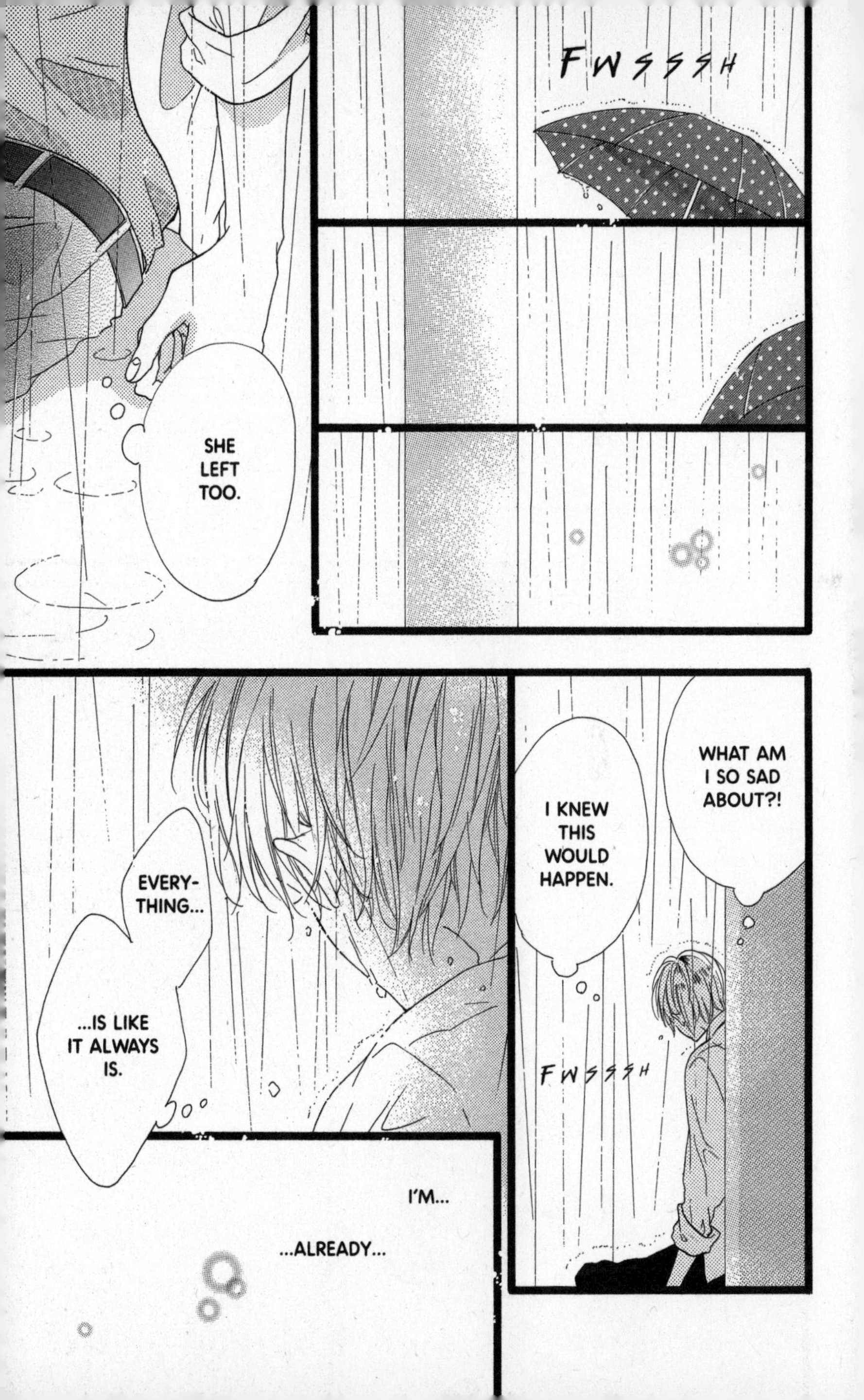
FWSSSH
SHE LEFT TOO.
WHAT AM I SO SAD ABOUT?!
I KNEW THIS WOULD HAPPEN.
FWSSSH
EVERY-THING...
...IS LIKE IT ALWAYS IS.
I'M...
...ALREADY...

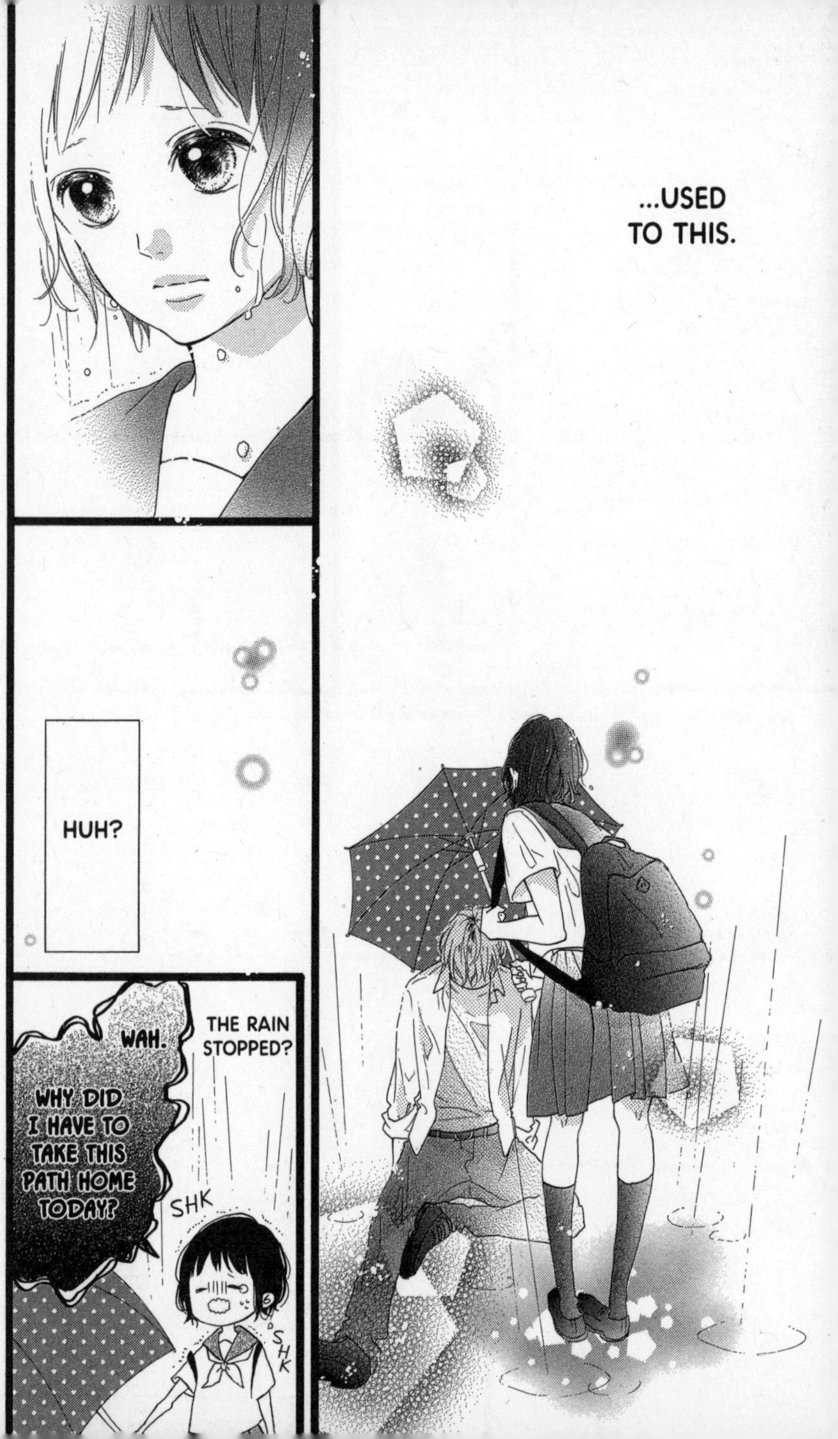
...USED TO THIS.
HUH?
THE RAIN STOPPED?
WAH.
WHY DID I HAVE TO TAKE THIS PATH HOME TODAY?
SHK
SHK

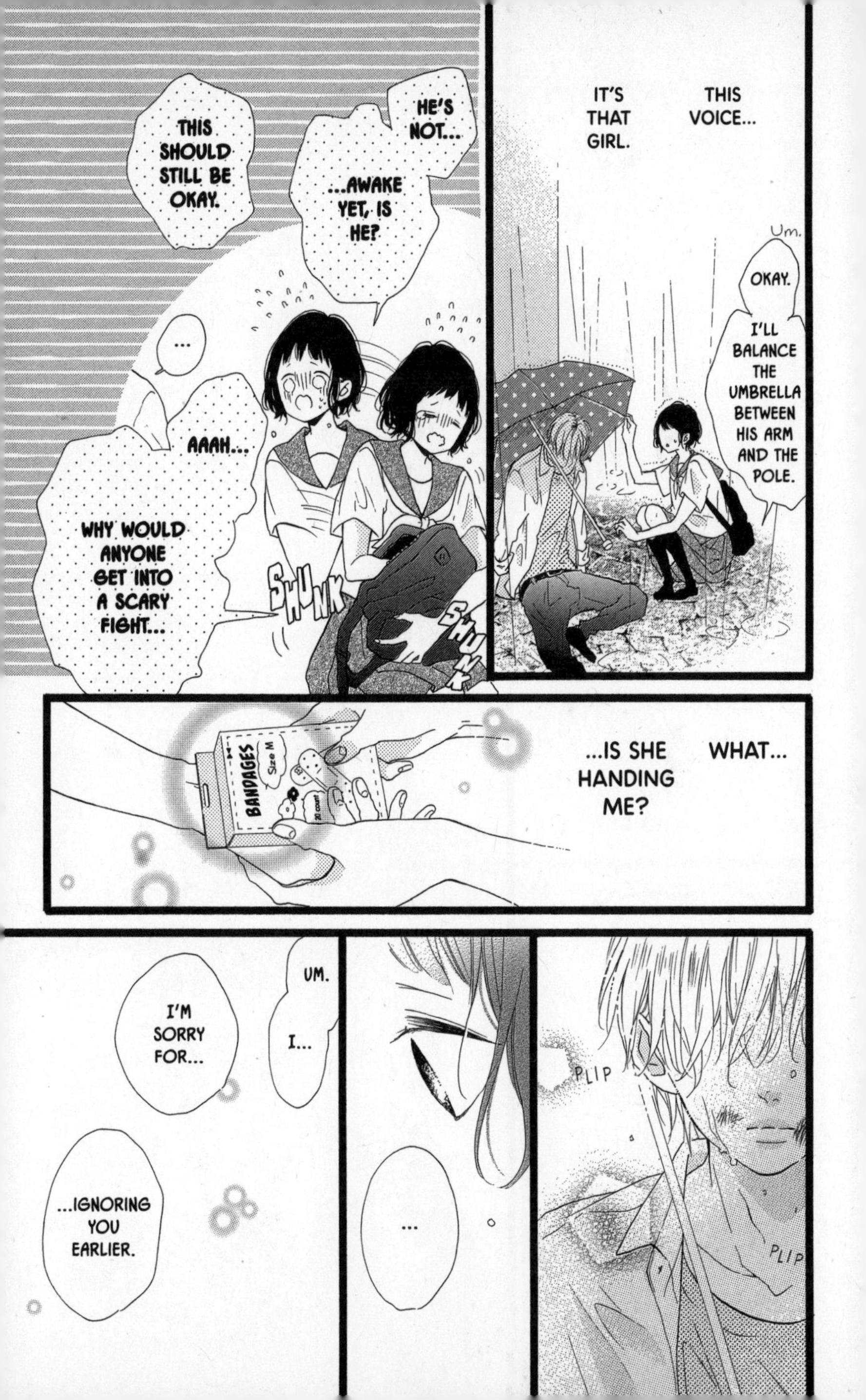
THIS VOICE...
IT'S THAT GIRL.
Um.
OKAY.
I'LL BALANCE THE UMBRELLA BETWEEN HIS ARM AND THE POLE.
HE'S NOT...
...AWAKE YET, IS HE?
THIS SHOULD STILL BE OKAY.
...
AAAH...
WHY WOULD ANYONE GET INTO A SCARY FIGHT...
SHUNK
SHUNK
BANDAGES
Size M
20 count
WHAT...
...IS SHE HANDING ME?
PLIP
PLIP
...
UM.
I...
I'M SORRY FOR...
...IGNORING YOU EARLIER.

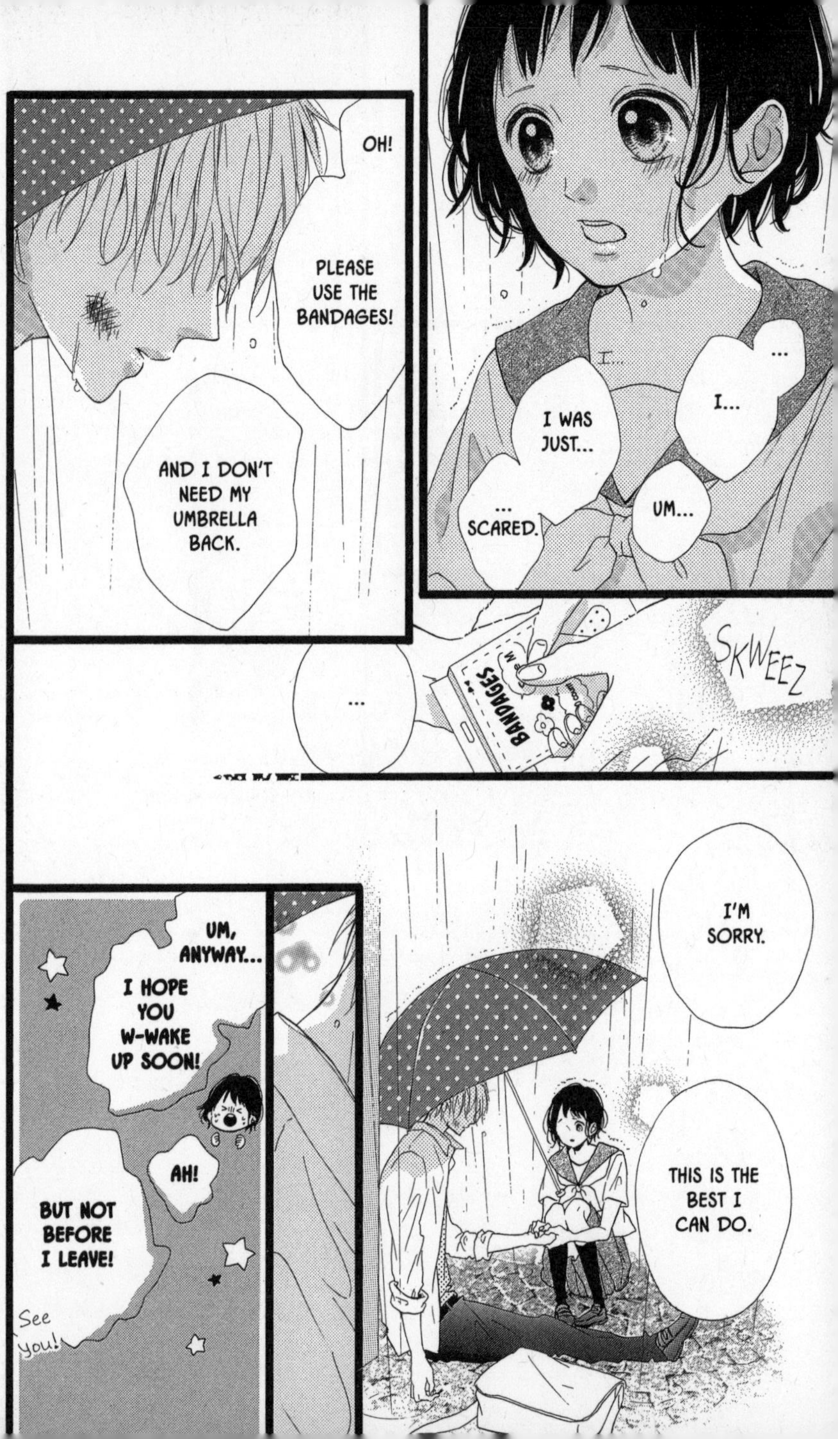
...
I...
I...
I WAS JUST...
UM...
... SCARED.
OH!
PLEASE USE THE BANDAGES!
AND I DON'T NEED MY UMBRELLA BACK.
SKWEEZ
BANDAGES
...
I'M SORRY.
THIS IS THE BEST I CAN DO.
UM, ANYWAY...
I HOPE YOU W-WAKE UP SOON!
AH!
BUT NOT BEFORE I LEAVE!
See you!

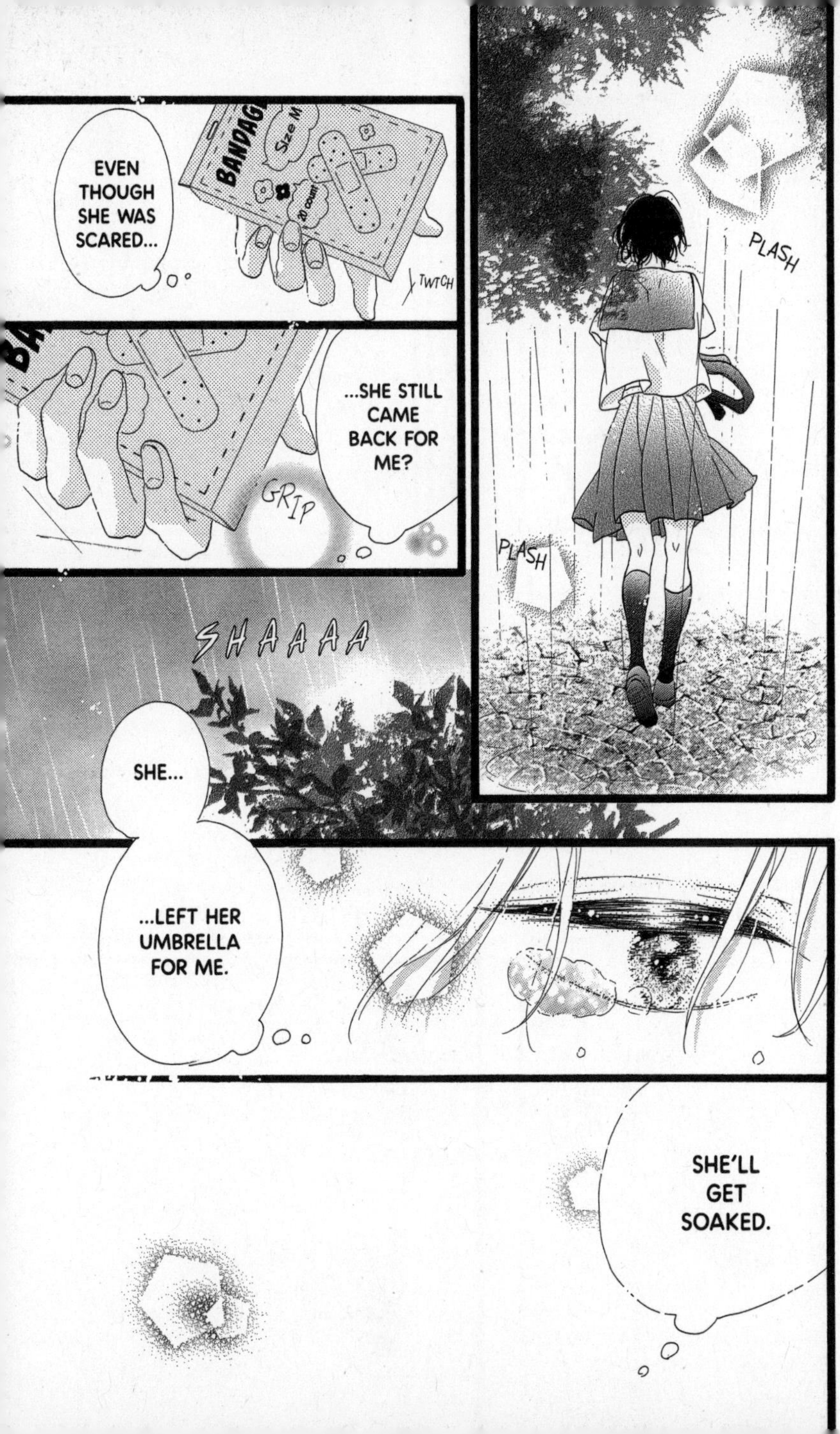
PLASH
PLASH
EVEN THOUGH SHE WAS SCARED...
TWITCH
Size M
...SHE STILL CAME BACK FOR ME?
GRIP
SHAAAA
SHE...
...LEFT HER UMBRELLA FOR ME.
SHE'LL GET SOAKED.

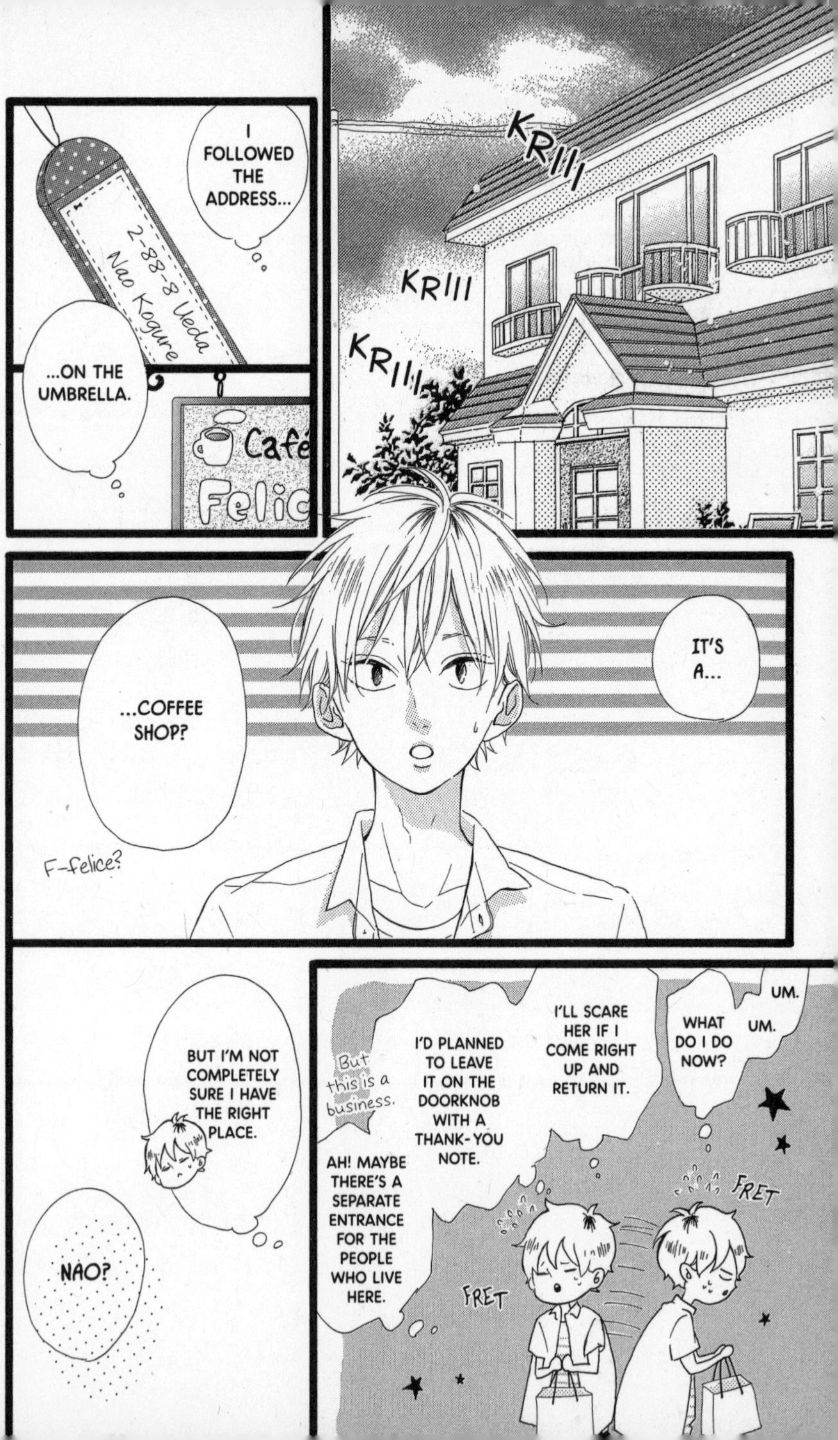
KRIII
KRIII
KRIII
I FOLLOWED THE ADDRESS...
2-88-8 Ueda Nao Kogure
Café Felic
...ON THE UMBRELLA.
IT'S A...
...COFFEE SHOP?
F-felice?
UM.
UM.
WHAT DO I DO NOW?
I'LL SCARE HER IF I COME RIGHT UP AND RETURN IT.
I'D PLANNED TO LEAVE IT ON THE DOORKNOB WITH A THANK-YOU NOTE.
But this is a business.
AH! MAYBE THERE'S A SEPARATE ENTRANCE FOR THE PEOPLE WHO LIVE HERE.
FRET
FRET
BUT I'M NOT COMPLETELY SURE I HAVE THE RIGHT PLACE.
NAO?

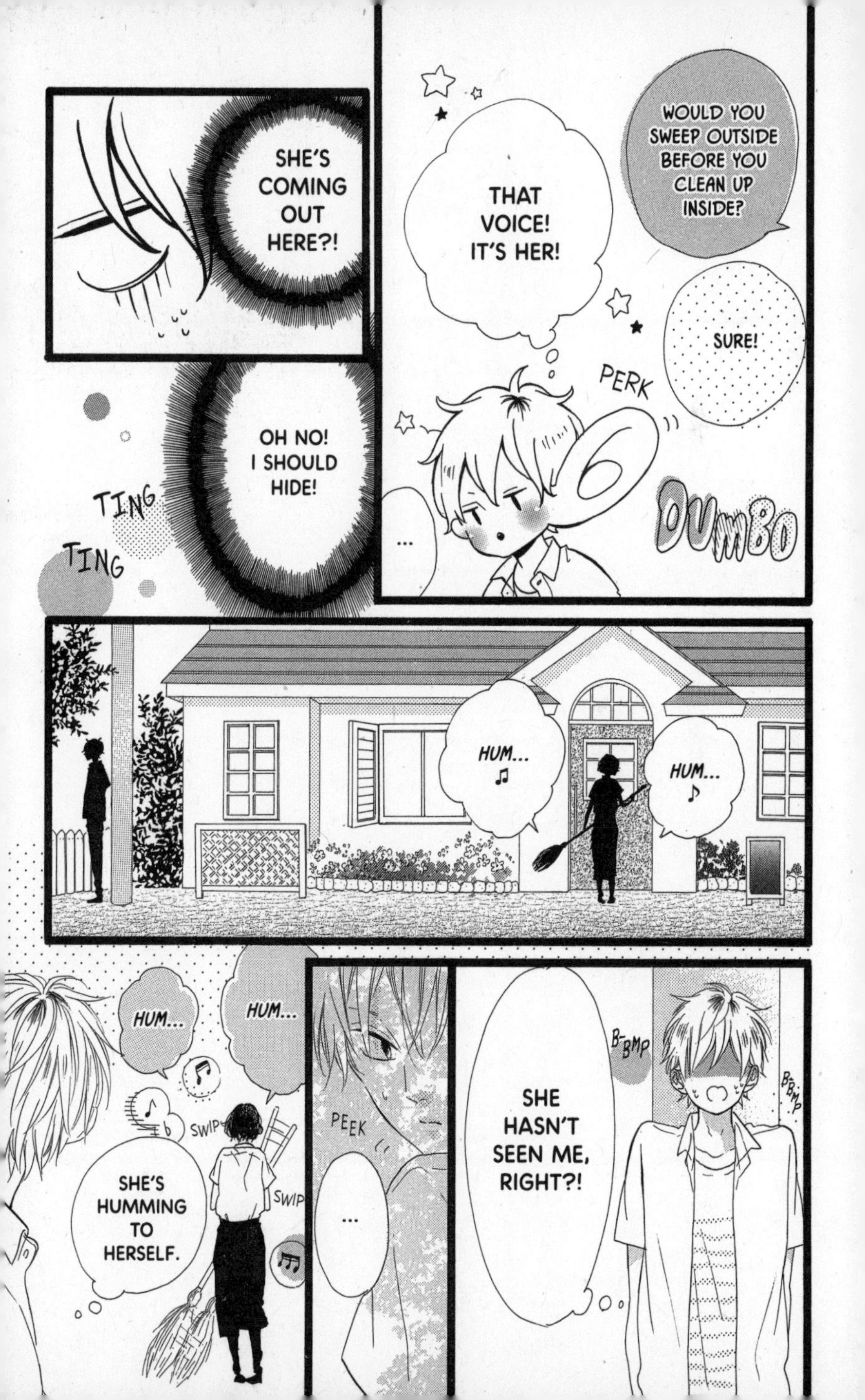
WOULD YOU SWEEP OUTSIDE BEFORE YOU CLEAN UP INSIDE?
THAT VOICE! IT'S HER!
SURE!
PERK
DUMBO
...
SHE'S COMING OUT HERE?!
OH NO! I SHOULD HIDE!
TING
TING
HUM... ♪
HUM... ♫
B-BMP
B-BMP
SHE HASN'T SEEN ME, RIGHT?!
PEEK
...
HUM...
HUM...
SWIP
SWIP
SHE'S HUMMING TO HERSELF.

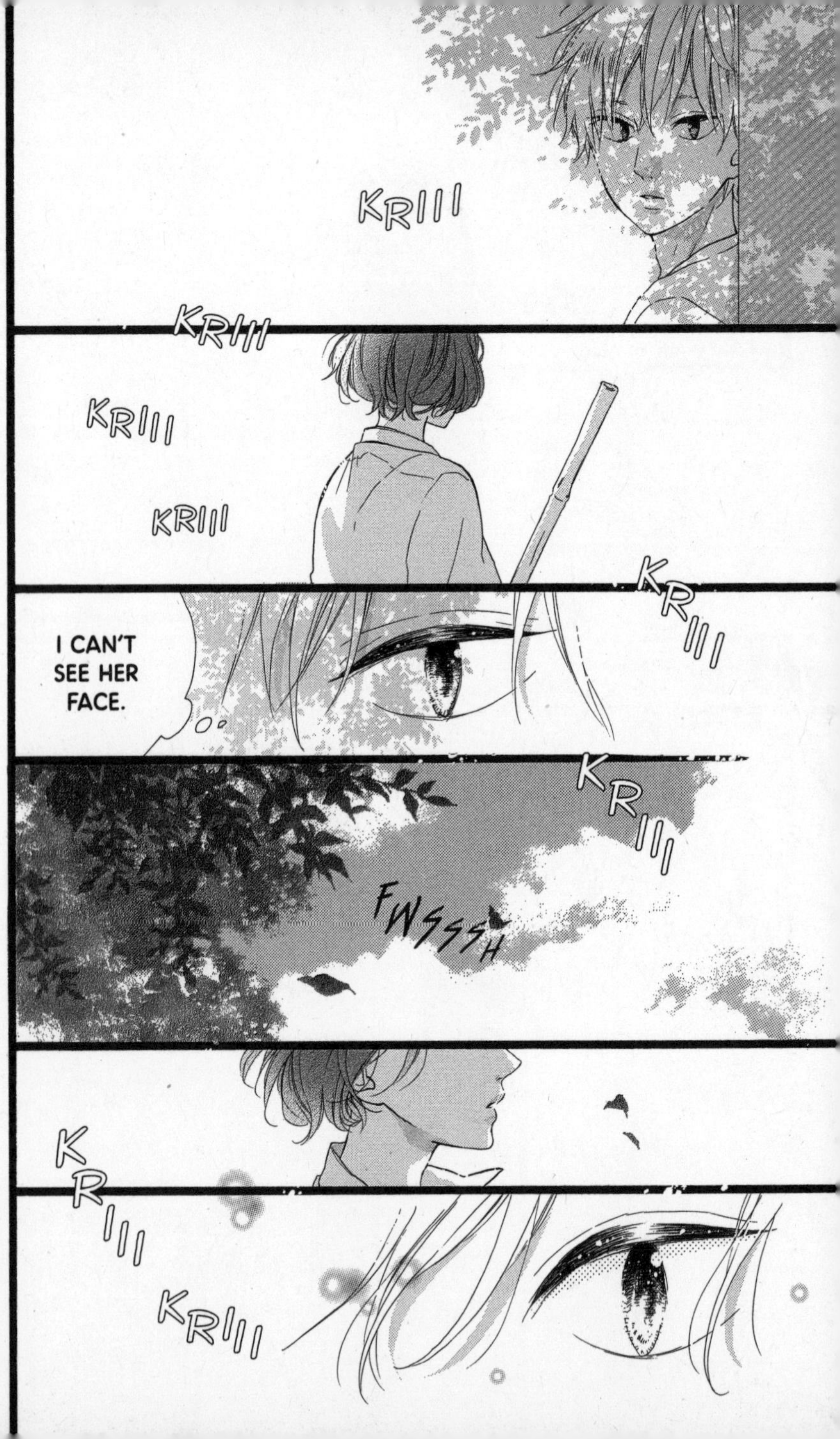
KRIII
KRIII
KRIII
KRIII
KRIII
I CAN'T SEE HER FACE.
KRIII
FWSSSH
KRIII
KRIII

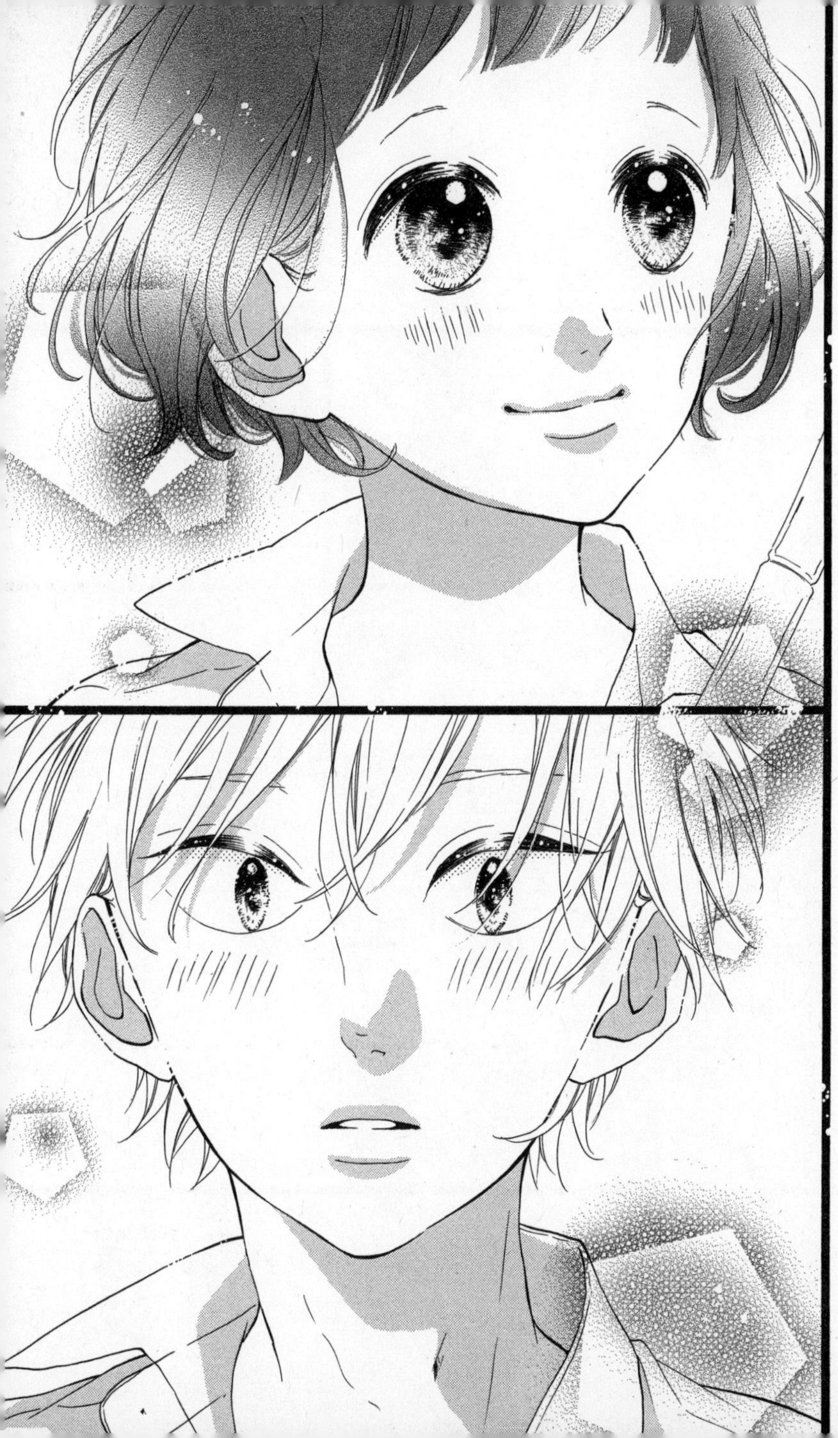

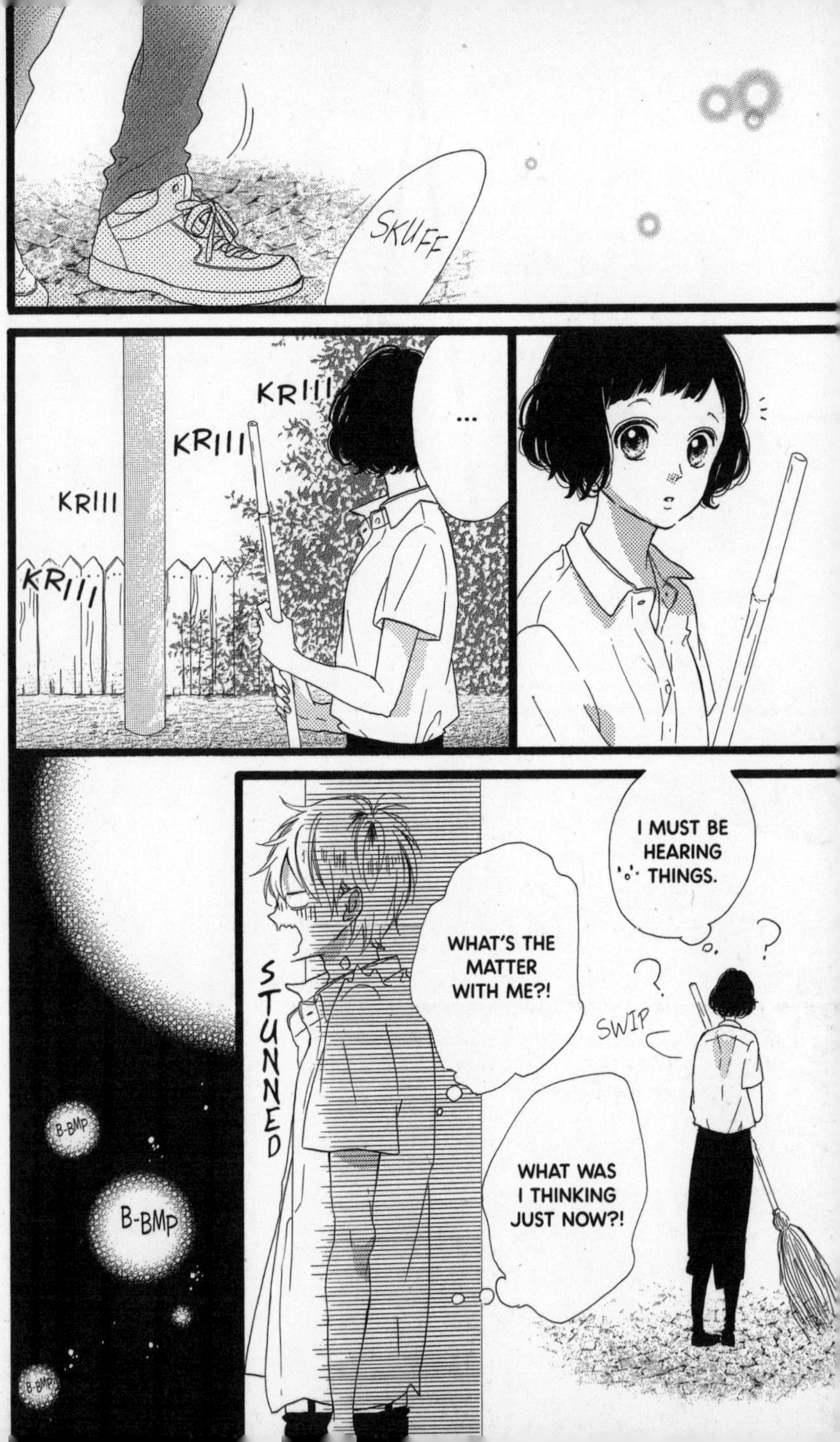
SKUFF
...
KRIII
KRIII
KRIII
KRIII
I MUST BE HEARING THINGS.
SWIP
WHAT'S THE MATTER WITH ME?!
STUNNED
WHAT WAS I THINKING JUST NOW?!
B-BMP
B-BMP
B-BMP

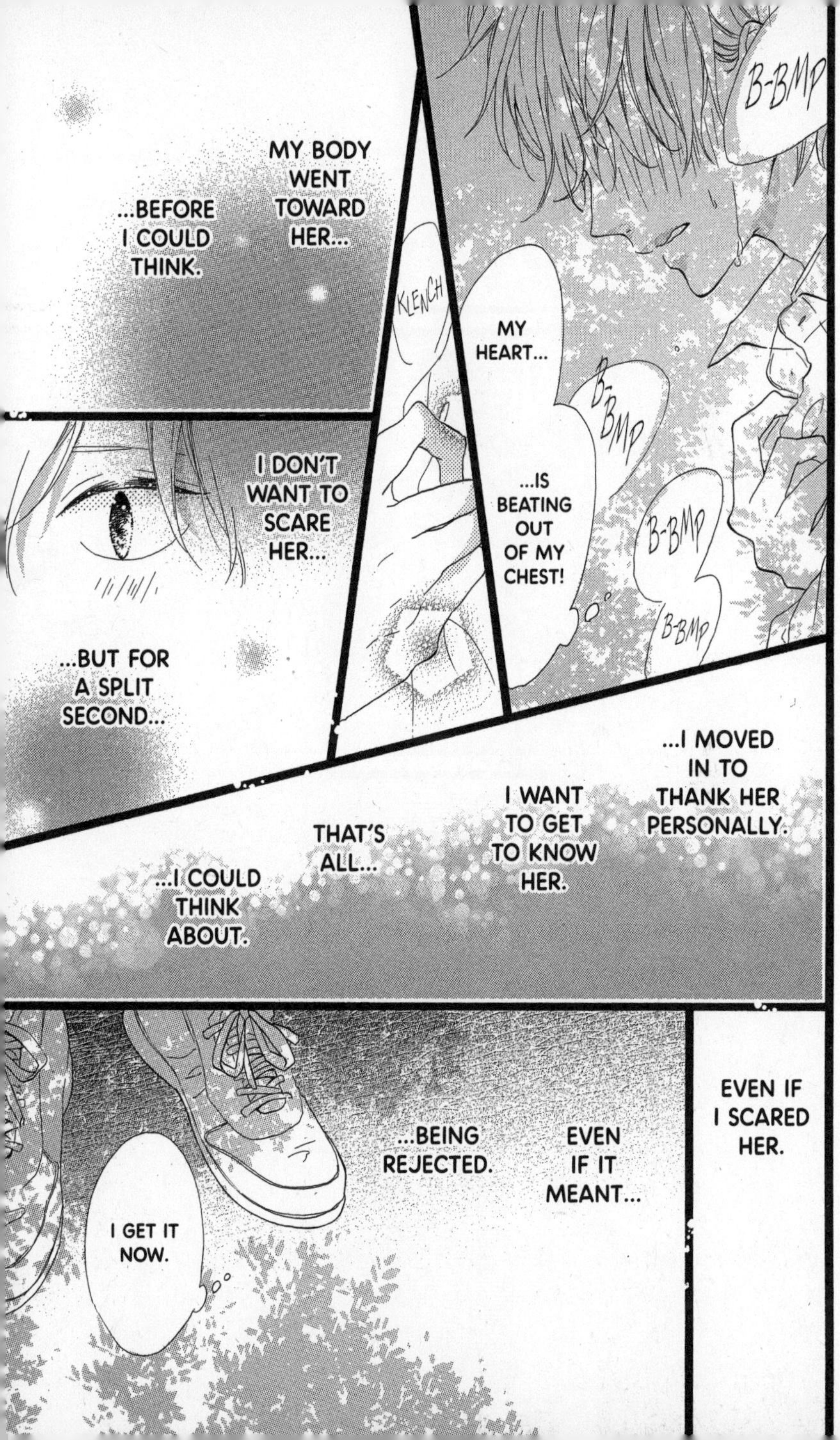
B-BMP
MY HEART...
B-BMP
...IS BEATING OUT OF MY CHEST!
B-BMP
B-BMP
KLENCH
MY BODY WENT TOWARD HER...
...BEFORE I COULD THINK.
I DON'T WANT TO SCARE HER...
...BUT FOR A SPLIT SECOND...
...I MOVED IN TO THANK HER PERSONALLY.
I WANT TO GET TO KNOW HER.
THAT'S ALL...
...I COULD THINK ABOUT.
EVEN IF I SCARED HER.
EVEN IF IT MEANT...
...BEING REJECTED.
I GET IT NOW.

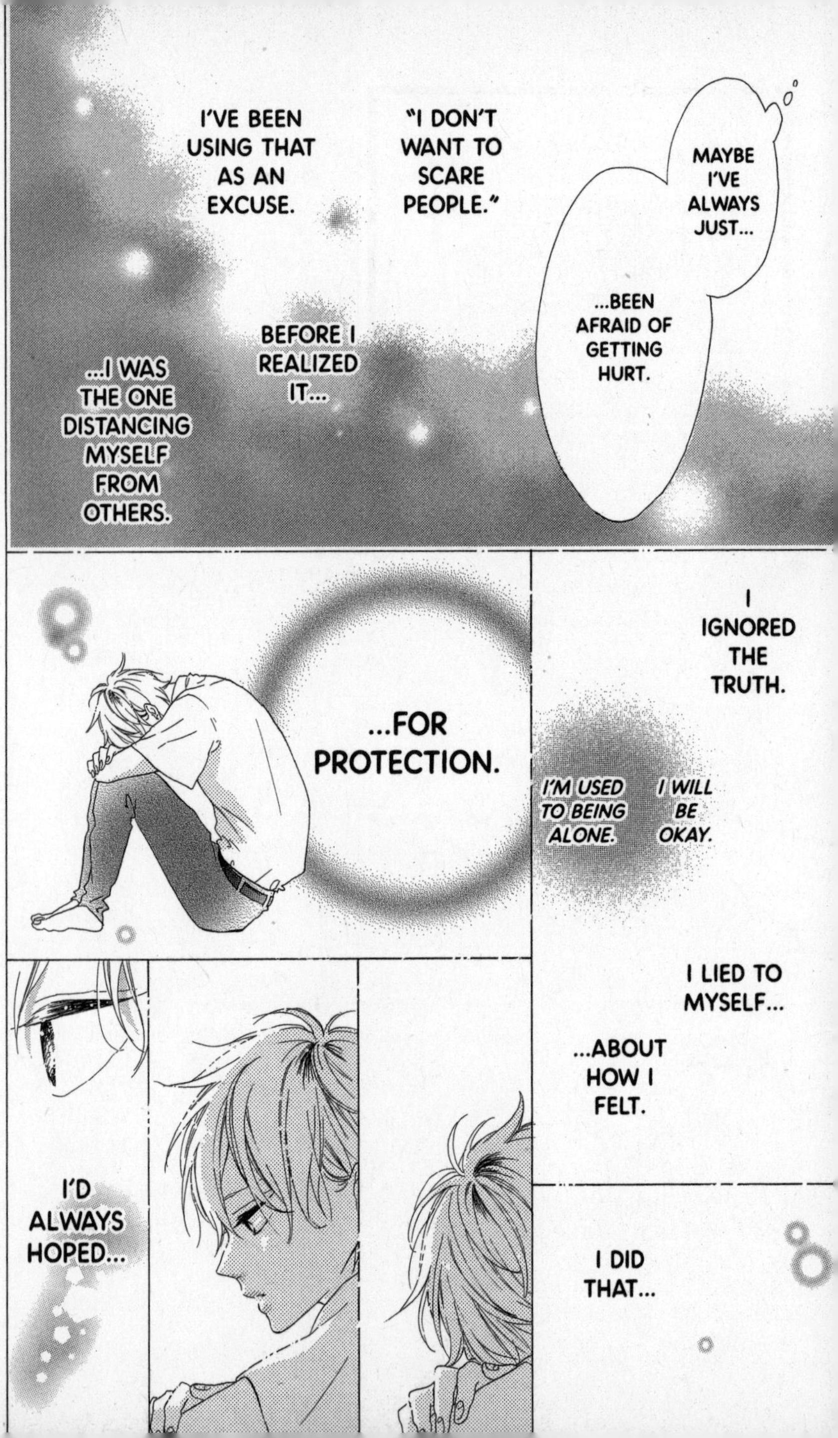
MAYBE I'VE ALWAYS JUST...
...BEEN AFRAID OF GETTING HURT.
"I DON'T WANT TO SCARE PEOPLE."
I'VE BEEN USING THAT AS AN EXCUSE.
BEFORE I REALIZED IT...
...I WAS THE ONE DISTANCING MYSELF FROM OTHERS.
I IGNORED THE TRUTH.
I WILL BE OKAY.
I'M USED TO BEING ALONE.
I LIED TO MYSELF...
...ABOUT HOW I FELT.
I DID THAT...
...FOR PROTECTION.
I'D ALWAYS HOPED...

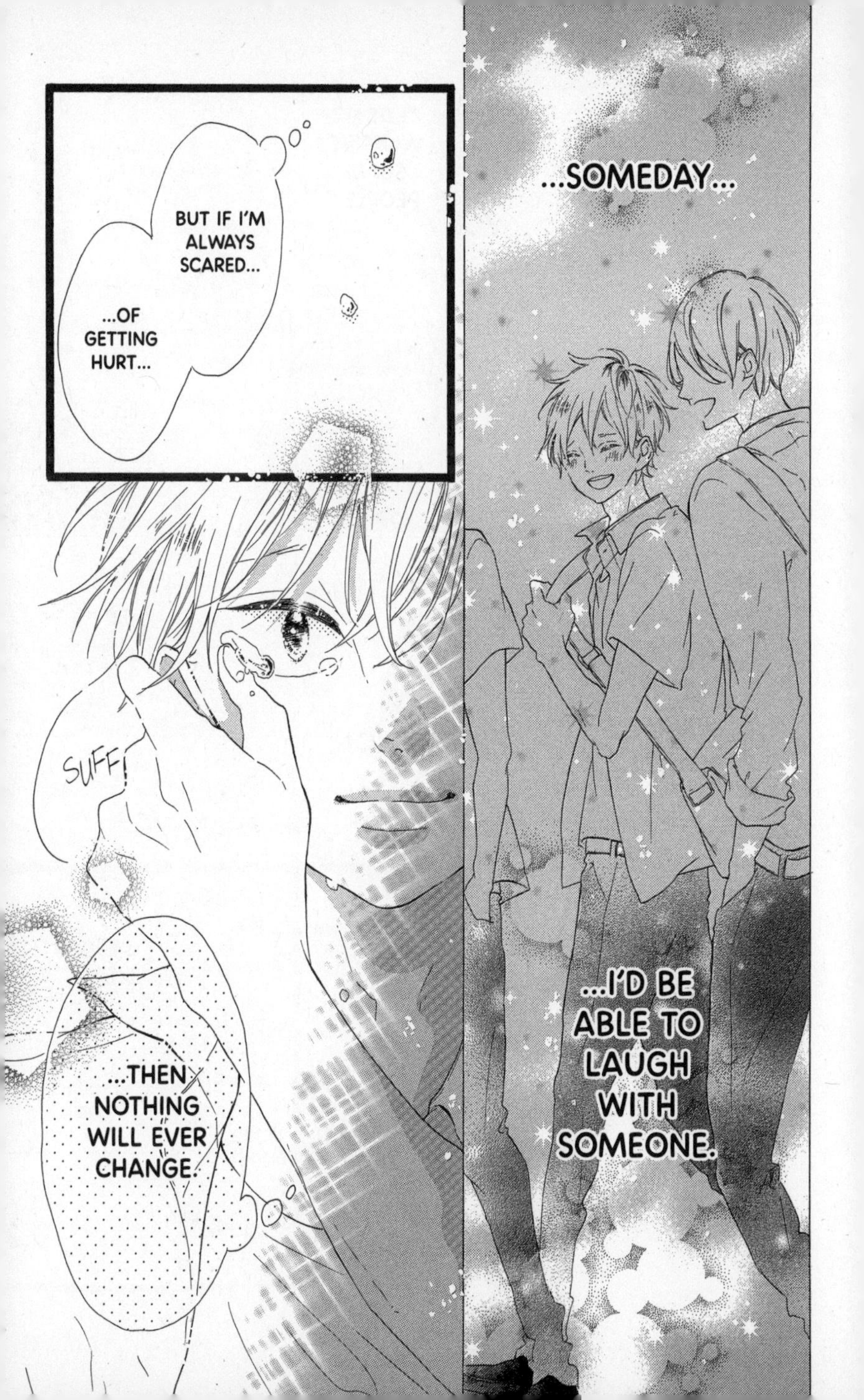
...SOMEDAY...
...I'D BE ABLE TO LAUGH WITH SOMEONE.
BUT IF I'M ALWAYS SCARED...
...OF GETTING HURT...
SUFF
...THEN NOTHING WILL EVER CHANGE.

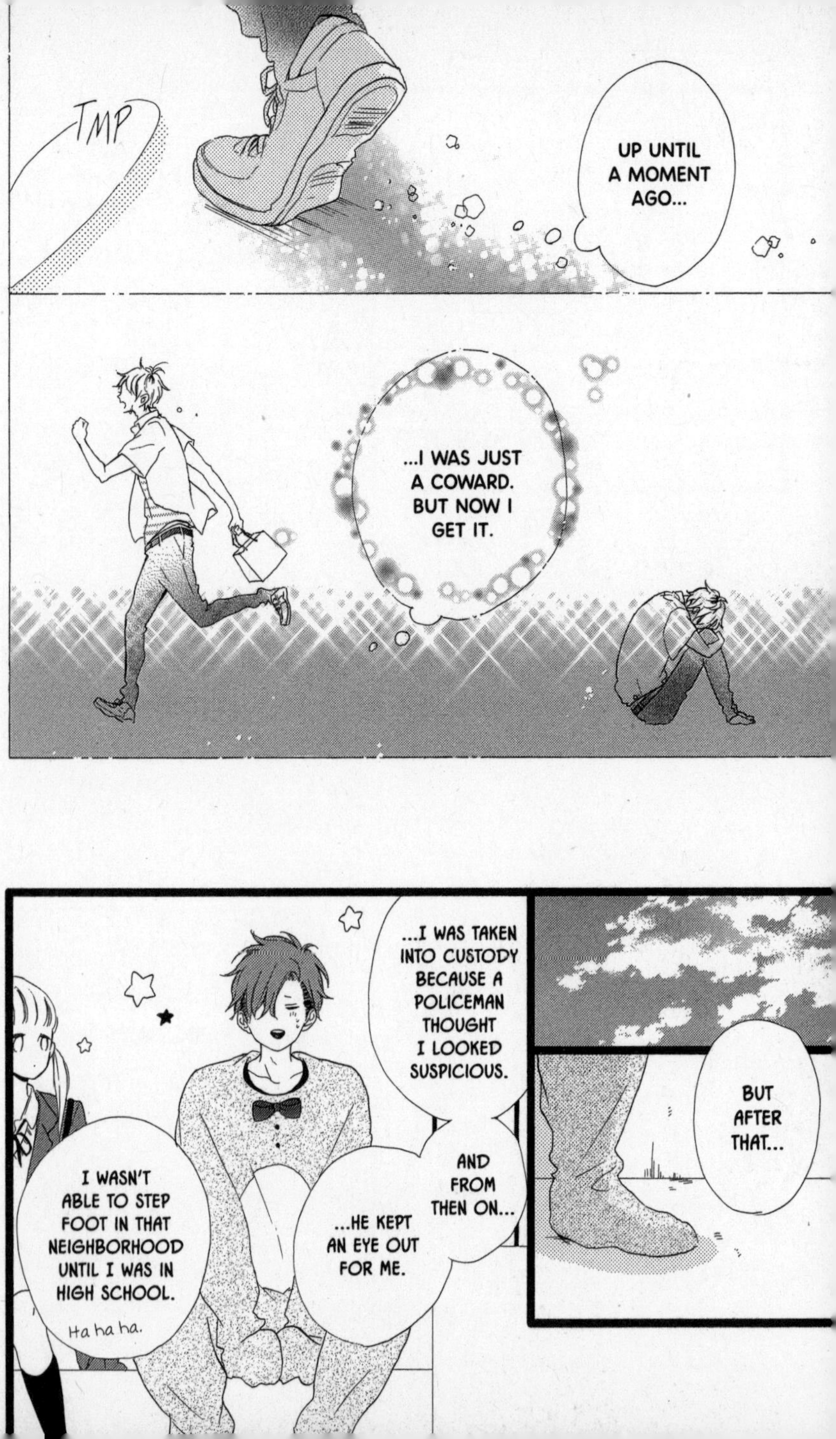
UP UNTIL A MOMENT AGO...
TMP
...I WAS JUST A COWARD. BUT NOW I GET IT.
BUT AFTER THAT...
...I WAS TAKEN INTO CUSTODY BECAUSE A POLICEMAN THOUGHT I LOOKED SUSPICIOUS.
AND FROM THEN ON...
...HE KEPT AN EYE OUT FOR ME.
I WASN'T ABLE TO STEP FOOT IN THAT NEIGHBORHOOD UNTIL I WAS IN HIGH SCHOOL.
Ha ha ha.

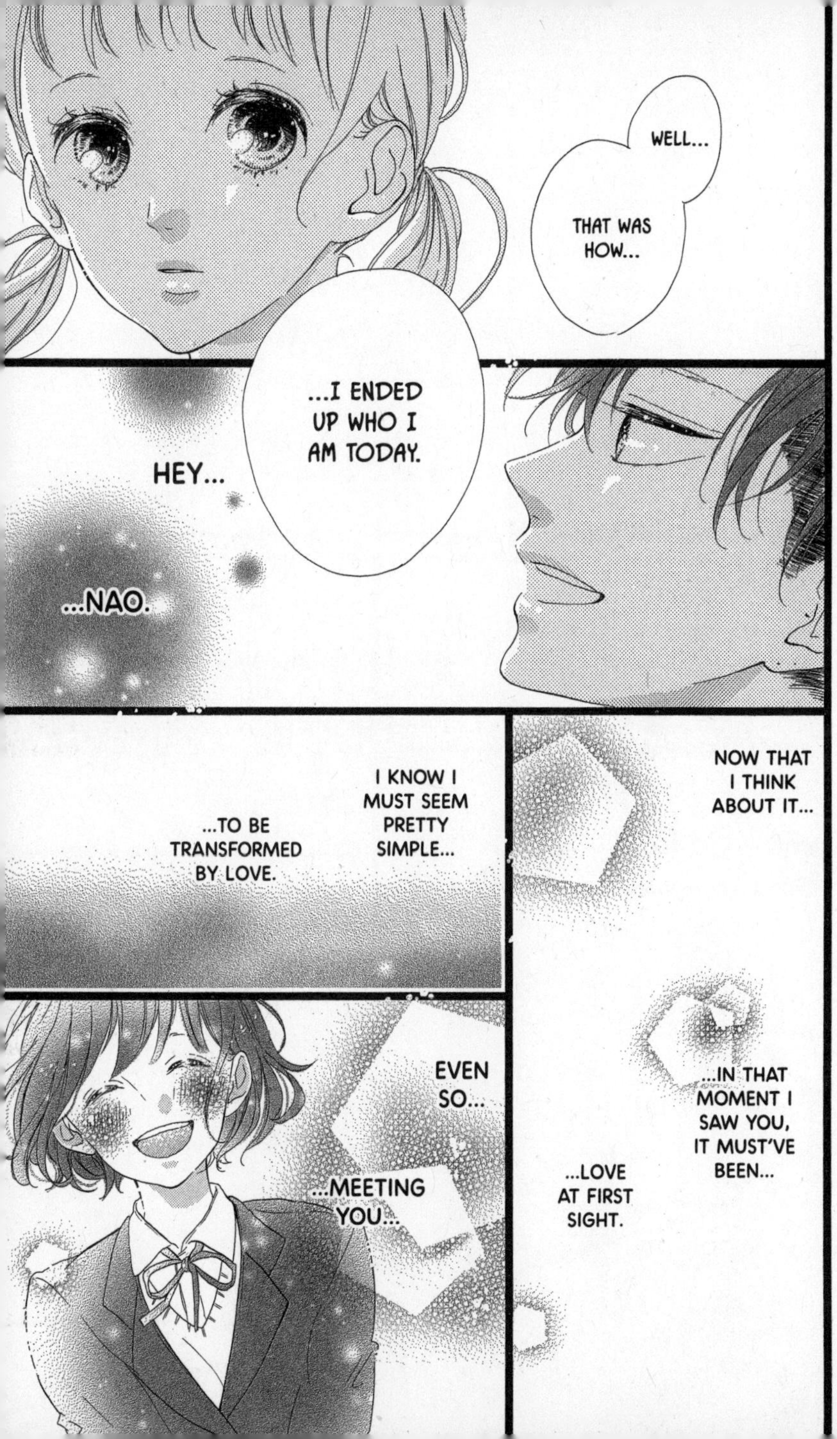
WELL...
THAT WAS HOW...
...I ENDED UP WHO I AM TODAY.
HEY...
...NAO.
NOW THAT I THINK ABOUT IT...
...IN THAT MOMENT I SAW YOU, IT MUST'VE BEEN...
...LOVE AT FIRST SIGHT.
I KNOW I MUST SEEM PRETTY SIMPLE...
...TO BE TRANSFORMED BY LOVE.
EVEN SO...
...MEETING YOU...

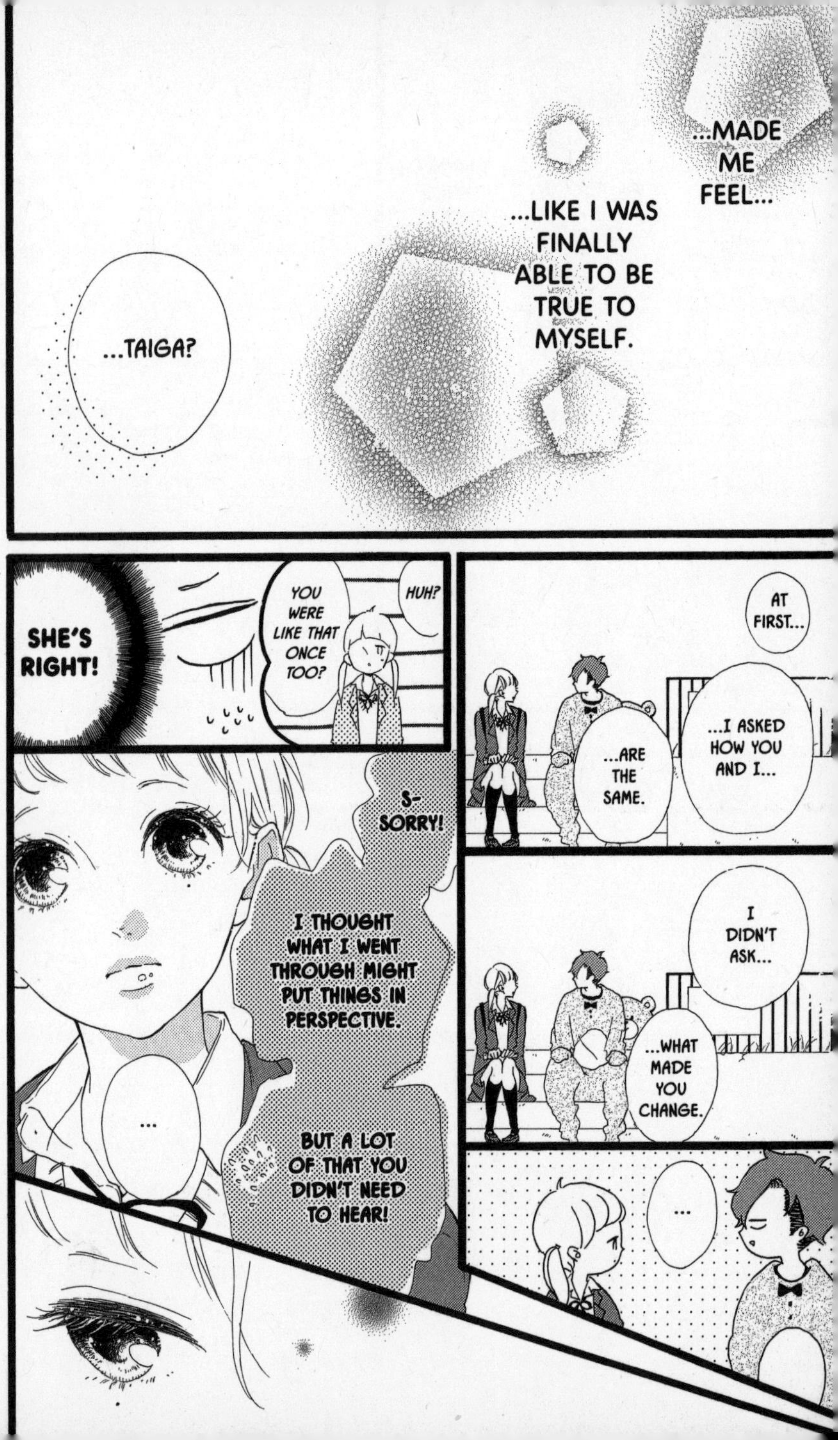
...MADE ME FEEL...
...LIKE I WAS FINALLY ABLE TO BE TRUE TO MYSELF.
...TAIGA?
AT FIRST...
...I ASKED HOW YOU AND I...
...ARE THE SAME.
I DIDN'T ASK...
...WHAT MADE YOU CHANGE.
...
HUH?
YOU WERE LIKE THAT ONCE TOO?
SHE'S RIGHT!
S-SORRY!
I THOUGHT WHAT I WENT THROUGH MIGHT PUT THINGS IN PERSPECTIVE.
BUT A LOT OF THAT YOU DIDN'T NEED TO HEAR!
...

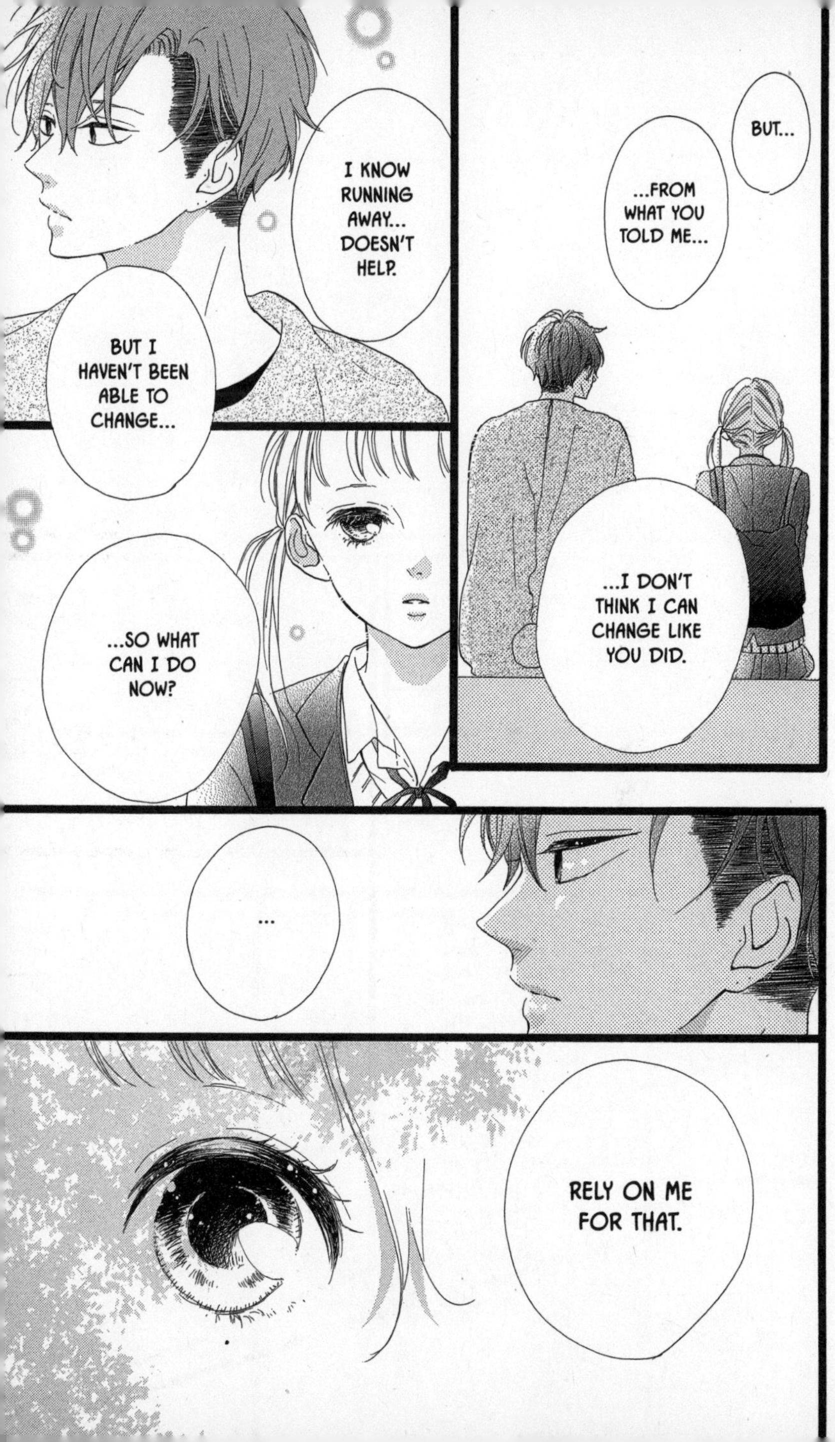
BUT...
...FROM WHAT YOU TOLD ME...
...I DON'T THINK I CAN CHANGE LIKE YOU DID.
I KNOW RUNNING AWAY... DOESN'T HELP.
BUT I HAVEN'T BEEN ABLE TO CHANGE...
...SO WHAT CAN I DO NOW?
...
RELY ON ME FOR THAT.

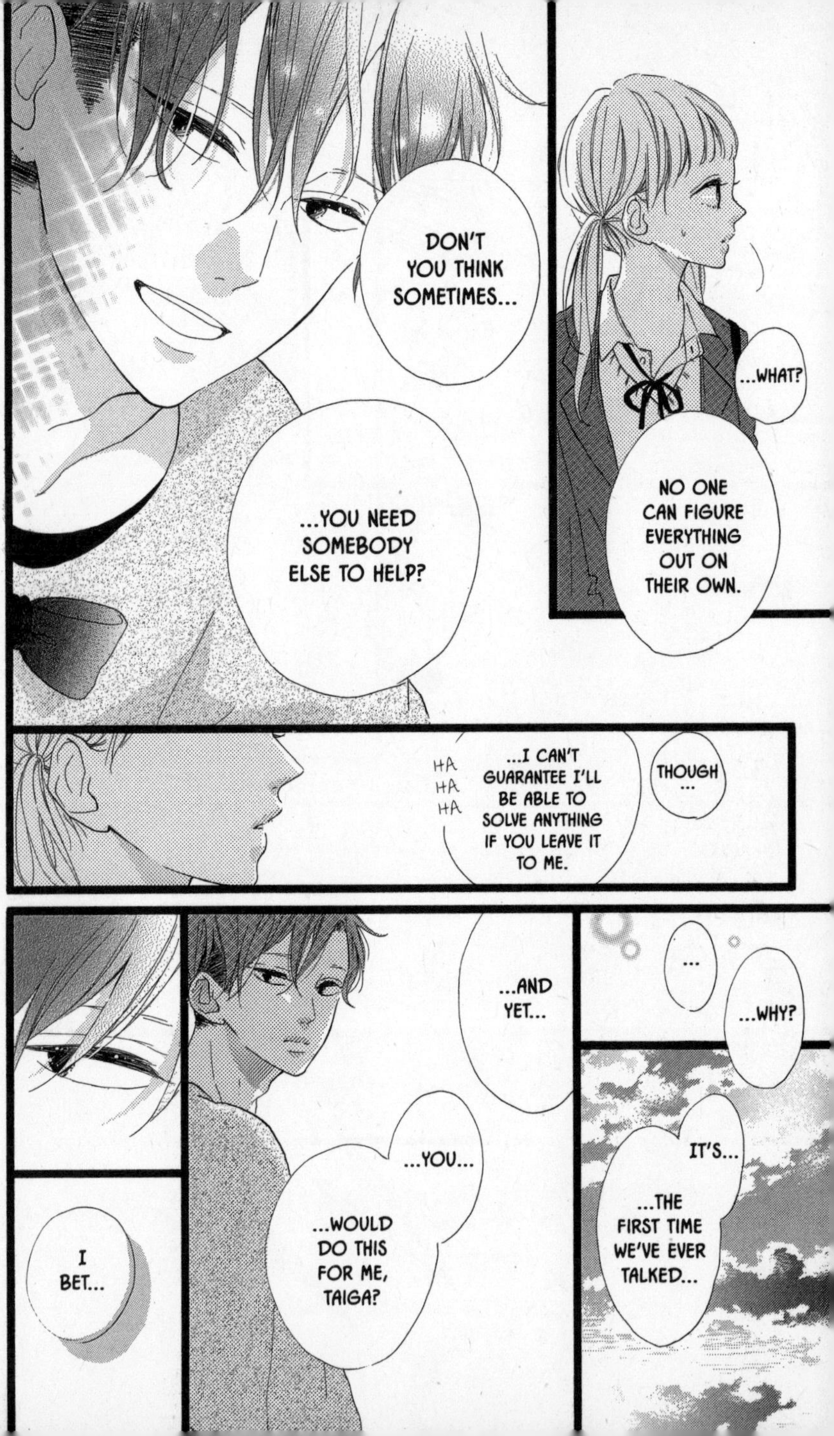
...WHAT?
NO ONE CAN FIGURE EVERYTHING OUT ON THEIR OWN.
DON'T YOU THINK SOMETIMES...
...YOU NEED SOMEBODY ELSE TO HELP?
THOUGH...
HA HA HA
...I CAN'T GUARANTEE I'LL BE ABLE TO SOLVE ANYTHING IF YOU LEAVE IT TO ME.
...
...WHY?
IT'S...
...THE FIRST TIME WE'VE EVER TALKED...
...AND YET...
...YOU...
...WOULD DO THIS FOR ME, TAIGA?
I BET...

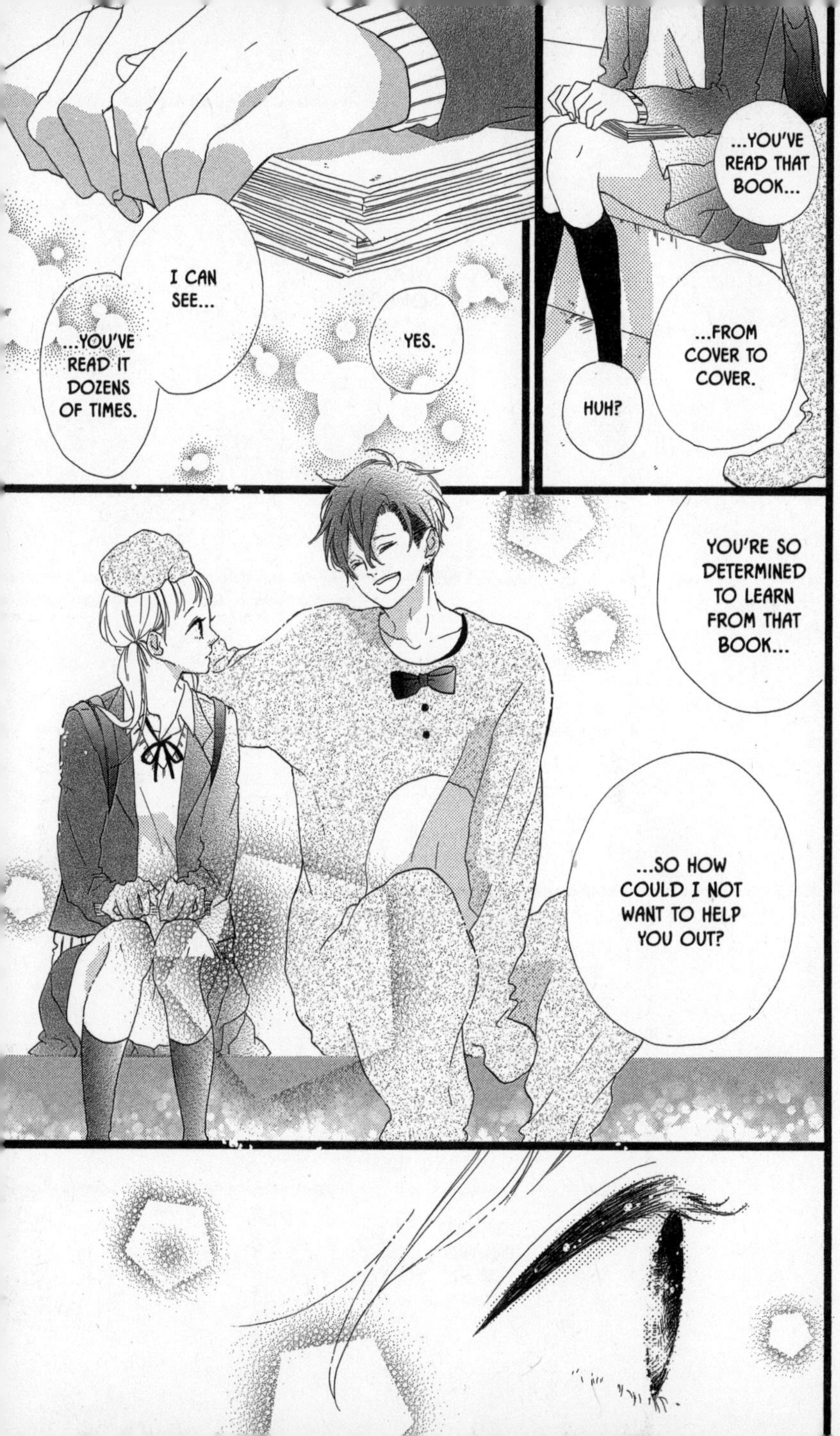
...YOU'VE READ THAT BOOK...
...FROM COVER TO COVER.
HUH?
I CAN SEE...
...YOU'VE READ IT DOZENS OF TIMES.
YES.
YOU'RE SO DETERMINED TO LEARN FROM THAT BOOK...
...SO HOW COULD I NOT WANT TO HELP YOU OUT?

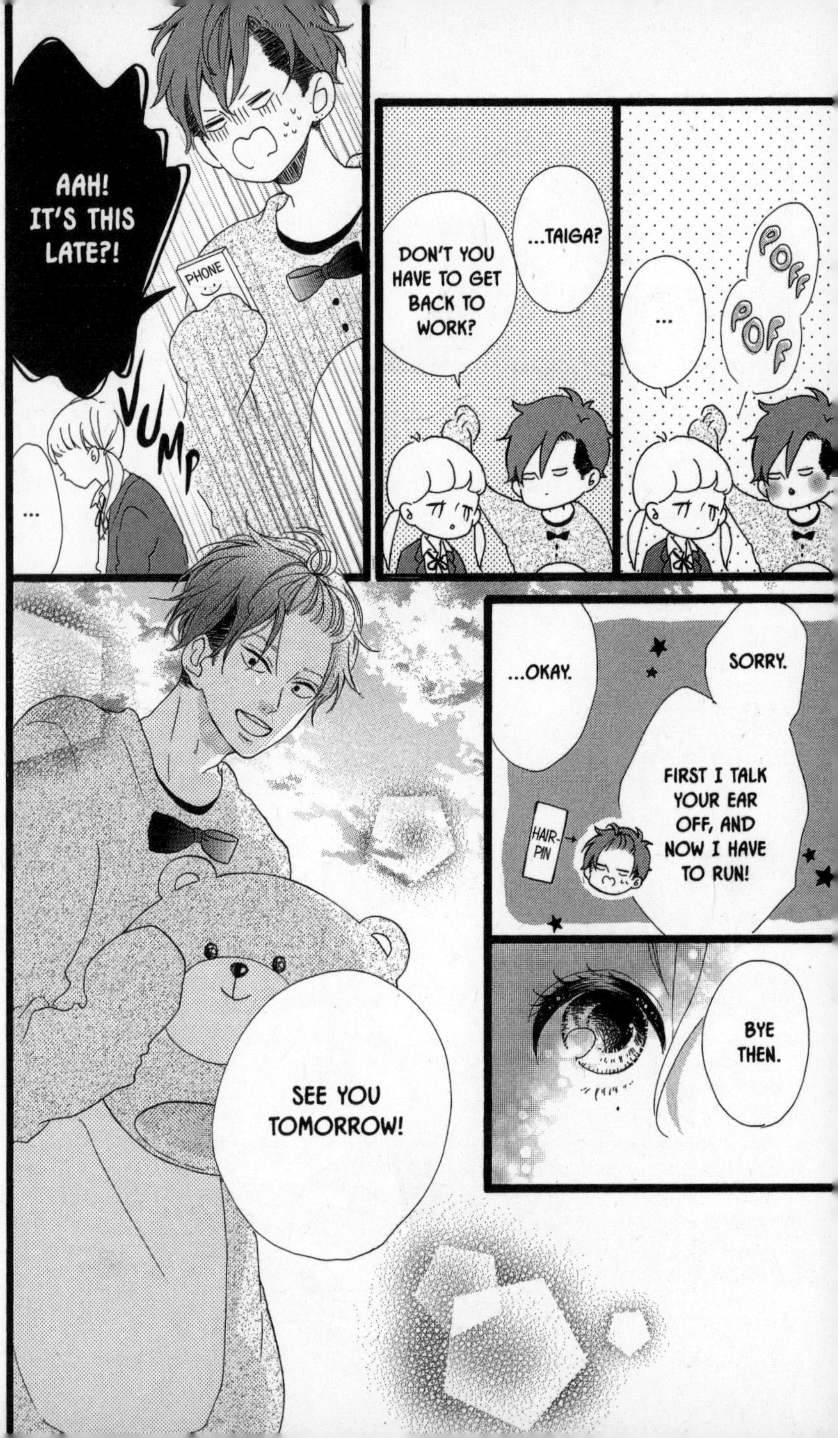
...
POFF POFF
...TAIGA?
DON'T YOU HAVE TO GET BACK TO WORK?
AAH! IT'S THIS LATE?!
PHONE
JUMP
...
SORRY.
FIRST I TALK YOUR EAR OFF, AND NOW I HAVE TO RUN!
HAIR-PIN
...OKAY.
BYE THEN.
SEE YOU TOMORROW!

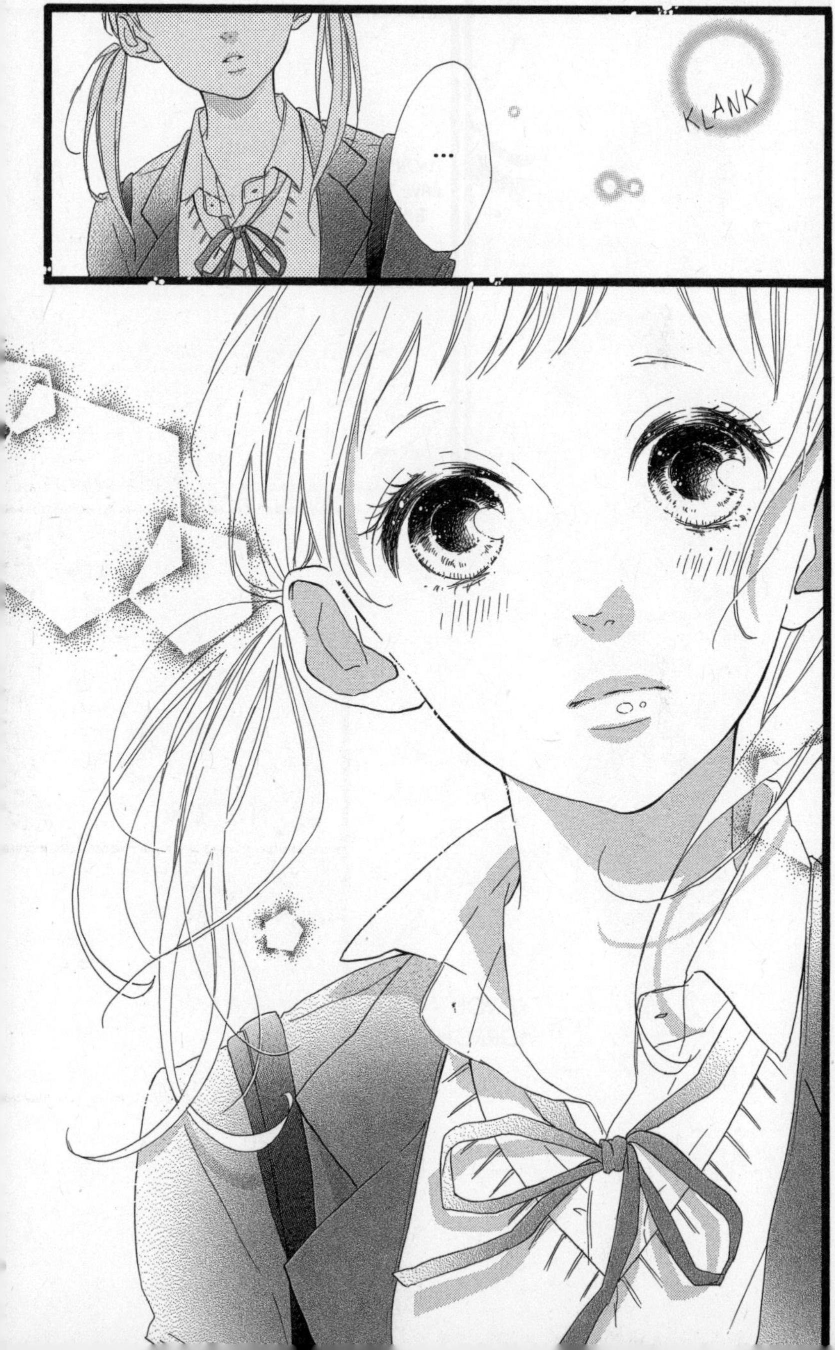
KLANK
...

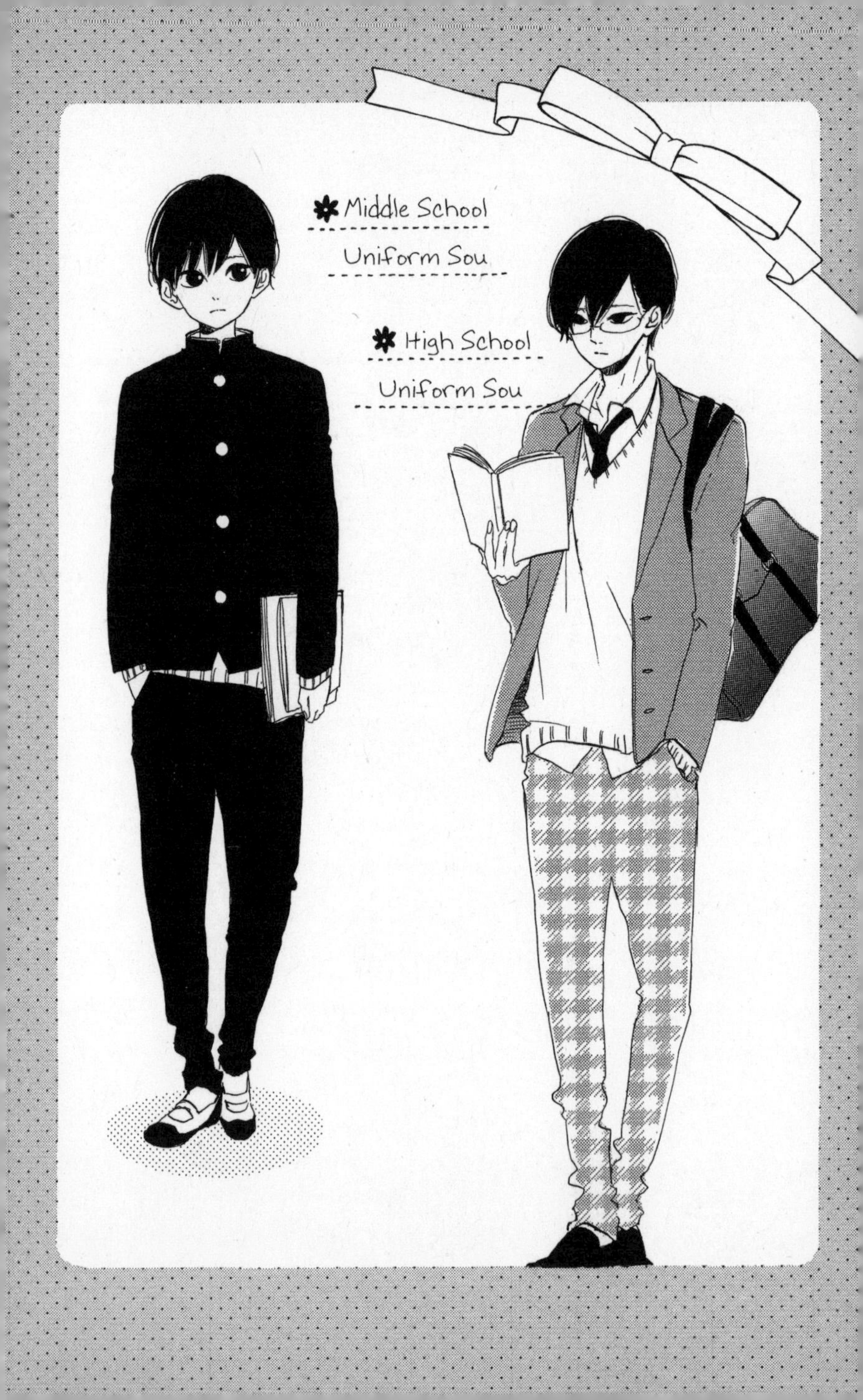
Middle School Uniform Sou
High School Uniform Sou

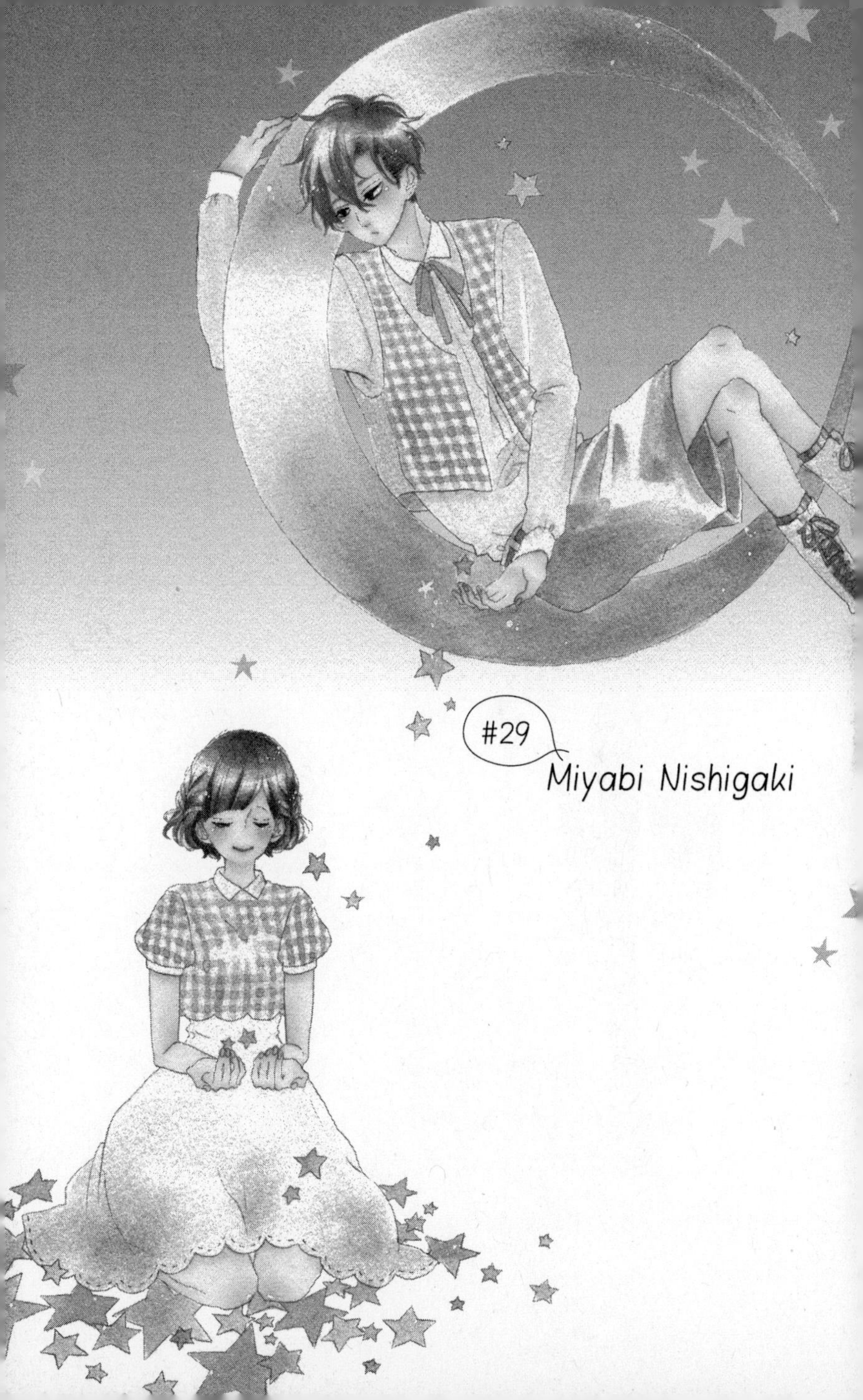
#29
Miyabi Nishigaki

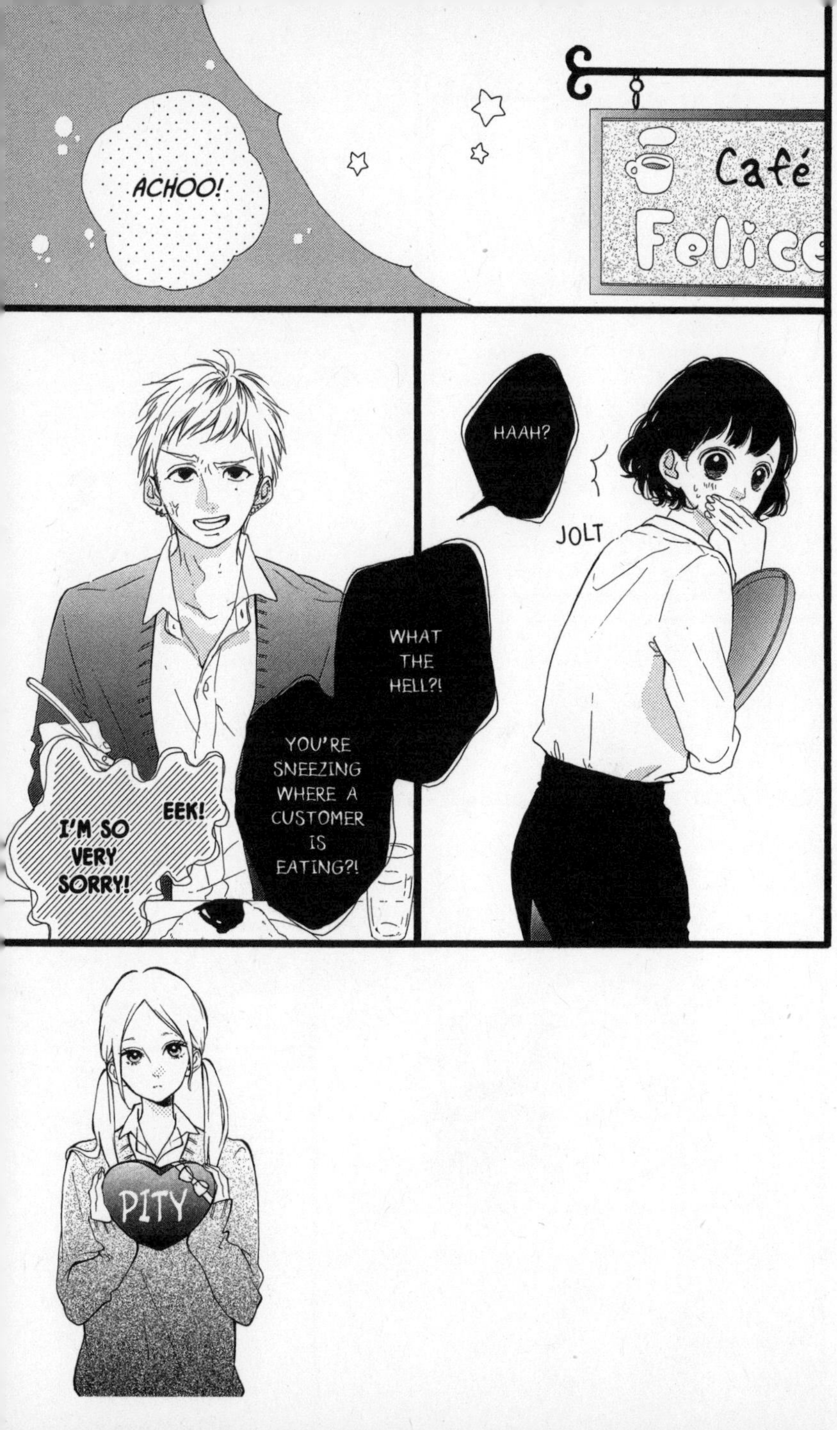
Café Felice
ACHOO!
HAAH?
JOLT
WHAT THE HELL?!
YOU'RE SNEEZING WHERE A CUSTOMER IS EATING?!
EEK!
I'M SO VERY SORRY!
PITY

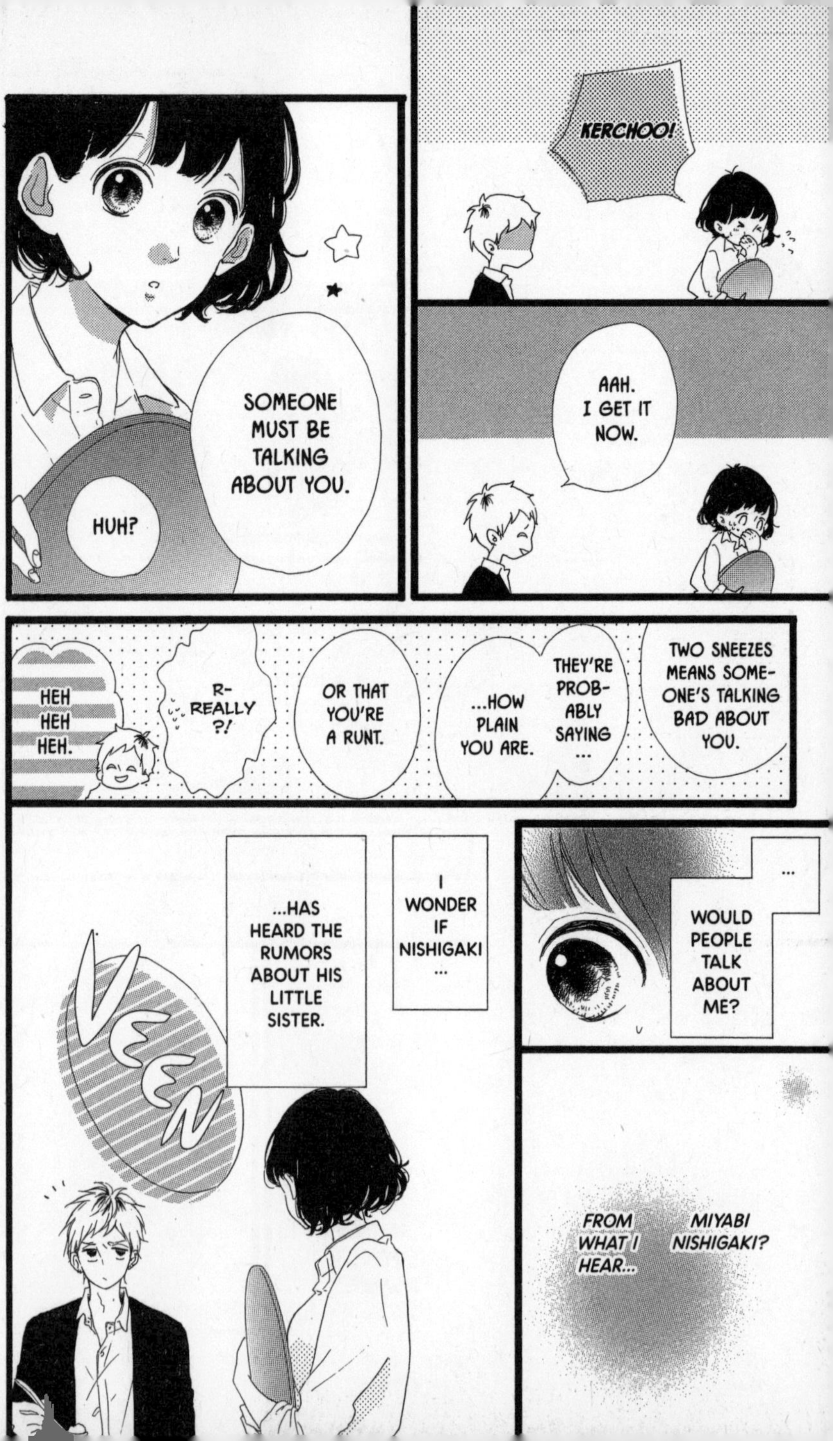
KERCHOO!
AAH. I GET IT NOW.
SOMEONE MUST BE TALKING ABOUT YOU.
HUH?
TWO SNEEZES MEANS SOME-ONE'S TALKING BAD ABOUT YOU.
THEY'RE PROB-ABLY SAYING ...
...HOW PLAIN YOU ARE.
OR THAT YOU'RE A RUNT.
R-REALLY?!
HEH HEH HEH.
...
WOULD PEOPLE TALK ABOUT ME?
MIYABI NISHIGAKI?
FROM WHAT I HEAR...
I WONDER IF NISHIGAKI ...
...HAS HEARD THE RUMORS ABOUT HIS LITTLE SISTER.
VEEN

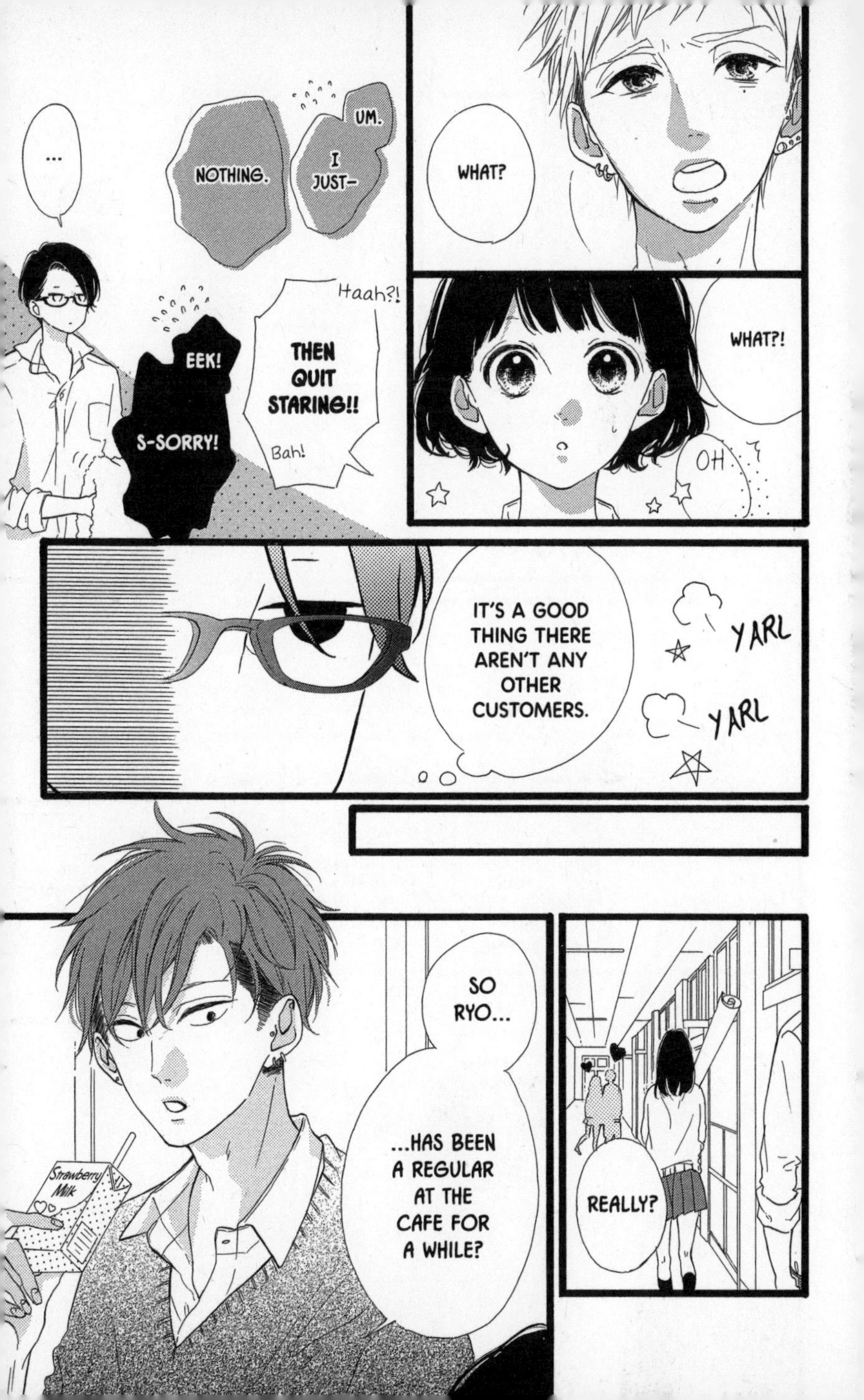
WHAT?
WHAT?!
OH
UM.
I JUST—
NOTHING.
...
Haah?!
THEN QUIT STARING!!
Bah!
EEK!
S-SORRY!
YARL
YARL
IT'S A GOOD THING THERE AREN'T ANY OTHER CUSTOMERS.
REALLY?
SO RYO...
...HAS BEEN A REGULAR AT THE CAFE FOR A WHILE?
Strawberry Milk

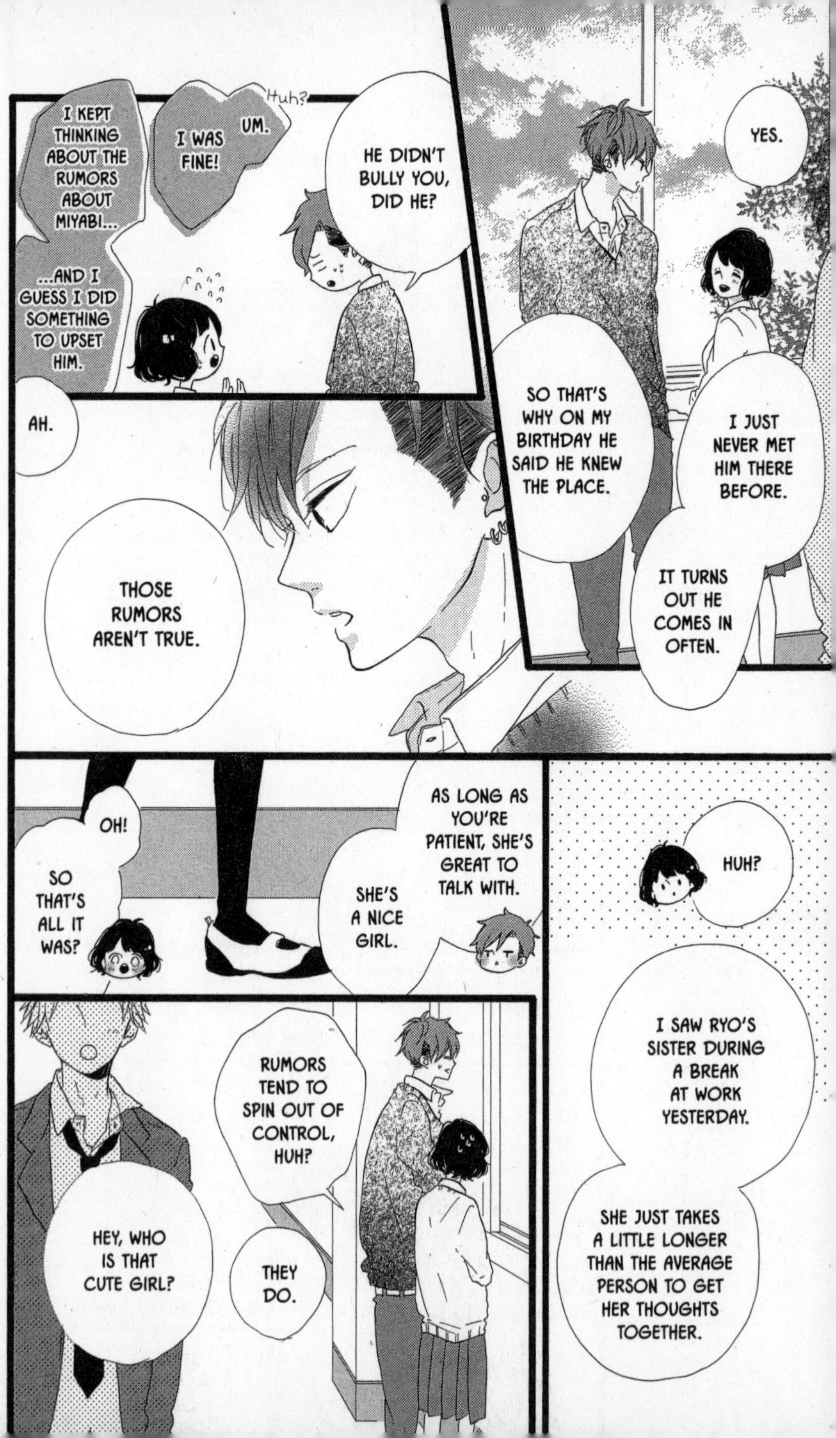
YES.
I JUST NEVER MET HIM THERE BEFORE.
IT TURNS OUT HE COMES IN OFTEN.
SO THAT'S WHY ON MY BIRTHDAY HE SAID HE KNEW THE PLACE.
HE DIDN'T BULLY YOU, DID HE?
Huh?
UM.
I WAS FINE!
I KEPT THINKING ABOUT THE RUMORS ABOUT MIYABI...
...AND I GUESS I DID SOMETHING TO UPSET HIM.
AH.
THOSE RUMORS AREN'T TRUE.
HUH?
I SAW RYO'S SISTER DURING A BREAK AT WORK YESTERDAY.
SHE JUST TAKES A LITTLE LONGER THAN THE AVERAGE PERSON TO GET HER THOUGHTS TOGETHER.
AS LONG AS YOU'RE PATIENT, SHE'S GREAT TO TALK WITH.
SHE'S A NICE GIRL.
OH!
SO THAT'S ALL IT WAS?
RUMORS TEND TO SPIN OUT OF CONTROL, HUH?
THEY DO.
HEY, WHO IS THAT CUTE GIRL?

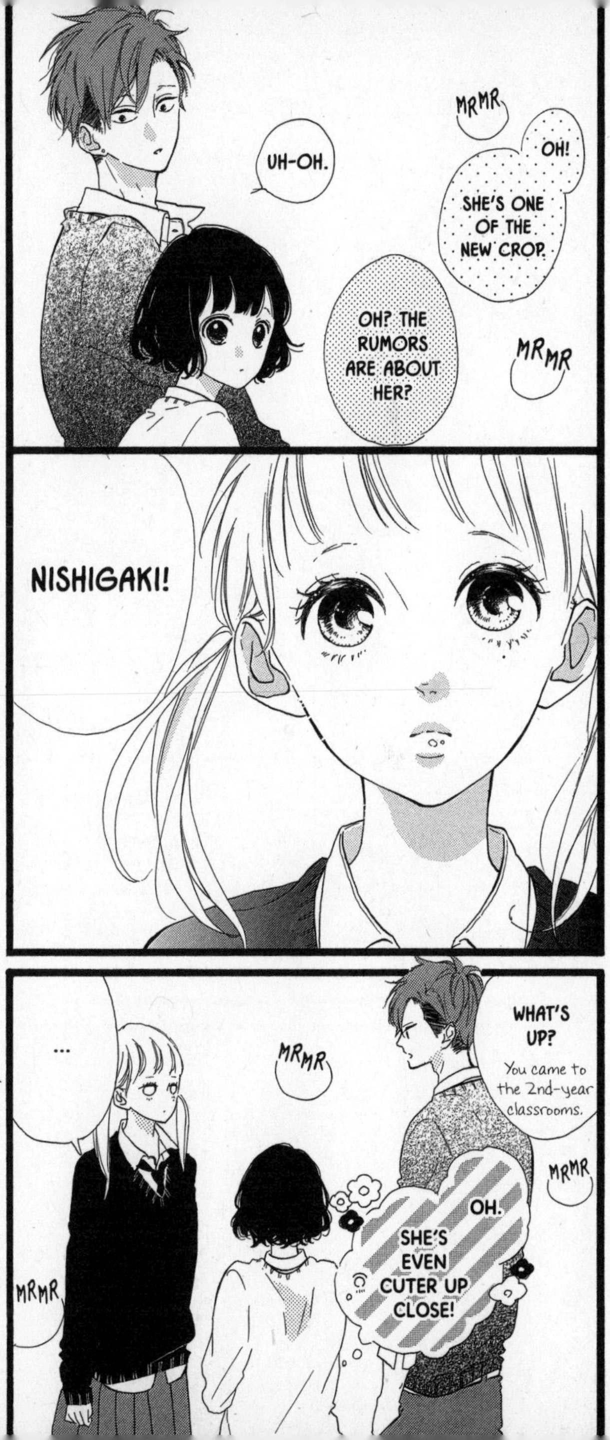
MRMR
OH!
SHE'S ONE OF THE NEW CROP.
UH-OH.
OH? THE RUMORS ARE ABOUT HER?
MRMR
NISHIGAKI!
WHAT'S UP?
You came to the 2nd-year classrooms.
MRMR
MRMR
...
OH.
SHE'S EVEN CUTER UP CLOSE!
MRMR
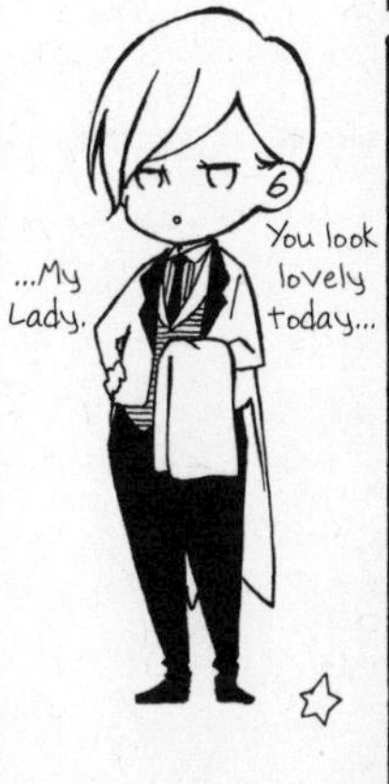
You look lovely today...
...My Lady.

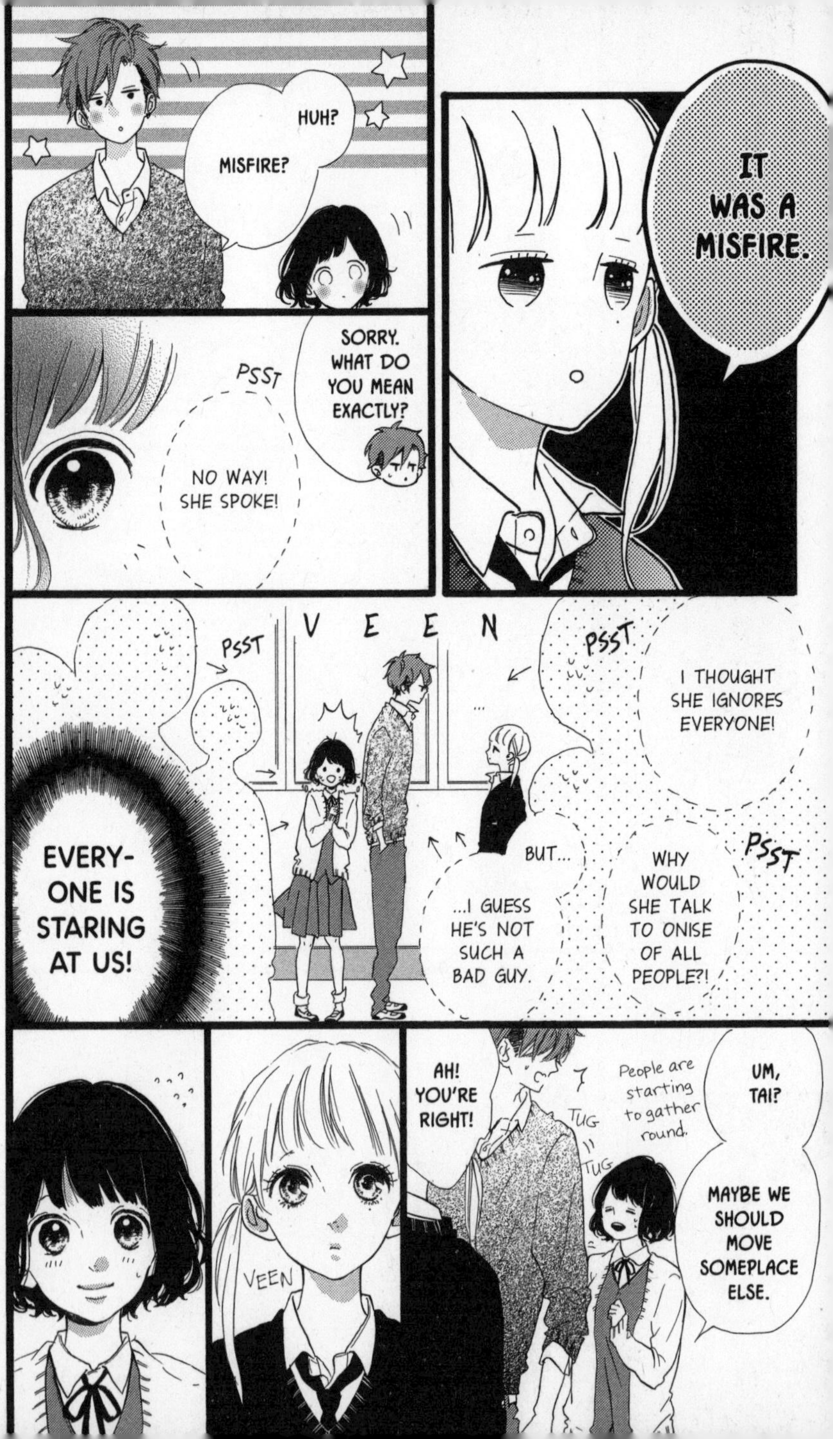
IT WAS A MISFIRE.
HUH?
MISFIRE?
SORRY. WHAT DO YOU MEAN EXACTLY?
PSST
NO WAY! SHE SPOKE!
PSST
I THOUGHT SHE IGNORES EVERYONE!
PSST
WHY WOULD SHE TALK TO ONISE OF ALL PEOPLE?!
BUT...
...I GUESS HE'S NOT SUCH A BAD GUY.
V E E N
...
PSST
EVERY-ONE IS STARING AT US!
UM, TAI?
MAYBE WE SHOULD MOVE SOMEPLACE ELSE.
People are starting to gather round.
TUG
TUG
AH! YOU'RE RIGHT!
VEEN

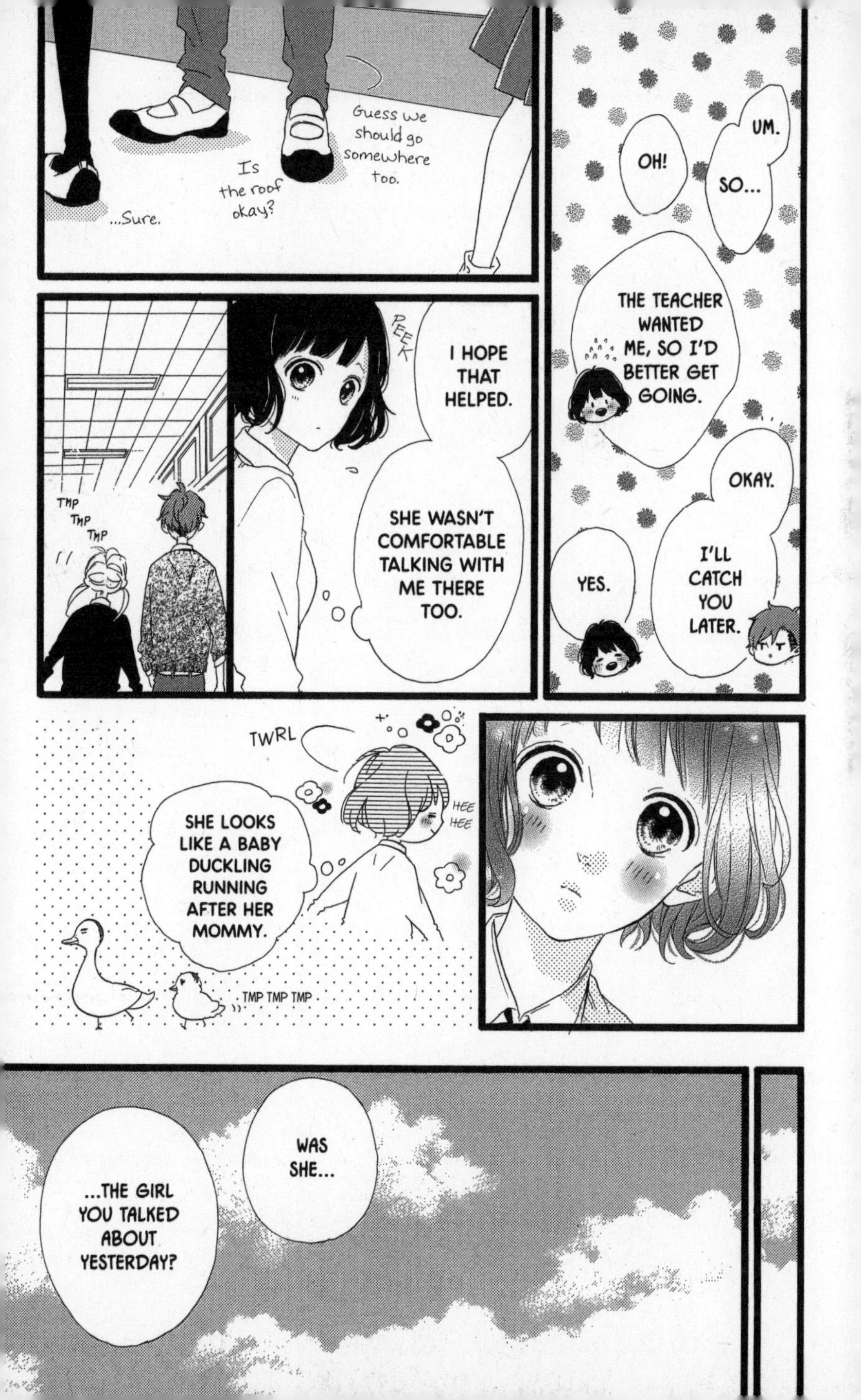
UM.
SO...
OH!
THE TEACHER WANTED ME, SO I'D BETTER GET GOING.
OKAY.
I'LL CATCH YOU LATER.
YES.
Guess we should go somewhere too.
Is the roof okay?
...Sure.
PEEK
I HOPE THAT HELPED.
SHE WASN'T COMFORTABLE TALKING WITH ME THERE TOO.
TMP
TMP
TMP
TWRL
HEE HEE
SHE LOOKS LIKE A BABY DUCKLING RUNNING AFTER HER MOMMY.
TMP TMP TMP
WAS SHE...
...THE GIRL YOU TALKED ABOUT YESTERDAY?

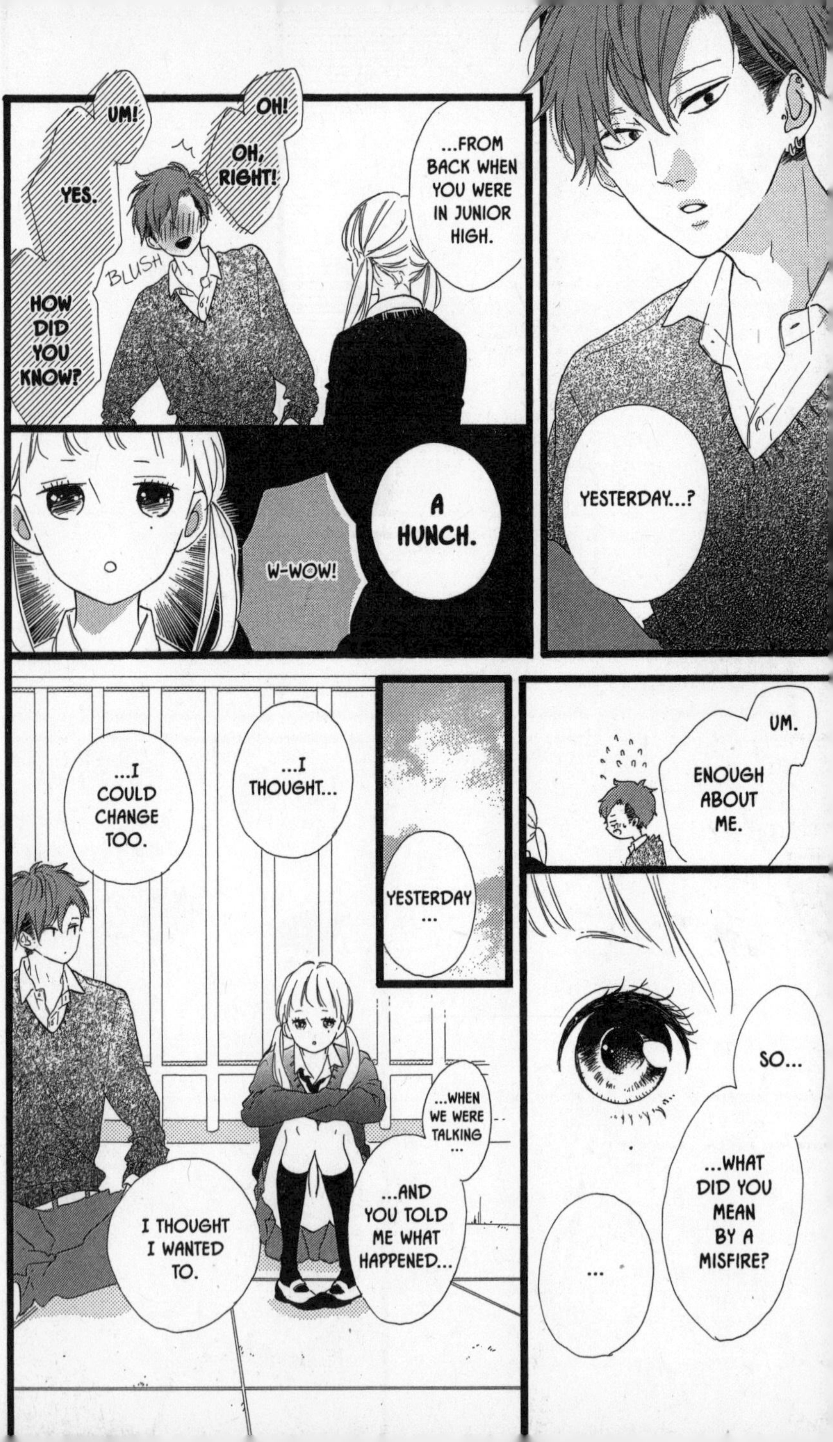
YESTERDAY...?
...FROM BACK WHEN YOU WERE IN JUNIOR HIGH.
OH!
OH, RIGHT!
UM!
YES.
BLUSH
HOW DID YOU KNOW?
A HUNCH.
W-WOW!
UM.
ENOUGH ABOUT ME.
SO...
...WHAT DID YOU MEAN BY A MISFIRE?
...
YESTERDAY...
...I THOUGHT...
...I COULD CHANGE TOO.
...WHEN WE WERE TALKING...
...AND YOU TOLD ME WHAT HAPPENED...
I THOUGHT I WANTED TO.

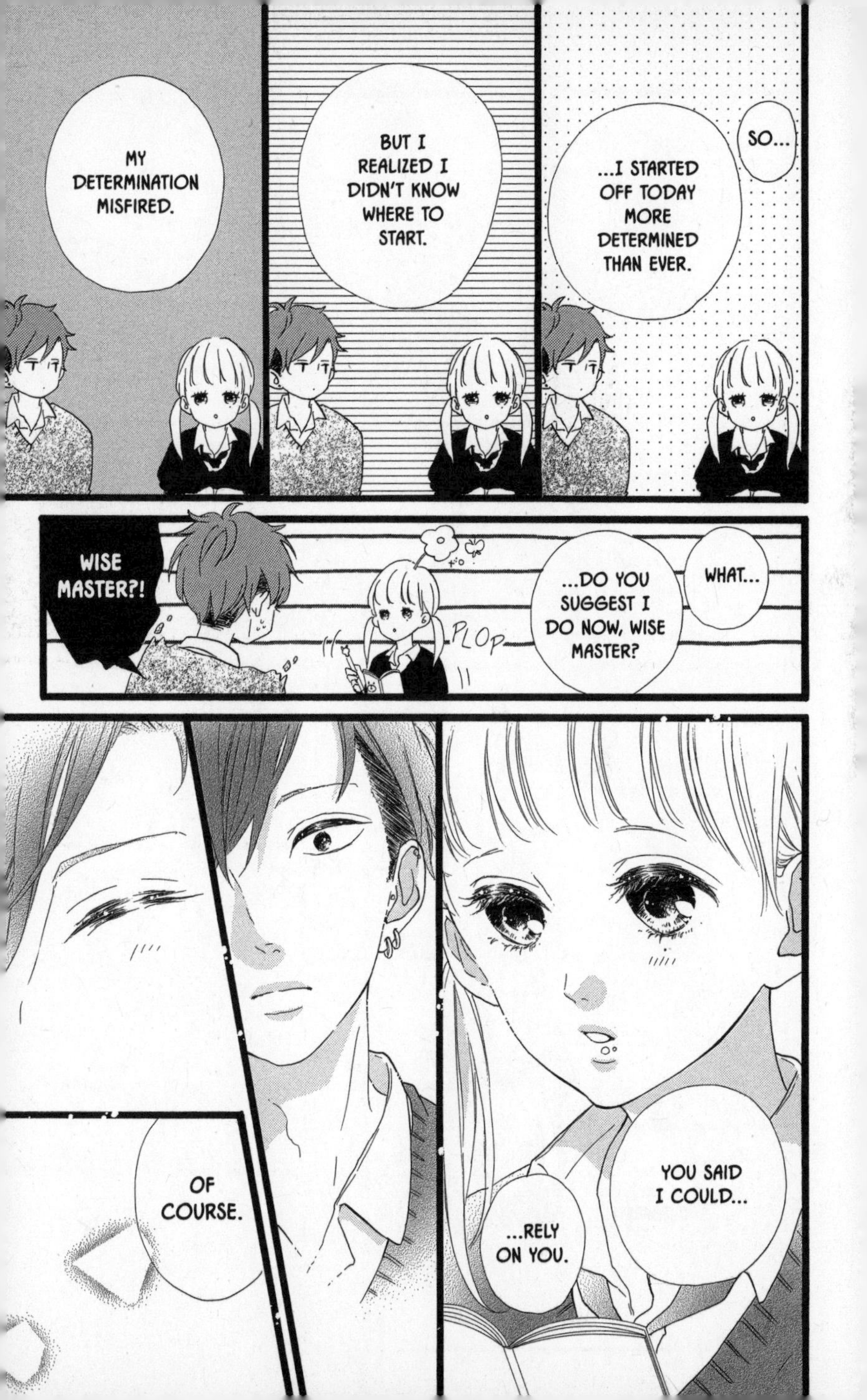
SO...
...I STARTED OFF TODAY MORE DETERMINED THAN EVER.
BUT I REALIZED I DIDN'T KNOW WHERE TO START.
MY DETERMINATION MISFIRED.
WHAT...
...DO YOU SUGGEST I DO NOW, WISE MASTER?
PLOP
WISE MASTER?!
YOU SAID I COULD...
...RELY ON YOU.
OF COURSE.

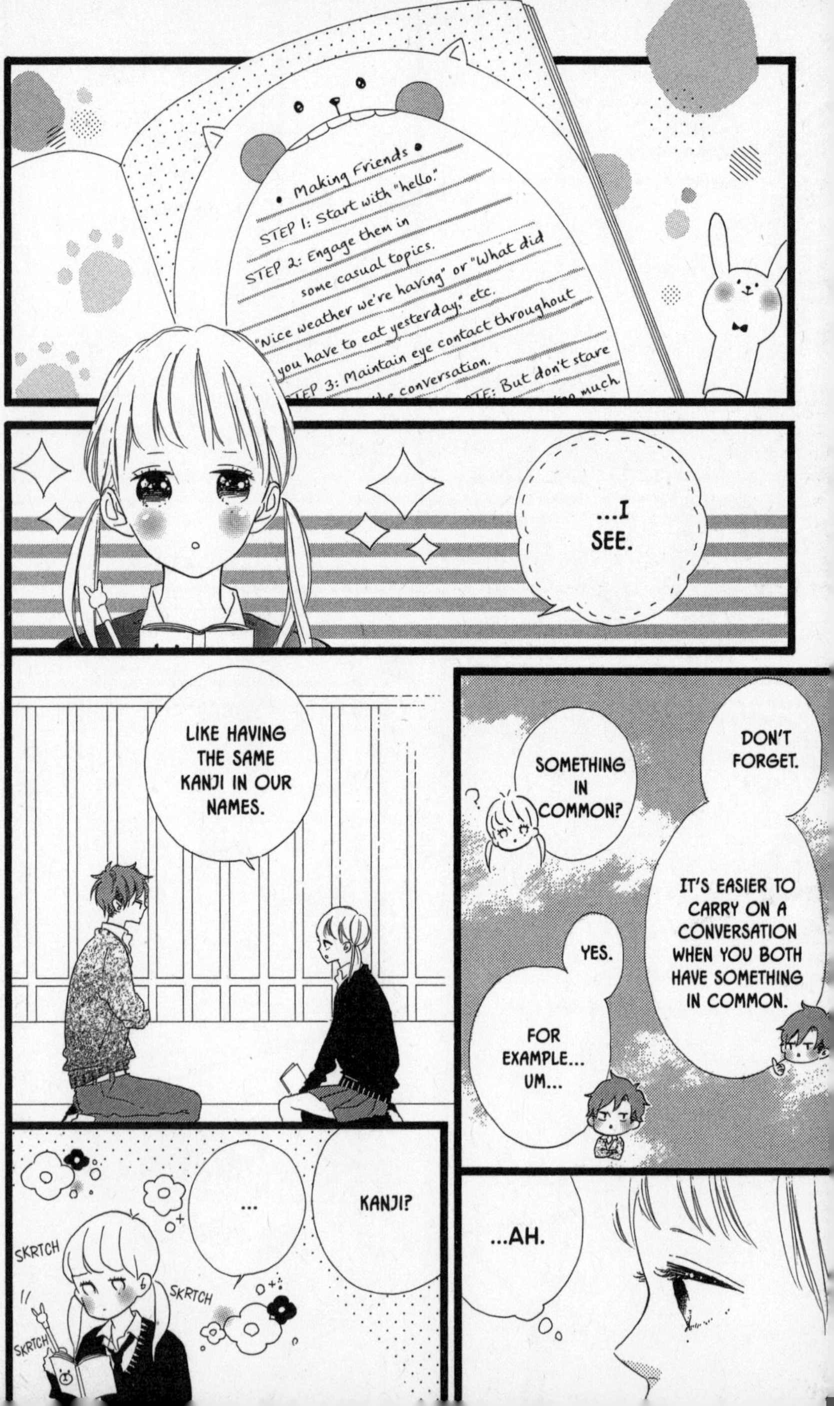

• Making Friends •
STEP 1: Start with "hello."
STEP 2: Engage them in some casual topics.
"Nice weather we're having" or "What did you have to eat yesterday," etc.
STEP 3: Maintain eye contact throughout the conversation.
But don't stare
...I SEE.
DON'T FORGET.
IT'S EASIER TO CARRY ON A CONVERSATION WHEN YOU BOTH HAVE SOMETHING IN COMMON.
SOMETHING IN COMMON?
YES.
FOR EXAMPLE... UM...
LIKE HAVING THE SAME KANJI IN OUR NAMES.
...AH.
KANJI?
...
SKRTCH
SKRTCH
SKRTCH

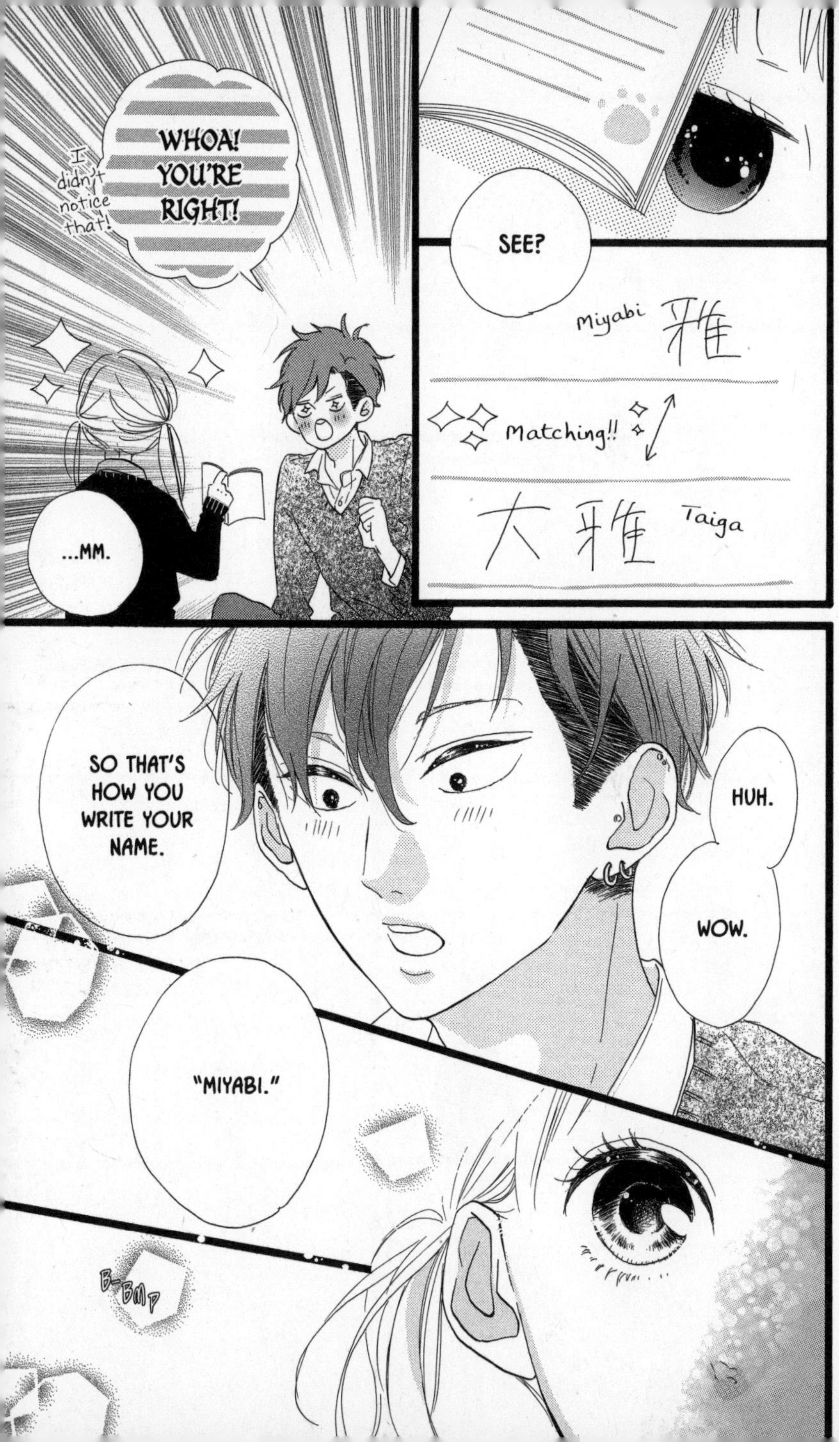
SEE?
Miyabi 雅
Matching!!
大雅 Taiga
WHOA! YOU'RE RIGHT!
I didn't notice that!
...MM.
HUH.
WOW.
SO THAT'S HOW YOU WRITE YOUR NAME.
"MIYABI."
B-BMP

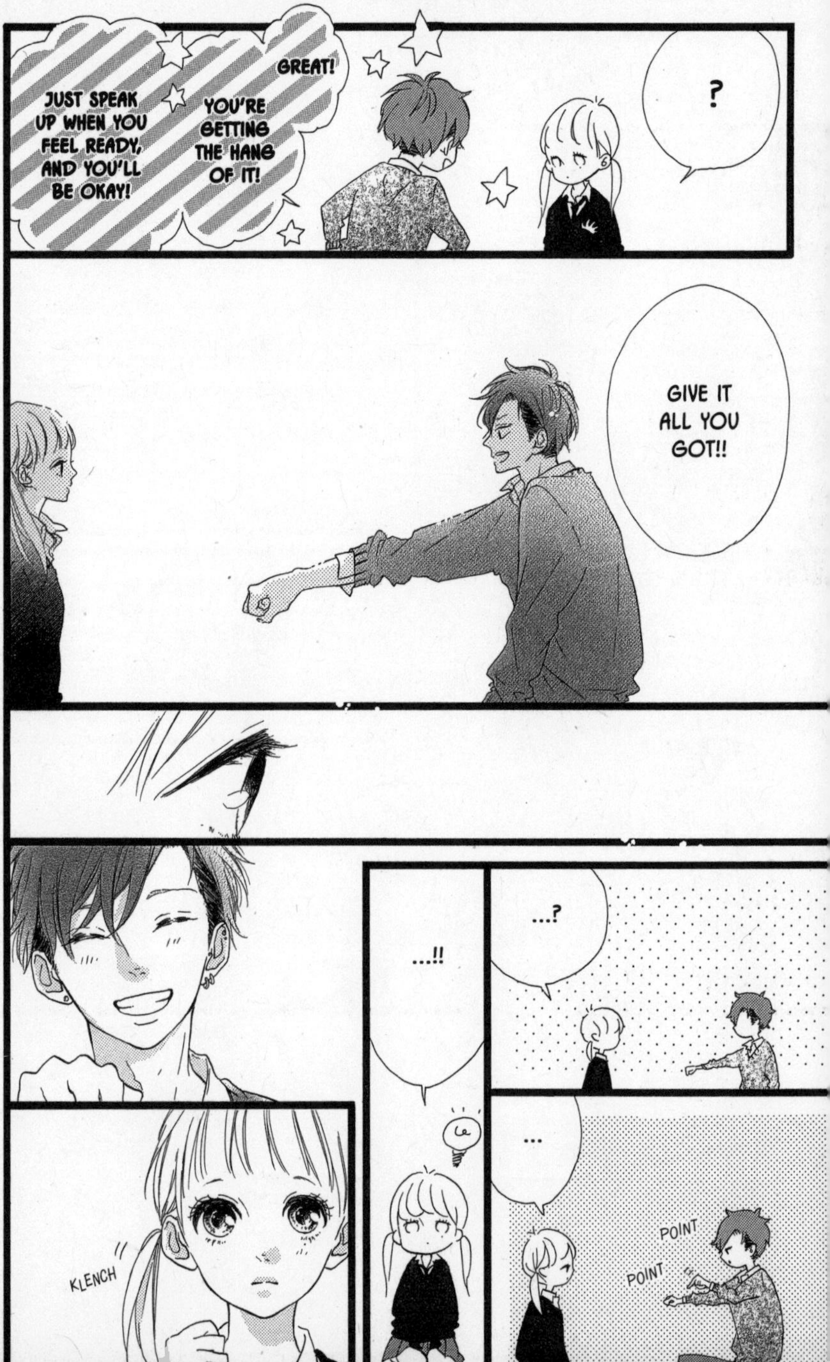
?
GREAT!
YOU'RE GETTING THE HANG OF IT!
JUST SPEAK UP WHEN YOU FEEL READY, AND YOU'LL BE OKAY!
GIVE IT ALL YOU GOT!!
...?
...
POINT
POINT
...!!
KLENCH

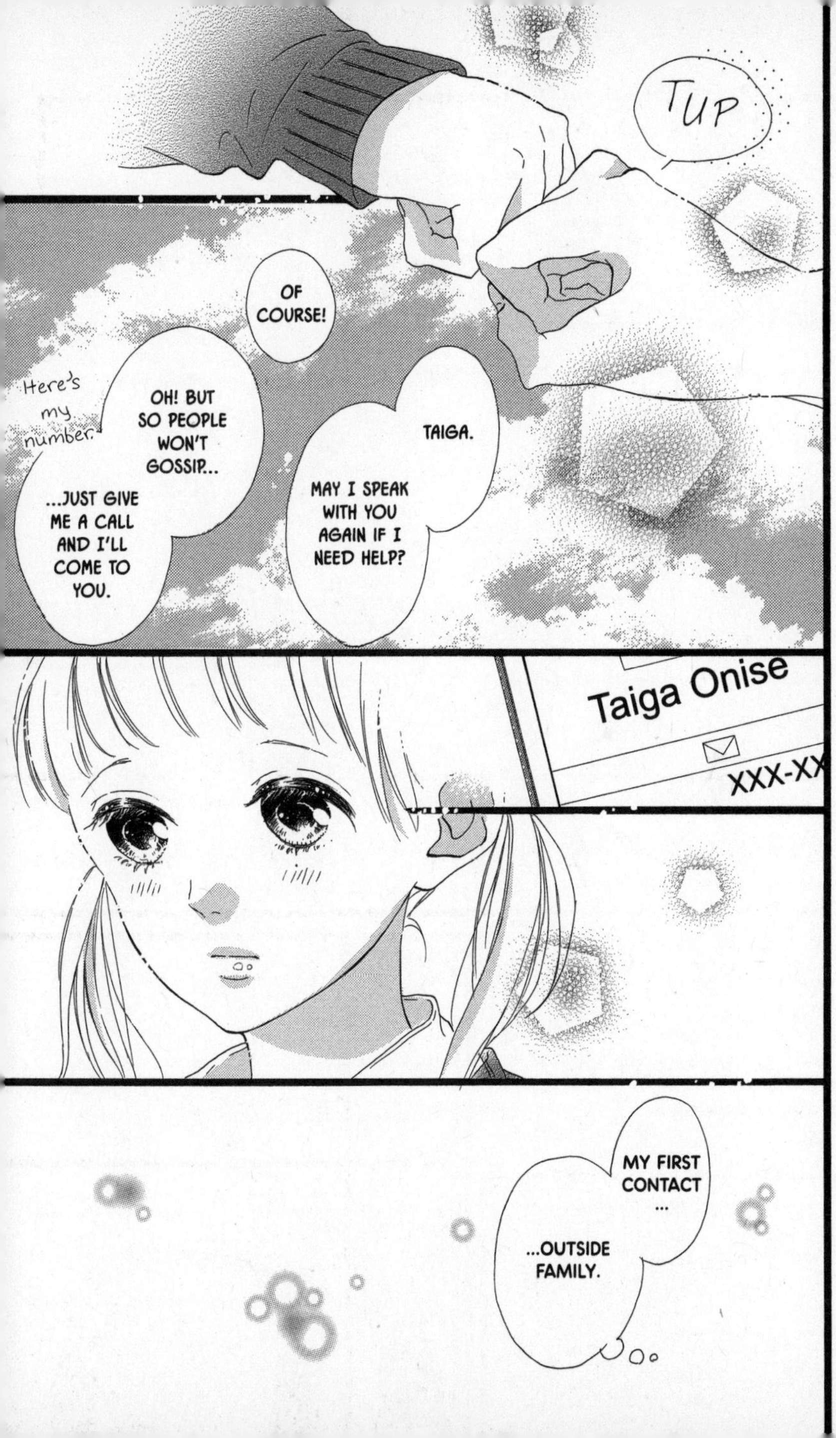
TUP
TAIGA.
MAY I SPEAK WITH YOU AGAIN IF I NEED HELP?
OF COURSE!
OH! BUT SO PEOPLE WON'T GOSSIP...
...JUST GIVE ME A CALL AND I'LL COME TO YOU.
Here's my number.
Taiga Onise
XXX-XX
MY FIRST CONTACT...
...OUTSIDE FAMILY.

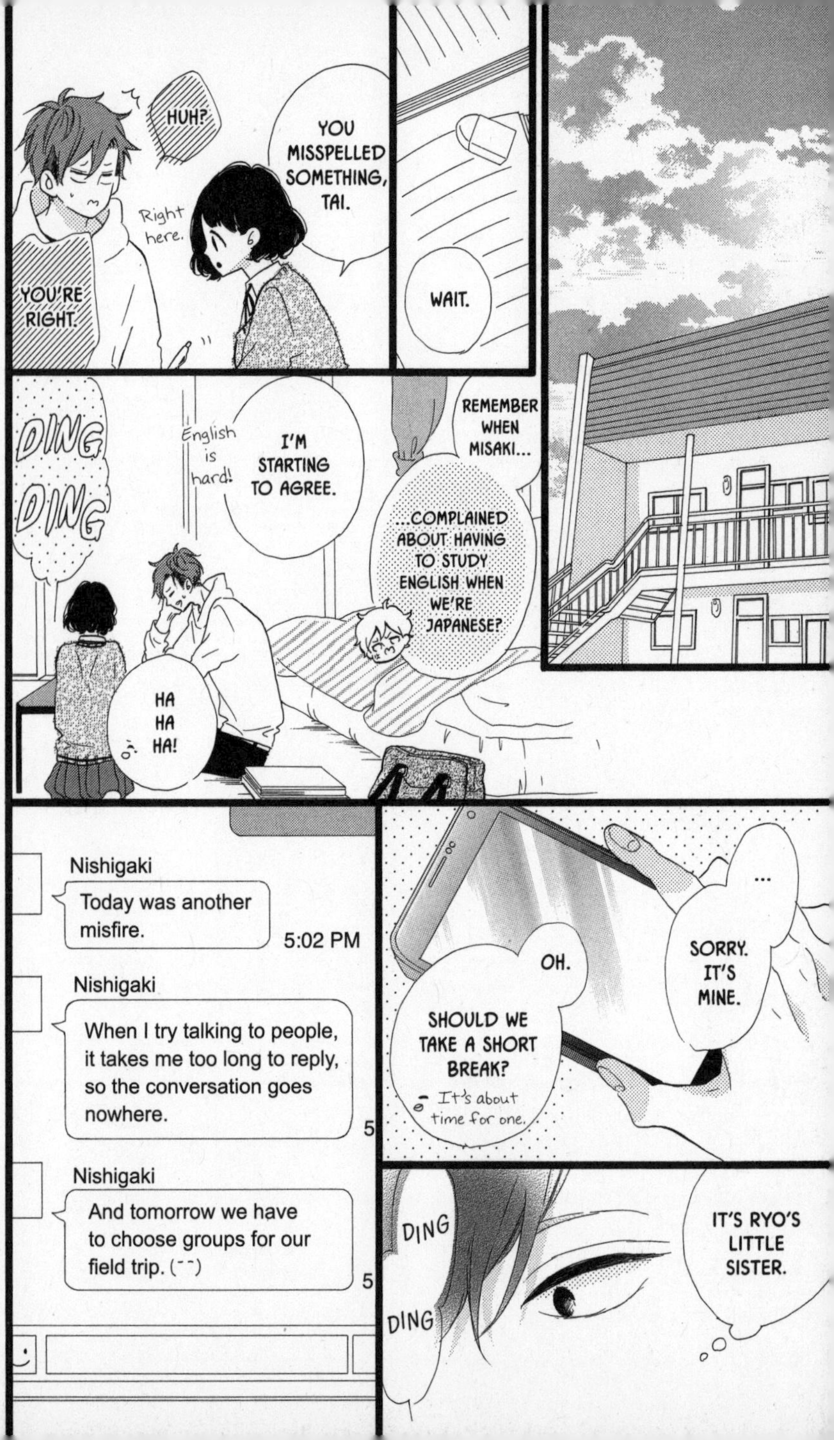
WAIT.
YOU MISSPELLED SOMETHING, TAI.
Right here.
HUH?
YOU'RE RIGHT.
REMEMBER WHEN MISAKI...
...COMPLAINED ABOUT HAVING TO STUDY ENGLISH WHEN WE'RE JAPANESE?
I'M STARTING TO AGREE.
English is hard!
DING DING
HA HA HA!
...
SORRY. IT'S MINE.
OH.
SHOULD WE TAKE A SHORT BREAK?
It's about time for one.
IT'S RYO'S LITTLE SISTER.
DING
DING
Nishigaki
Today was another misfire.
5:02 PM
Nishigaki
When I try talking to people, it takes me too long to reply, so the conversation goes nowhere.
5
Nishigaki
And tomorrow we have to choose groups for our field trip. (¯¯)
5

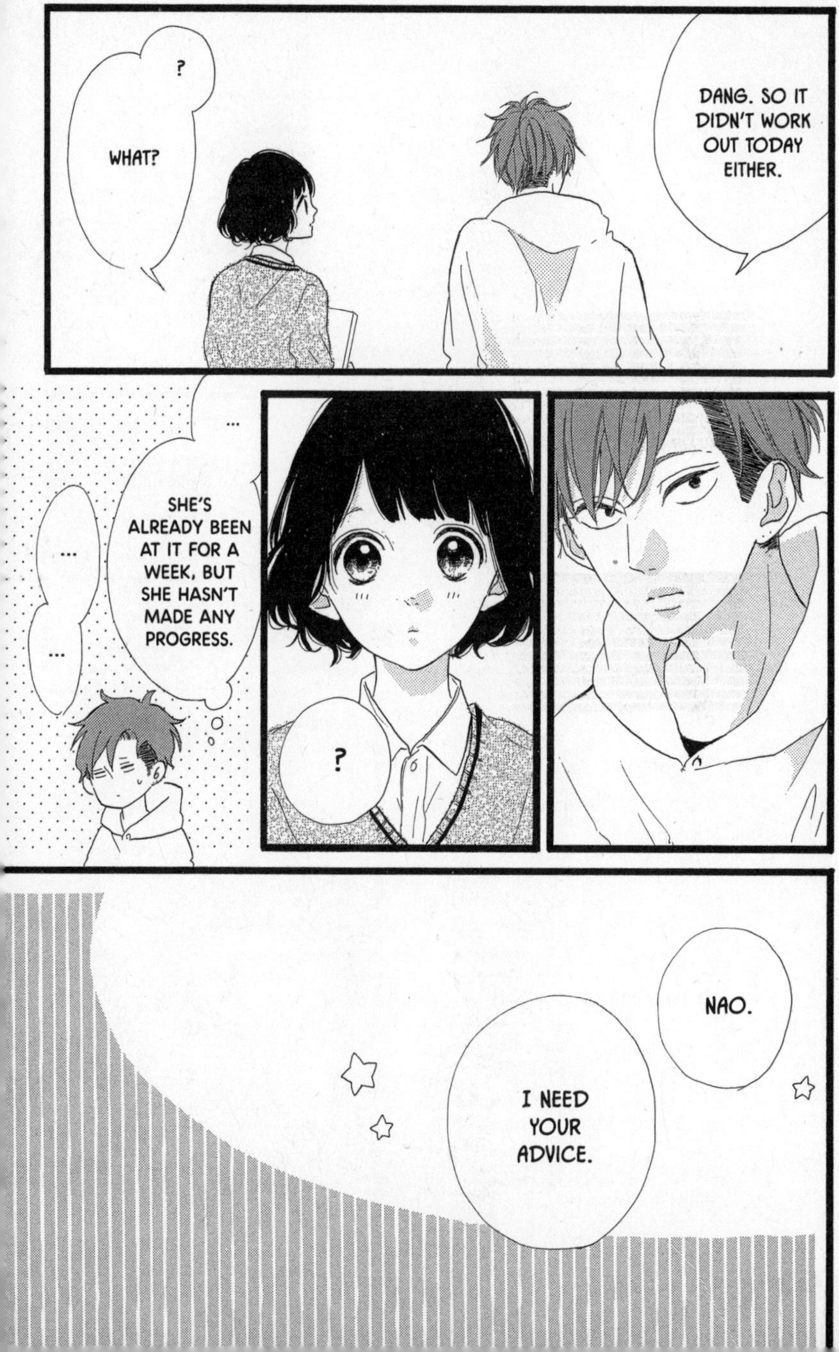
DANG. SO IT DIDN'T WORK OUT TODAY EITHER.
? WHAT?
?
... SHE'S ALREADY BEEN AT IT FOR A WEEK, BUT SHE HASN'T MADE ANY PROGRESS.
...
...
NAO.
I NEED YOUR ADVICE.

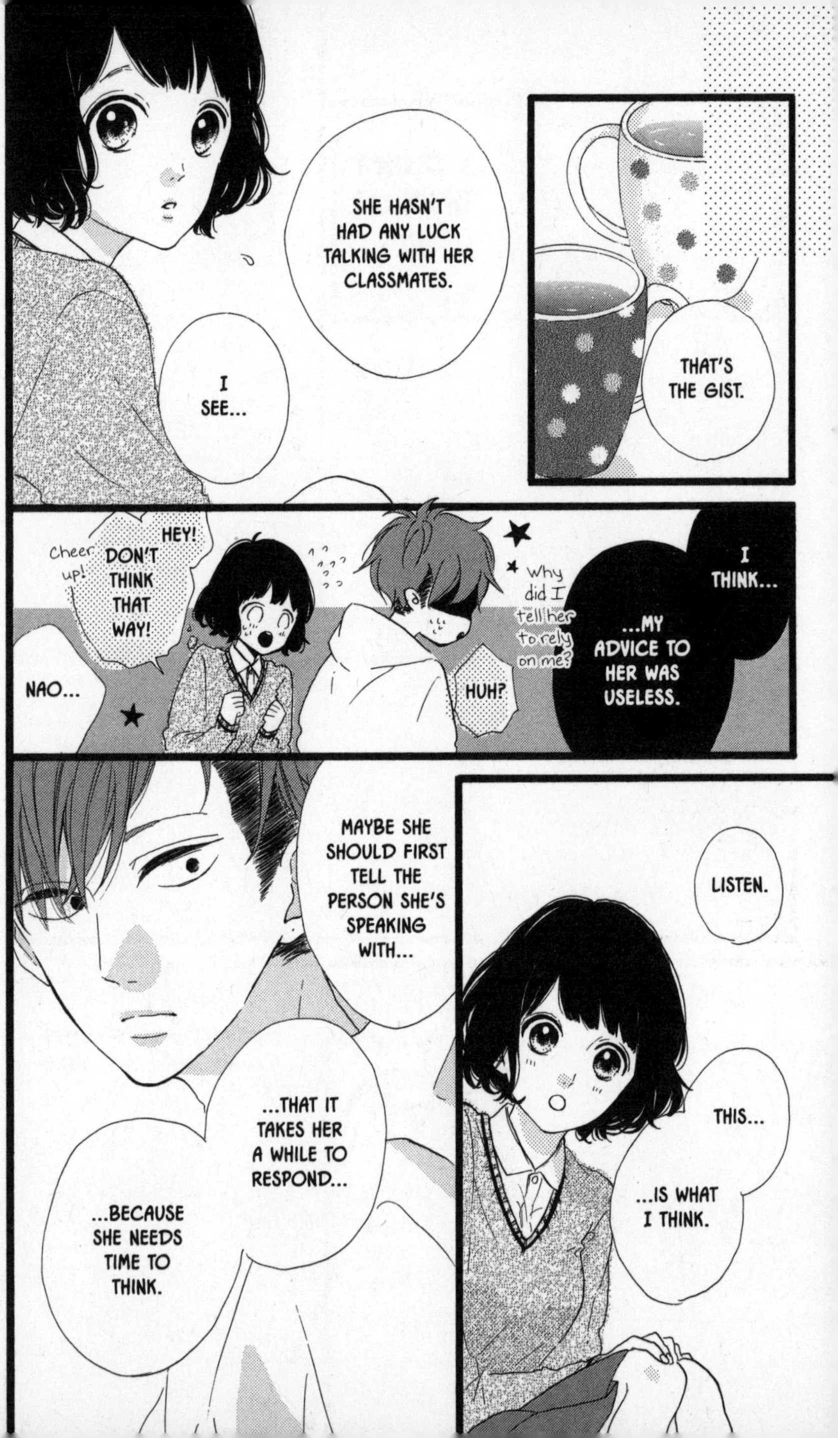
THAT'S THE GIST.
SHE HASN'T HAD ANY LUCK TALKING WITH HER CLASSMATES.
I SEE...
I THINK...
...MY ADVICE TO HER WAS USELESS.
Why did I tell her to rely on me?
HUH?
HEY! DON'T THINK THAT WAY!
Cheer up!
NAO...
LISTEN.
THIS...
...IS WHAT I THINK.
MAYBE SHE SHOULD FIRST TELL THE PERSON SHE'S SPEAKING WITH...
...THAT IT TAKES HER A WHILE TO RESPOND...
...BECAUSE SHE NEEDS TIME TO THINK.

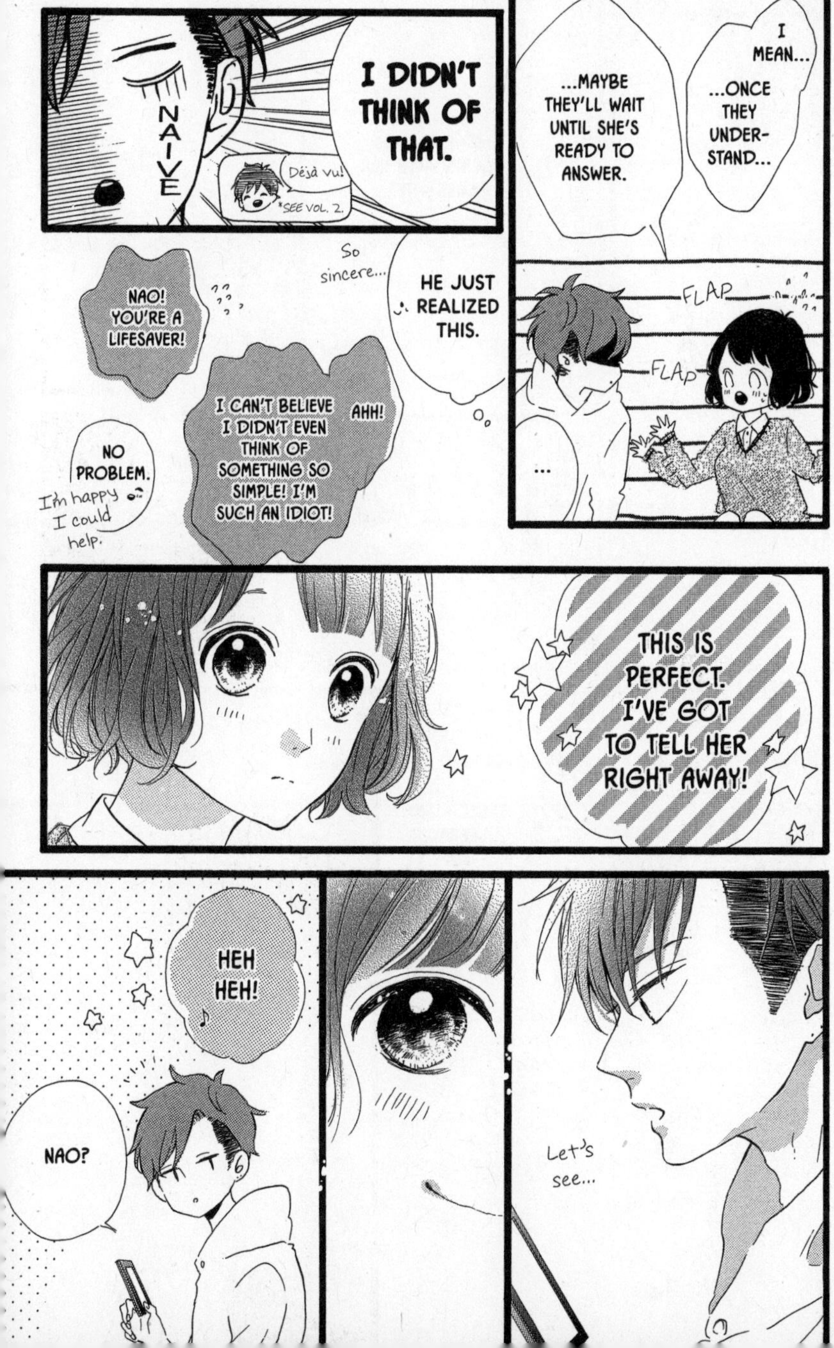
I MEAN...
...ONCE THEY UNDERSTAND...
...MAYBE THEY'LL WAIT UNTIL SHE'S READY TO ANSWER.
I DIDN'T THINK OF THAT.
NAIVE
Déjà vu!
*SEE VOL. 2.
FLAP
FLAP
...
HE JUST REALIZED THIS.
So sincere...
AHH!
I CAN'T BELIEVE I DIDN'T EVEN THINK OF SOMETHING SO SIMPLE! I'M SUCH AN IDIOT!
NAO! YOU'RE A LIFESAVER!
NO PROBLEM.
I'm happy I could help.
THIS IS PERFECT. I'VE GOT TO TELL HER RIGHT AWAY!
Let's see...
HEH HEH!
NAO?

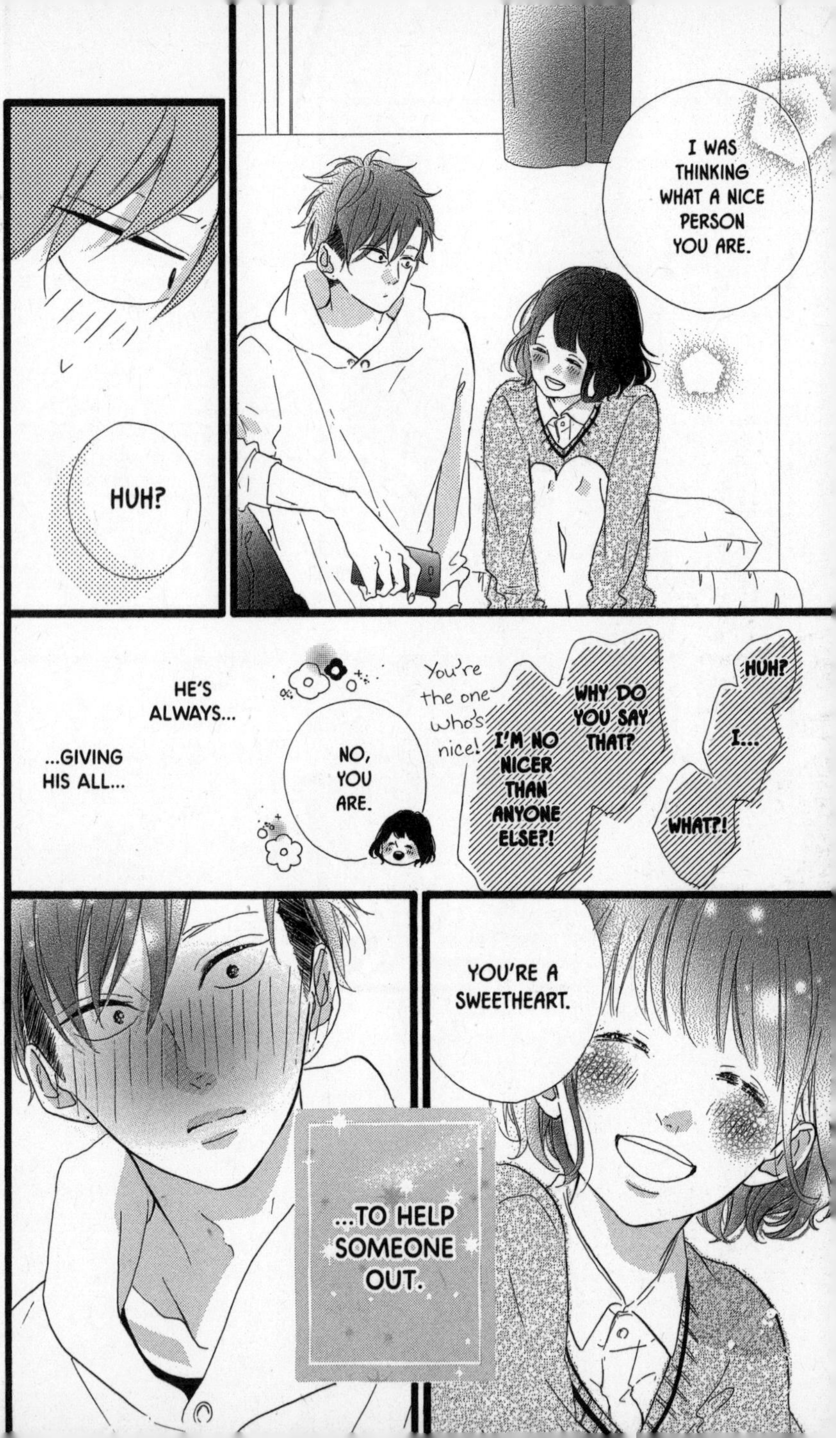
I WAS THINKING WHAT A NICE PERSON YOU ARE.
HUH?
HUH?
I...
WHAT?!
WHY DO YOU SAY THAT?
I'M NO NICER THAN ANYONE ELSE?!
You're the one who's nice!
NO, YOU ARE.
HE'S ALWAYS...
...GIVING HIS ALL...
YOU'RE A SWEETHEART.
...TO HELP SOMEONE OUT.

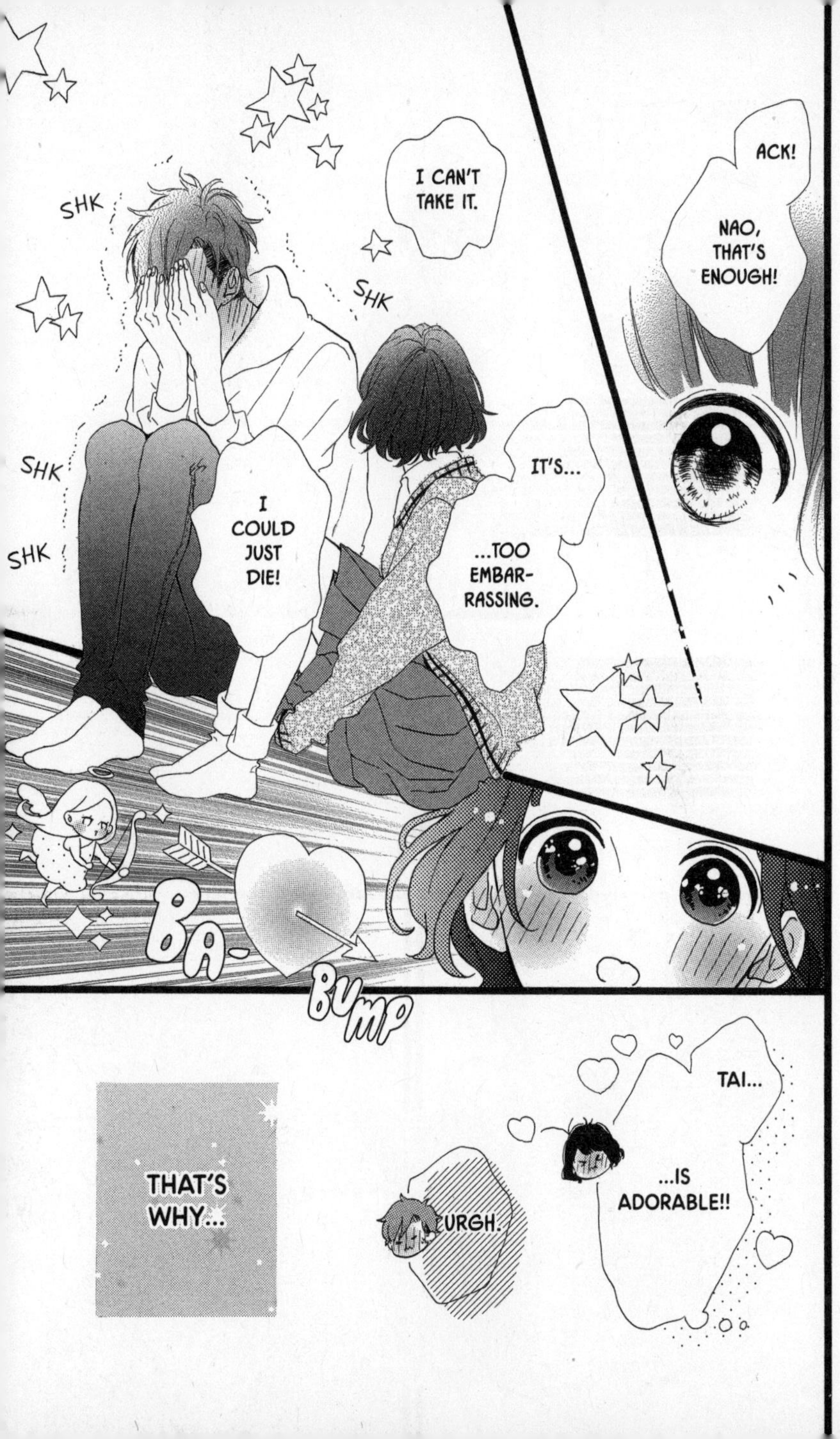
ACK!
NAO, THAT'S ENOUGH!
I CAN'T TAKE IT.
SHK
SHK
IT'S...
...TOO EMBARRASSING.
I COULD JUST DIE!
SHK
SHK
BA-BUMP
TAI...
...IS ADORABLE!!
URGH.
THAT'S WHY...

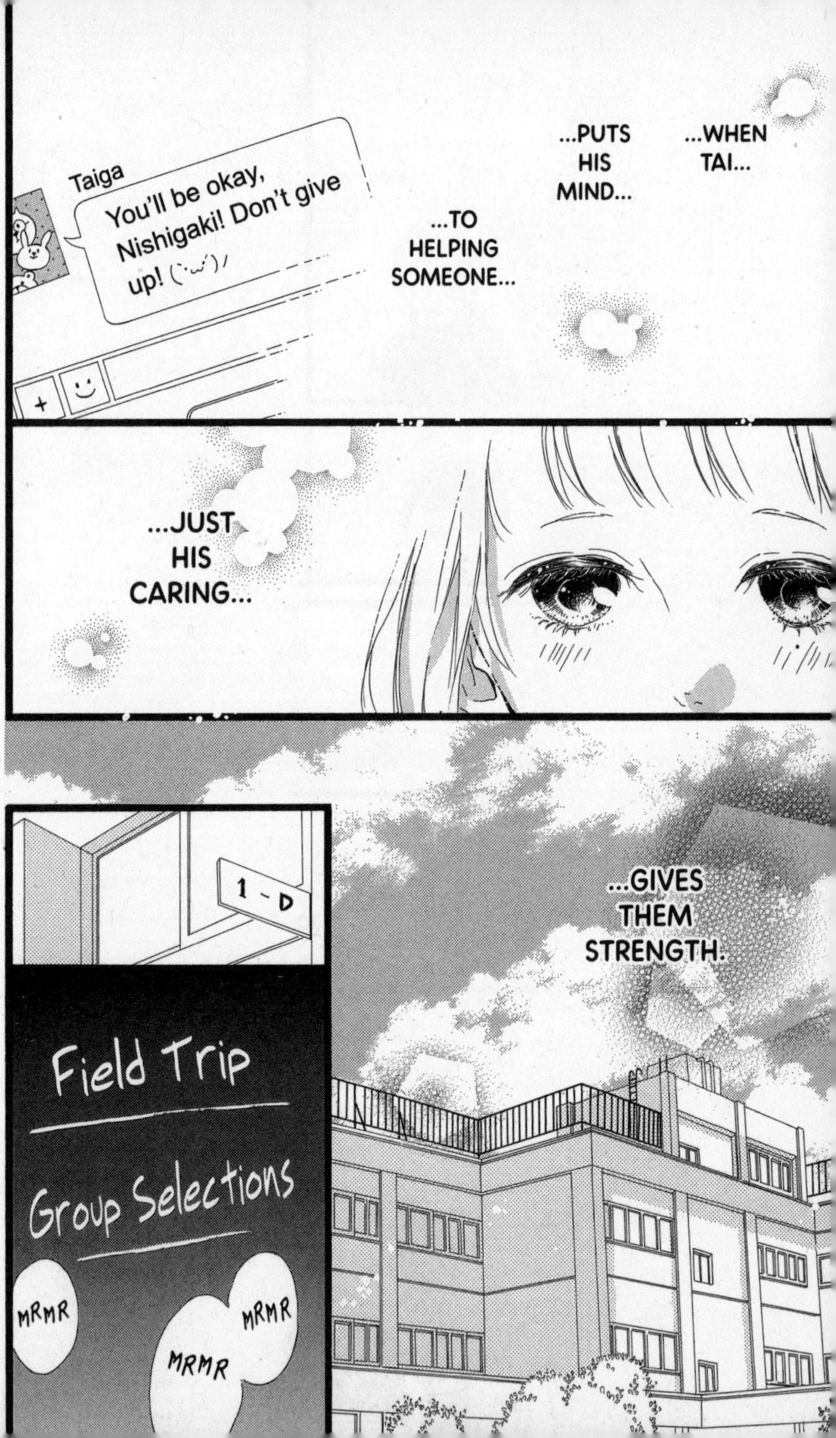
...WHEN TAI...
...PUTS HIS MIND...
...TO HELPING SOMEONE...
Taiga
You'll be okay, Nishigaki! Don't give up! (`･ω･´)/
...JUST HIS CARING...
...GIVES THEM STRENGTH.
1-D
Field Trip
Group Selections
MRMR
MRMR
MRMR

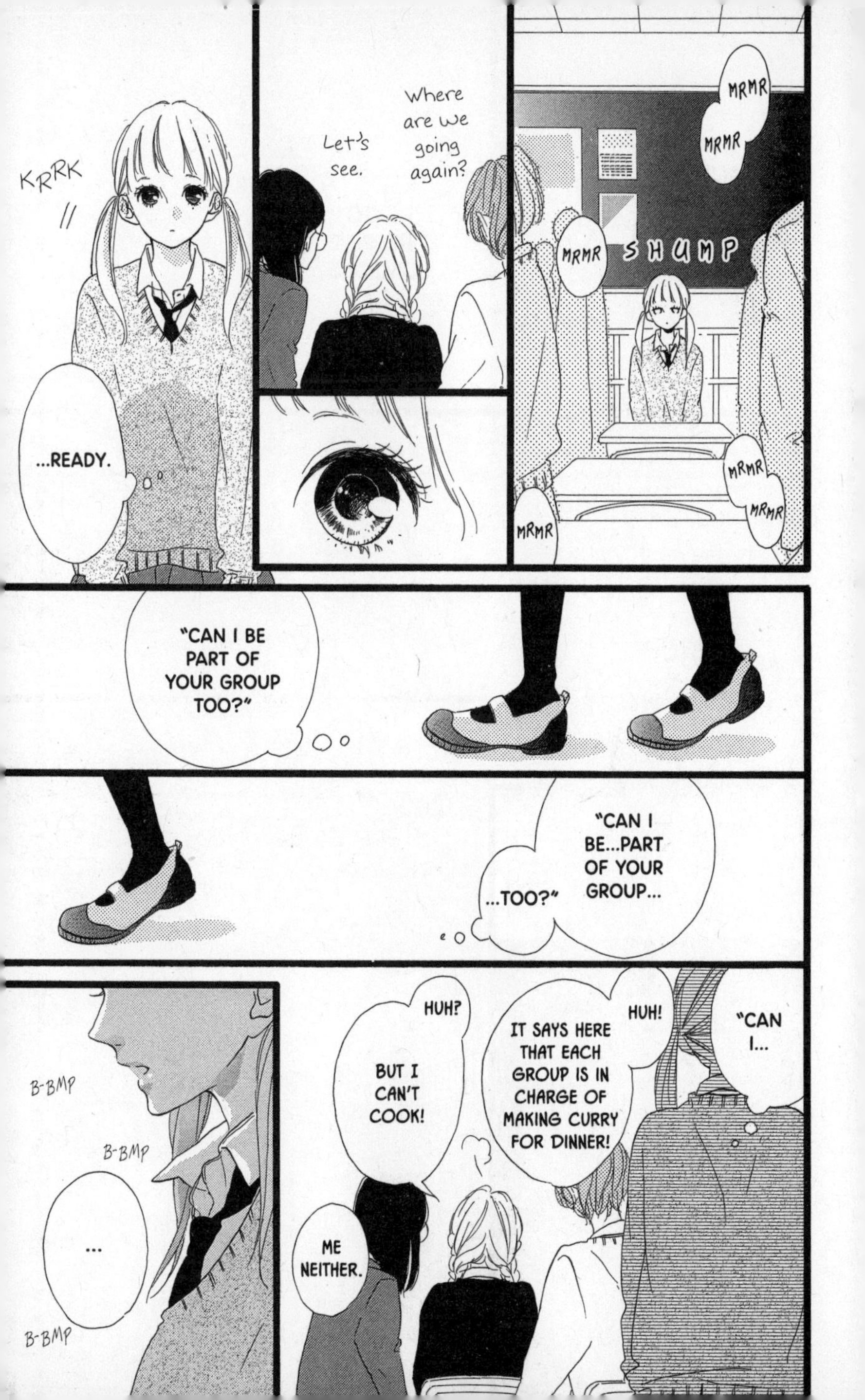
MRMR
MRMR
MRMR
SHUMP
MRMR
MRMR
MRMR
Where are we going again?
Let's see.
KRRK
...READY.
"CAN I BE PART OF YOUR GROUP TOO?"
"CAN I BE...PART OF YOUR GROUP...
...TOO?"
"CAN I...
HUH!
IT SAYS HERE THAT EACH GROUP IS IN CHARGE OF MAKING CURRY FOR DINNER!
HUH?
BUT I CAN'T COOK!
ME NEITHER.
B-BMP
B-BMP
...
B-BMP

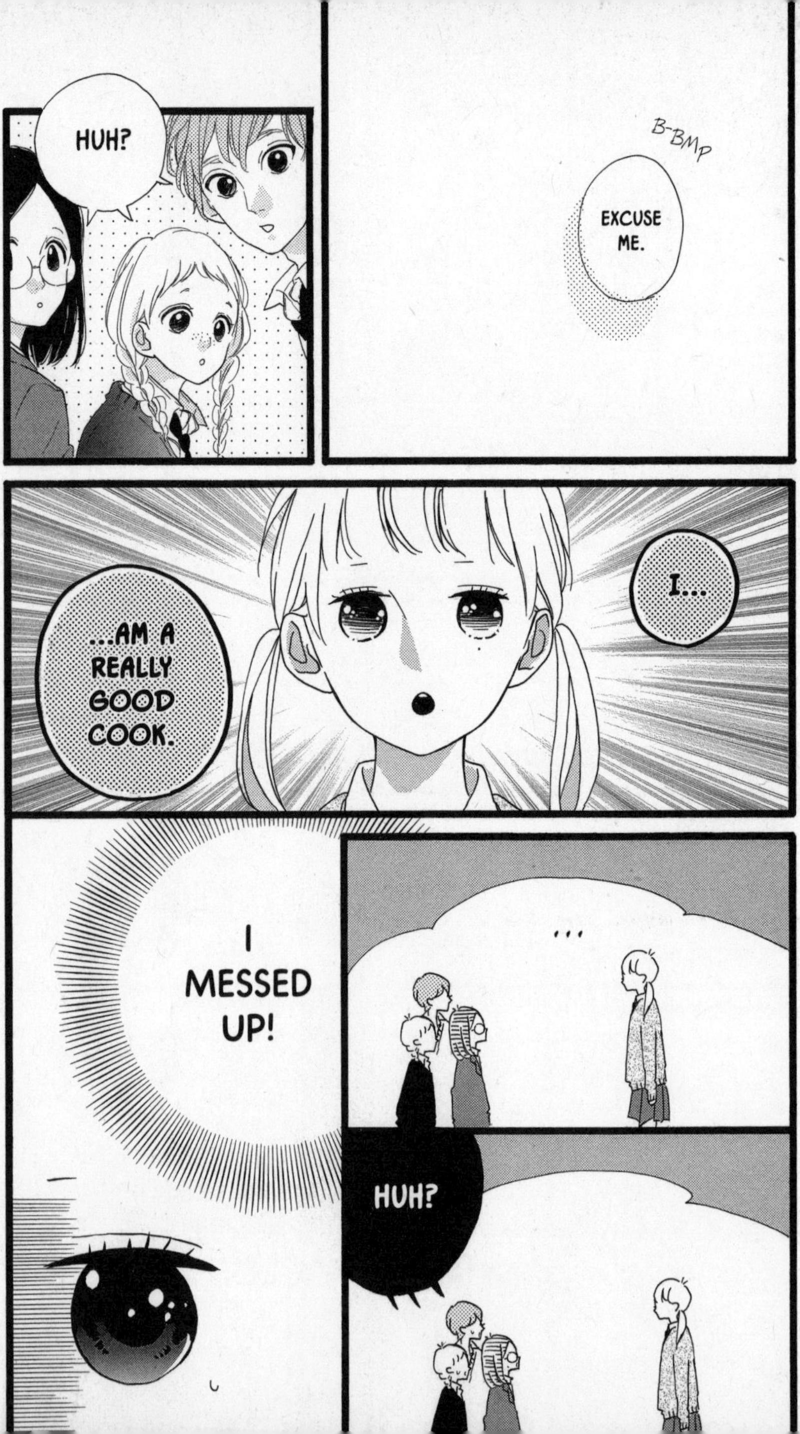
B-BMP
EXCUSE ME.
HUH?
I...
...AM A REALLY GOOD COOK.
...
HUH?
I MESSED UP!

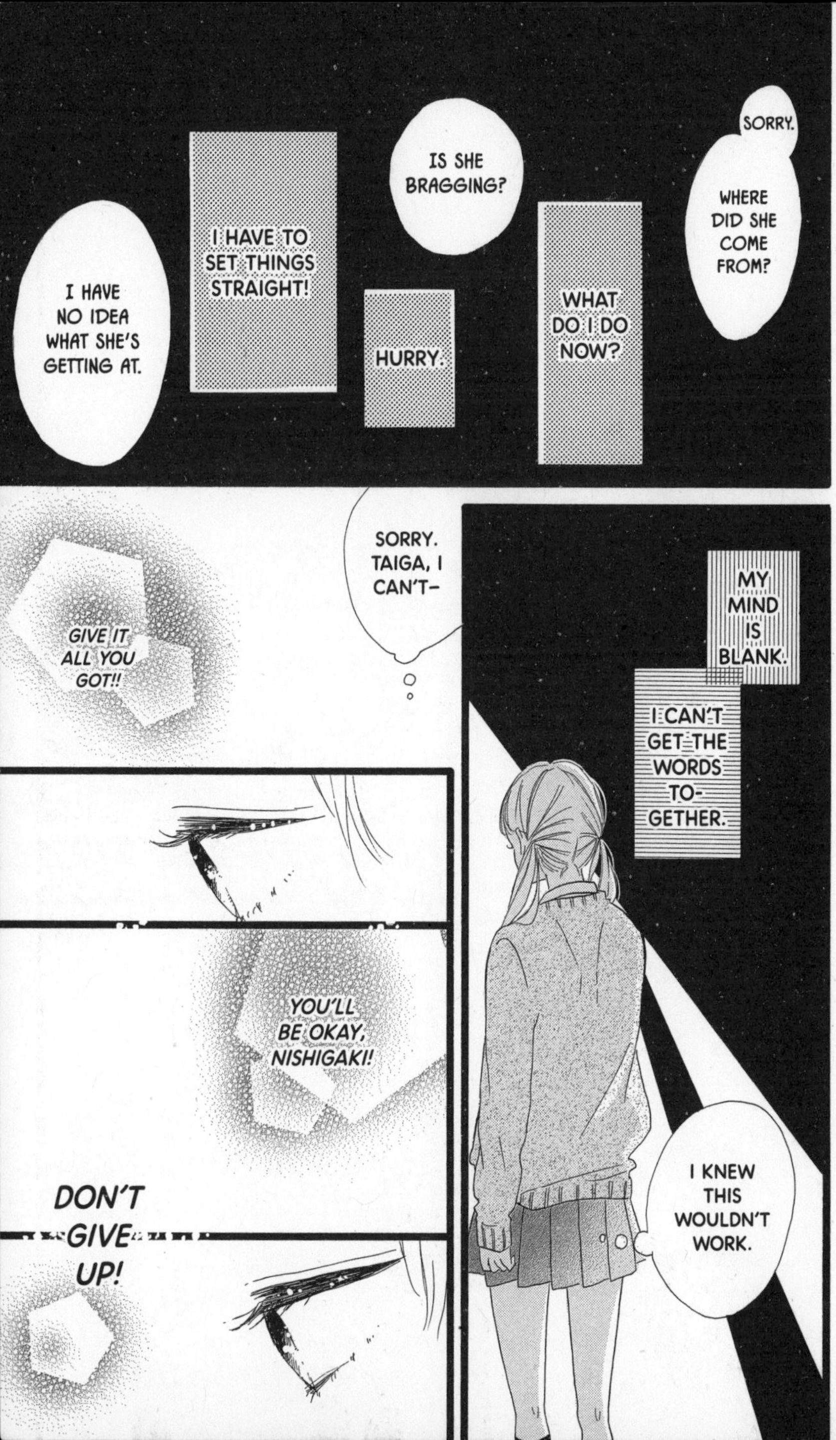
SORRY.
WHERE DID SHE COME FROM?
WHAT DO I DO NOW?
IS SHE BRAGGING?
HURRY.
I HAVE TO SET THINGS STRAIGHT!
I HAVE NO IDEA WHAT SHE'S GETTING AT.
MY MIND IS BLANK.
I CAN'T GET THE WORDS TO-GETHER.
I KNEW THIS WOULDN'T WORK.
SORRY. TAIGA, I CAN'T–
GIVE IT ALL YOU GOT!!
YOU'LL BE OKAY, NISHIGAKI!
DON'T GIVE UP!

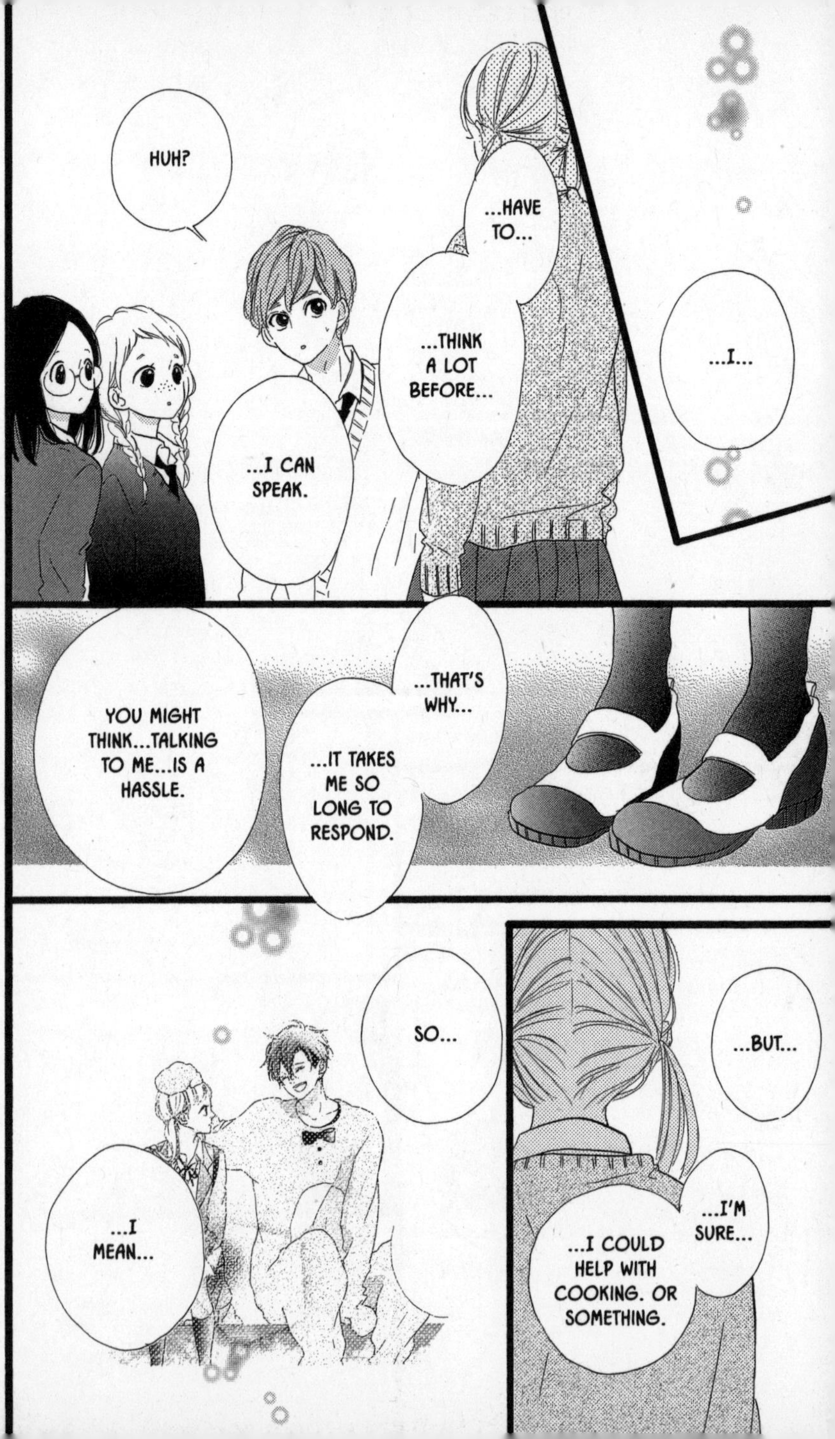
...I...
...HAVE TO...
...THINK A LOT BEFORE...
...I CAN SPEAK.
HUH?
...THAT'S WHY...
...IT TAKES ME SO LONG TO RESPOND.
YOU MIGHT THINK...TALKING TO ME...IS A HASSLE.
...BUT...
...I'M SURE...
...I COULD HELP WITH COOKING. OR SOMETHING.
SO...
...I MEAN...

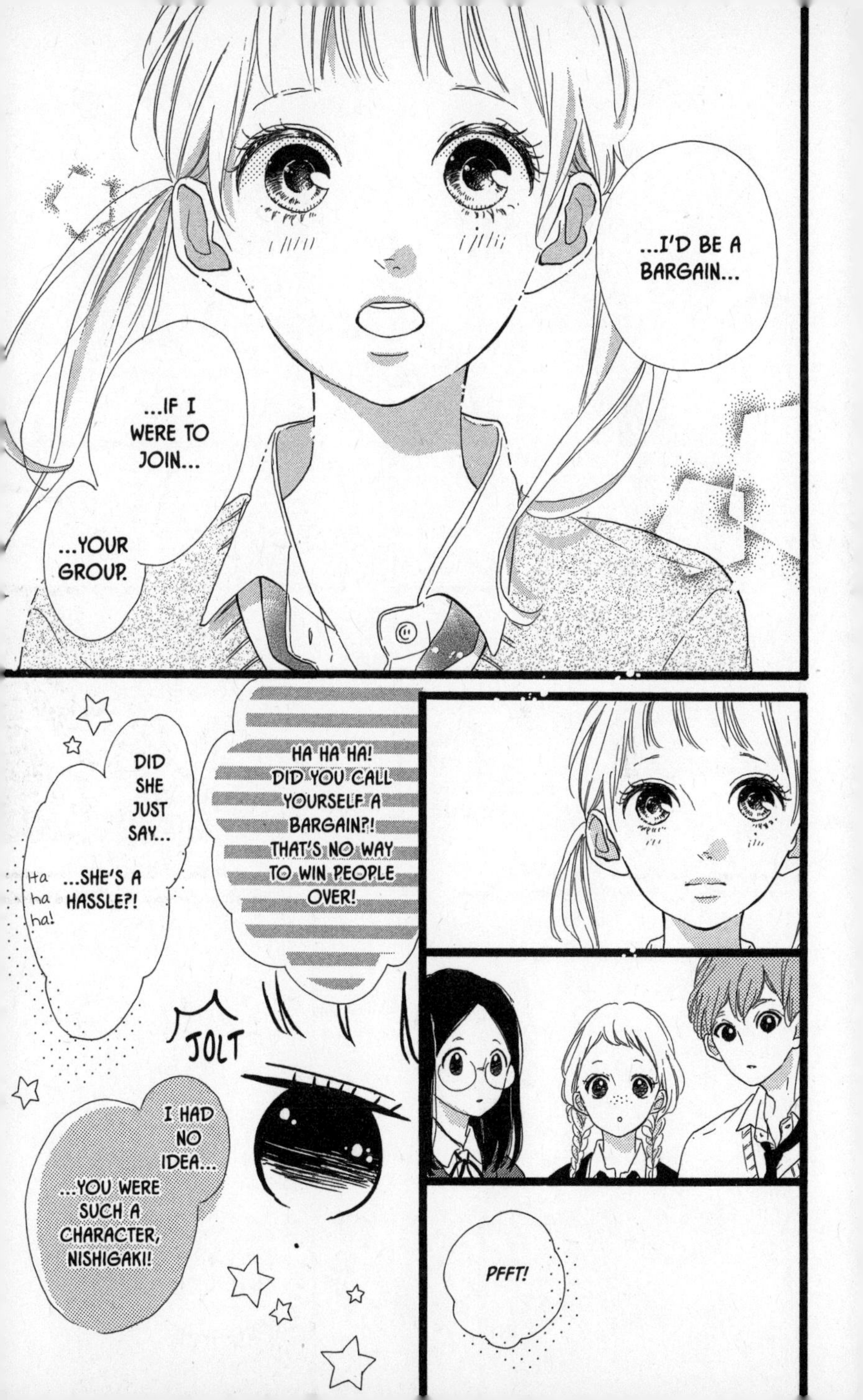
...I'D BE A BARGAIN...
...IF I WERE TO JOIN...
...YOUR GROUP.
PFFT!
HA HA HA! DID YOU CALL YOURSELF A BARGAIN?! THAT'S NO WAY TO WIN PEOPLE OVER!
DID SHE JUST SAY...
...SHE'S A HASSLE?!
Ha ha ha!
JOLT
I HAD NO IDEA...
...YOU WERE SUCH A CHARACTER, NISHIGAKI!

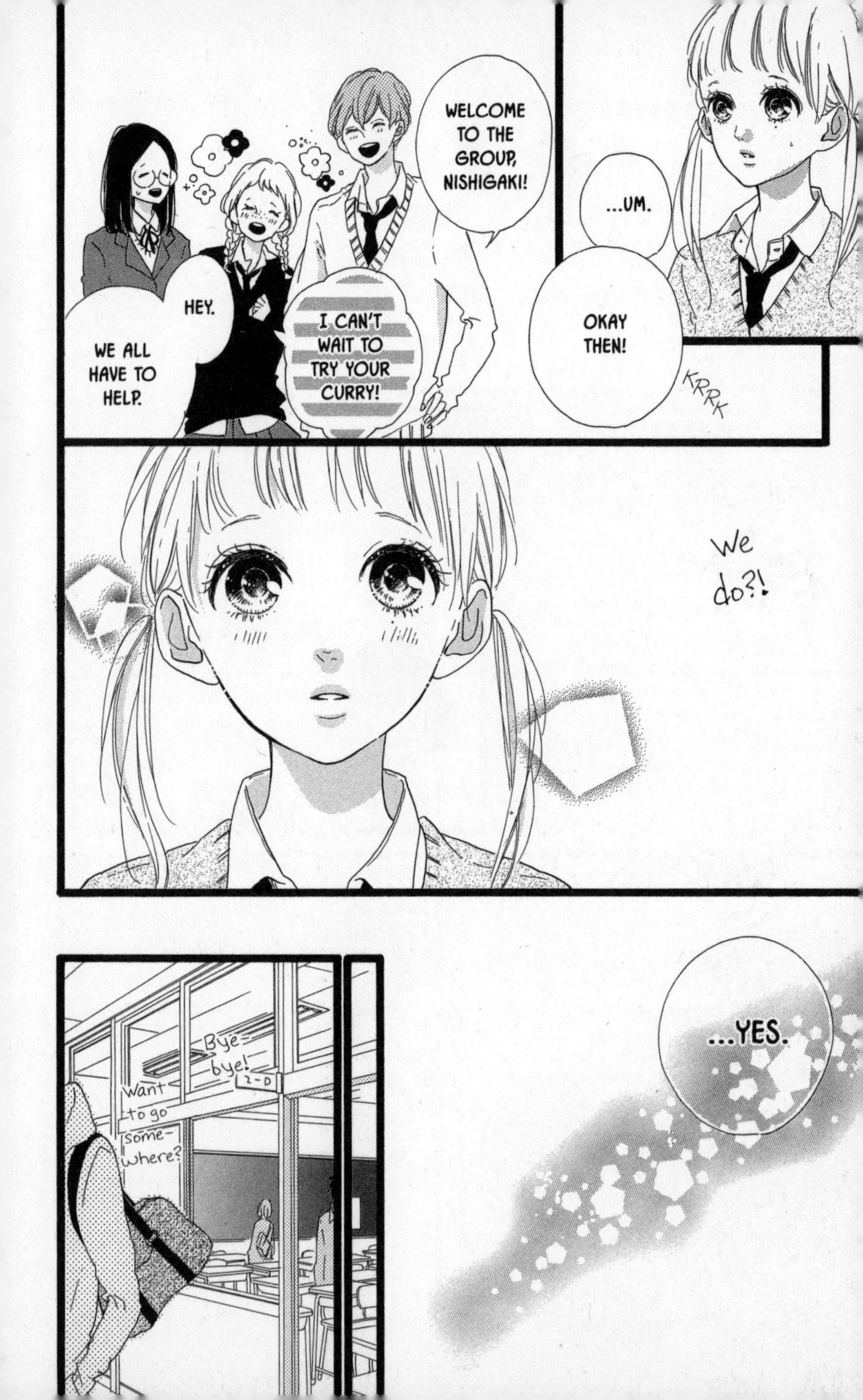
...UM.
OKAY THEN!
KRRK
WELCOME TO THE GROUP, NISHIGAKI!
I CAN'T WAIT TO TRY YOUR CURRY!
HEY.
WE ALL HAVE TO HELP.
We do?!
...YES.
Bye bye!
2-D
Want to go somewhere?

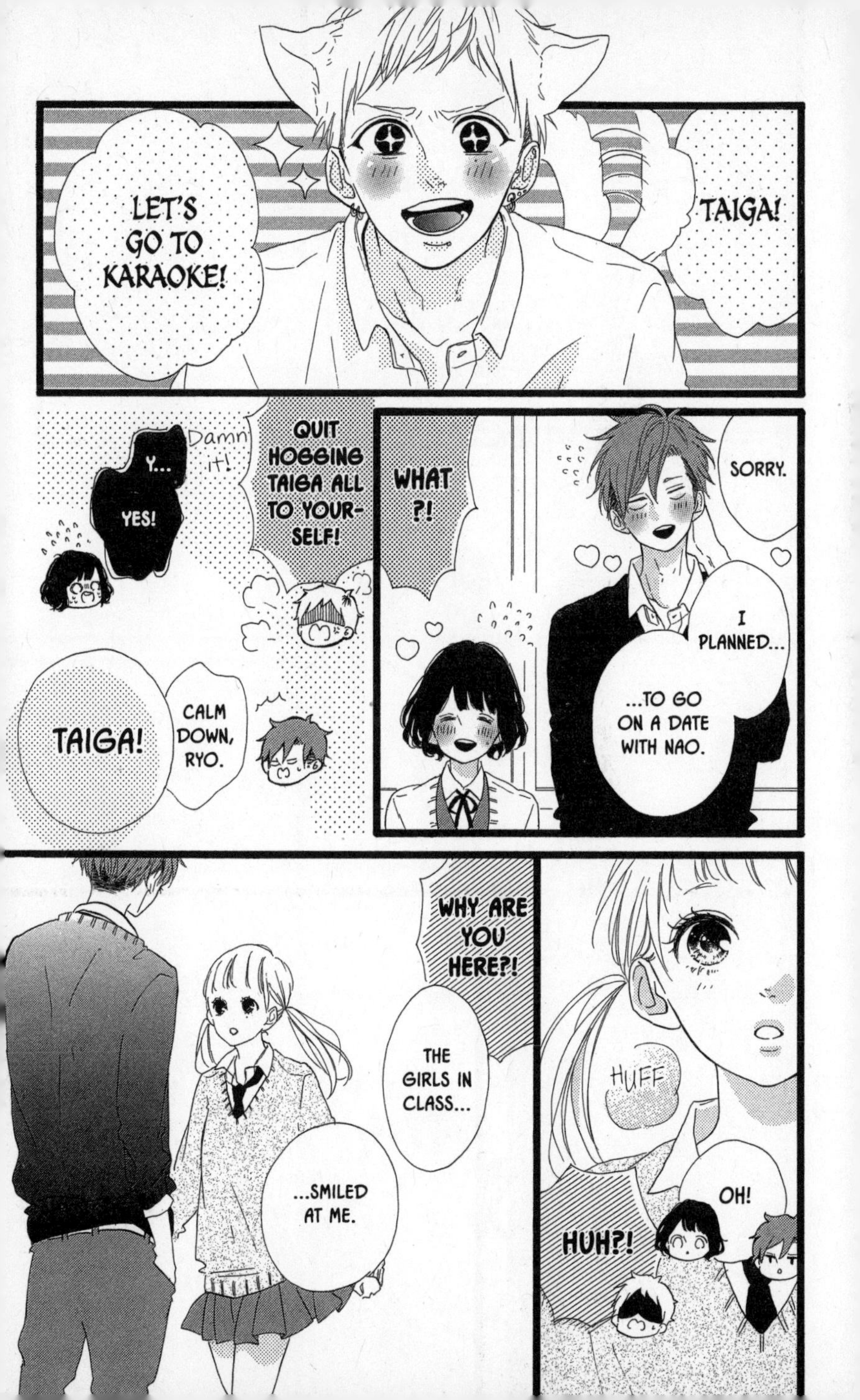
TAIGA!
LET'S GO TO KARAOKE!
SORRY.
I PLANNED...
...TO GO ON A DATE WITH NAO.
WHAT?!
QUIT HOGGING TAIGA ALL TO YOURSELF!
Damn it!
Y... YES!
CALM DOWN, RYO.
TAIGA!
HUFF
OH!
HUH?!
WHY ARE YOU HERE?!
THE GIRLS IN CLASS...
...SMILED AT ME.

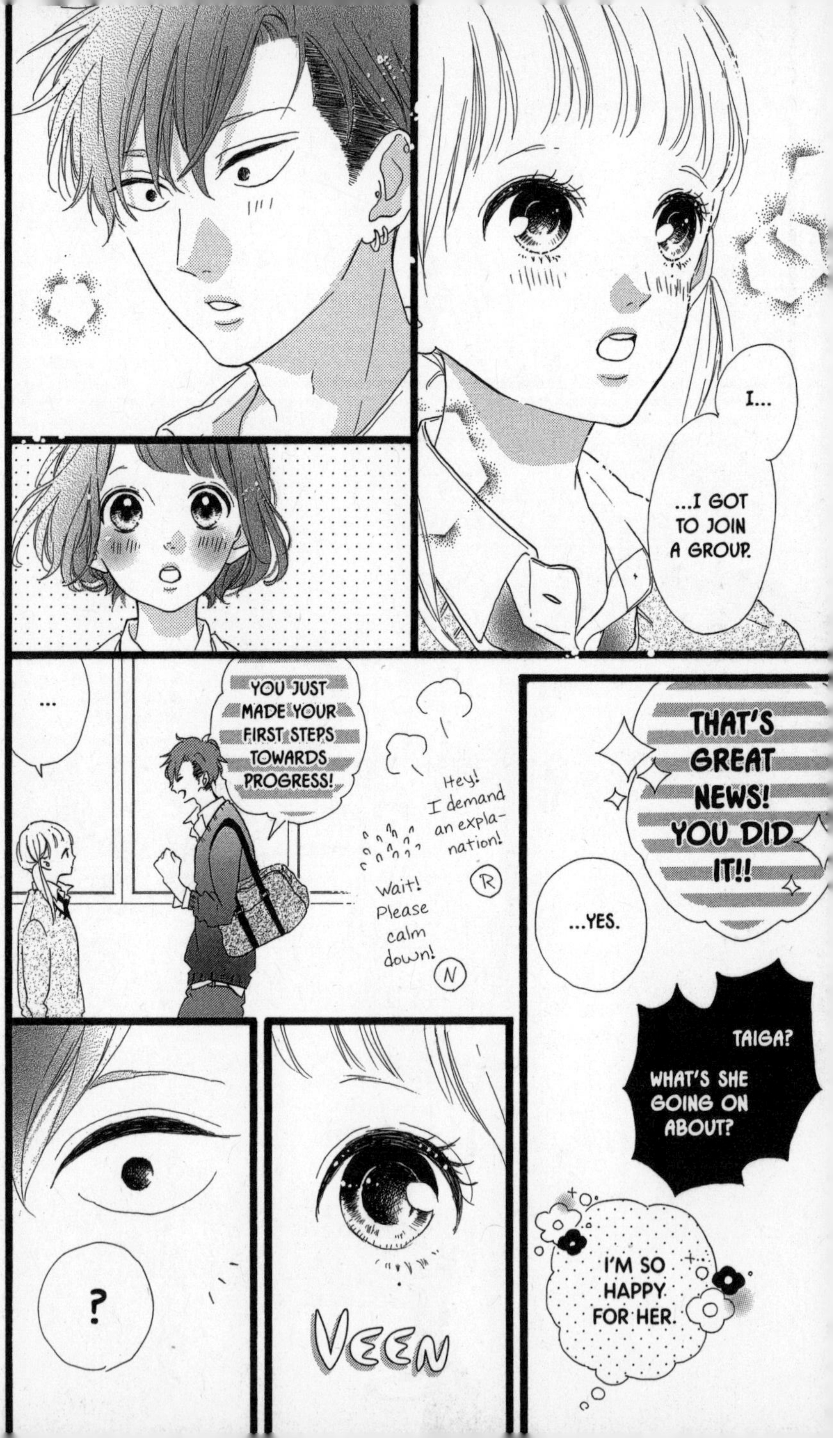
I...
...I GOT TO JOIN A GROUP.
THAT'S GREAT NEWS! YOU DID IT!!
...YES.
TAIGA?
WHAT'S SHE GOING ON ABOUT?
I'M SO HAPPY FOR HER.
...
YOU JUST MADE YOUR FIRST STEPS TOWARDS PROGRESS!
Hey! I demand an explanation! R
Wait! Please calm down! N
VEEN
?

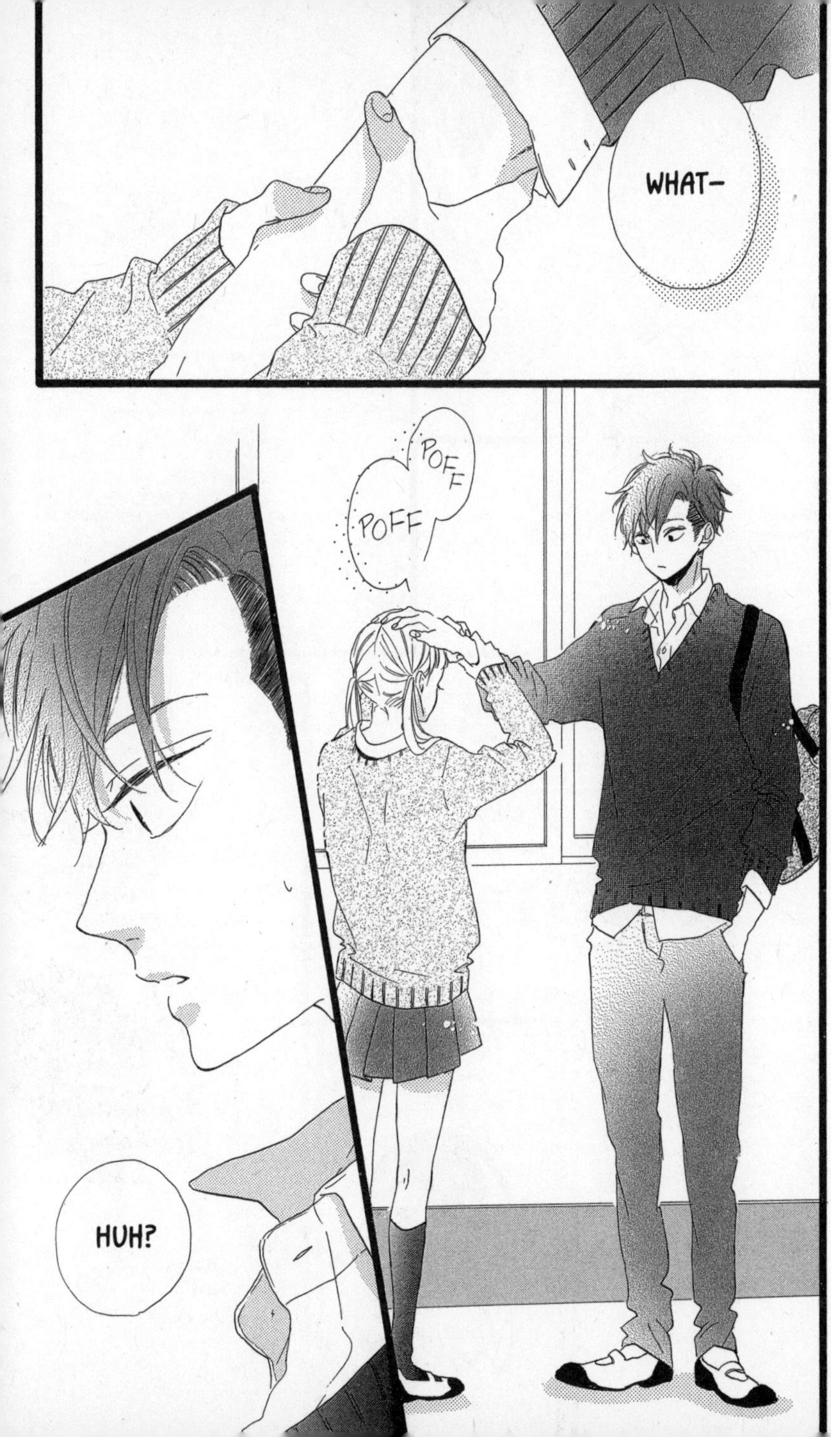
WHAT-
POFF
POFF
HUH?

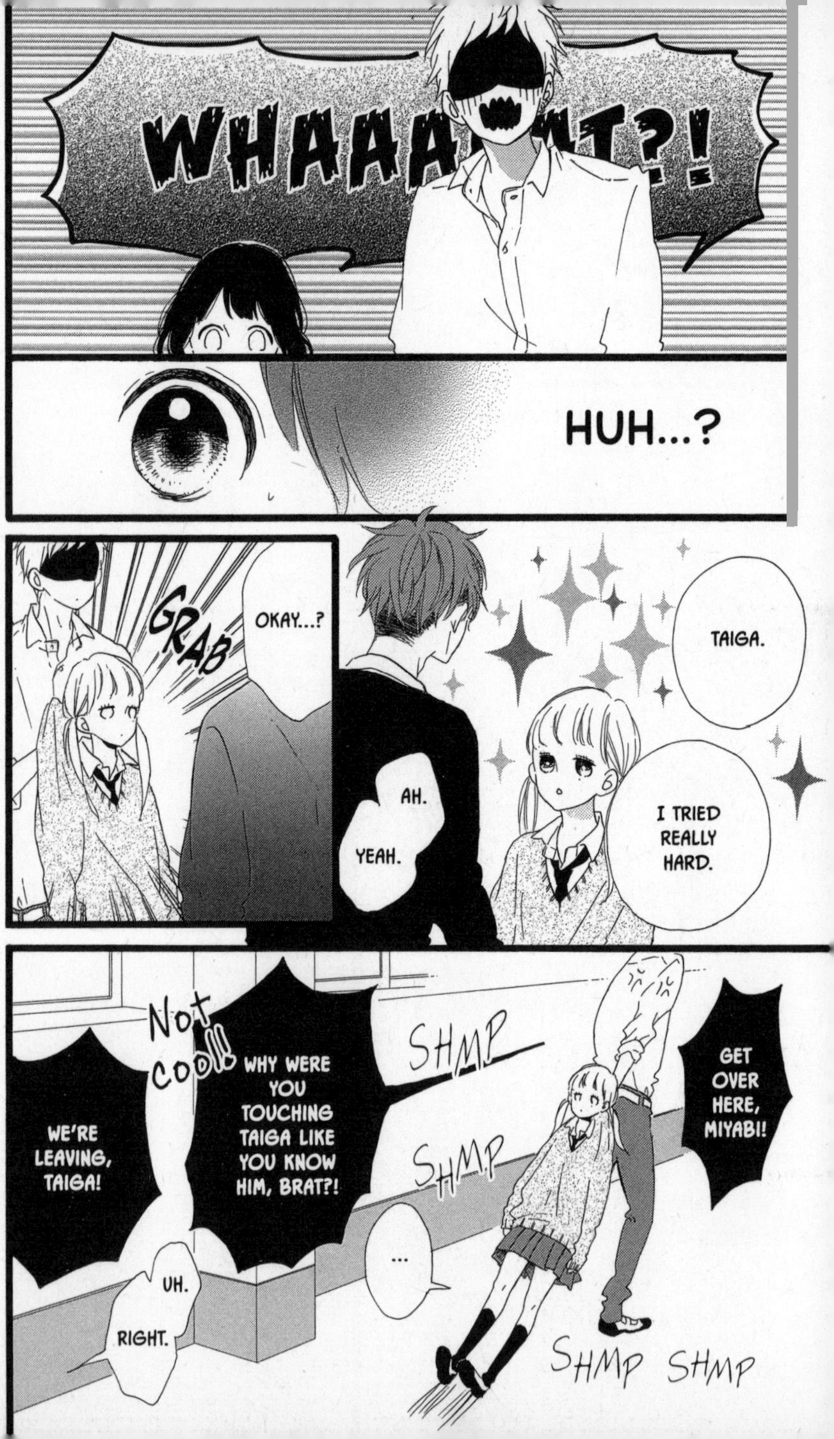
WHAAA
T?!
HUH...?
TAIGA.
I TRIED REALLY HARD.
AH.
YEAH.
OKAY...?
GRAB
GET OVER HERE, MIYABI!
SHMP
SHMP
SHMP SHMP
...
WHY WERE YOU TOUCHING TAIGA LIKE YOU KNOW HIM, BRAT?!
Not cool!!
WE'RE LEAVING, TAIGA!
UH.
RIGHT.

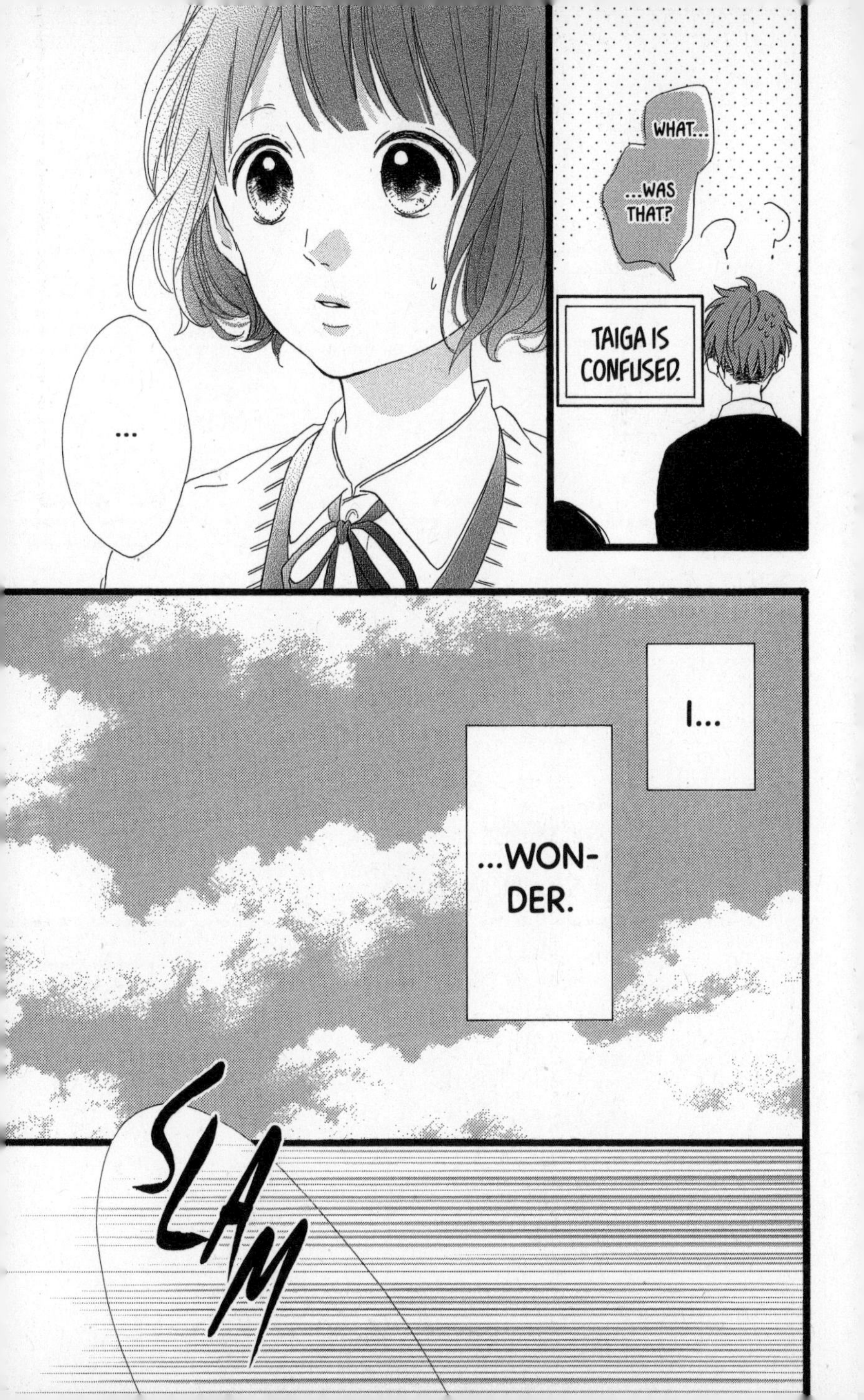
WHAT...
...WAS THAT?
TAIGA IS CONFUSED.
...
I...
...WON-DER.
SLAM

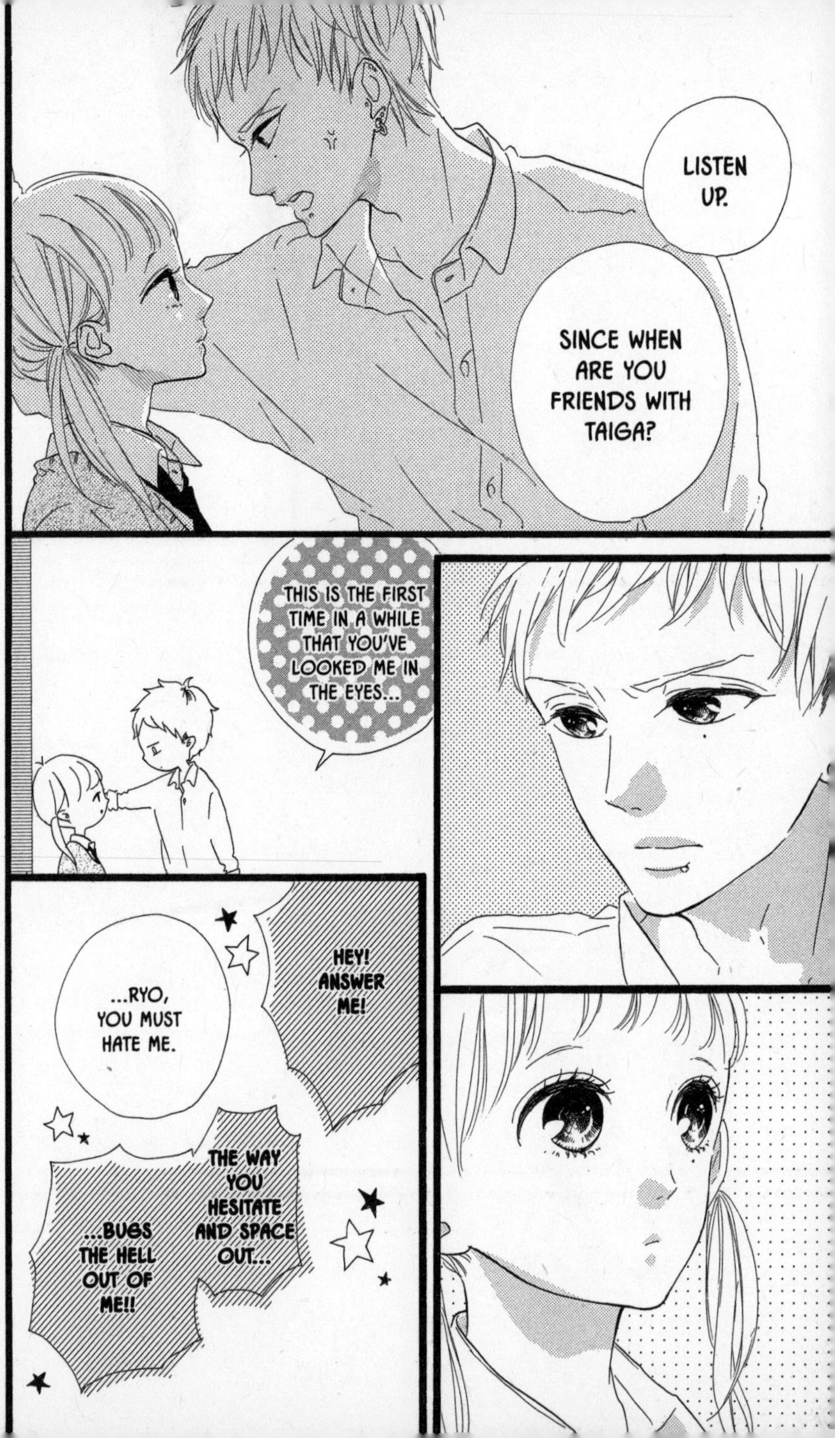
LISTEN UP.
SINCE WHEN ARE YOU FRIENDS WITH TAIGA?
THIS IS THE FIRST TIME IN A WHILE THAT YOU'VE LOOKED ME IN THE EYES...
HEY! ANSWER ME!
THE WAY YOU HESITATE AND SPACE OUT...
...BUGS THE HELL OUT OF ME!!
...RYO, YOU MUST HATE ME.

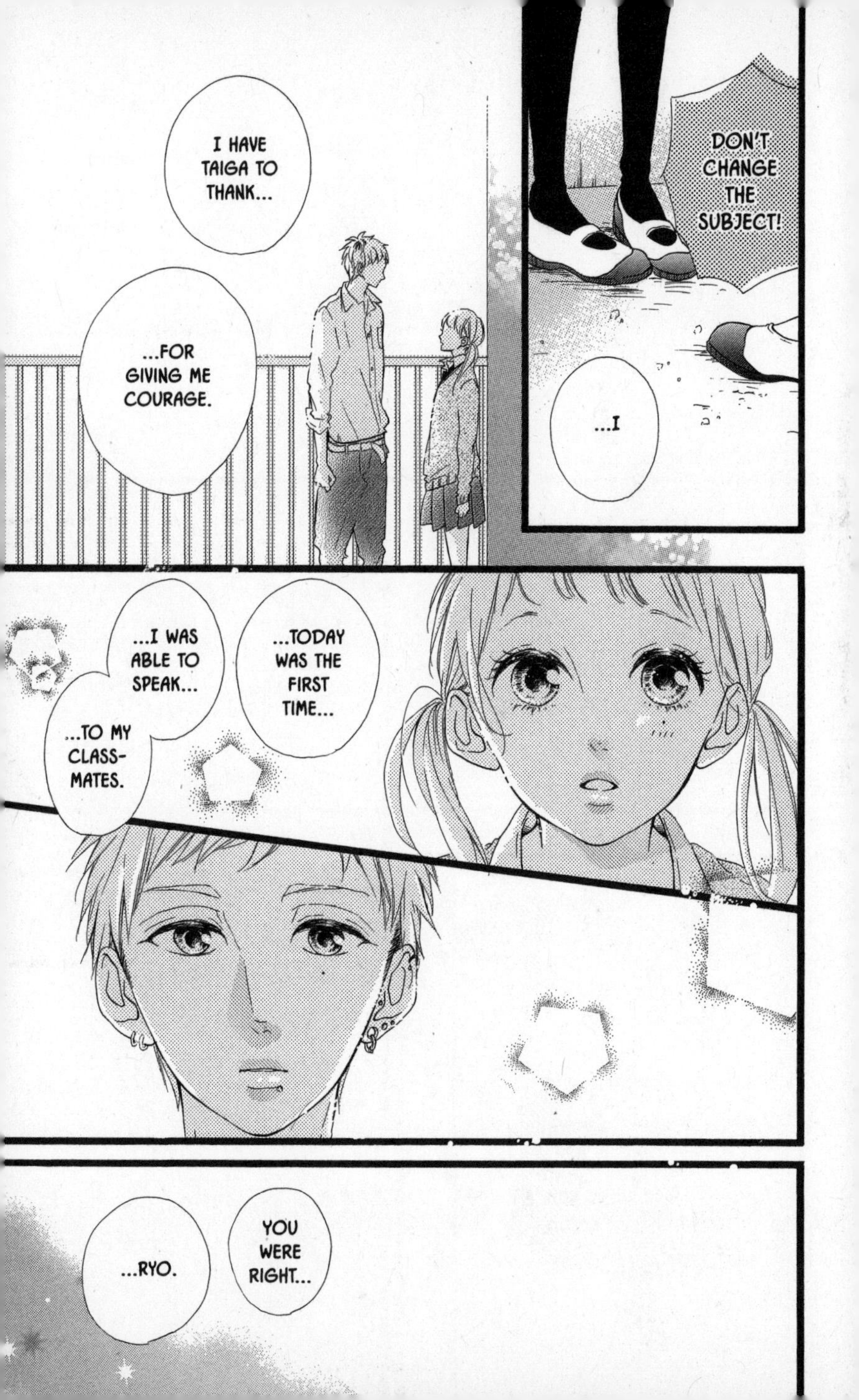
DON'T CHANGE THE SUBJECT!
...I
I HAVE TAIGA TO THANK...
...FOR GIVING ME COURAGE.
...TODAY WAS THE FIRST TIME...
...I WAS ABLE TO SPEAK...
...TO MY CLASS-MATES.
YOU WERE RIGHT...
...RYO.

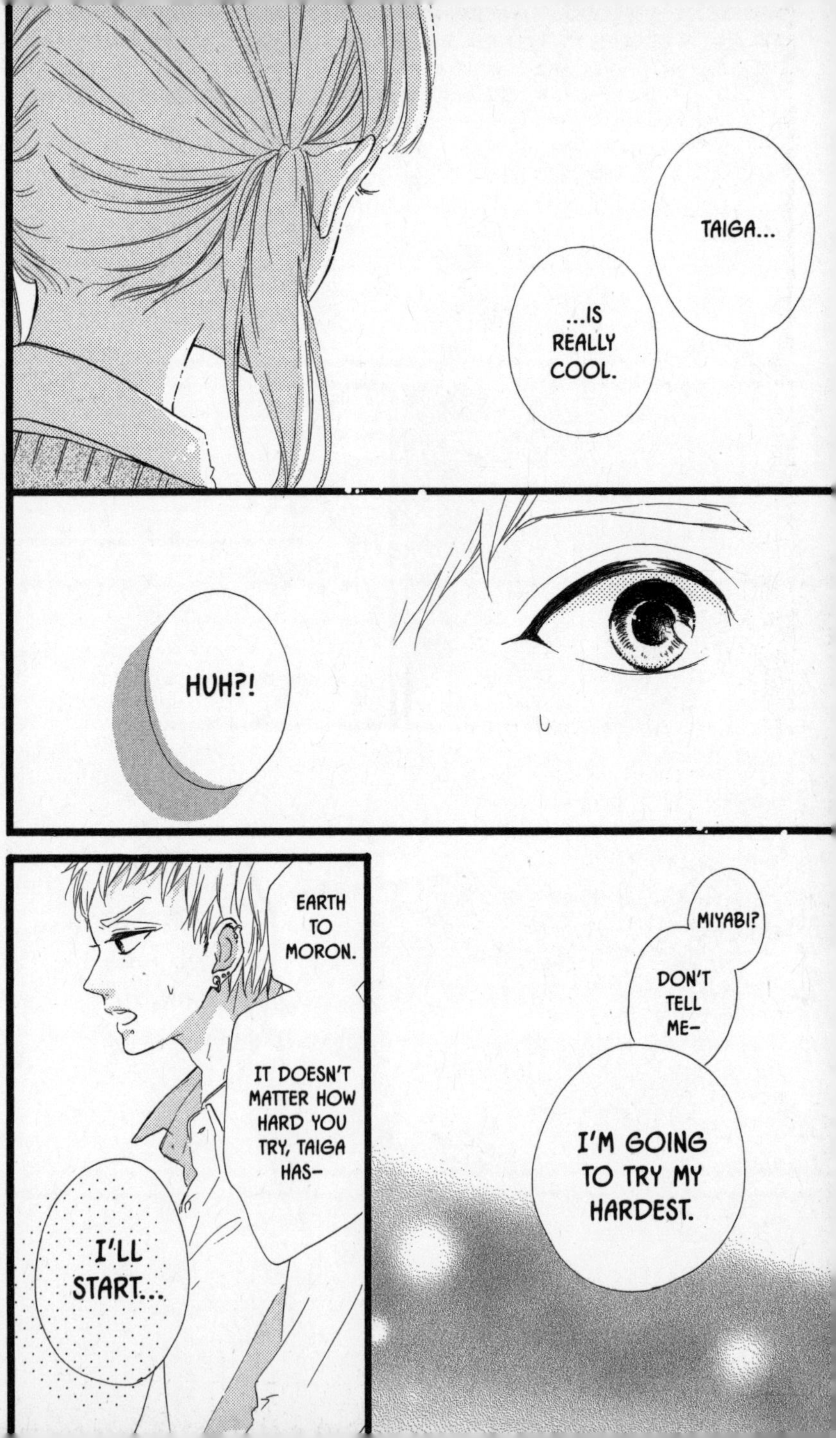
TAIGA...
...IS REALLY COOL.
HUH?!
MIYABI?
DON'T TELL ME-
I'M GOING TO TRY MY HARDEST.
EARTH TO MORON.
IT DOESN'T MATTER HOW HARD YOU TRY, TAIGA HAS-
I'LL START...

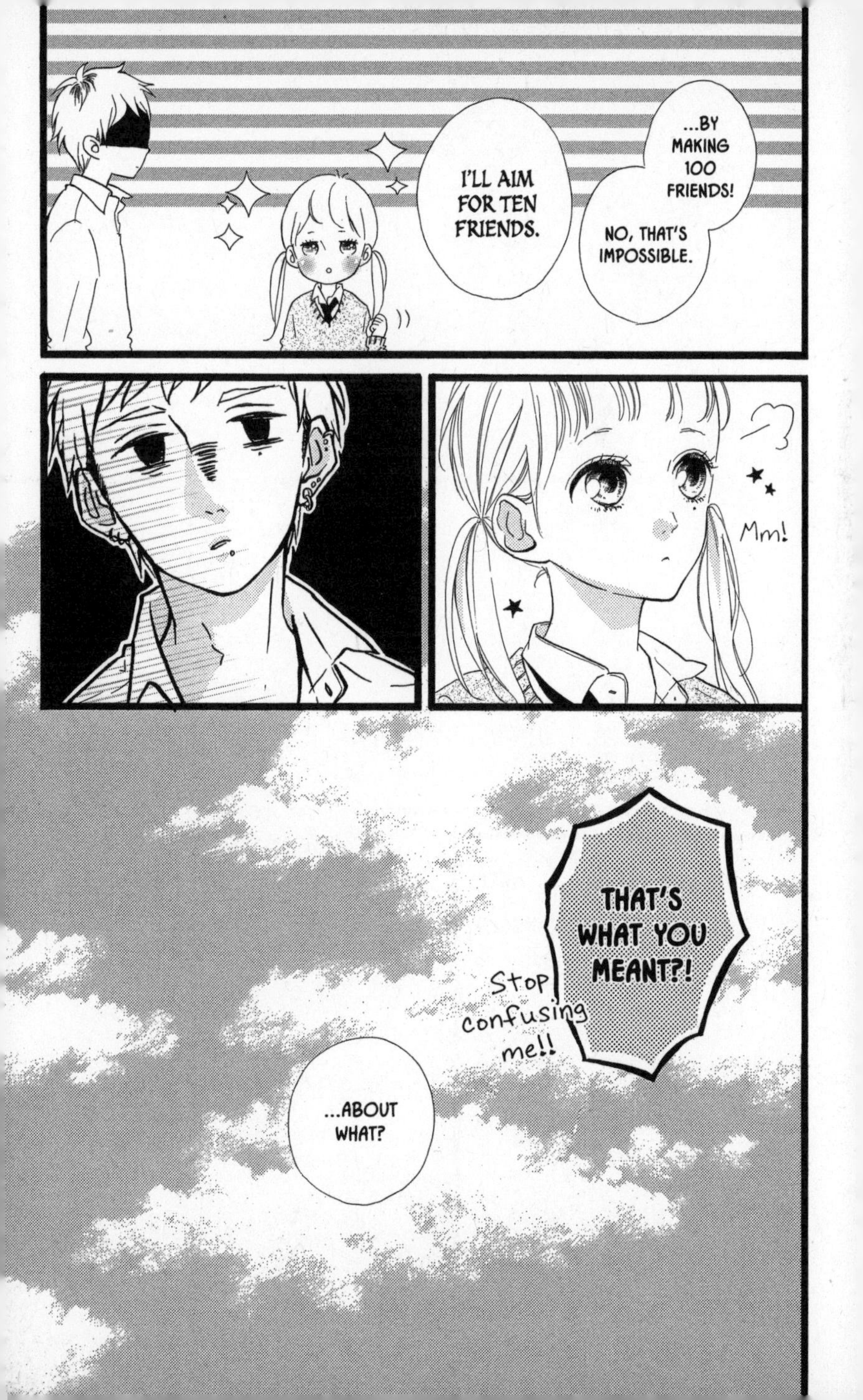
...BY MAKING 100 FRIENDS!
NO, THAT'S IMPOSSIBLE.
I'LL AIM FOR TEN FRIENDS.
Mm!
THAT'S WHAT YOU MEANT?!
Stop confusing me!!
...ABOUT WHAT?

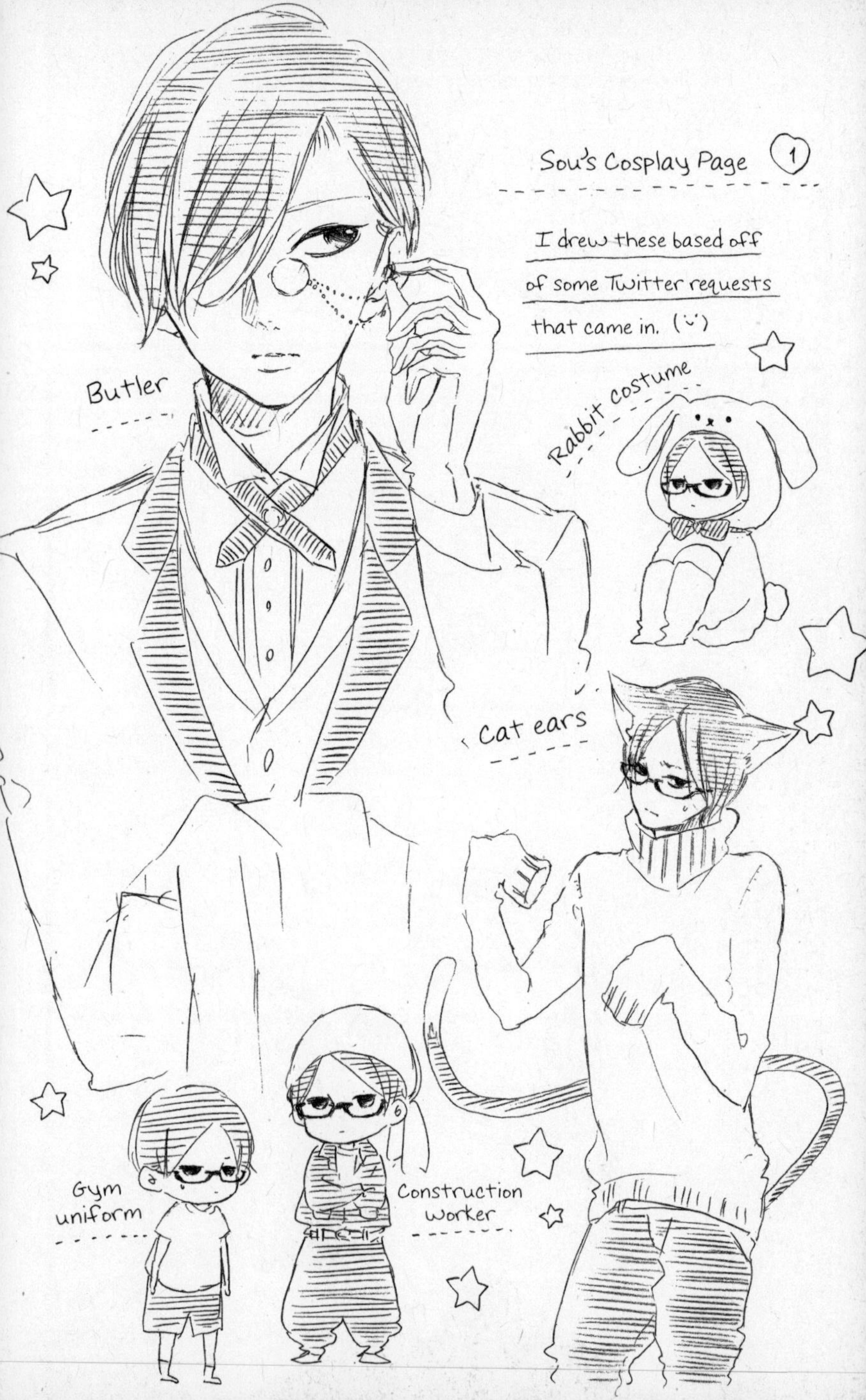
Sou's Cosplay Page 1
I drew these based off of some Twitter requests that came in.
Butler
Rabbit costume
Cat ears
Gym uniform
Construction worker

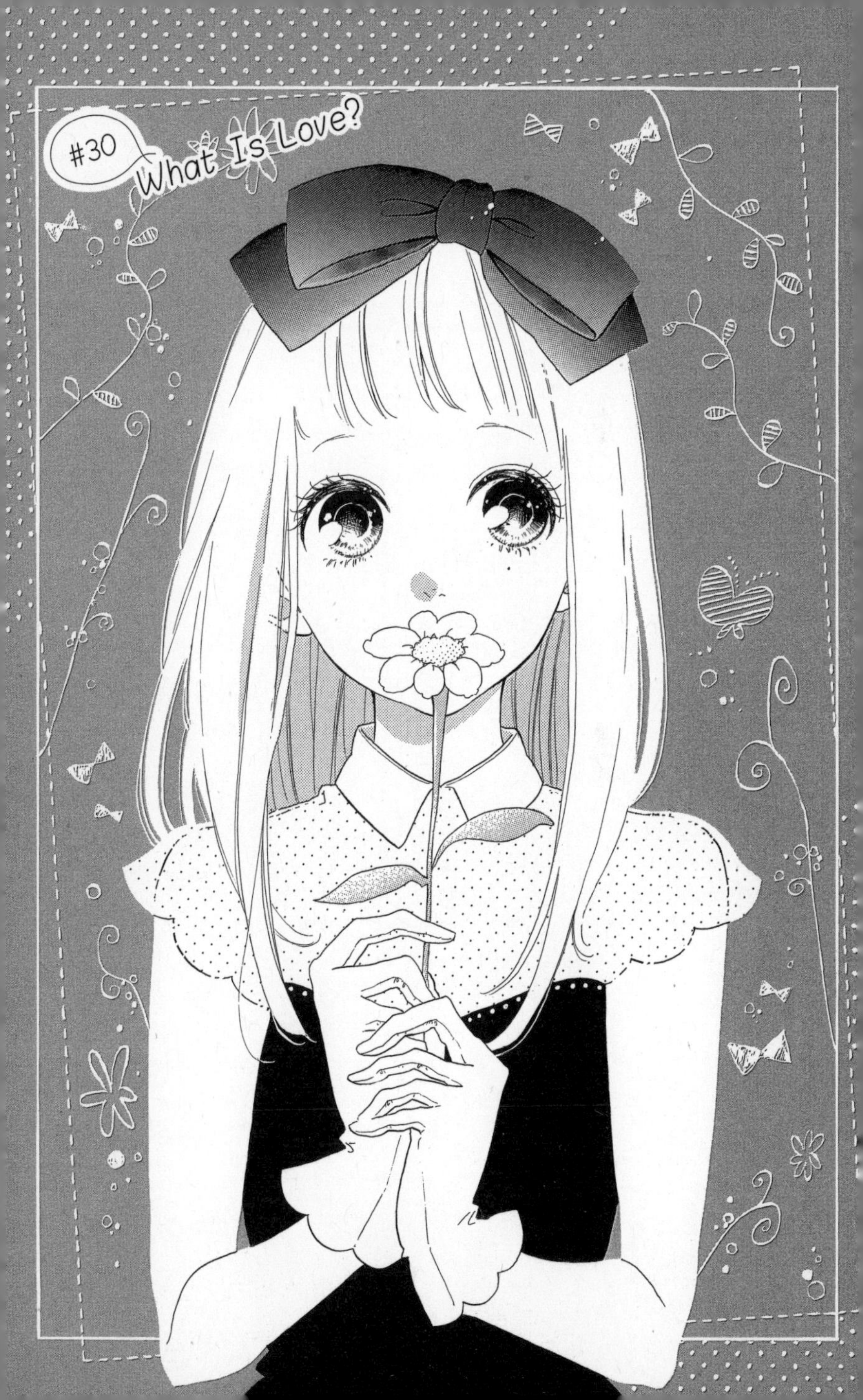
#30
What Is Love?

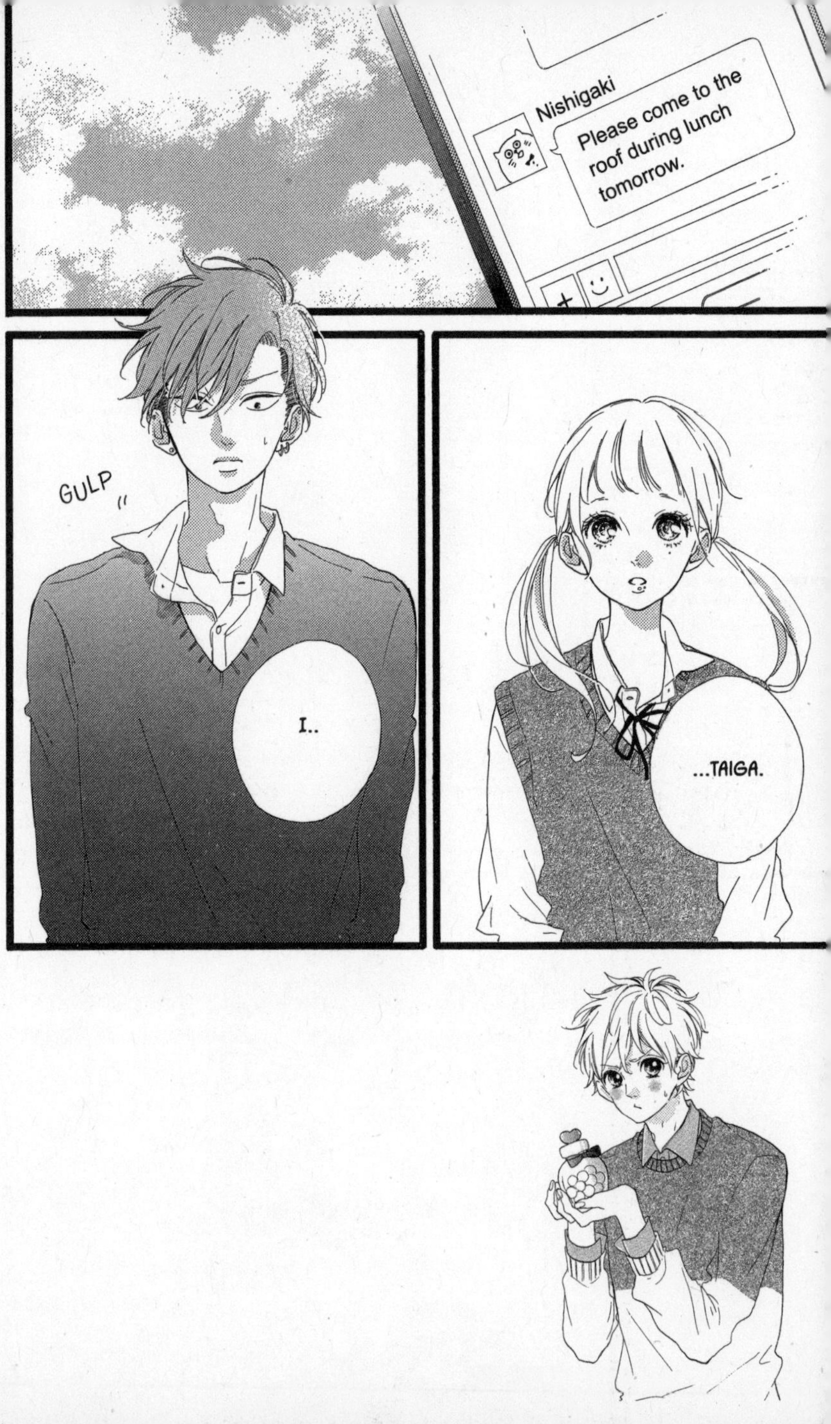
Nishigaki
Please come to the roof during lunch tomorrow.
...TAIGA.
GULP
I..

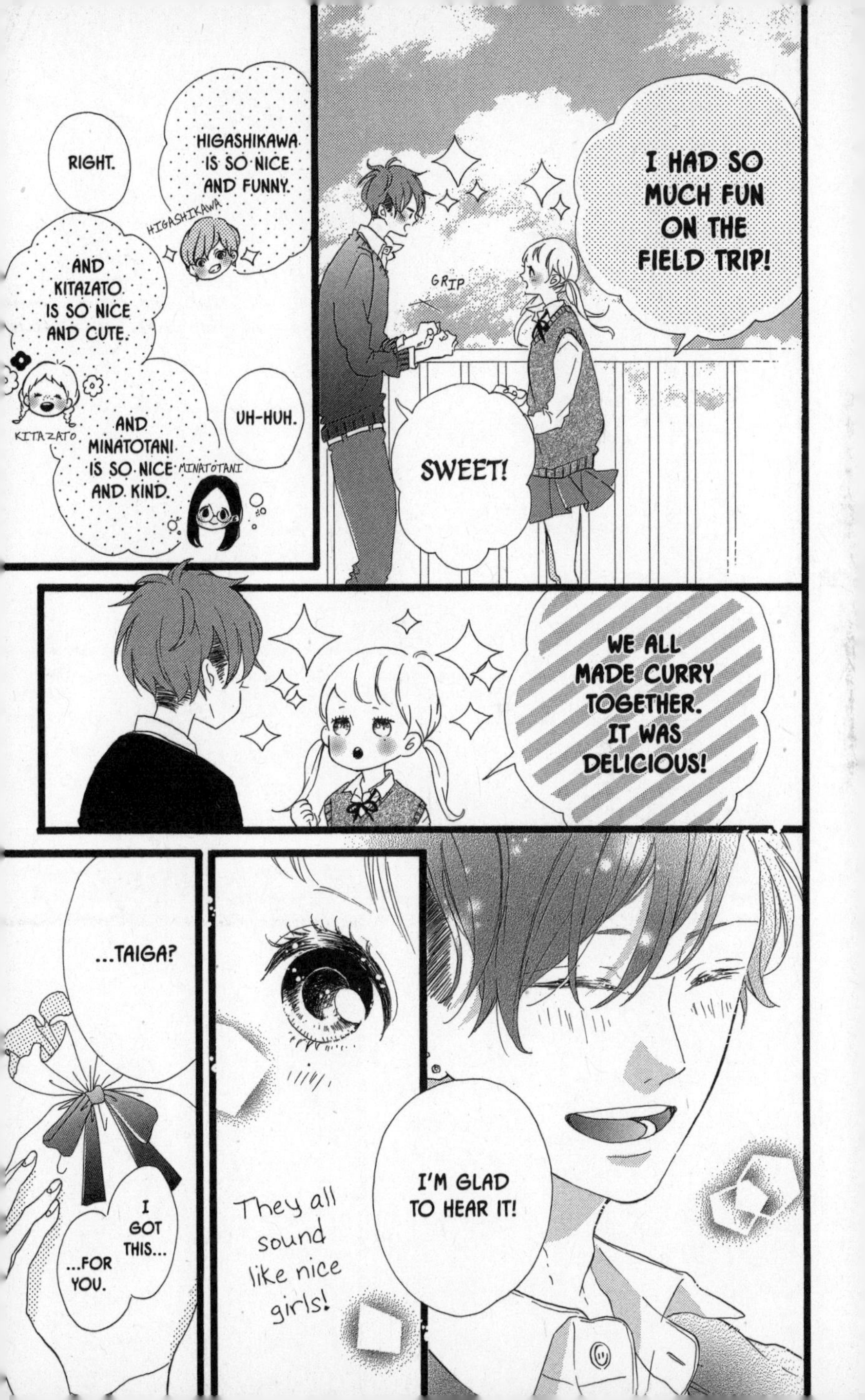
I HAD SO MUCH FUN ON THE FIELD TRIP!
GRIP
SWEET!
HIGASHIKAWA IS SO NICE AND FUNNY.
HIGASHIKAWA
RIGHT.
AND KITAZATO IS SO NICE AND CUTE.
KITAZATO
UH-HUH.
AND MINATOTANI IS SO NICE AND KIND.
MINATOTANI
WE ALL MADE CURRY TOGETHER. IT WAS DELICIOUS!
I'M GLAD TO HEAR IT!
They all sound like nice girls!
...TAIGA?
I GOT THIS...
...FOR YOU.

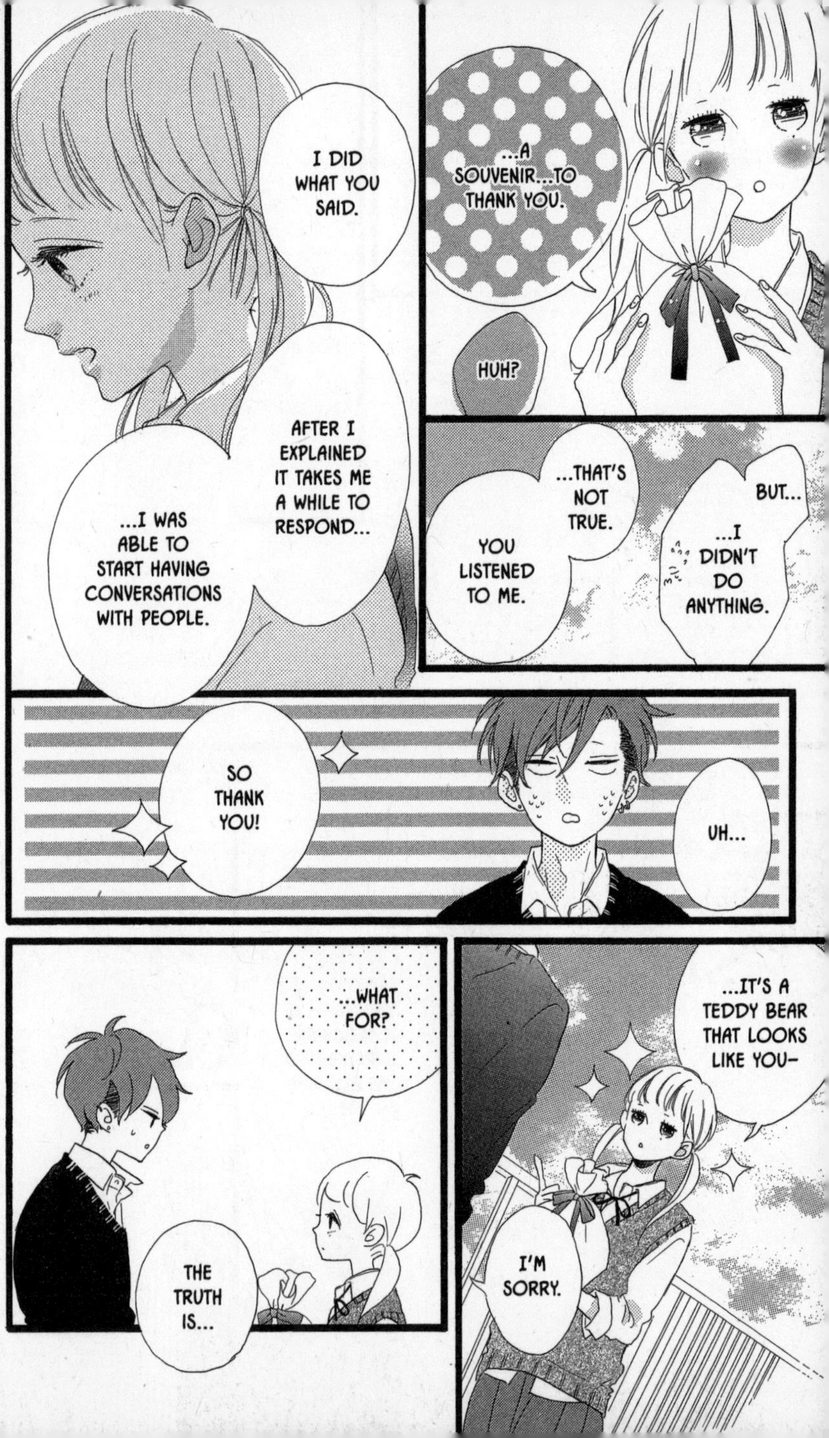
...A SOUVENIR...TO THANK YOU.
HUH?
BUT... ...I DIDN'T DO ANYTHING.
...THAT'S NOT TRUE.
YOU LISTENED TO ME.
I DID WHAT YOU SAID.
AFTER I EXPLAINED IT TAKES ME A WHILE TO RESPOND...
...I WAS ABLE TO START HAVING CONVERSATIONS WITH PEOPLE.
SO THANK YOU!
UH...
...IT'S A TEDDY BEAR THAT LOOKS LIKE YOU—
I'M SORRY.
...WHAT FOR?
THE TRUTH IS...

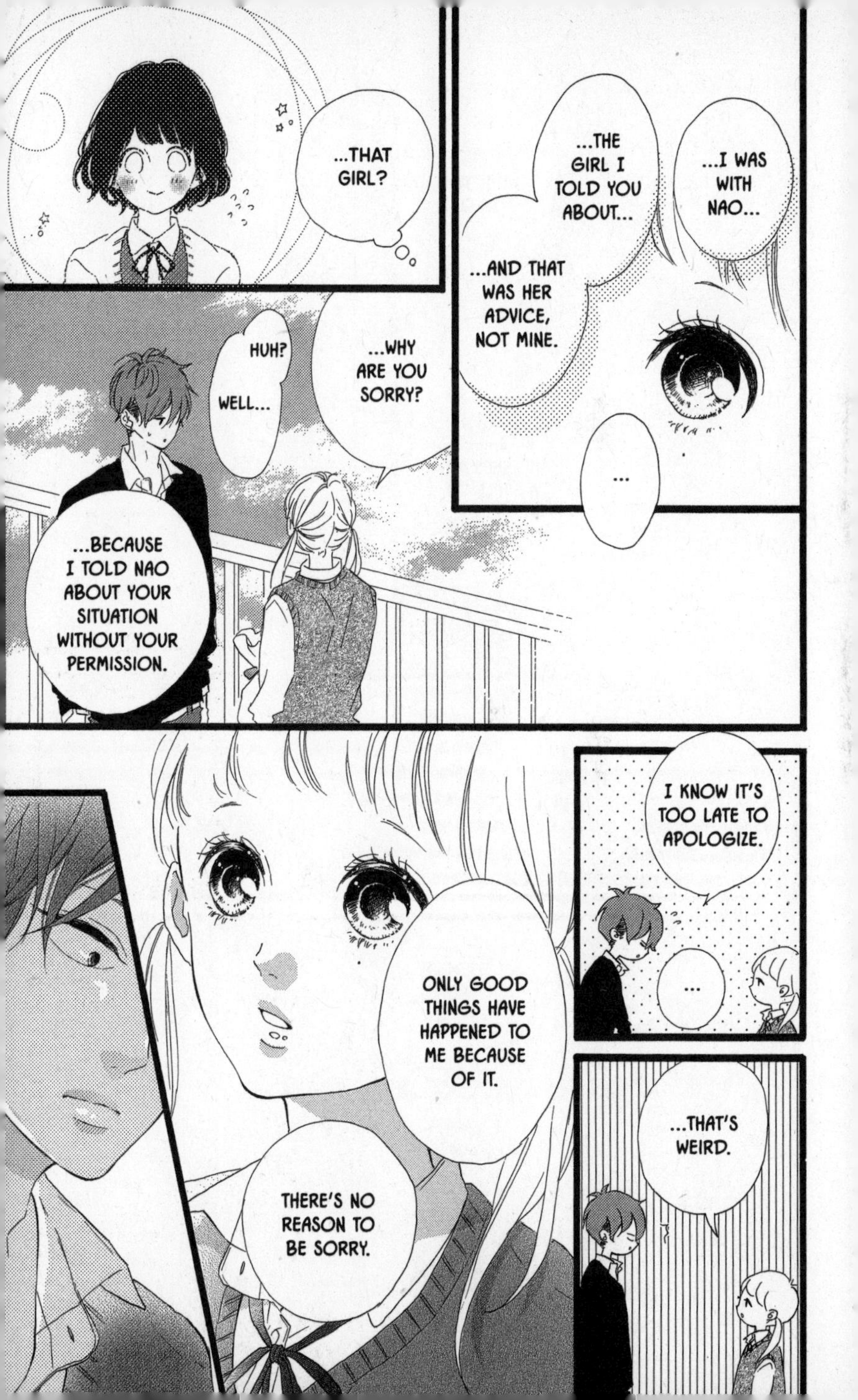
...I WAS WITH NAO...
...THE GIRL I TOLD YOU ABOUT...
...AND THAT WAS HER ADVICE, NOT MINE.
...
...THAT GIRL?
...WHY ARE YOU SORRY?
HUH? WELL...
...BECAUSE I TOLD NAO ABOUT YOUR SITUATION WITHOUT YOUR PERMISSION.
I KNOW IT'S TOO LATE TO APOLOGIZE.
...
...THAT'S WEIRD.
ONLY GOOD THINGS HAVE HAPPENED TO ME BECAUSE OF IT.
THERE'S NO REASON TO BE SORRY.

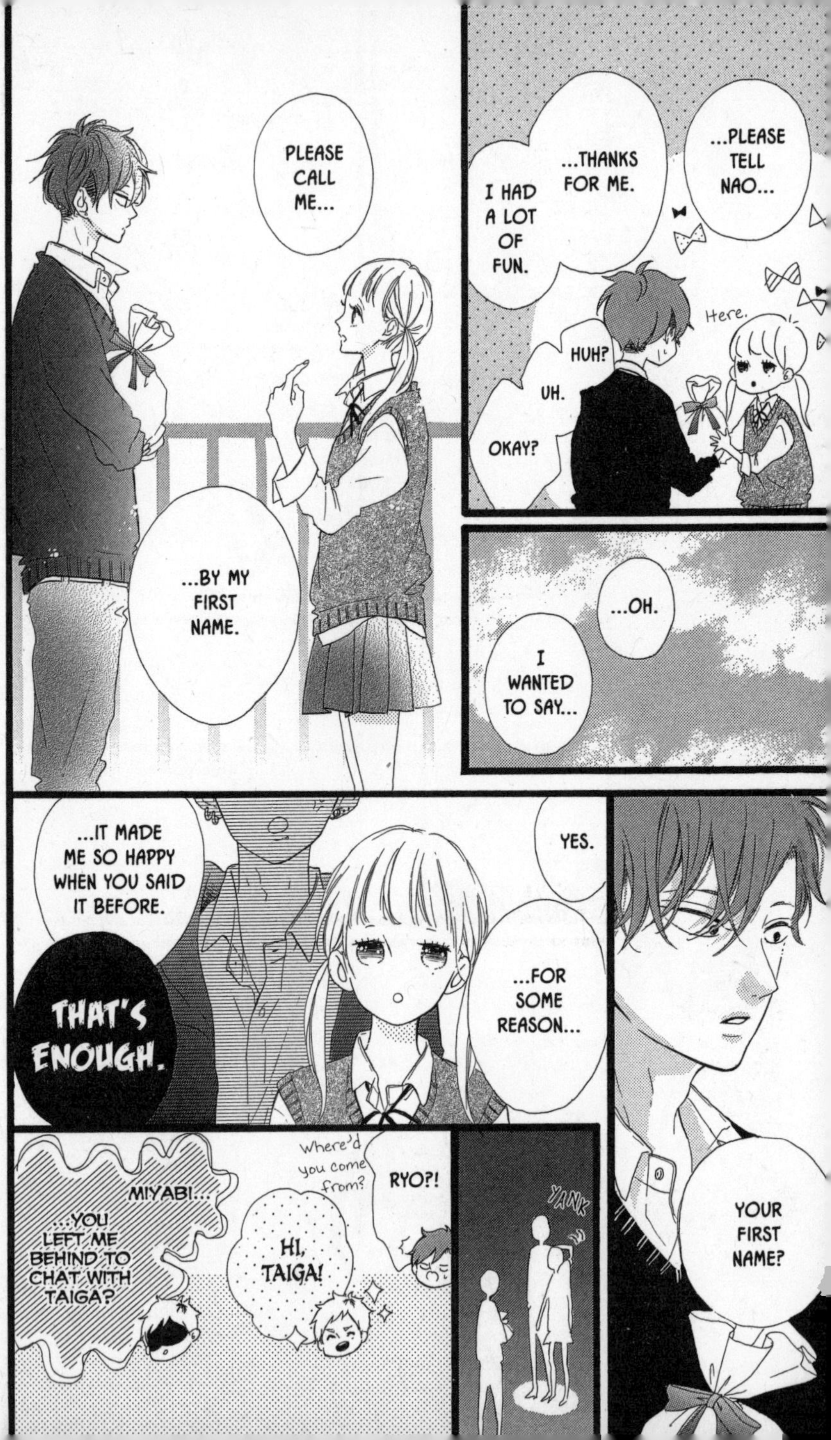
...PLEASE TELL NAO...
...THANKS FOR ME.
I HAD A LOT OF FUN.
Here.
HUH?
UH.
OKAY?
...OH.
I WANTED TO SAY...
PLEASE CALL ME...
...BY MY FIRST NAME.
YOUR FIRST NAME?
YES.
...FOR SOME REASON...
...IT MADE ME SO HAPPY WHEN YOU SAID IT BEFORE.
THAT'S ENOUGH.
YANK
RYO?!
Where'd you come from?
HI, TAIGA!
MIYABI...
...YOU LEFT ME BEHIND TO CHAT WITH TAIGA?

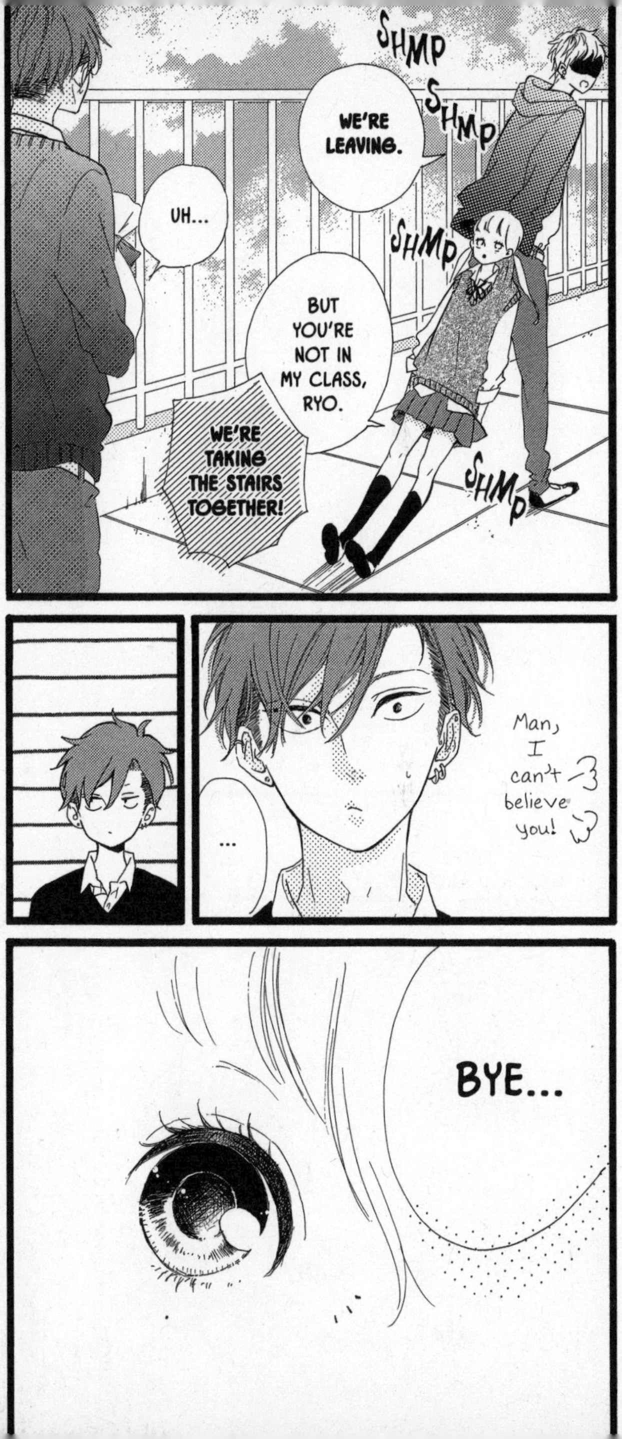
SHMP
SHMP
WE'RE LEAVING.
SHMP
BUT YOU'RE NOT IN MY CLASS, RYO.
UH...
WE'RE TAKING THE STAIRS TOGETHER!
SHMP
...
Man, I can't believe you!
BYE...
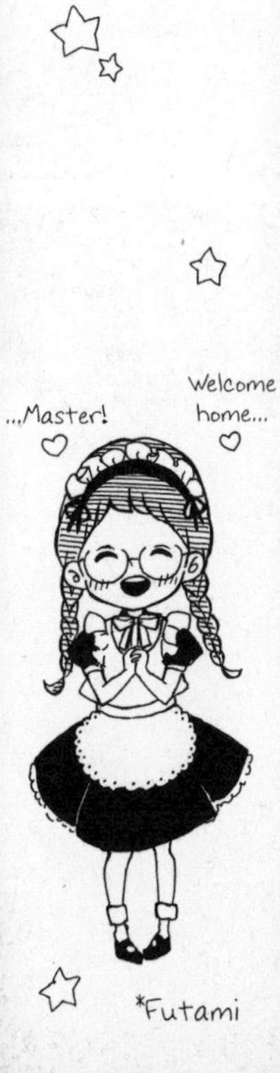
Welcome home...
...Master!
*Futami

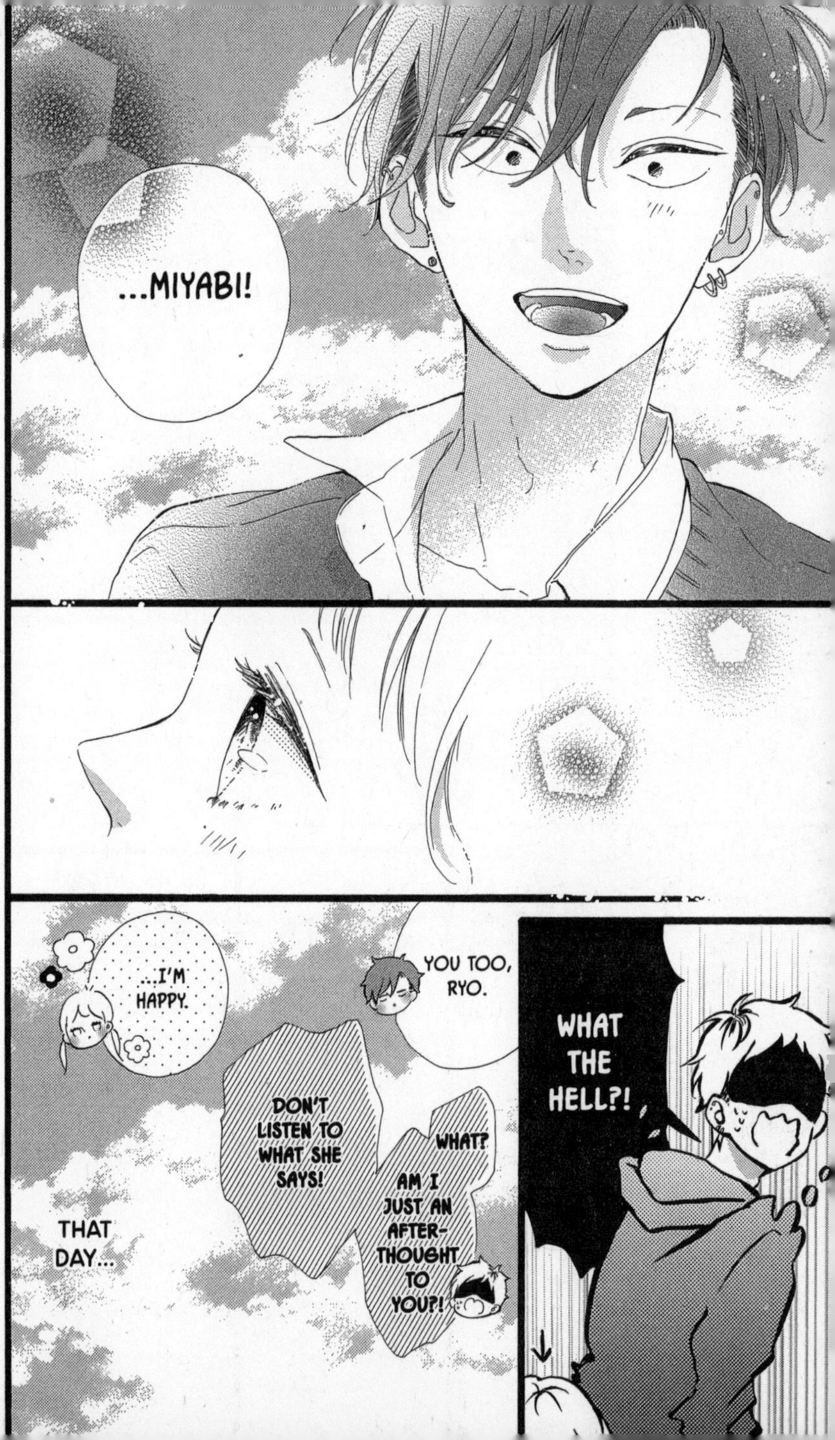
...MIYABI!
WHAT THE HELL?!
YOU TOO, RYO.
...I'M HAPPY.
WHAT? AM I JUST AN AFTER-THOUGHT TO YOU?!
DON'T LISTEN TO WHAT SHE SAYS!
THAT DAY...

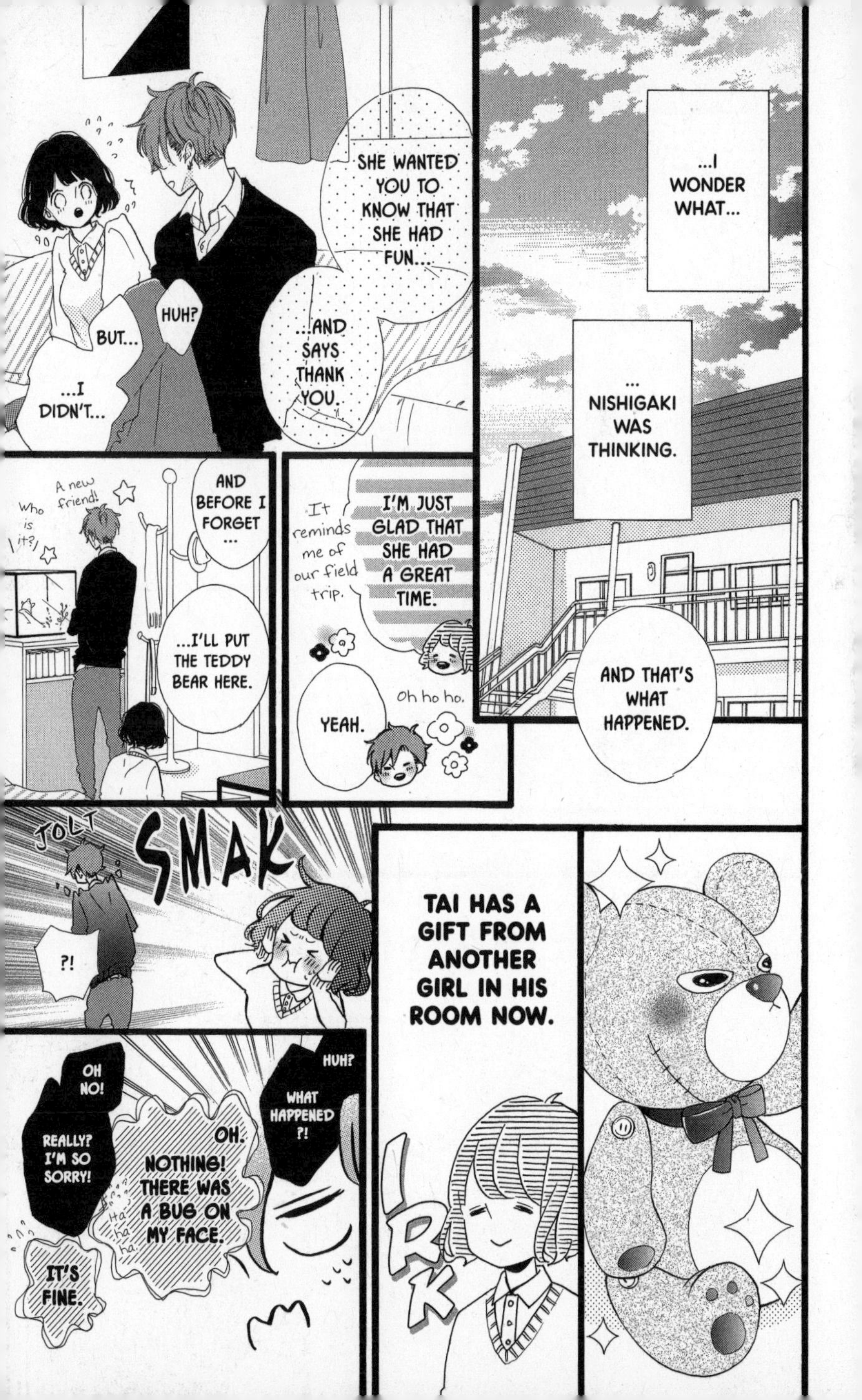
...I WONDER WHAT...
...NISHIGAKI WAS THINKING.
AND THAT'S WHAT HAPPENED.
SHE WANTED YOU TO KNOW THAT SHE HAD FUN...
...AND SAYS THANK YOU.
HUH?
BUT...
...I DIDN'T...
I'M JUST GLAD THAT SHE HAD A GREAT TIME.
It reminds me of our field trip.
Oh ho ho.
YEAH.
A new friend!
Who is it?!
AND BEFORE I FORGET...
...I'LL PUT THE TEDDY BEAR HERE.
TAI HAS A GIFT FROM ANOTHER GIRL IN HIS ROOM NOW.
IRK
JOLT
SMAK
?!
HUH?
WHAT HAPPENED?!
OH.
NOTHING! THERE WAS A BUG ON MY FACE.
Ha ha ha.
OH NO!
REALLY? I'M SO SORRY!
IT'S FINE.

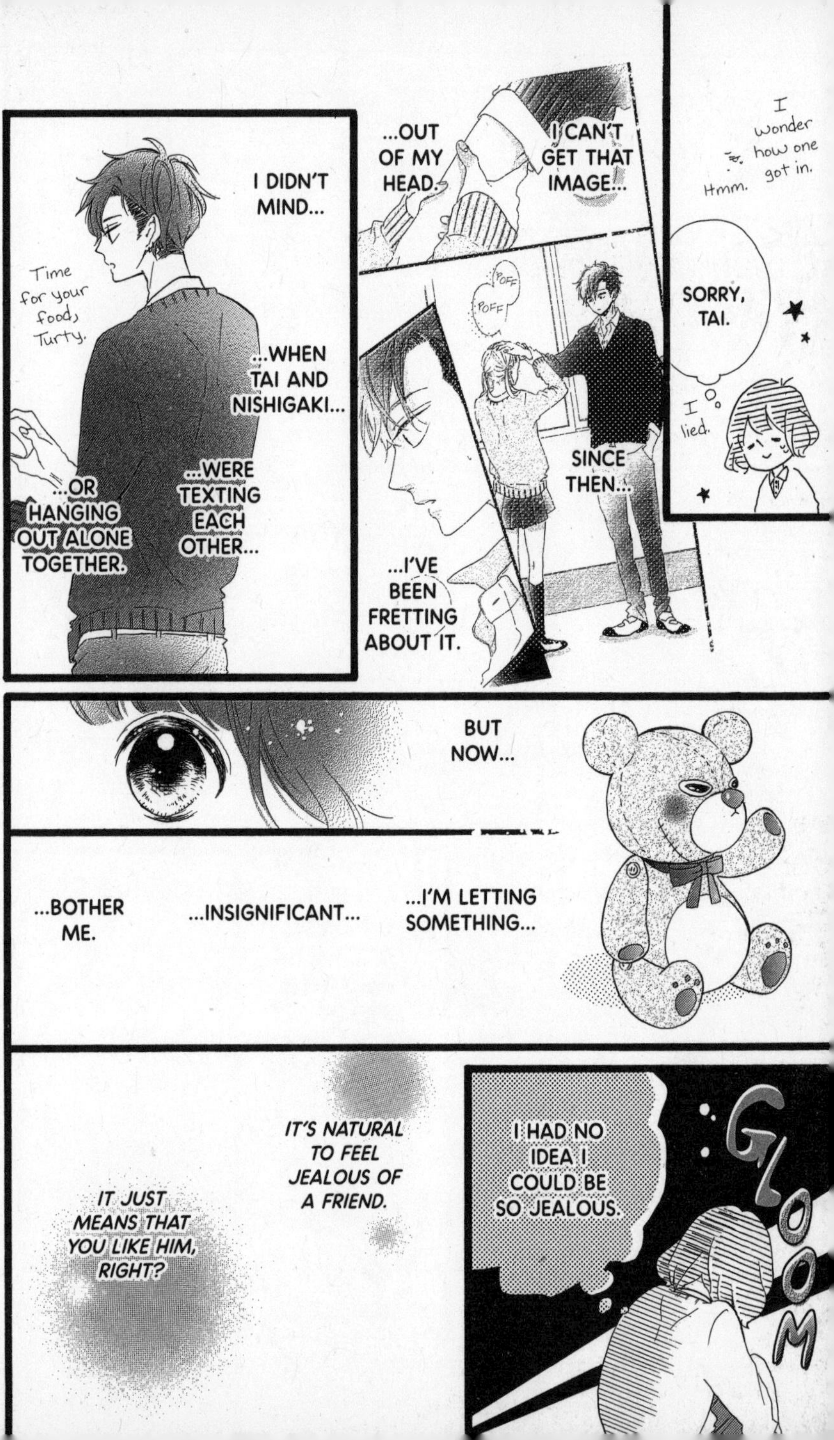
I wonder how one got in.
Hmm.
SORRY, TAI.
I lied.
I CAN'T GET THAT IMAGE...
...OUT OF MY HEAD.
POFF
POFF
SINCE THEN...
...I'VE BEEN FRETTING ABOUT IT.
I DIDN'T MIND...
...WHEN TAI AND NISHIGAKI...
...WERE TEXTING EACH OTHER...
...OR HANGING OUT ALONE TOGETHER.
Time for your food, Turty.
BUT NOW...
...I'M LETTING SOMETHING...
...INSIGNIFICANT...
...BOTHER ME.
GLOOM
I HAD NO IDEA I COULD BE SO JEALOUS.
IT'S NATURAL TO FEEL JEALOUS OF A FRIEND.
IT JUST MEANS THAT YOU LIKE HIM, RIGHT?

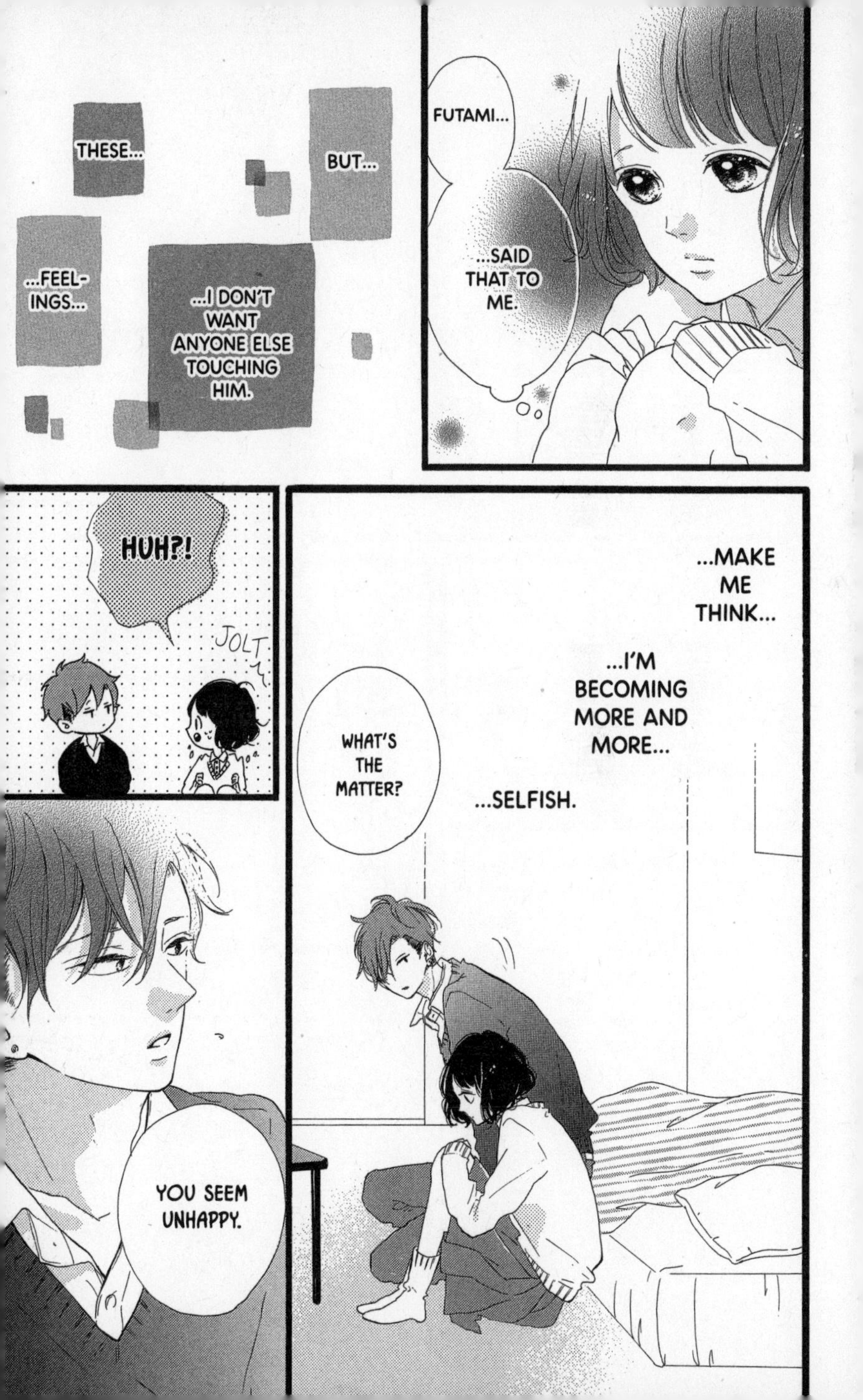
FUTAMI...
...SAID THAT TO ME.
BUT...
...I DON'T WANT ANYONE ELSE TOUCHING HIM.
THESE...
...FEEL-INGS...
...MAKE ME THINK...
...I'M BECOMING MORE AND MORE...
...SELFISH.
WHAT'S THE MATTER?
HUH?!
JOLT
YOU SEEM UNHAPPY.

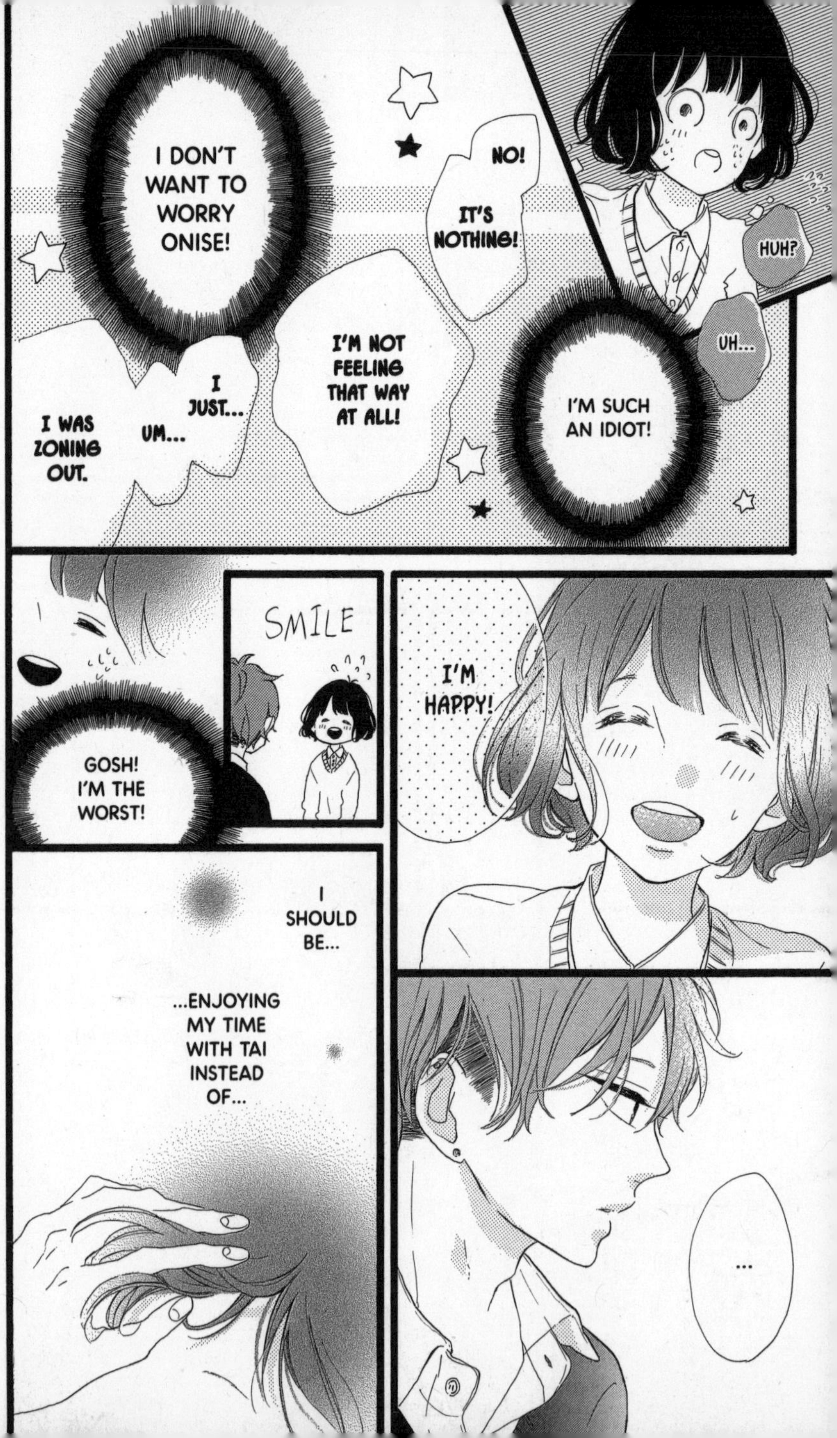
HUH?
UH...
NO!
IT'S NOTHING!
I'M SUCH AN IDIOT!
I DON'T WANT TO WORRY ONISE!
I'M NOT FEELING THAT WAY AT ALL!
I JUST...
UM...
I WAS ZONING OUT.
I'M HAPPY!
SMILE
GOSH! I'M THE WORST!
...
I SHOULD BE...
...ENJOYING MY TIME WITH TAI INSTEAD OF...

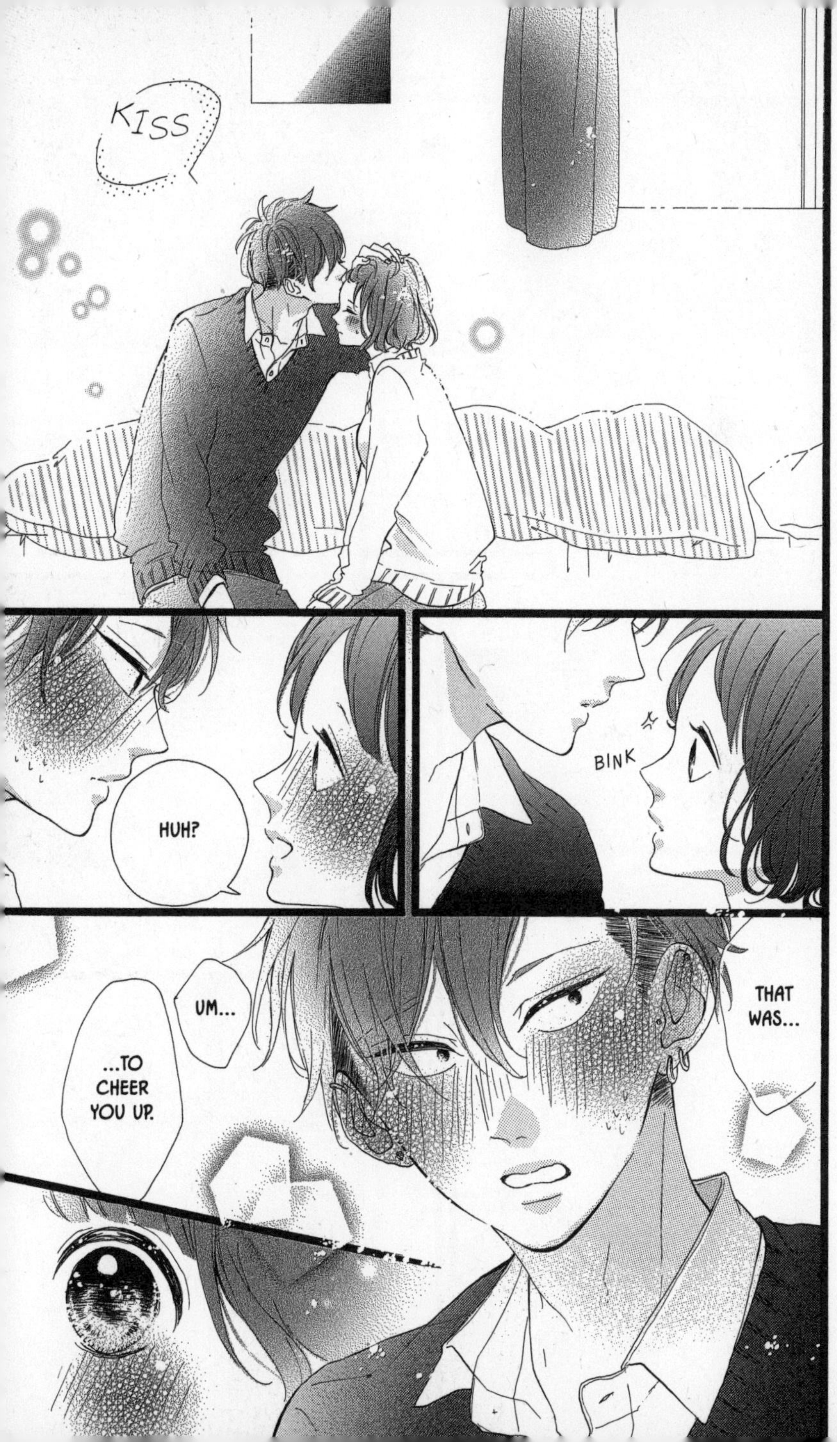
KISS
BINK
HUH?
THAT WAS...
UM...
...TO CHEER YOU UP.

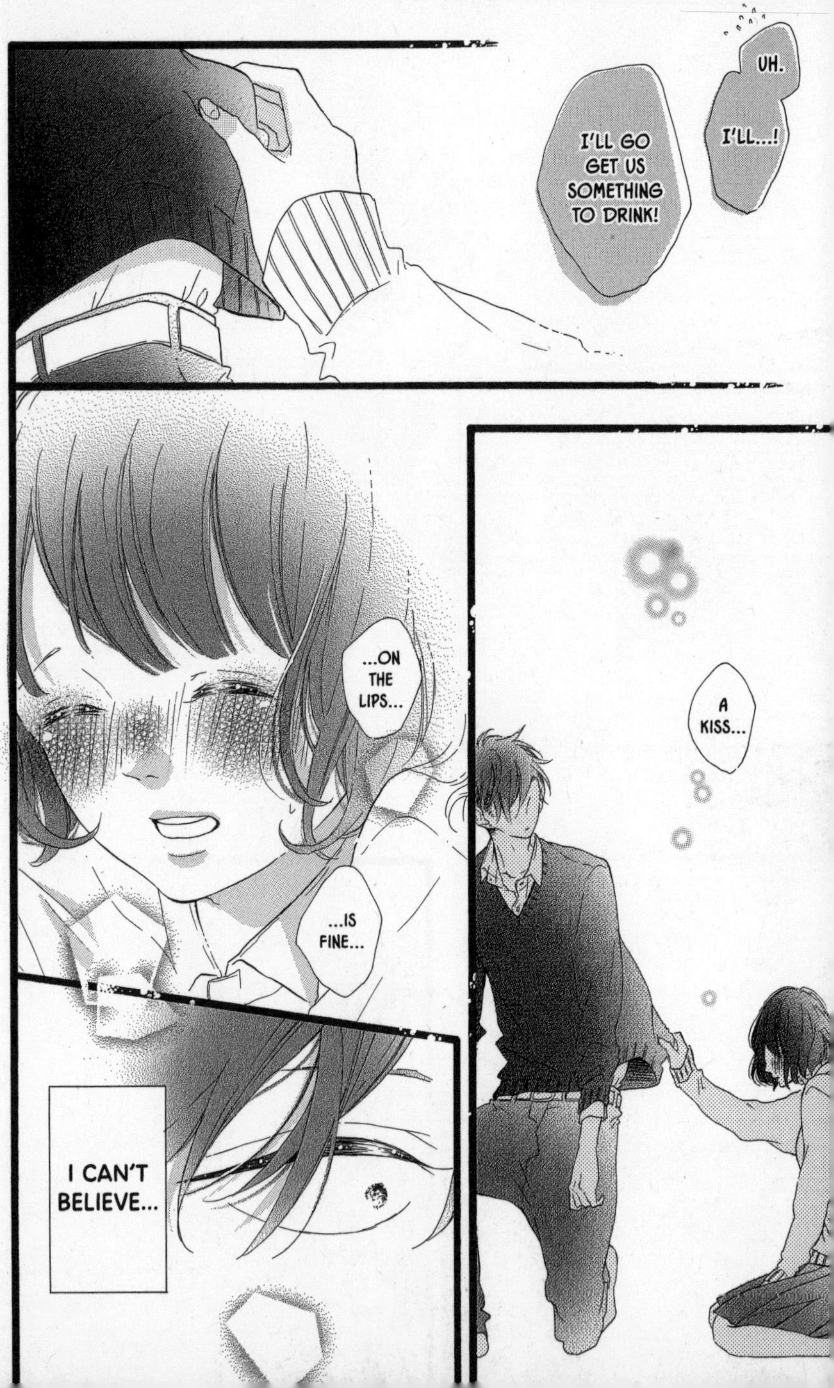
UH.
I'LL...!
I'LL GO GET US SOMETHING TO DRINK!
A KISS...
...ON THE LIPS...
...IS FINE...
I CAN'T BELIEVE...

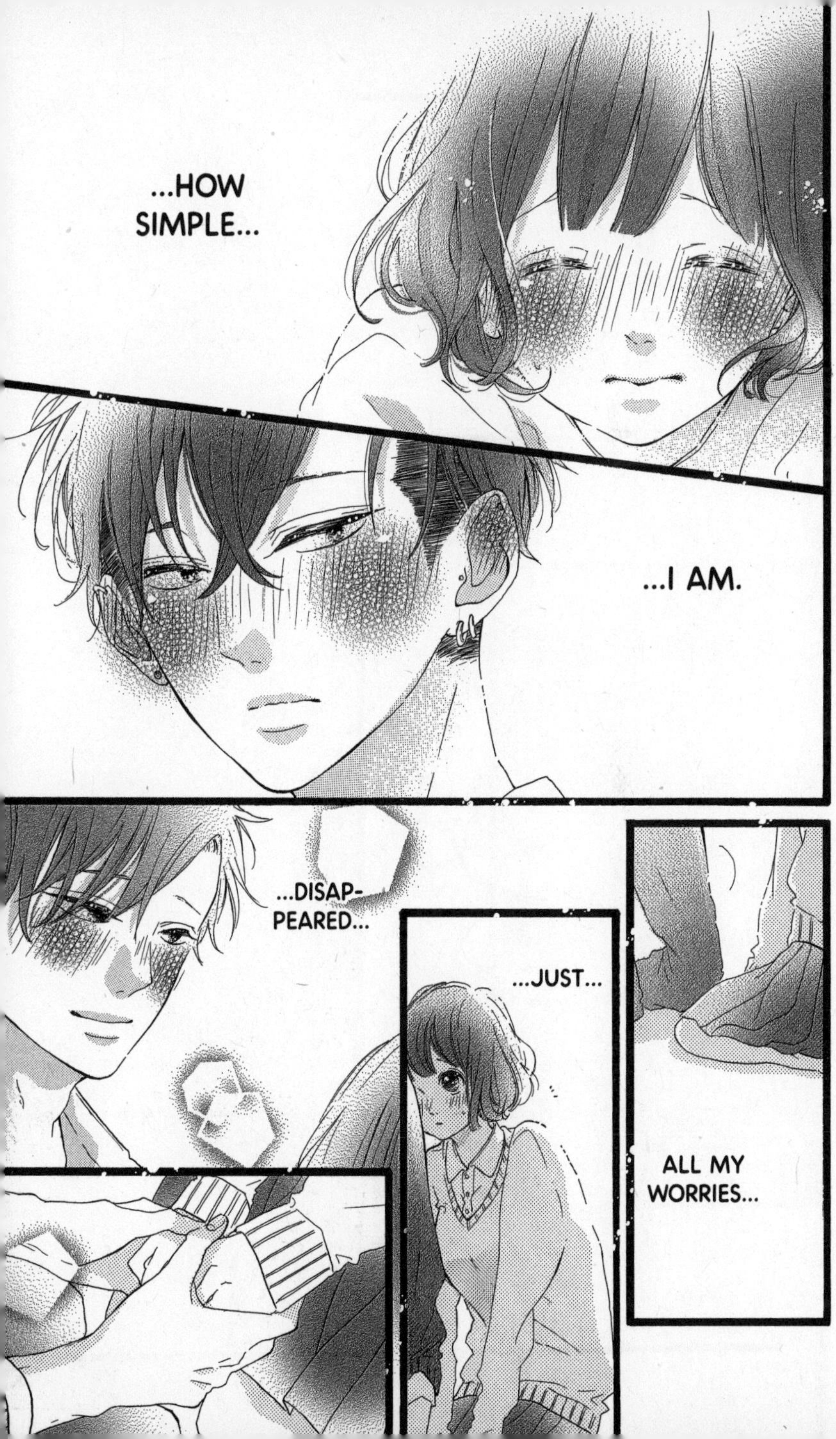
...HOW SIMPLE...
...I AM.
ALL MY WORRIES...
...JUST...
...DISAP-PEARED...

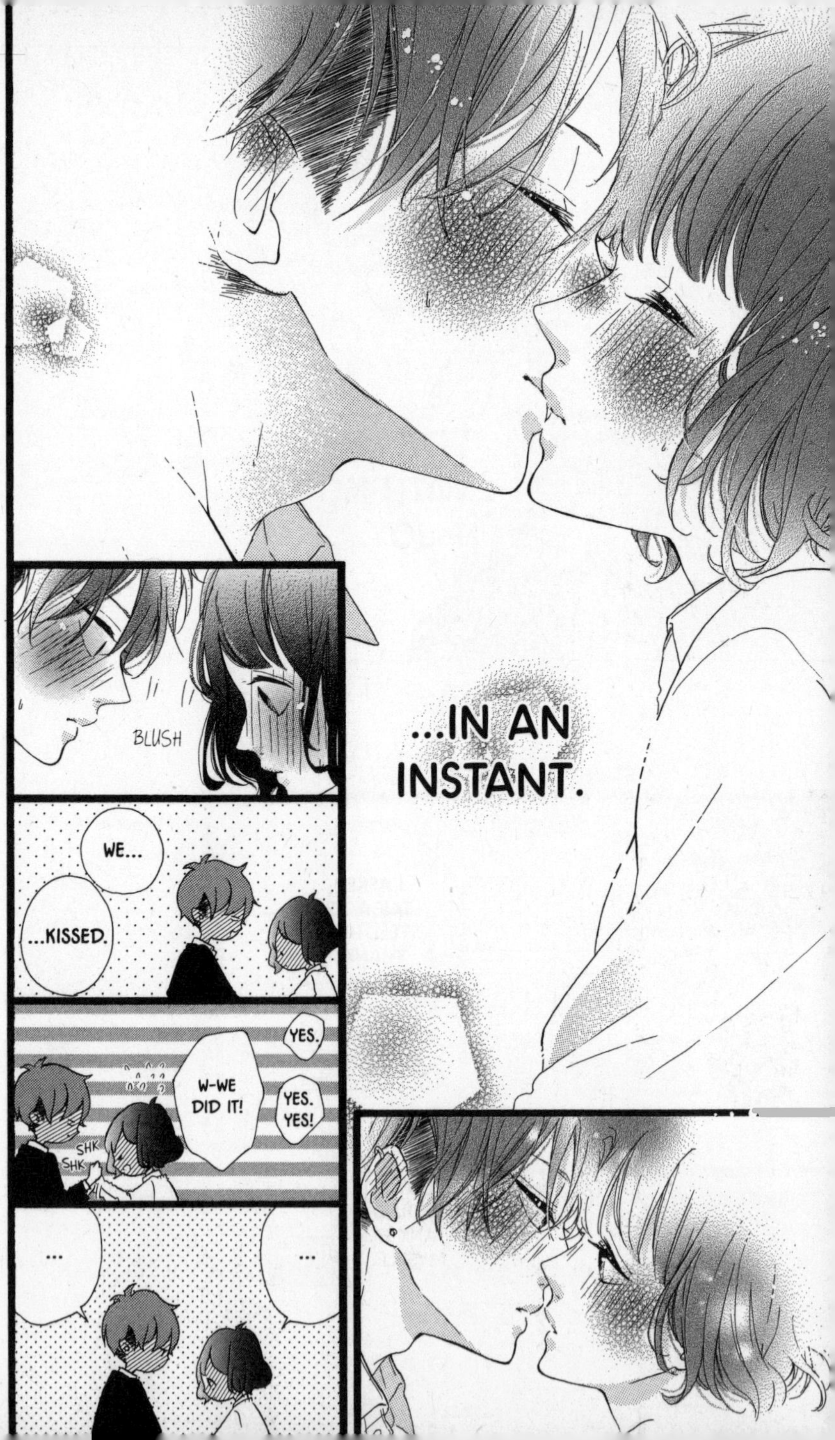

...IN AN INSTANT.
BLUSH
WE...
...KISSED.
YES.
YES. YES!
W-WE DID IT!
SHK SHK
...
...

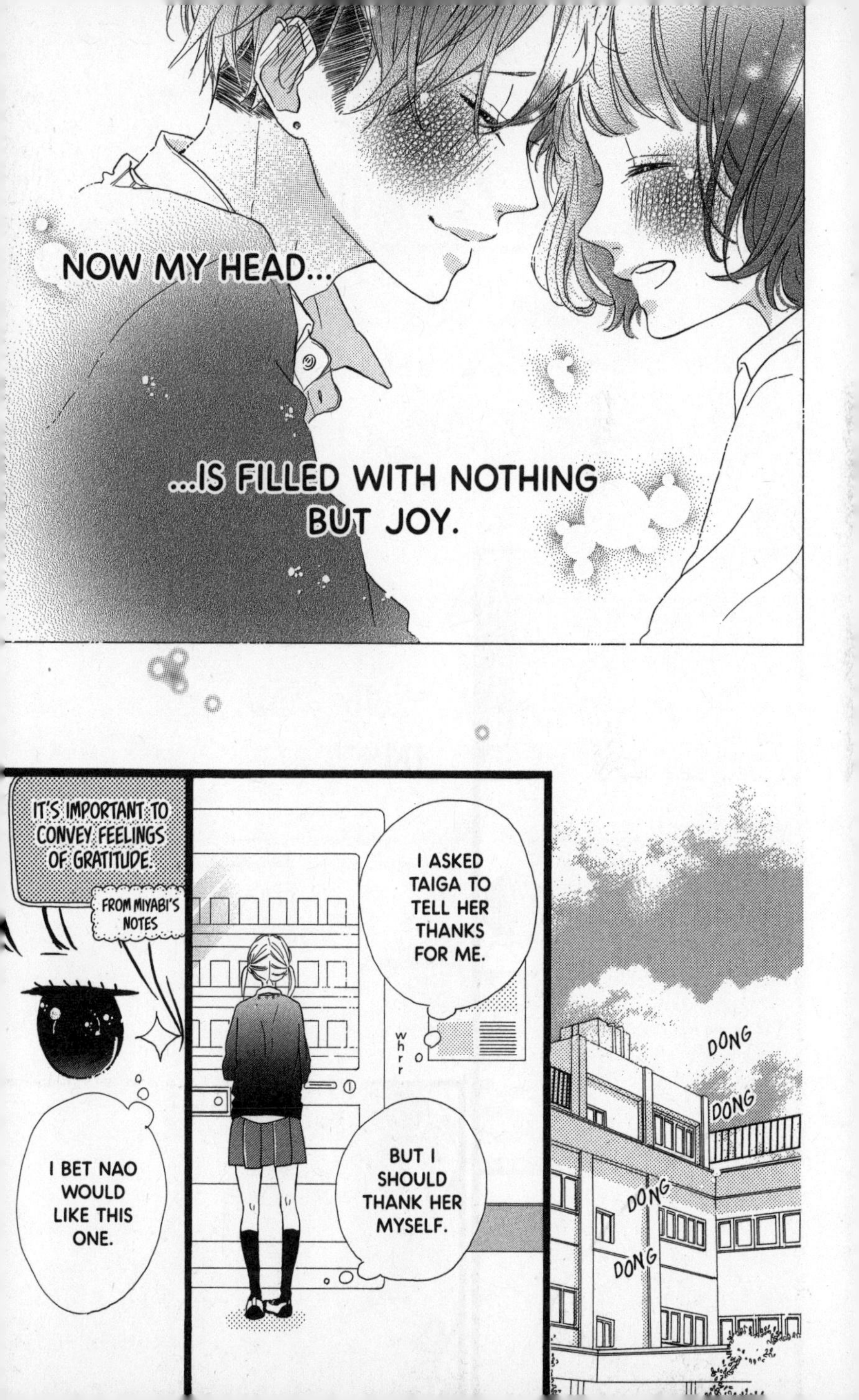
NOW MY HEAD...
...IS FILLED WITH NOTHING BUT JOY.
DONG
DONG
DONG
DONG
I ASKED TAIGA TO TELL HER THANKS FOR ME.
BUT I SHOULD THANK HER MYSELF.
whrr
IT'S IMPORTANT TO CONVEY FEELINGS OF GRATITUDE.
FROM MIYABI'S NOTES
I BET NAO WOULD LIKE THIS ONE.

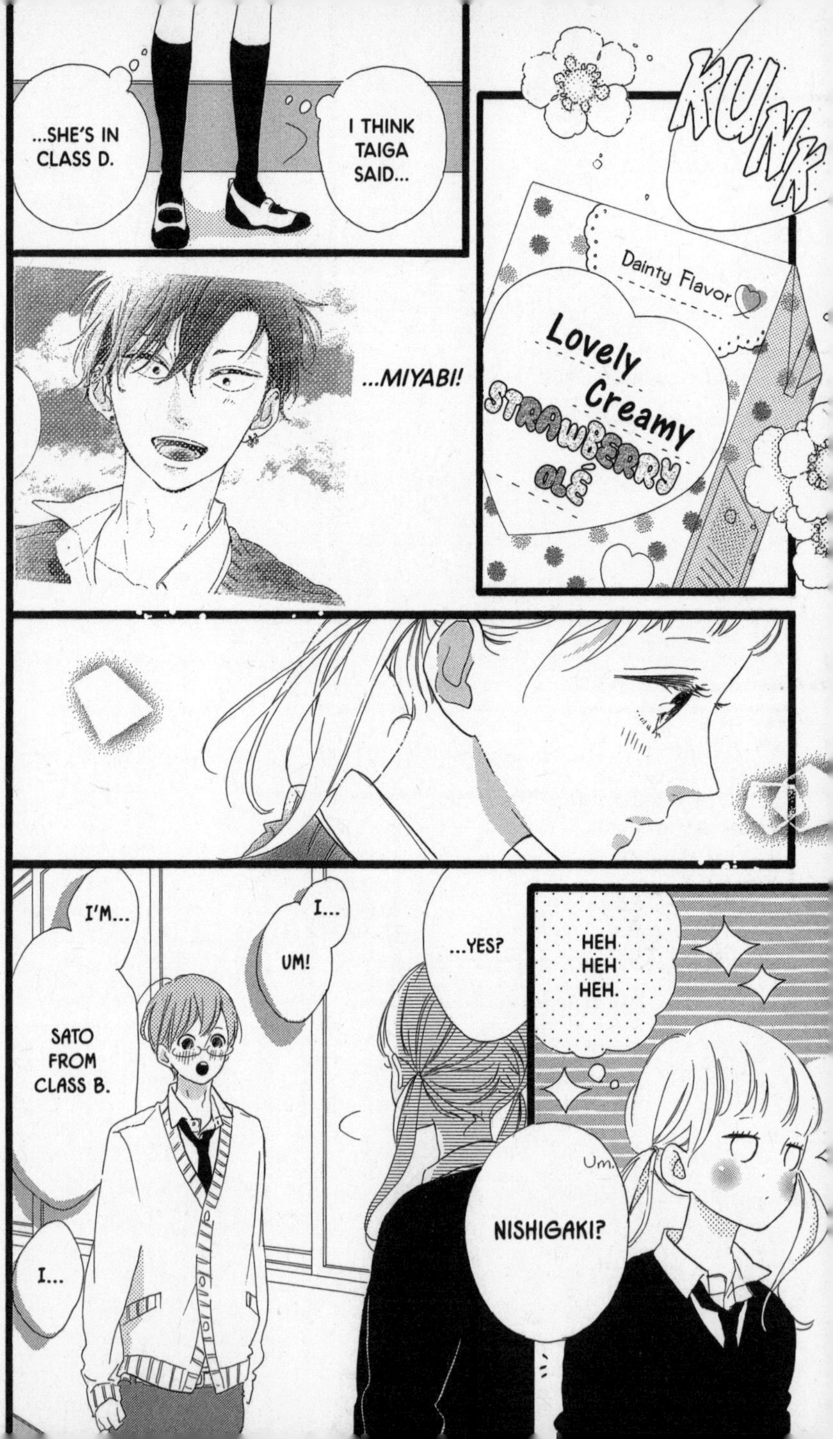
KUNK
Dainty Flavor
Lovely Creamy
STRAWBERRY OLÉ
I THINK TAIGA SAID...
...SHE'S IN CLASS D.
...MIYABI!
HEH HEH HEH.
Um.
NISHIGAKI?
...YES?
I...
UM!
I'M...
SATO FROM CLASS B.
I...

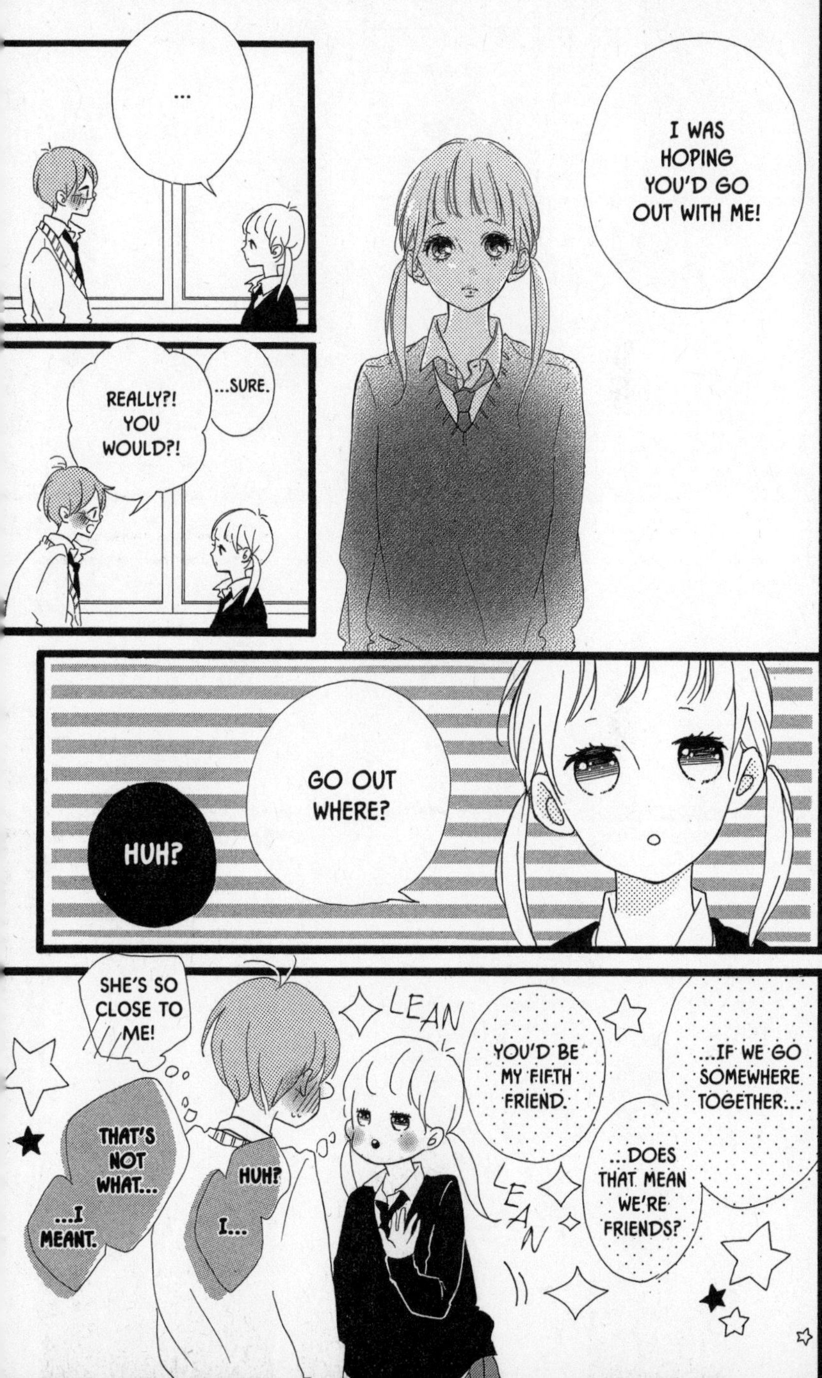
I WAS HOPING YOU'D GO OUT WITH ME!
...
...SURE.
REALLY?! YOU WOULD?!
GO OUT WHERE?
HUH?
...IF WE GO SOMEWHERE TOGETHER...
...DOES THAT MEAN WE'RE FRIENDS?
YOU'D BE MY FIFTH FRIEND.
LEAN
LEAN
SHE'S SO CLOSE TO ME!
HUH?
I...
THAT'S NOT WHAT...
...I MEANT.

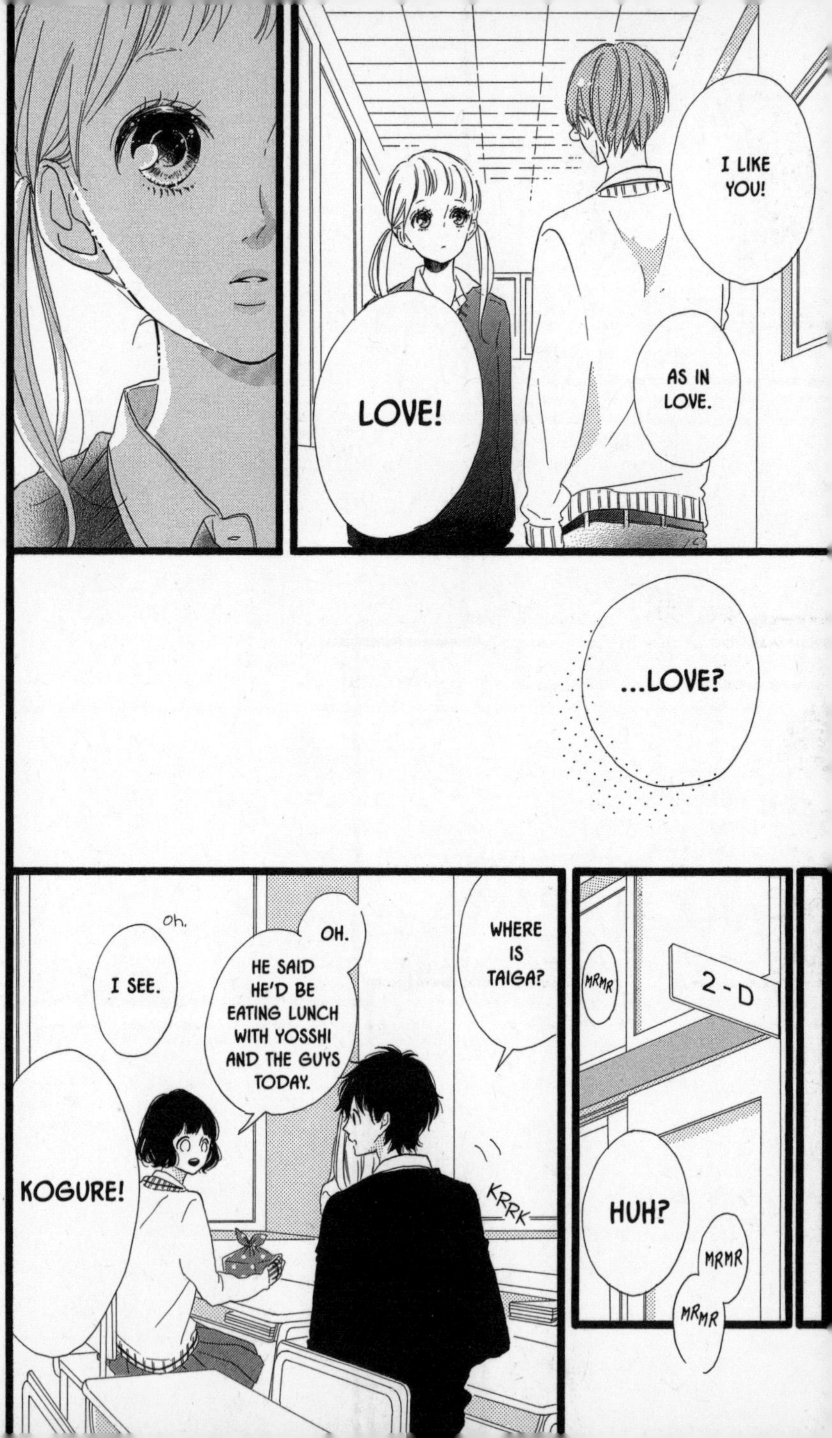
I LIKE YOU!
AS IN LOVE.
LOVE!
...LOVE?
2 - D
MRMR
HUH?
MRMR
MRMR
WHERE IS TAIGA?
OH.
HE SAID HE'D BE EATING LUNCH WITH YOSSHI AND THE GUYS TODAY.
Oh.
I SEE.
KRRK
KOGURE!

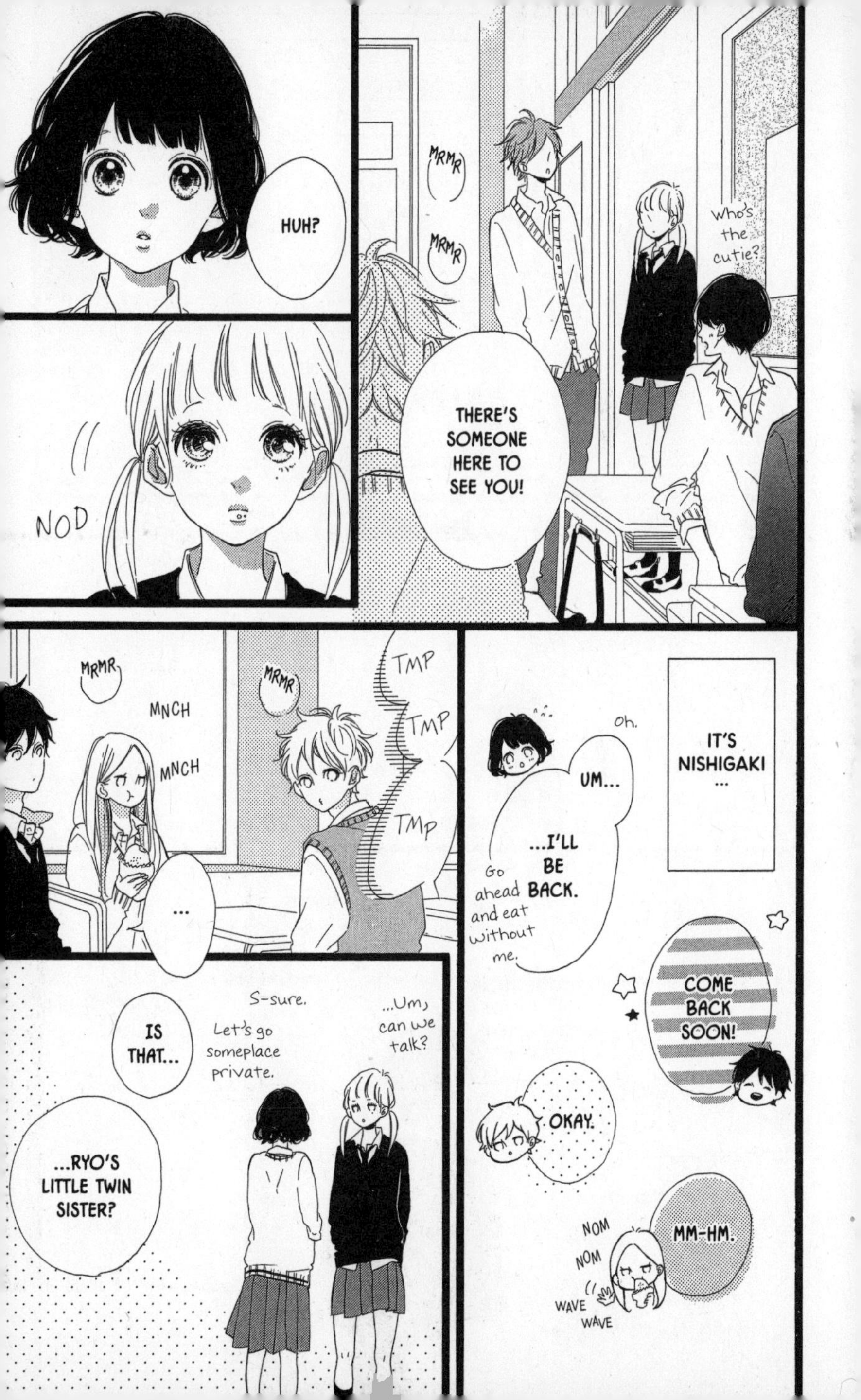
MRMR
MRMR
Who's the cutie?
THERE'S SOMEONE HERE TO SEE YOU!
HUH?
NOD
IT'S NISHIGAKI...
Oh.
UM...
...I'LL BE BACK.
Go ahead and eat without me.
COME BACK SOON!
OKAY.
MM-HM.
NOM NOM
WAVE WAVE
TMP TMP TMP
MRMR
MNCH MNCH
MRMR
...
...Um, can we talk?
S-sure.
Let's go someplace private.
IS THAT...
...RYO'S LITTLE TWIN SISTER?

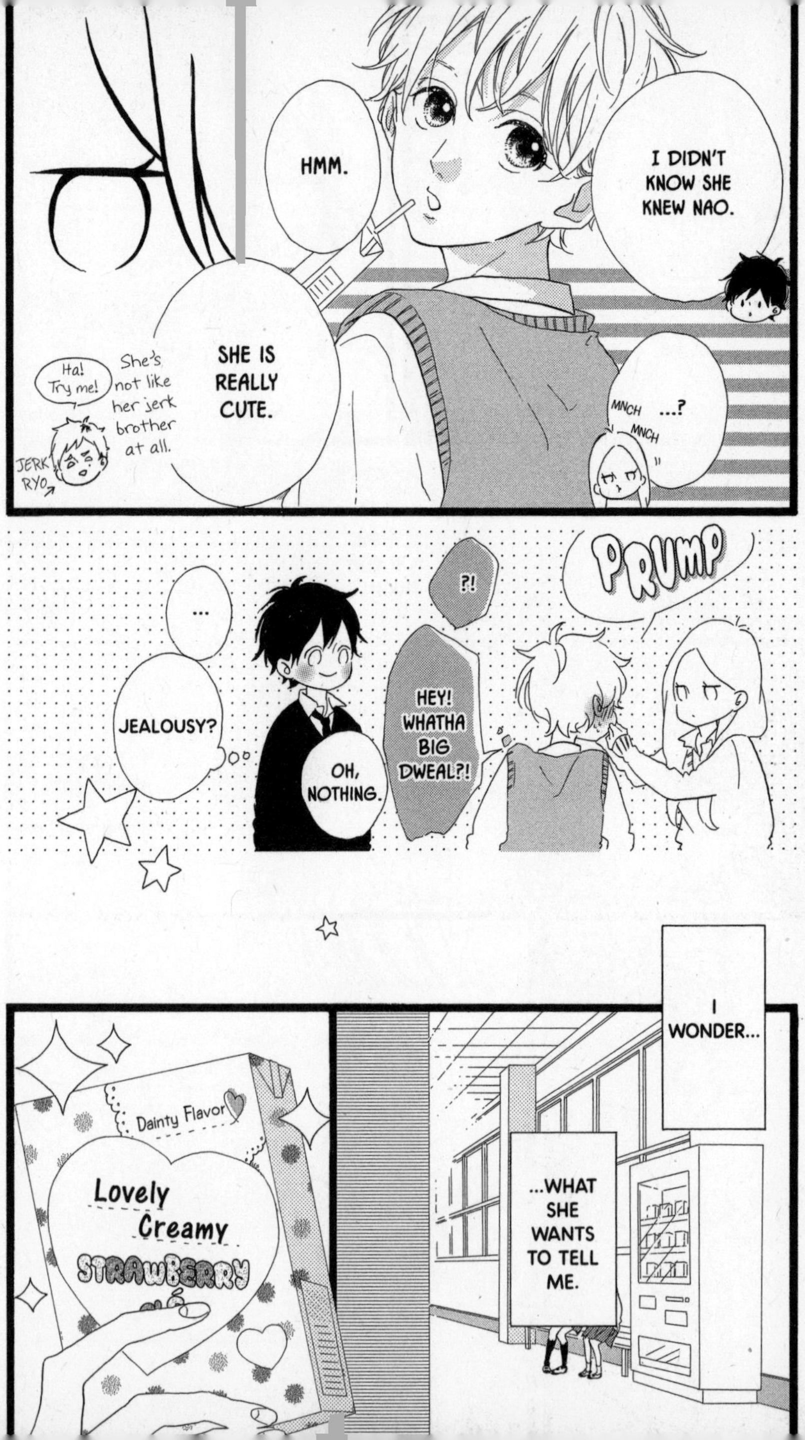
I DIDN'T KNOW SHE KNEW NAO.
HMM.
MNCH MNCH
...?
SHE IS REALLY CUTE.
She's not like her jerk brother at all.
Ha! Try me!
JERK RYO
PRUMP
?!
HEY! WHATHA BIG DWEAL?!
OH, NOTHING.
...
JEALOUSY?
I WONDER...
...WHAT SHE WANTS TO TELL ME.
Dainty Flavor
Lovely Creamy
STRAWBERRY

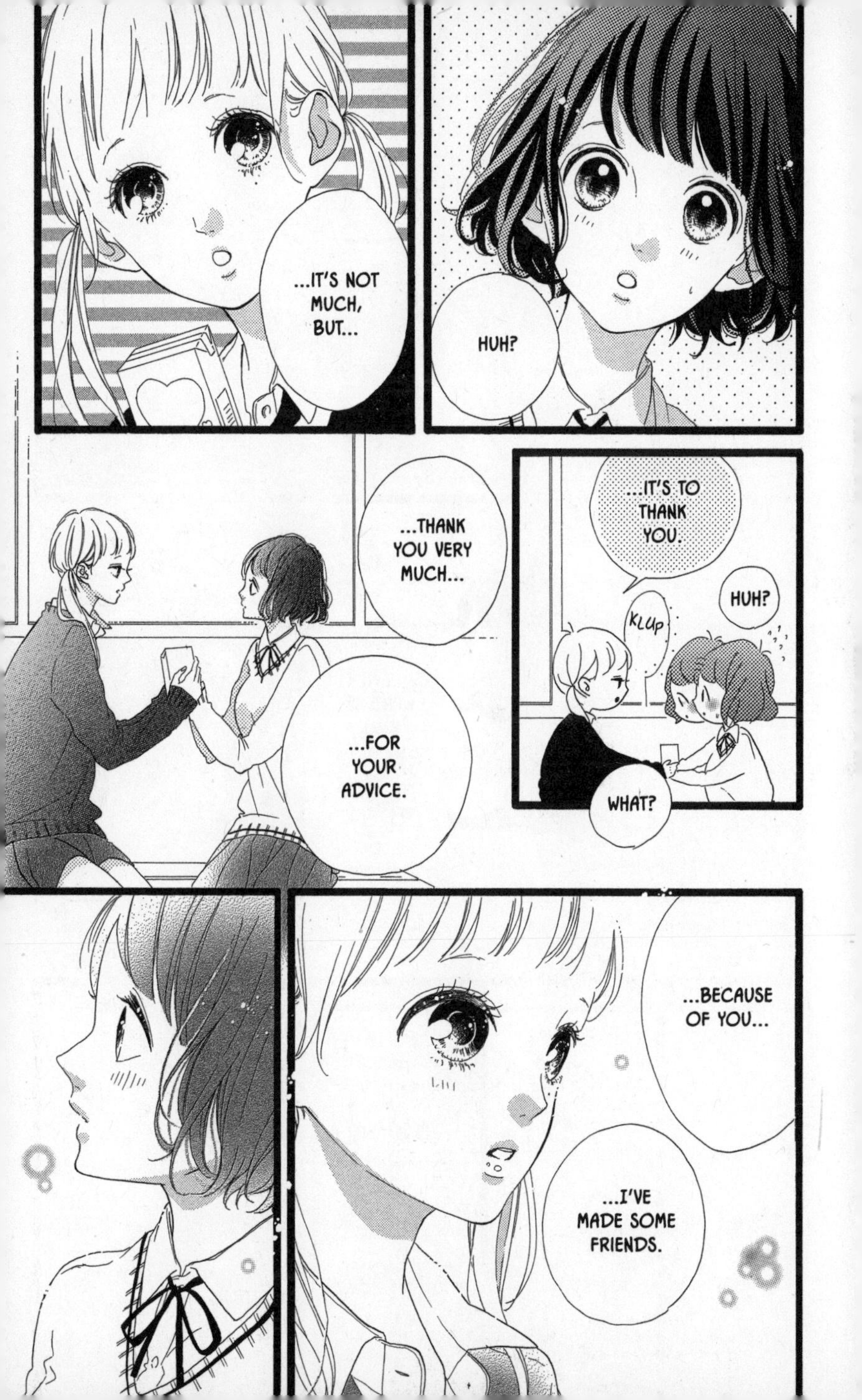
HUH?
...IT'S NOT MUCH, BUT...
...IT'S TO THANK YOU.
HUH?
KLUP
WHAT?
...THANK YOU VERY MUCH...
...FOR YOUR ADVICE.
...BECAUSE OF YOU...
...I'VE MADE SOME FRIENDS.

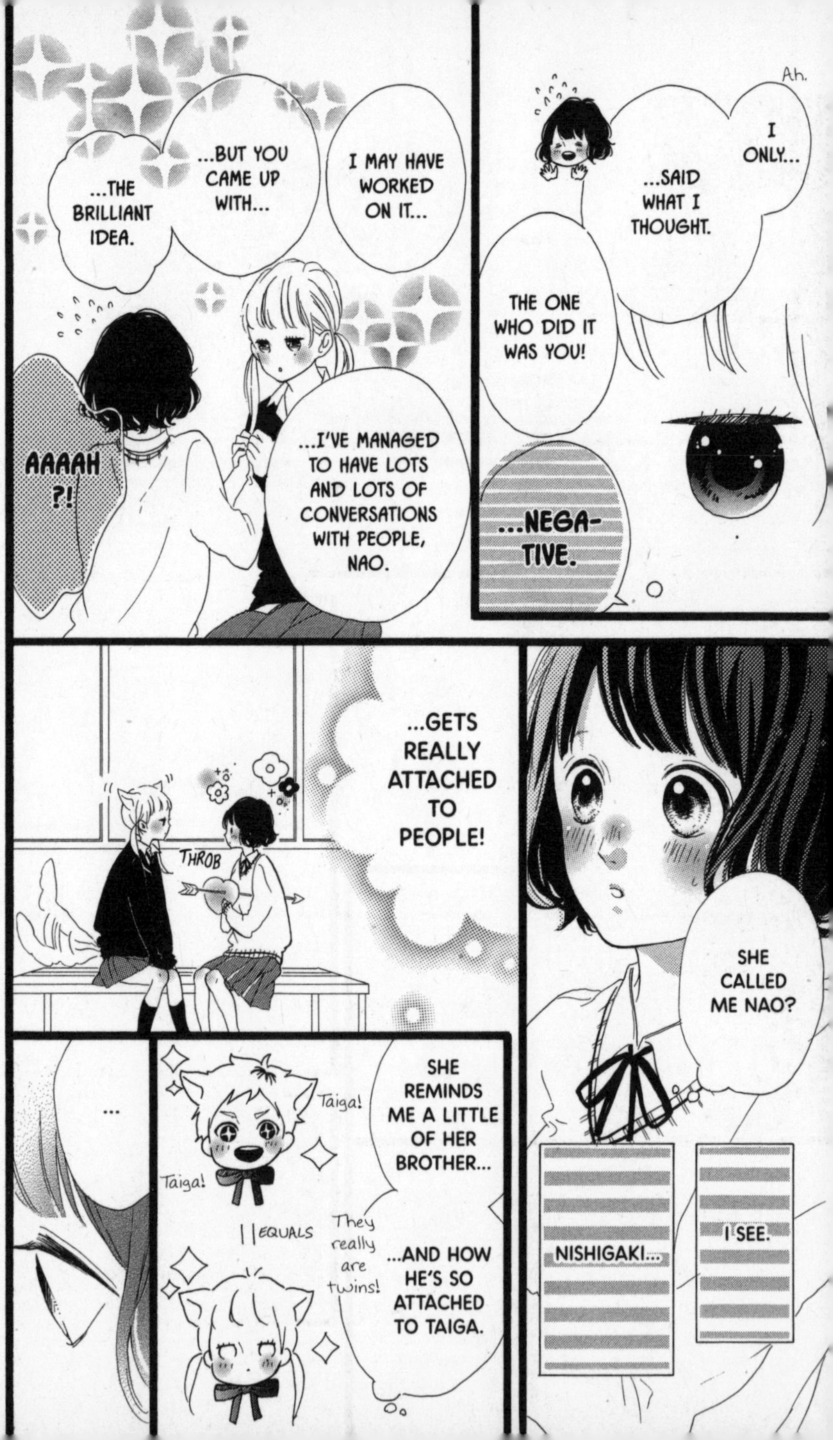
Ah.
I ONLY...
...SAID WHAT I THOUGHT.
THE ONE WHO DID IT WAS YOU!
...NEGA-TIVE.
I MAY HAVE WORKED ON IT...
...BUT YOU CAME UP WITH...
...THE BRILLIANT IDEA.
AAAAH ?!
...I'VE MANAGED TO HAVE LOTS AND LOTS OF CONVERSATIONS WITH PEOPLE, NAO.
SHE CALLED ME NAO?
I SEE.
NISHIGAKI...
...GETS REALLY ATTACHED TO PEOPLE!
THROB
SHE REMINDS ME A LITTLE OF HER BROTHER...
Taiga!
Taiga!
EQUALS
They really are twins!
...AND HOW HE'S SO ATTACHED TO TAIGA.
...

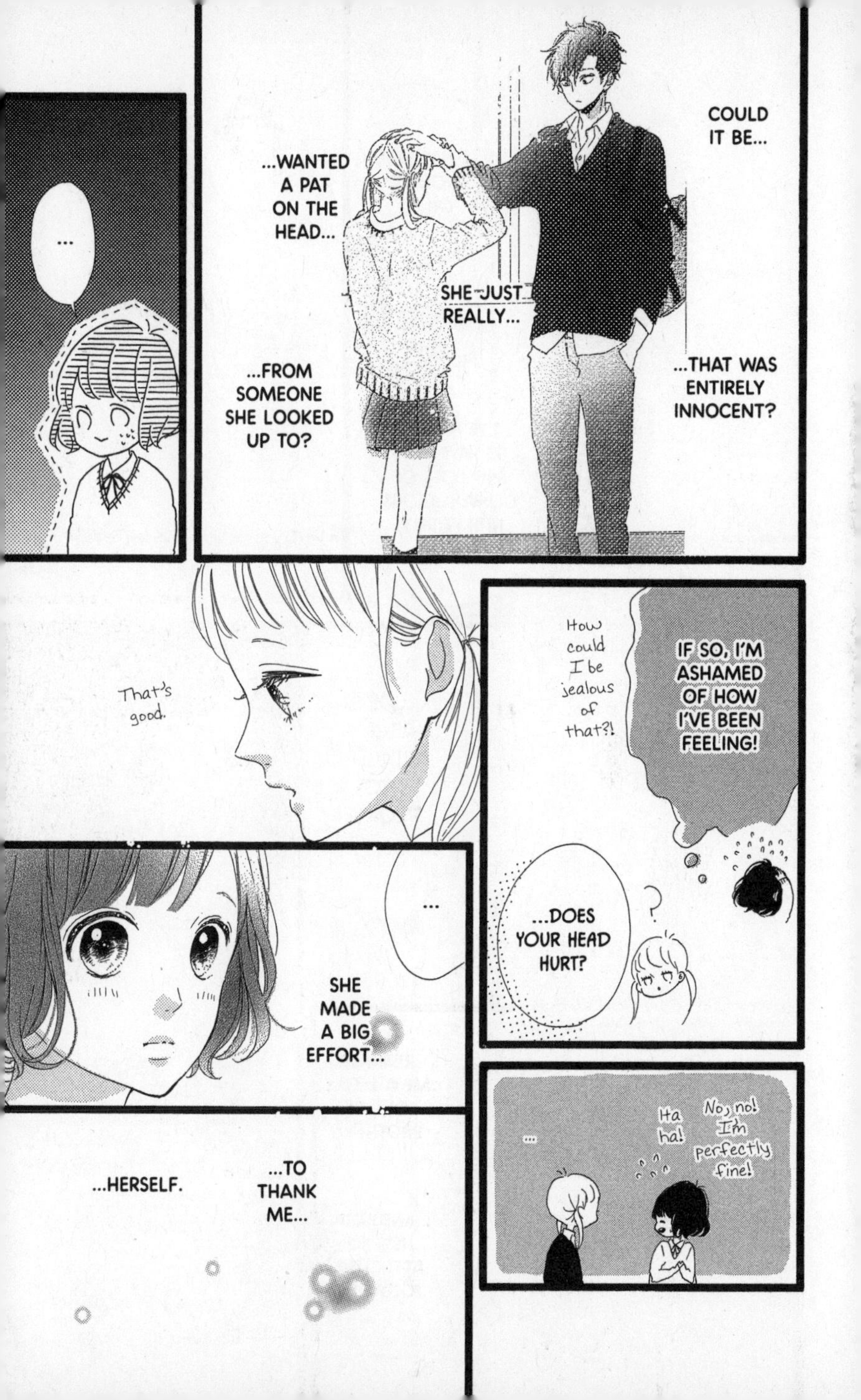
COULD IT BE...
...THAT WAS ENTIRELY INNOCENT?
SHE JUST REALLY...
...WANTED A PAT ON THE HEAD...
...FROM SOMEONE SHE LOOKED UP TO?
...
IF SO, I'M ASHAMED OF HOW I'VE BEEN FEELING!
How could I be jealous of that?!
...DOES YOUR HEAD HURT?
No, no! I'm perfectly fine!
Ha ha!
...
That's good.
...
SHE MADE A BIG EFFORT...
...TO THANK ME...
...HERSELF.

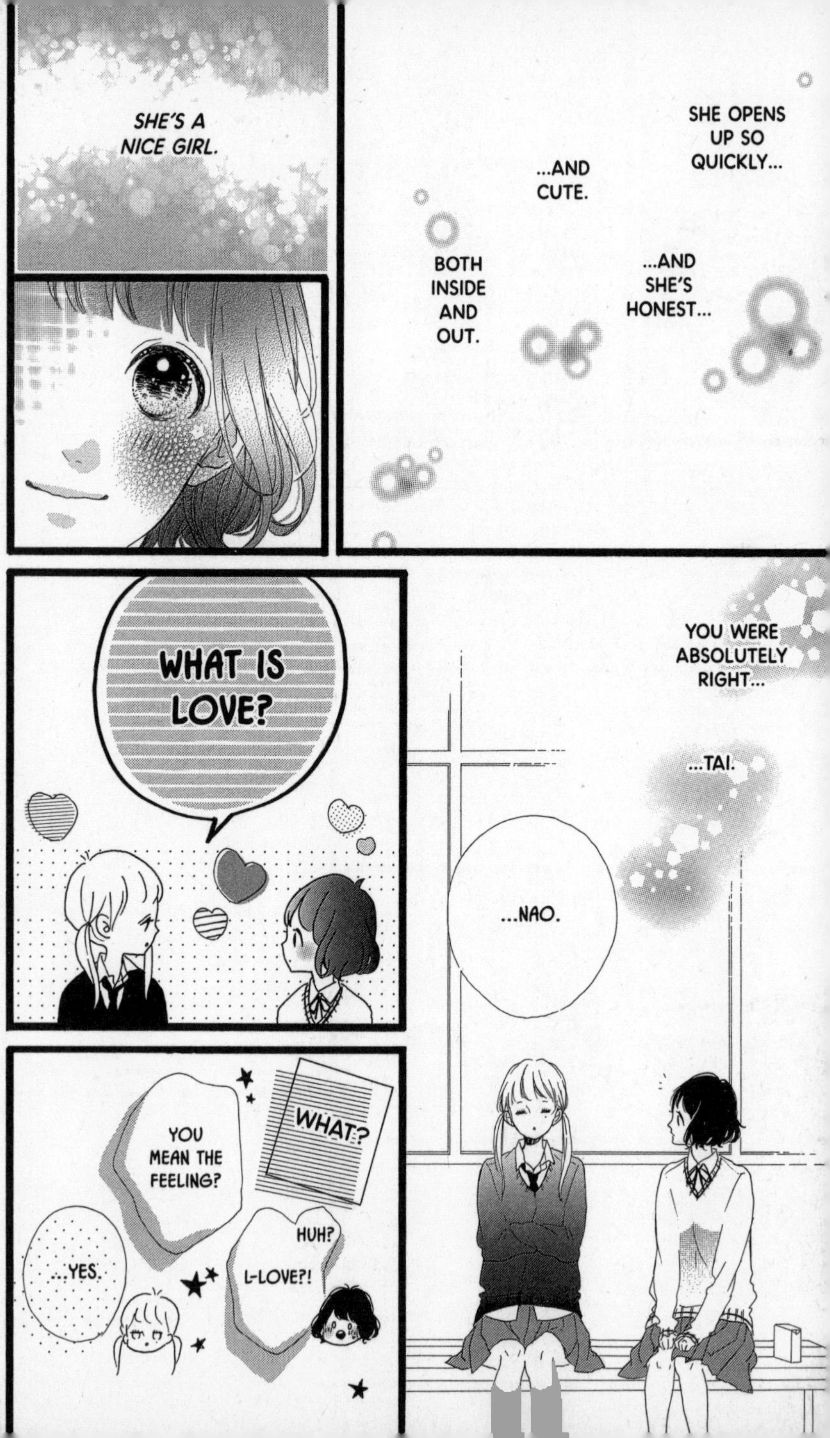
SHE OPENS UP SO QUICKLY...
...AND SHE'S HONEST...
...AND CUTE.
BOTH INSIDE AND OUT.
SHE'S A NICE GIRL.
YOU WERE ABSOLUTELY RIGHT...
...TAI.
...NAO.
WHAT IS LOVE?
WHAT?
YOU MEAN THE FEELING?
HUH?
L-LOVE?!
...YES.

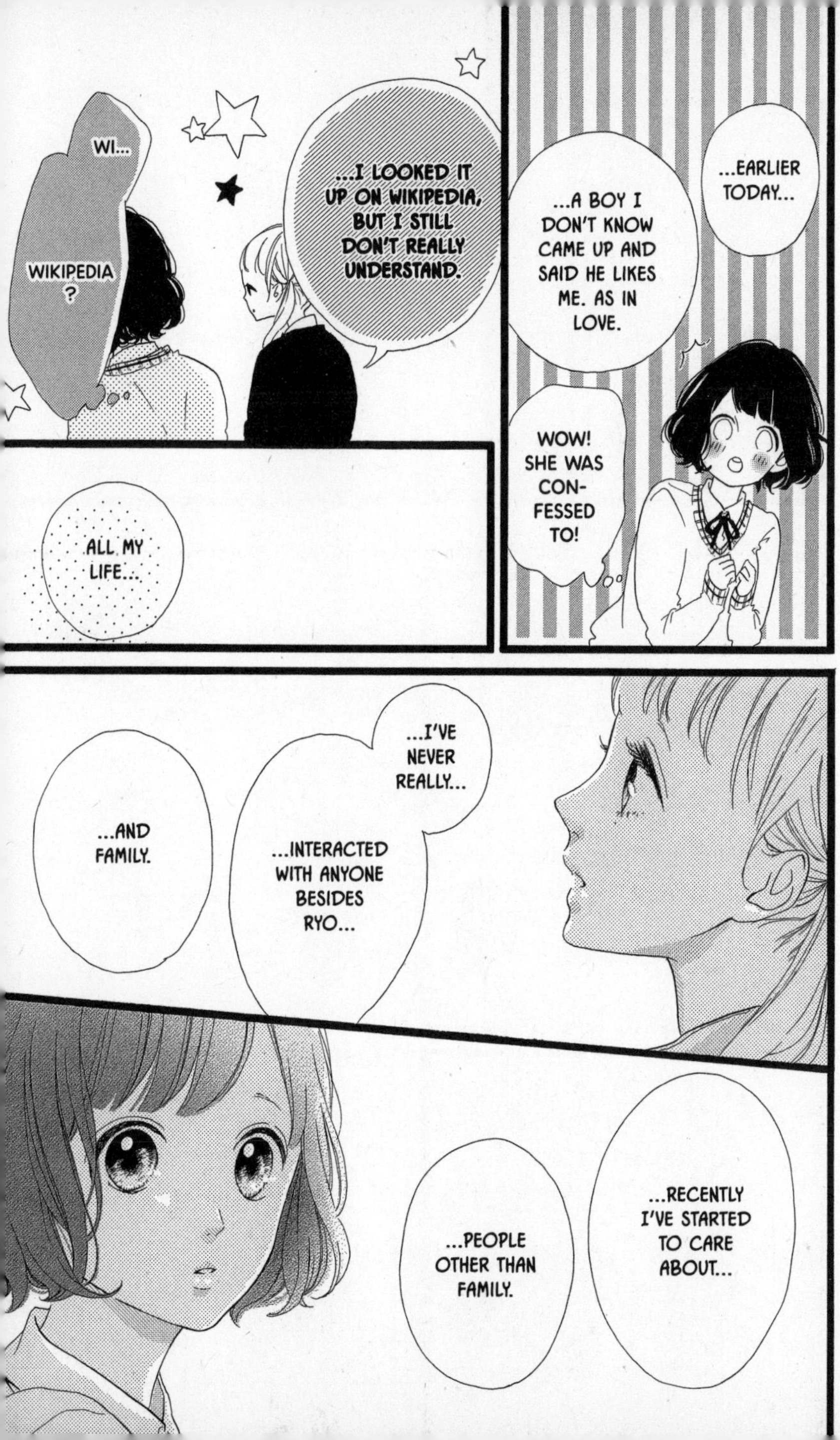
...EARLIER TODAY...
...A BOY I DON'T KNOW CAME UP AND SAID HE LIKES ME. AS IN LOVE.
WOW! SHE WAS CON-FESSED TO!
...I LOOKED IT UP ON WIKIPEDIA, BUT I STILL DON'T REALLY UNDERSTAND.
WI...
WIKIPEDIA?
ALL MY LIFE...
...I'VE NEVER REALLY...
...INTERACTED WITH ANYONE BESIDES RYO...
...AND FAMILY.
...RECENTLY I'VE STARTED TO CARE ABOUT...
...PEOPLE OTHER THAN FAMILY.

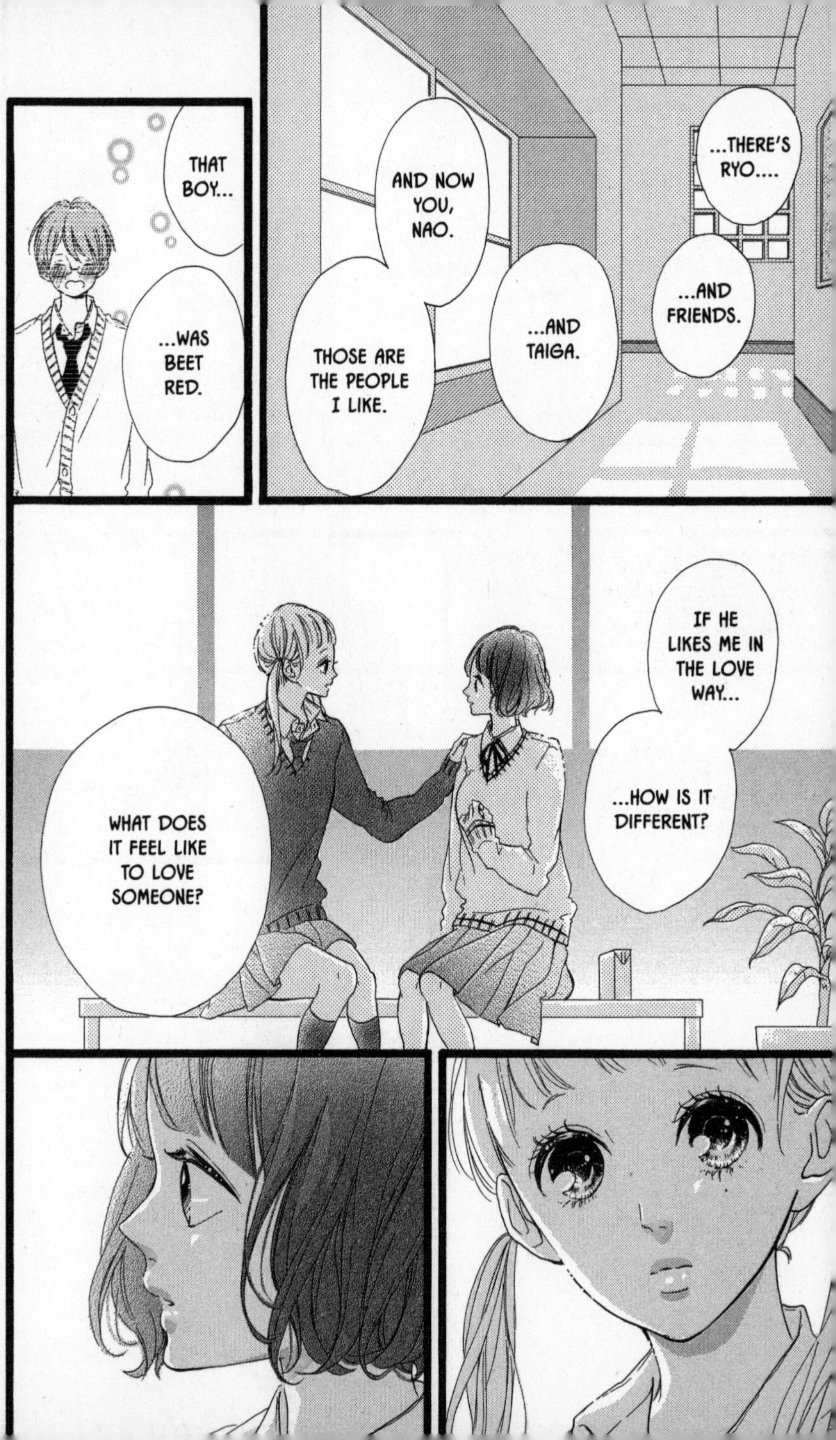
...THERE'S RYO....
...AND FRIENDS.
...AND TAIGA.
AND NOW YOU, NAO.
THOSE ARE THE PEOPLE I LIKE.
THAT BOY...
...WAS BEET RED.
IF HE LIKES ME IN THE LOVE WAY...
...HOW IS IT DIFFERENT?
WHAT DOES IT FEEL LIKE TO LOVE SOMEONE?

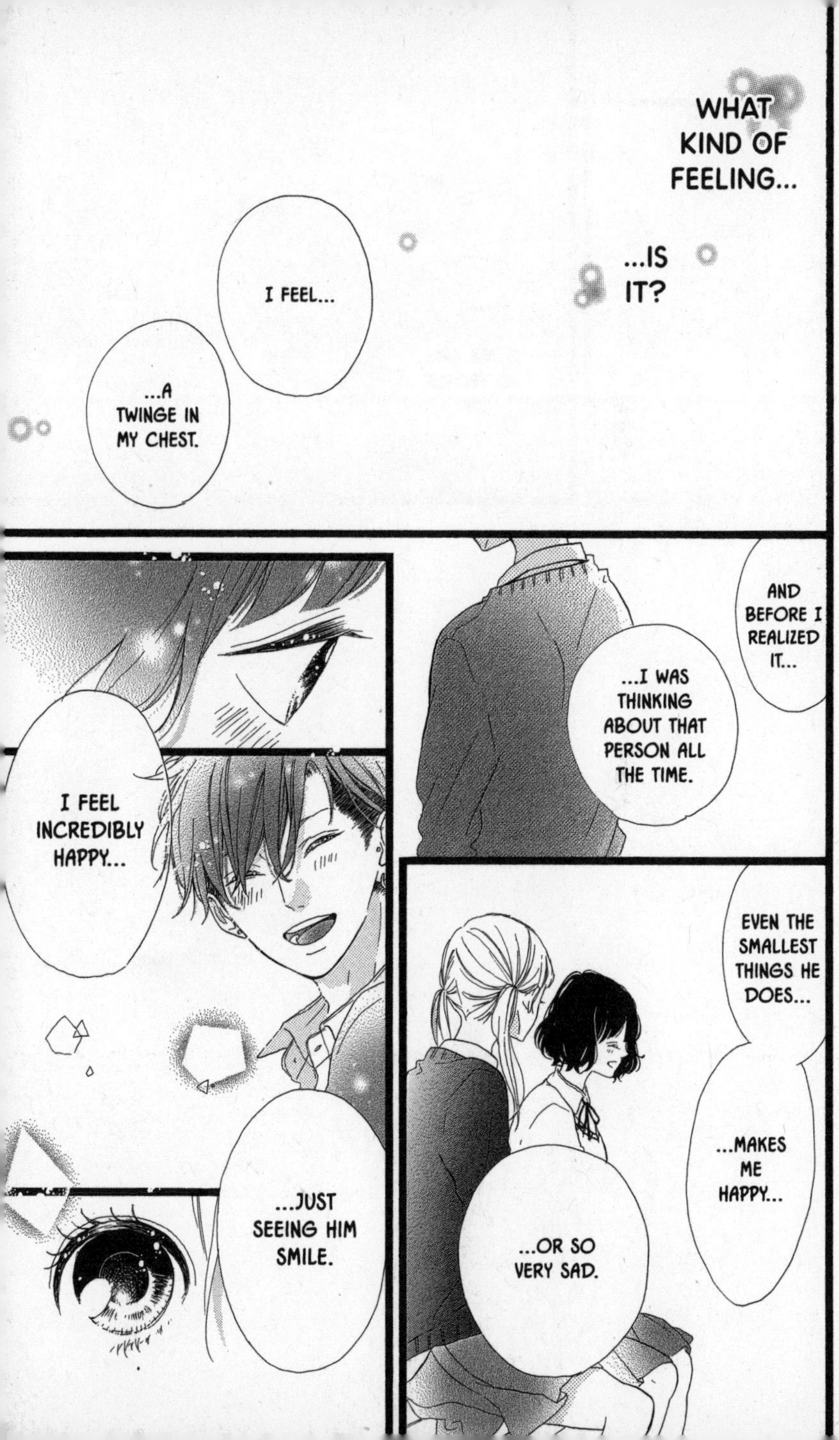
WHAT KIND OF FEELING...
...IS IT?
I FEEL...
...A TWINGE IN MY CHEST.
AND BEFORE I REALIZED IT...
...I WAS THINKING ABOUT THAT PERSON ALL THE TIME.
EVEN THE SMALLEST THINGS HE DOES...
...MAKES ME HAPPY...
...OR SO VERY SAD.
I FEEL INCREDIBLY HAPPY...
...JUST SEEING HIM SMILE.

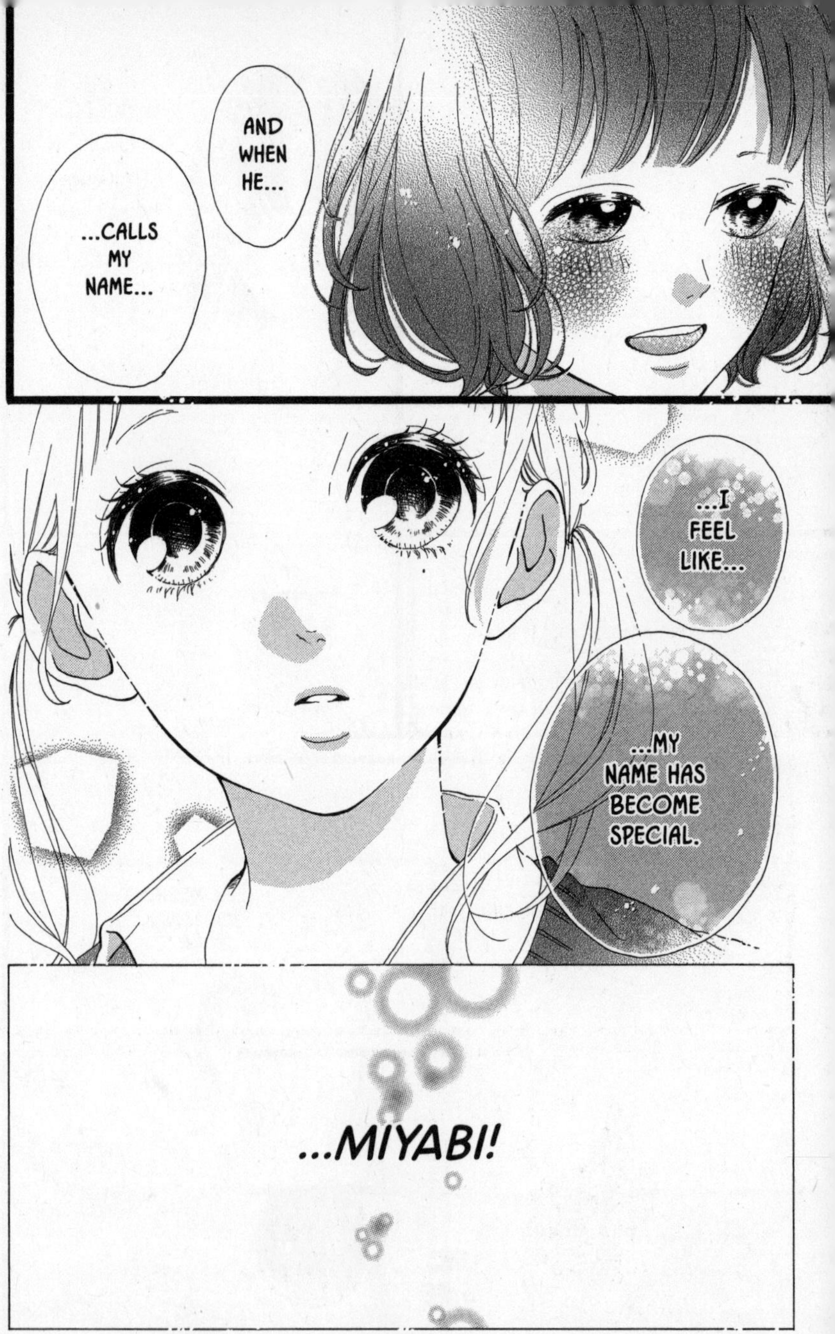
AND WHEN HE...
...CALLS MY NAME...
...I FEEL LIKE...
...MY NAME HAS BECOME SPECIAL.
...MIYABI!

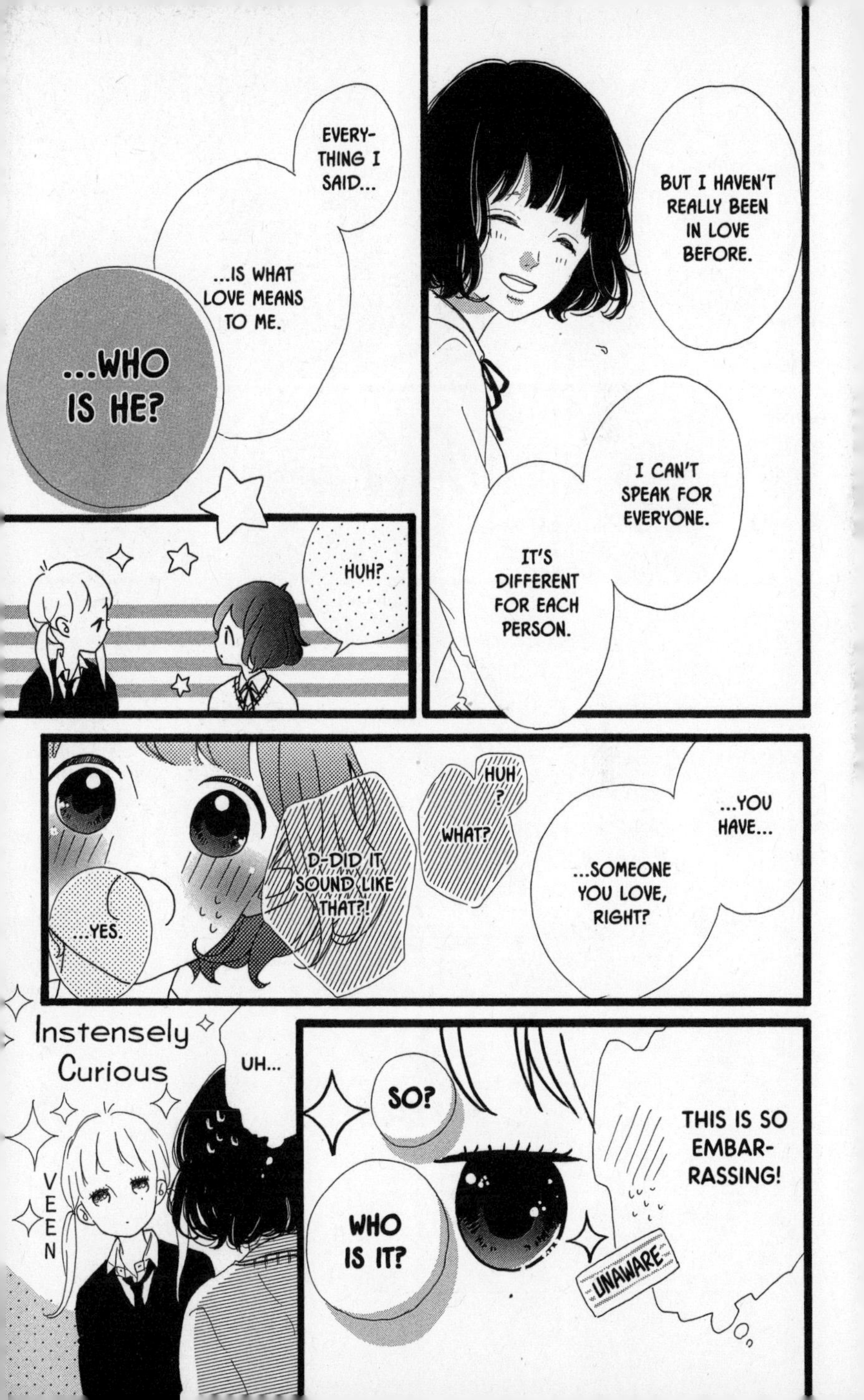
BUT I HAVEN'T REALLY BEEN IN LOVE BEFORE.
I CAN'T SPEAK FOR EVERYONE.
IT'S DIFFERENT FOR EACH PERSON.
EVERY-THING I SAID...
...IS WHAT LOVE MEANS TO ME.
...WHO IS HE?
HUH?
...YOU HAVE...
...SOMEONE YOU LOVE, RIGHT?
HUH?
WHAT?
D-DID IT SOUND LIKE THAT?!
...YES.
THIS IS SO EMBAR-RASSING!
SO?
WHO IS IT?
UNAWARE
UH...
Instensely Curious
VEEN

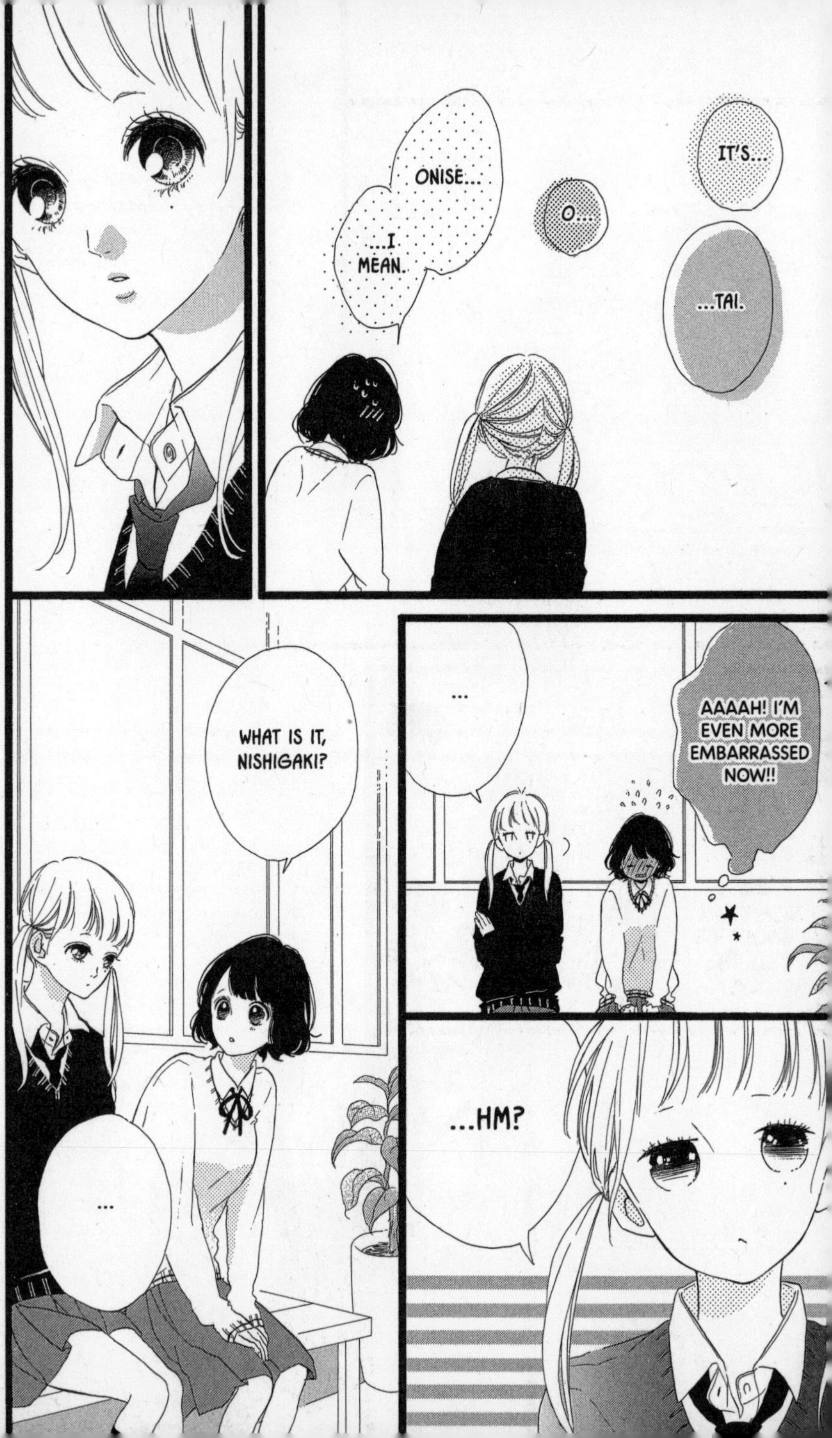
IT'S...
...TAI.
O...
ONISE...
...I MEAN.
AAAAH! I'M EVEN MORE EMBARRASSED NOW!!
...
...HM?
WHAT IS IT, NISHIGAKI?
...

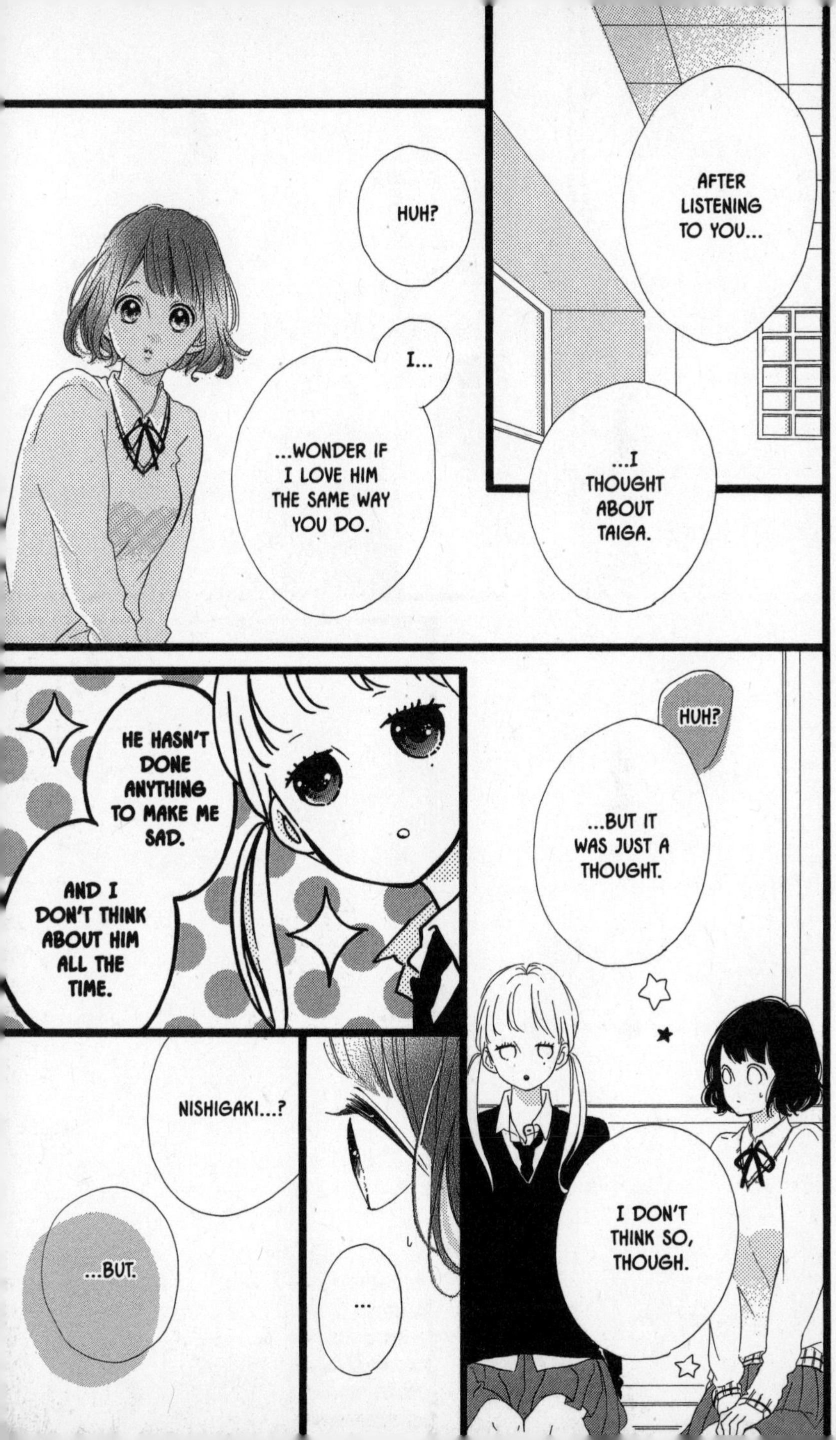
AFTER LISTENING TO YOU...
...I THOUGHT ABOUT TAIGA.
HUH?
I...
...WONDER IF I LOVE HIM THE SAME WAY YOU DO.
HUH?
...BUT IT WAS JUST A THOUGHT.
I DON'T THINK SO, THOUGH.
HE HASN'T DONE ANYTHING TO MAKE ME SAD.
AND I DON'T THINK ABOUT HIM ALL THE TIME.
NISHIGAKI...?
...
...BUT.

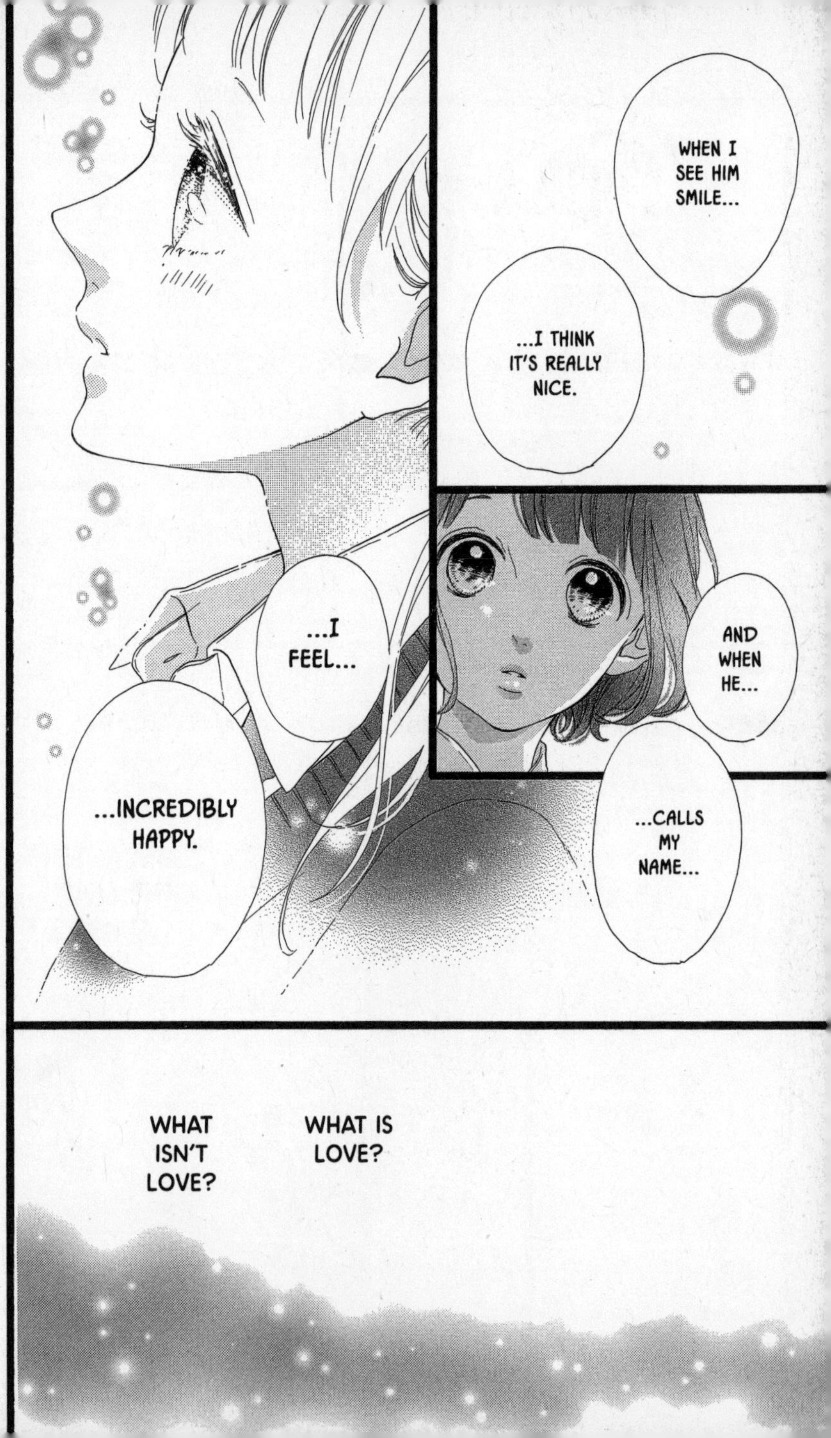
WHEN I SEE HIM SMILE...
...I THINK IT'S REALLY NICE.
AND WHEN HE...
...CALLS MY NAME...
...I FEEL...
...INCREDIBLY HAPPY.
WHAT IS LOVE?
WHAT ISN'T LOVE?

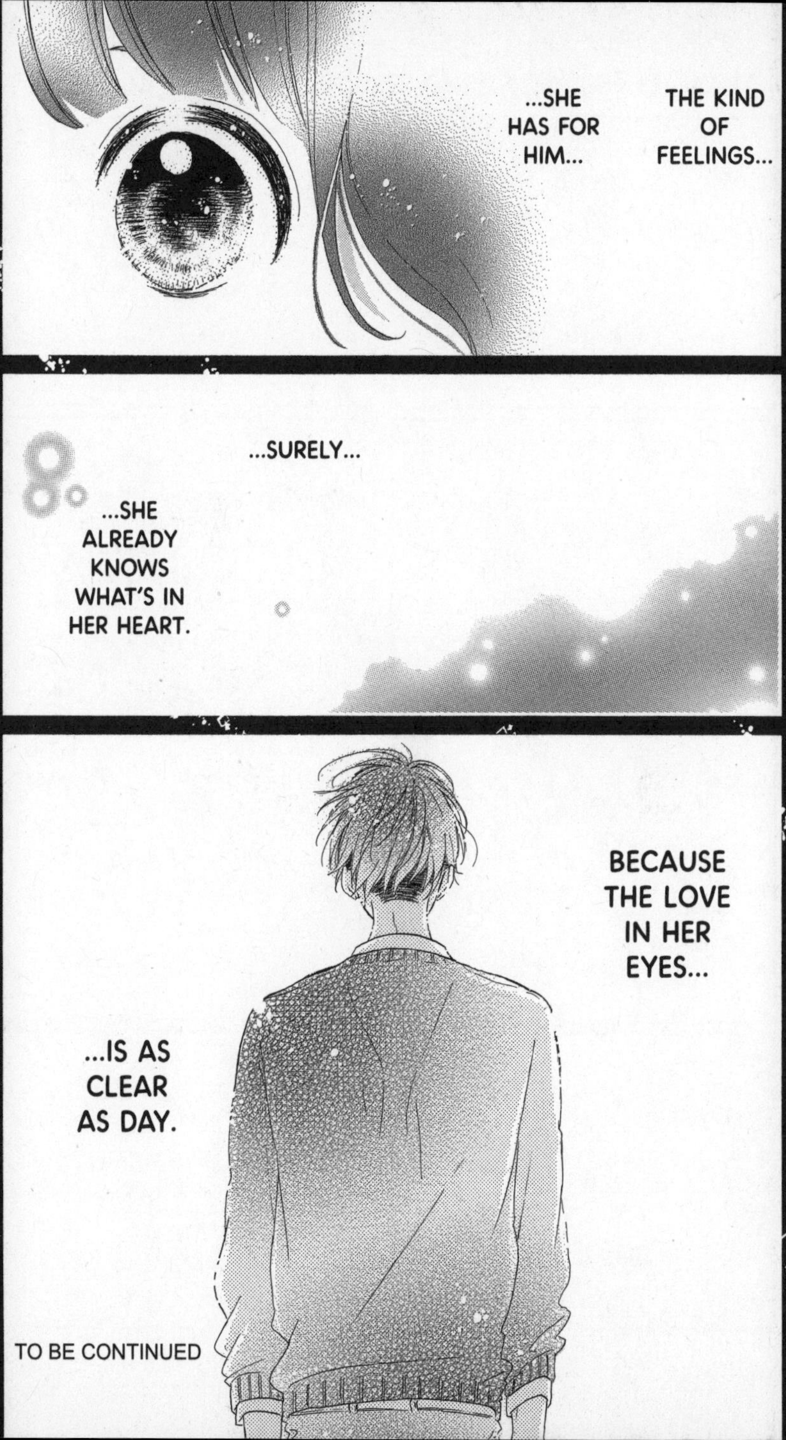
THE KIND OF FEELINGS...
...SHE HAS FOR HIM...
...SURELY...
...SHE ALREADY KNOWS WHAT'S IN HER HEART.
BECAUSE THE LOVE IN HER EYES...
...IS AS CLEAR AS DAY.
TO BE CONTINUED

The Night After the Kiss ①

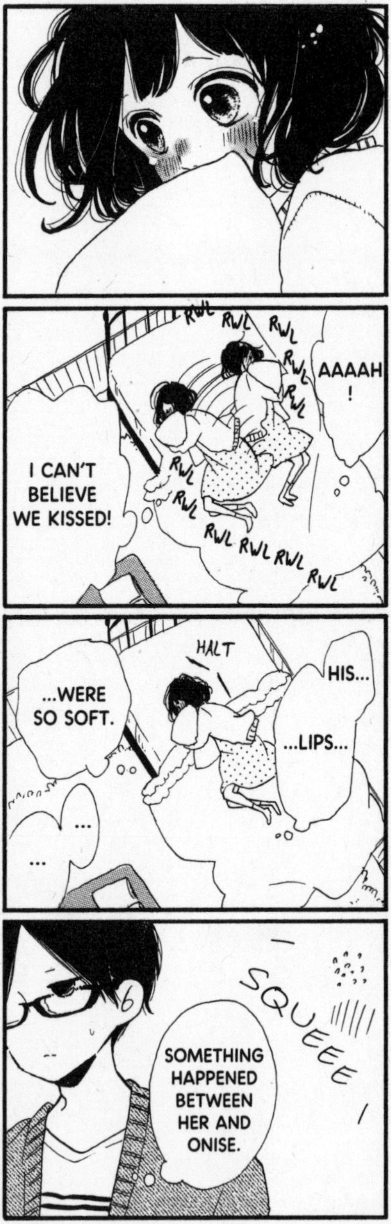
RWL RWL RWL RWL RWL
AAAAH!
I CAN'T BELIEVE WE KISSED!
RWL RWL
RWL RWL RWL RWL
HALT
HIS...
...LIPS...
...WERE SO SOFT.
...
...
SQUEEE
SOMETHING HAPPENED BETWEEN HER AND ONISE.

The Night After the Kiss ②

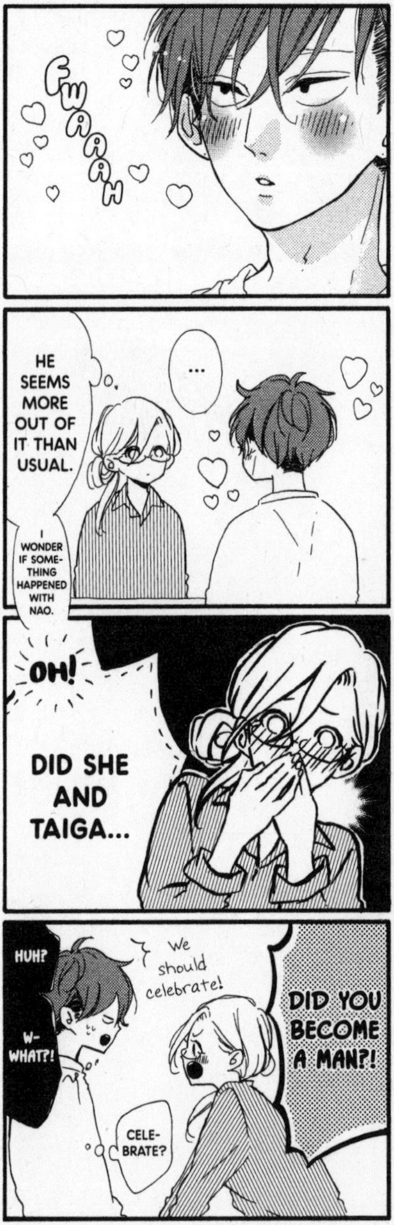
FWAAAAH
...
HE SEEMS MORE OUT OF IT THAN USUAL.
I WONDER IF SOME-THING HAPPENED WITH NAO.
OH!
DID SHE AND TAIGA...
DID YOU BECOME A MAN?!
We should celebrate!
HUH?
W-WHAT?!
CELE-BRATE?

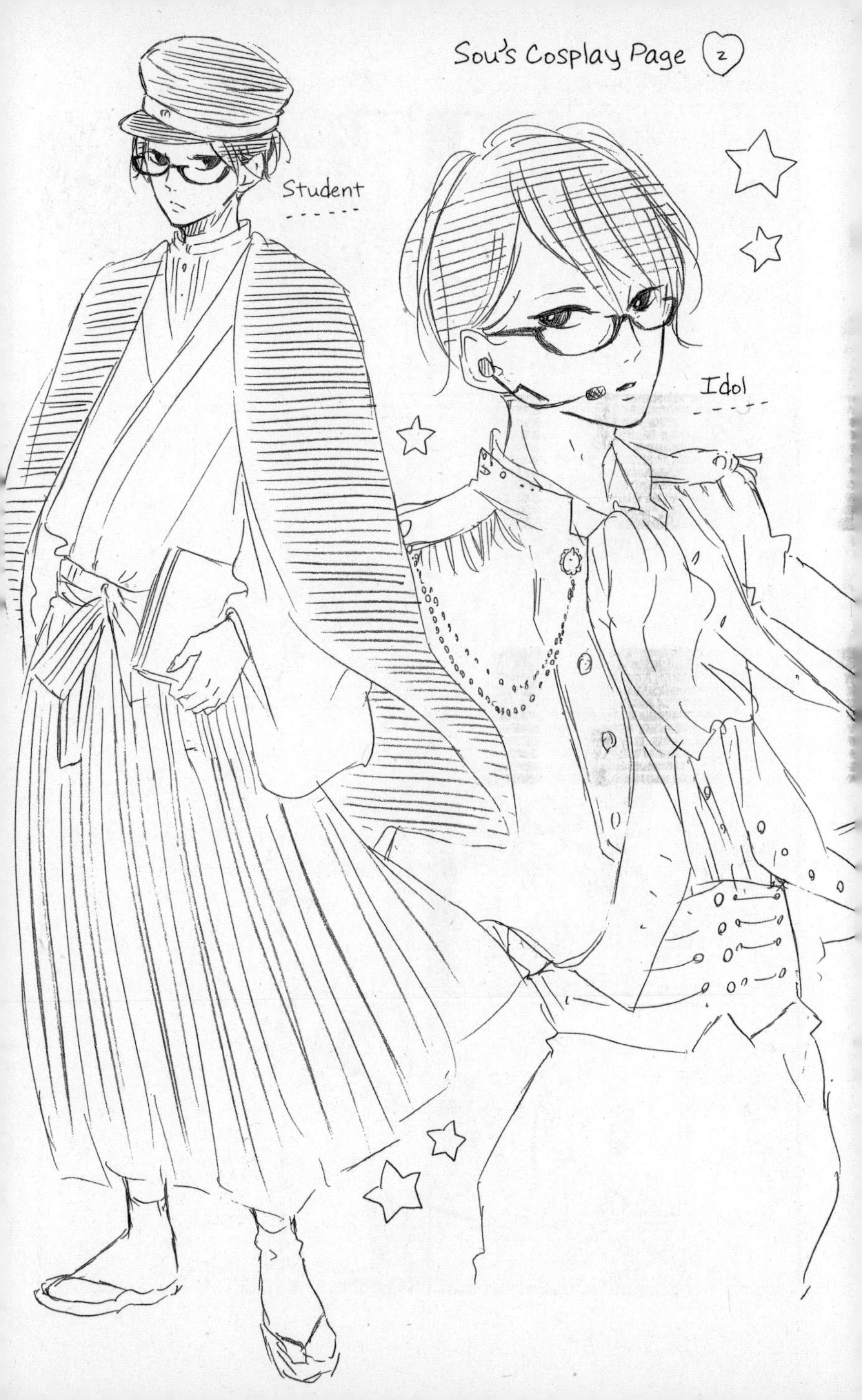
Sou's Cosplay Page 2
Student
Idol

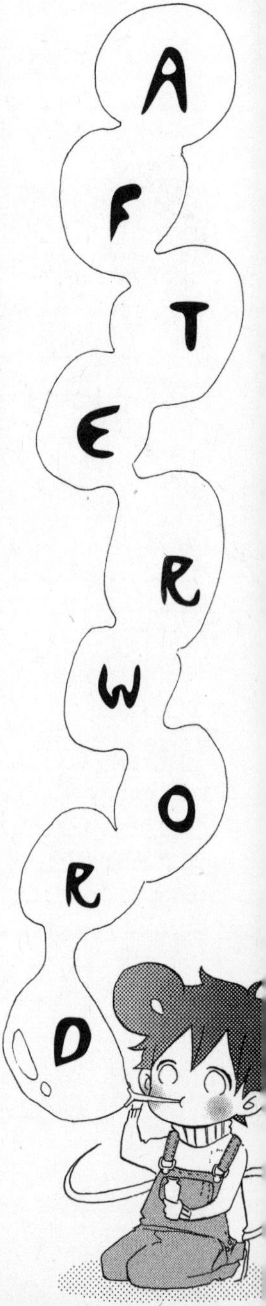
AFTERWORD

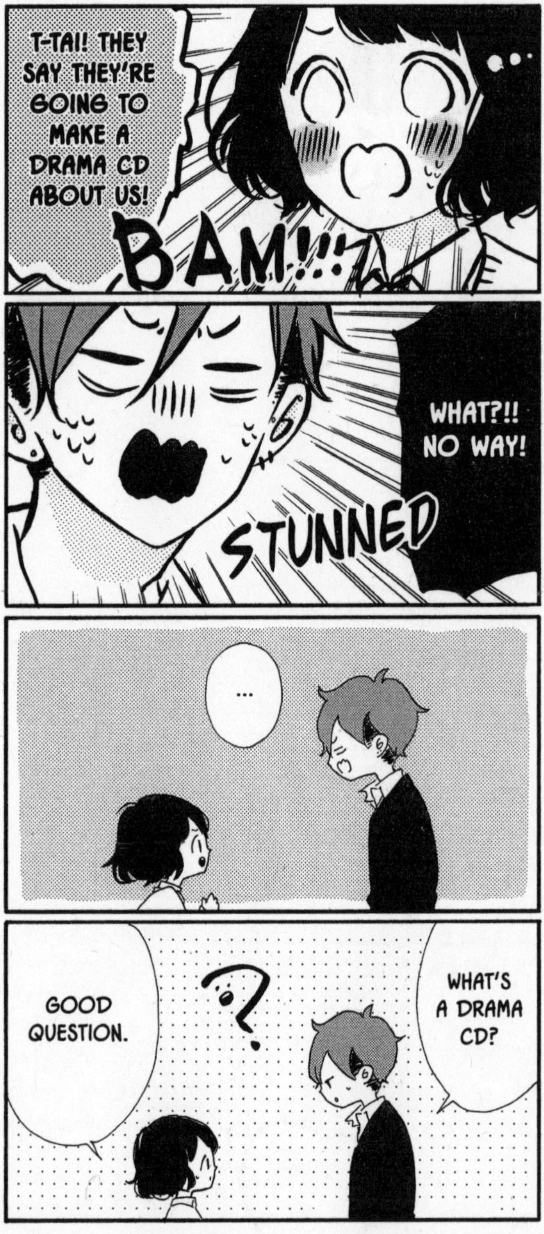
T-TAI! THEY SAY THEY'RE GOING TO MAKE A DRAMA CD ABOUT US!
BAM!!!
WHAT?!! NO WAY!
STUNNED
...
WHAT'S A DRAMA CD?
?
GOOD QUESTION.

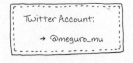

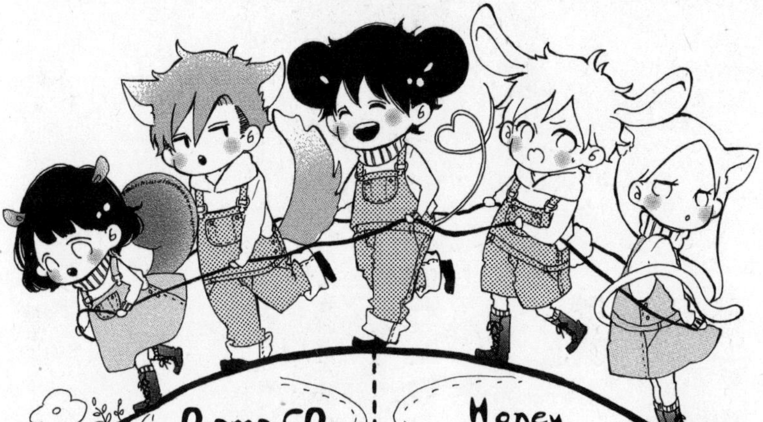

Drama CD News

You heard right! They're going to make *Honey So Sweet* into a drama CD! Woo hoo! HSS was originally planned to be two volumes, but it's lasted for so long! And now this! I couldn't be happier!

This is all thanks to my beloved readers, my supportive family, my editor, and everyone who was involved in the creation of this book! I cannot thank you all enough!

July is still a long way off, but if you're dying to hear Nao and Onise talk, reserve your copy of the CD today! (˘◡˘)♡ Supplies are limited!

Once I find out more about the voice actors aside from Nao and the other information, I'll be sure to announce it on Twitter.

Twitter Account:

→ @meguro_mu

Honey News

We've got two new characters, the Nishigaki twins! I also had a pair of twins in my other story, "Mismatched Planet," because I can't get enough of them! Even though I've played around with the idea of writing a story that starred twins, I can't seem to find the determination to do it! (*laugh*) Sou hardly makes an appearance in the story in this volume, so I dedicated all the bonus pages to him. It's a Sou festival! There are lots of readers who like Sou best (˘◡˘), so I had a lot of fun dressing him in all sorts of costumes. If I have the opportunity to, I'd like to do the same with another character! (˘◡˘)♡

And with that, thank you for reading volume 6!

Goodbye until we meet again in volume 7!

2/2015

MEGURO Amu ♡

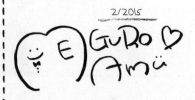

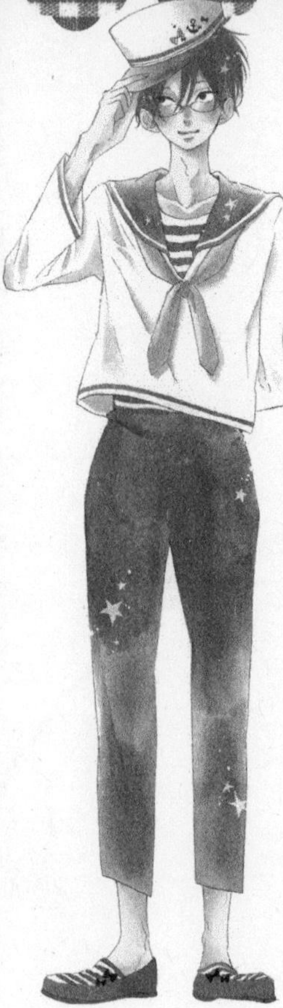

Recently my niece and I have started dancing to *Yo-Kai Exercise 1* and a certain anime theme music that's out. My niece is so incredibly adorable when she's dancing. Just watching her revives me. She's an angel.

—Amu Meguro

Newcomer Amu Meguro debuted with the one-shot manga *Makka na Ringo ni Kuchizuke O* (A Kiss for a Bright Red Apple). Born in Hokkaido, her hobbies are playing with her niece and eating. *Honey So Sweet* is her current series in *Bessatsu Margaret* magazine.

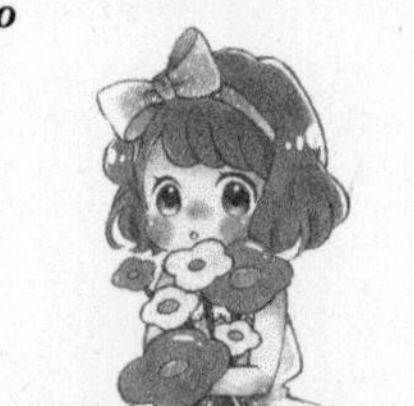

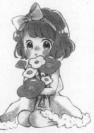

Honey So Sweet

Shojo Beat Edition

Volume 6

STORY AND ART BY
Amu Meguro

Translation/Katherine Schilling
Touch-Up Art & Lettering/Inori Fukuda Trant
Design/Izumi Evers
Editor/Nancy Thistlethwaite

Published by VIZ Media, LLC
P.O. Box 77010
San Francisco, CA 94107

10 9 8 7 6 5 4 3 2 1
First printing, April 2017

 VIZ media
www.viz.com

 Shojo **Beat**
www.shojobeat.com

You may be reading the wrong way!

This book reads right to left to maintain the original presentation and art of the Japanese edition, so action, sound effects and word balloons are reversed. This diagram shows how to follow the panels. Turn to the other side of the book to begin.

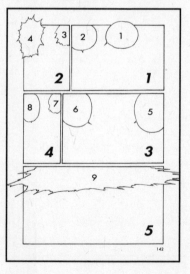